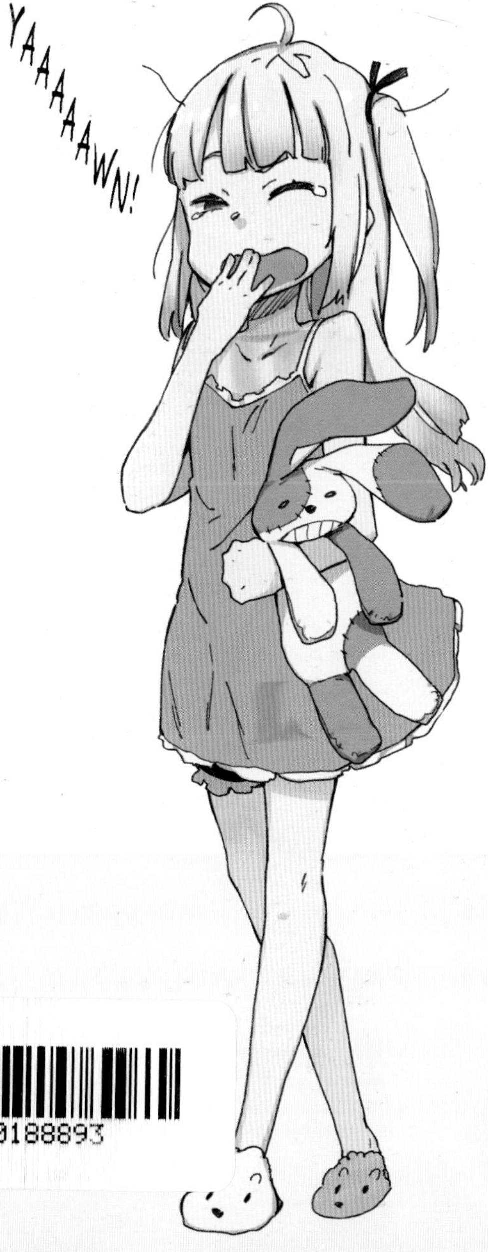
YAAAAAWN!

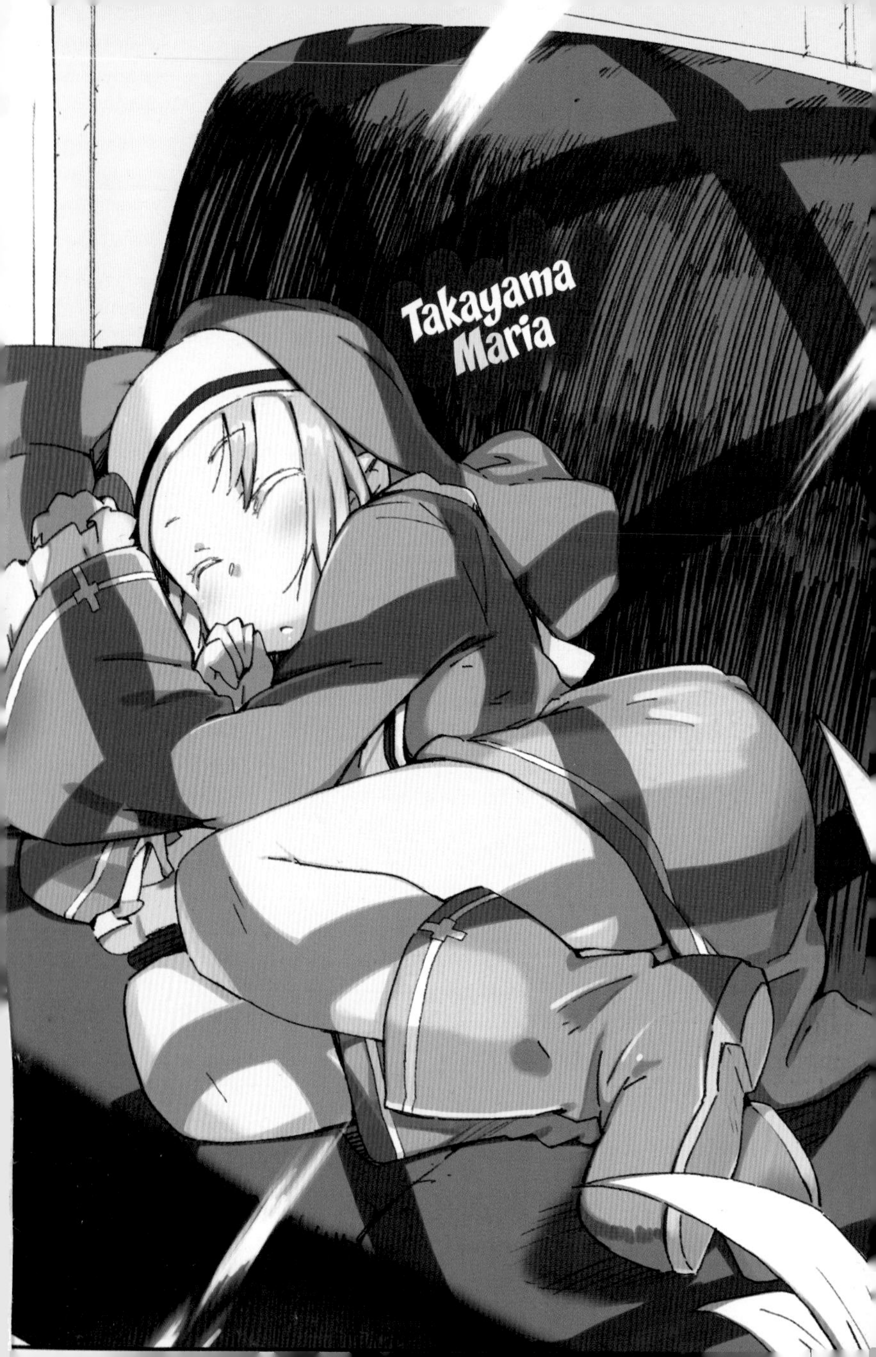
Takayama
Maria

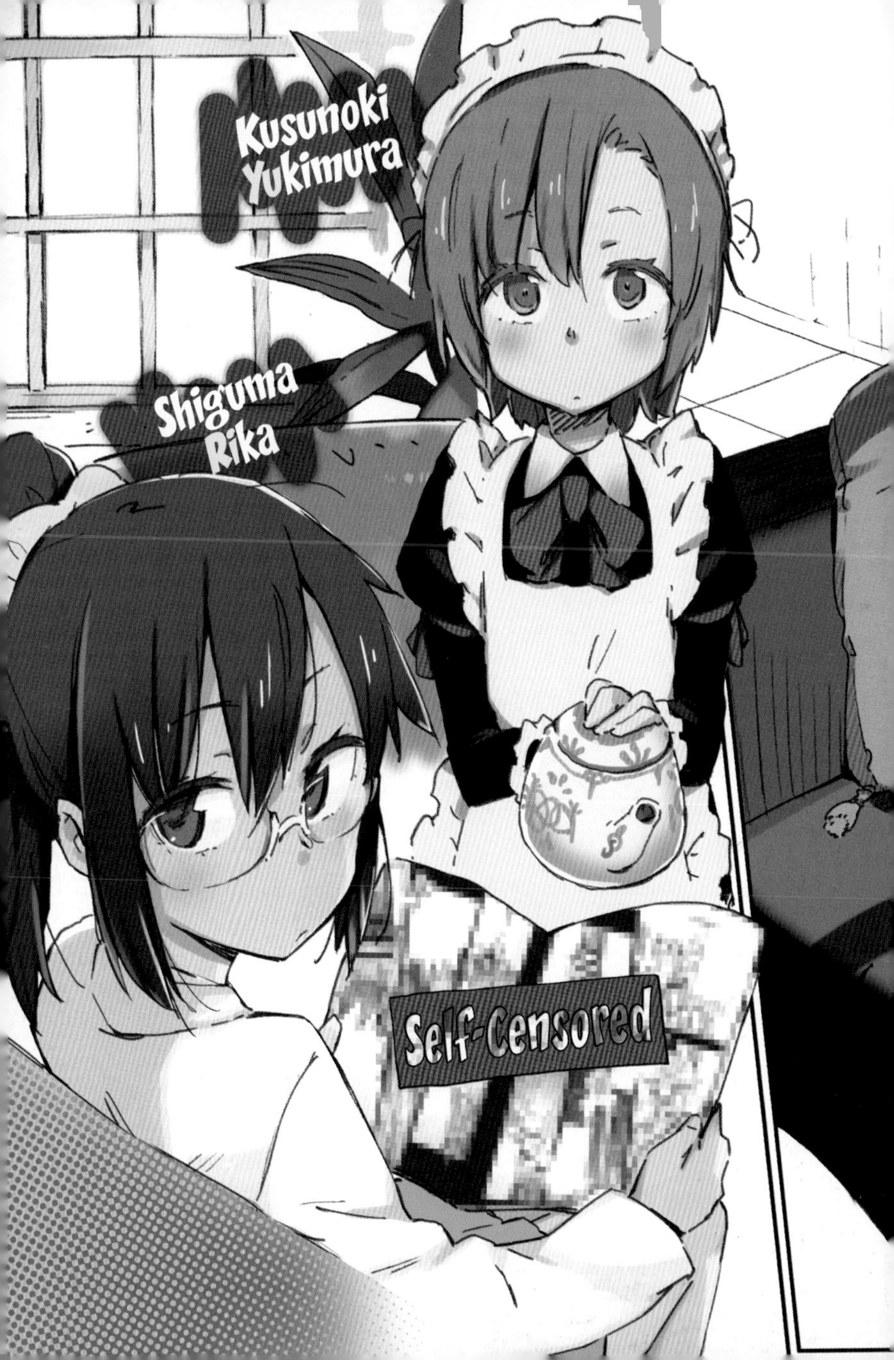
Kusunoki
Yukimura
Shiguma
Rika
Self-Censored

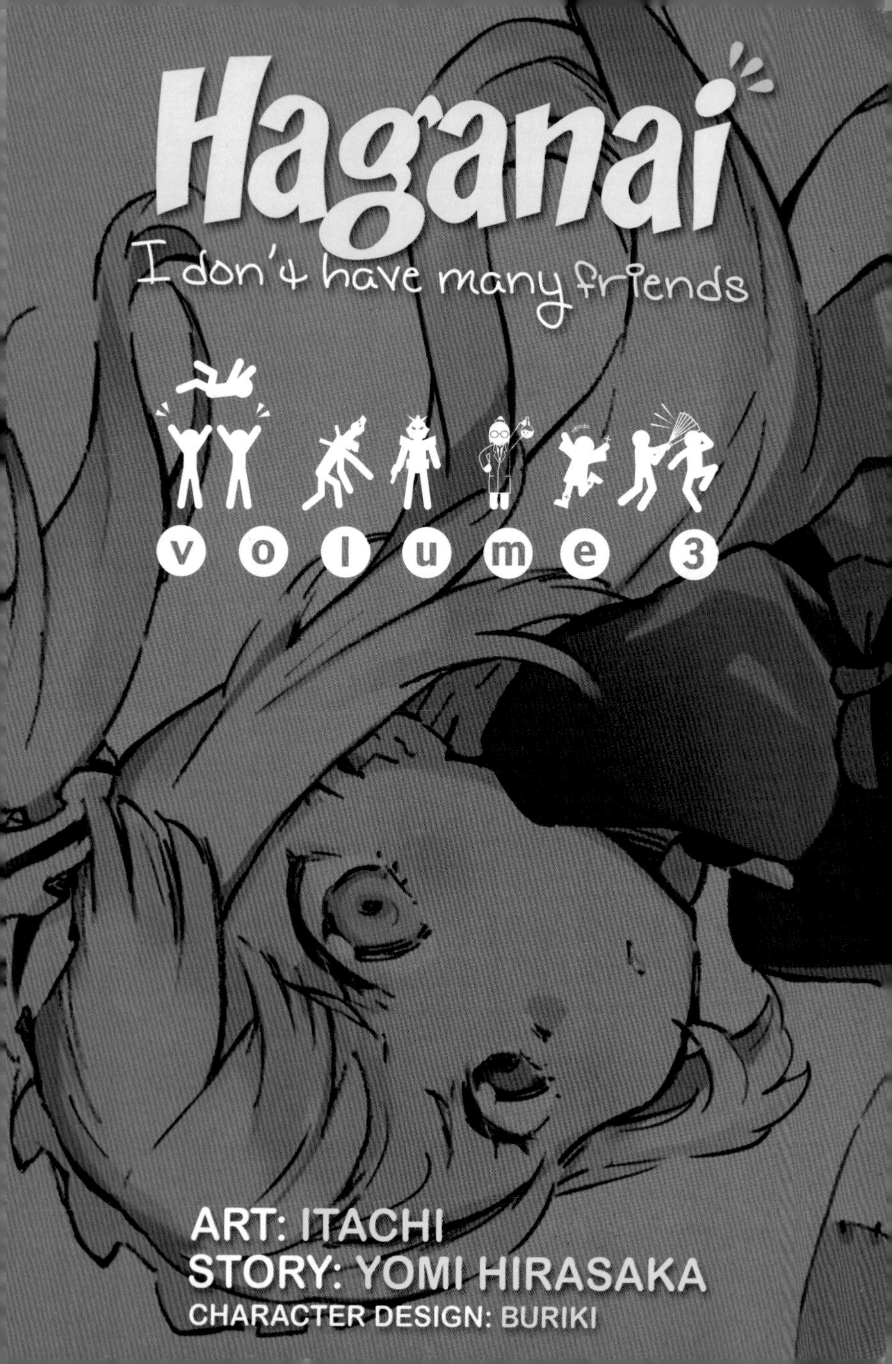

Haganai

I don't have many friends

volume 3

ART: ITACHI
STORY: YOMI HIRASAKA
CHARACTER DESIGN: BURIKI

HAGANAI

MEET THE CAST

羽瀬川 小鷹
Hasegawa Kodaka

A second-year student at Saint Chronica Academy. He looks like a thug. Doesn't have many friends.

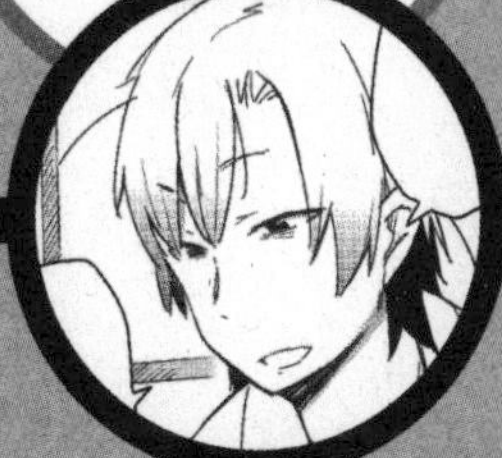

三日月 夜空
Mikazuki Yozora

Kodaka's classmate. Other than her looks, she doesn't have much going for her. Doesn't have many friends.

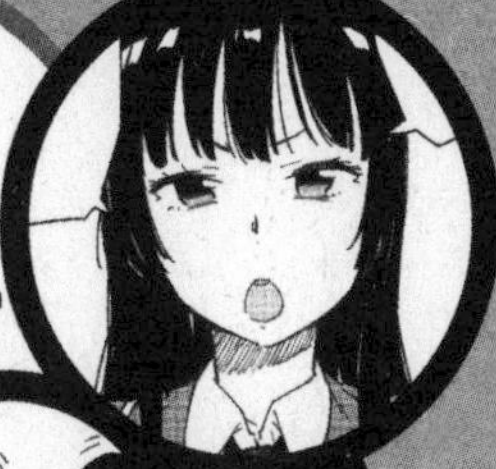

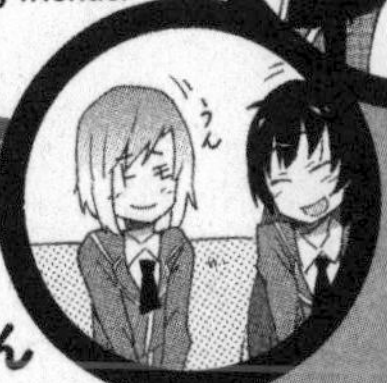

トモちゃん
Tomo-chan

Yozora's "air friend."

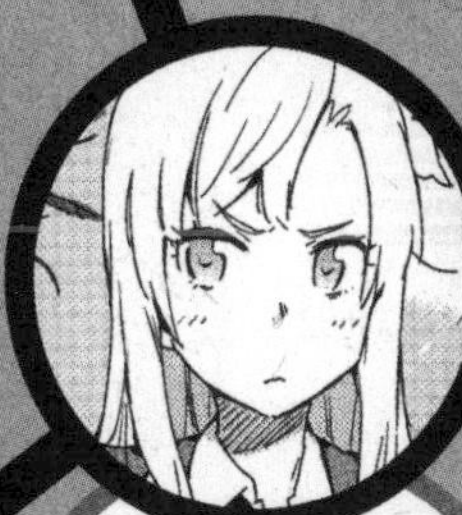

柏崎 星奈
Kashiwazaki Sena

The daughter of Saint Chronica Academy's director. Perfect in every way... except for her personality. Doesn't have many friends.

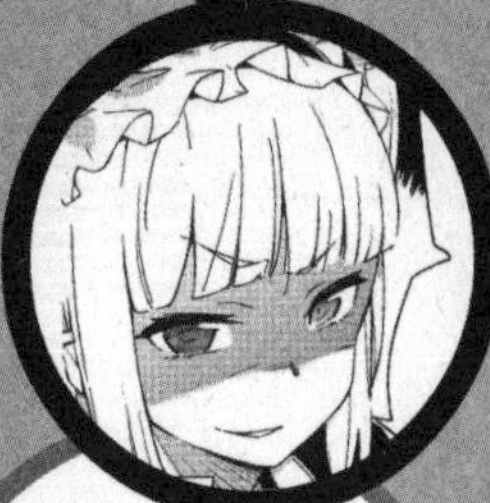

羽瀬川 小鳩
Hasegawa Kobato

Kodaka's kid sister. She's a student at Saint Chronica Academy's middle school, and she has some... unfortunate ideas. Her unusual style of clothing and speech stems from her persona as a vampire.

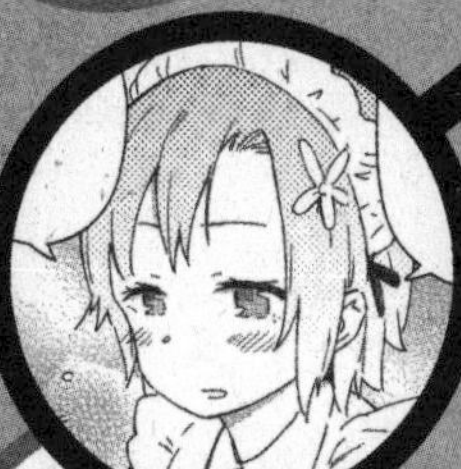

楠 幸村
Kusunoki Yukimura

A first-year student at Saint Chronica Academy. A kouhai to the rest of the club. Don't be fooled by the maid costume--Yukimura dreams of being a "fine Japanese boy."

The Neighbors Club

Previous club activity logs:

Hasegawa Kodaka, a lone wolf at a new school, happens to come across his gloomy classmate Mikazuki Yozora chattering happily away by herself. The two of them discuss the process of making friends, and Yozora, who's got energy to spare for the oddest things, spontaneously creates a new club for unfortunate souls who desperately need to make friends. The club's ranks quickly expand to include Kashiwazaki Sena, who's obsessed with bishoujo games and who happens to be the daughter of the academy director, and Kusunoki Yukimura, who constantly strives toward the noble ideal of manhoodwhile wearing a maid costume. The Neighbors Club is on a roll!

Haganai

I don't have many friends

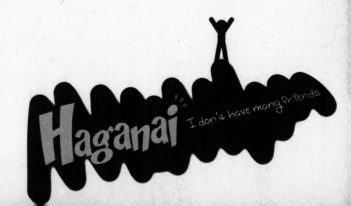

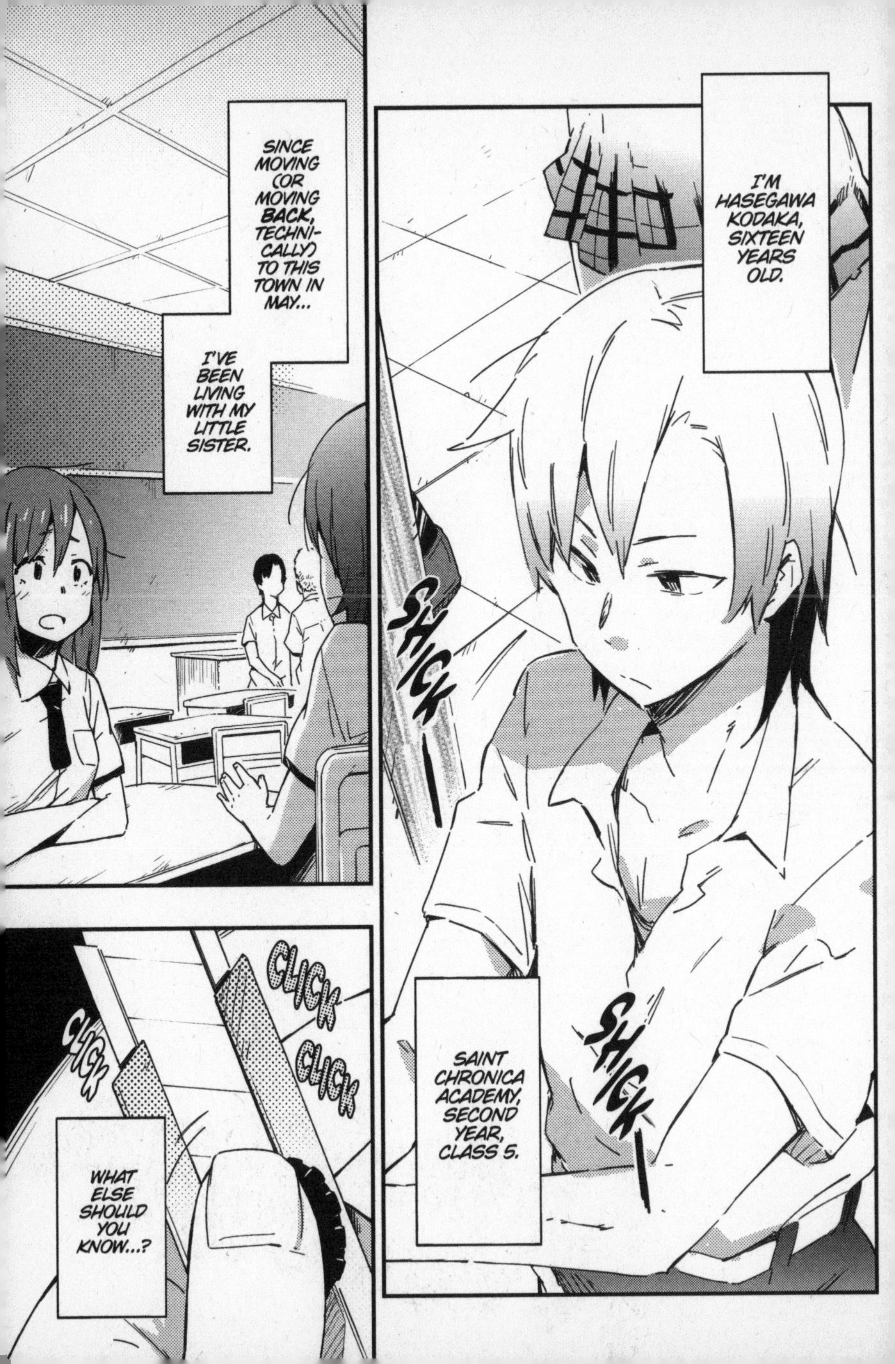
I'M HASEGAWA KODAKA, SIXTEEN YEARS OLD.
SHICK
SAINT CHRONICA ACADEMY, SECOND YEAR, CLASS 5.
SHICK
SINCE MOVING (OR MOVING BACK, TECHNICALLY) TO THIS TOWN IN MAY...
I'VE BEEN LIVING WITH MY LITTLE SISTER.
CLICK
CLICK
CLICK
WHAT ELSE SHOULD YOU KNOW...?

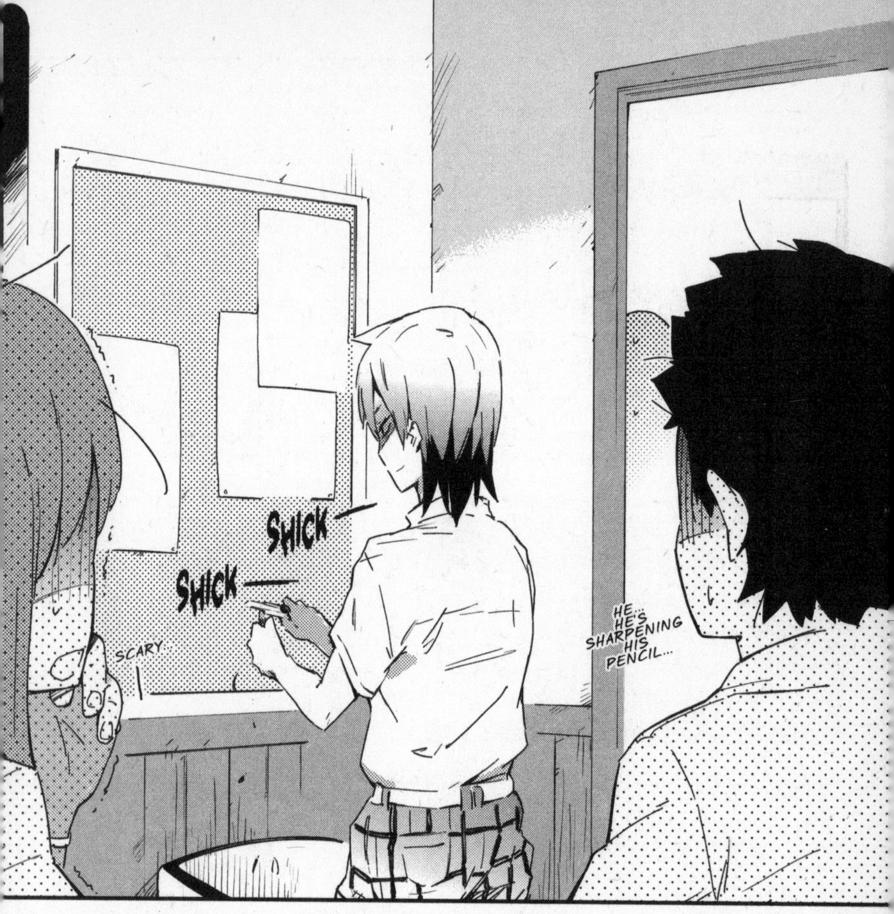
HE... HE'S SHARPENING HIS PENCIL...
SHICK
SHICK
SCARY...

Club Activity Log 11: LOL

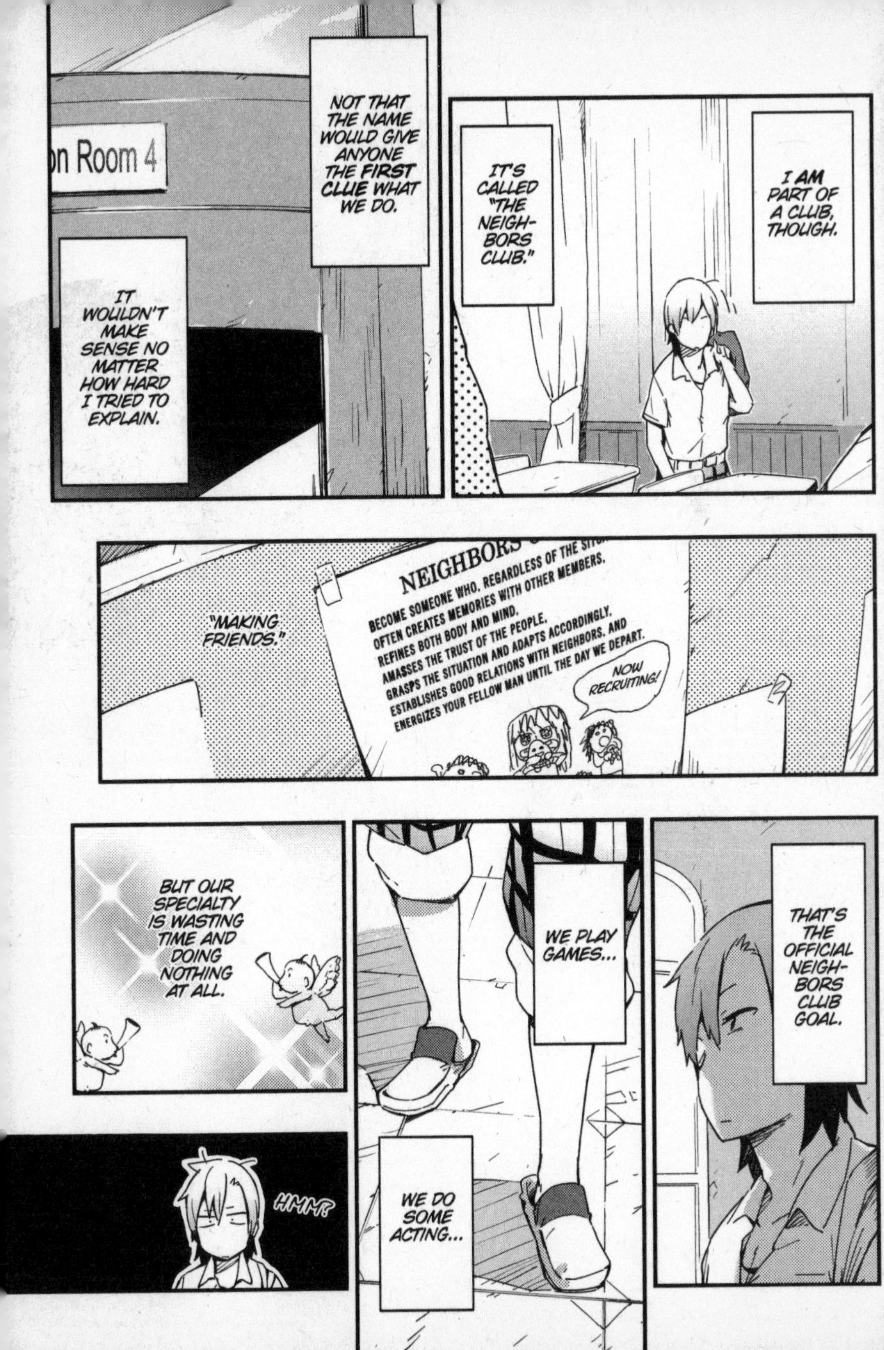
I AM PART OF A CLUB, THOUGH.
IT'S CALLED "THE NEIGH-BORS CLUB."
on Room 4
NOT THAT THE NAME WOULD GIVE ANYONE THE FIRST CLUE WHAT WE DO.
IT WOULDN'T MAKE SENSE NO MATTER HOW HARD I TRIED TO EXPLAIN.
NEIGHBORS
BECOME SOMEONE WHO, REGARDLESS OF THE SITU
OFTEN CREATES MEMORIES WITH OTHER MEMBERS.
REFINES BOTH BODY AND MIND.
AMASSES THE TRUST OF THE PEOPLE.
GRASPS THE SITUATION AND ADAPTS ACCORDINGLY.
ESTABLISHES GOOD RELATIONS WITH NEIGHBORS, AND
ENERGIZES YOUR FELLOW MAN UNTIL THE DAY WE DEPART.
NOW RECRUITING!
"MAKING FRIENDS."
THAT'S THE OFFICIAL NEIGH-BORS CLUB GOAL.
WE PLAY GAMES...
WE DO SOME ACTING...
BUT OUR SPECIALTY IS WASTING TIME AND DOING NOTHING AT ALL.
HMM?

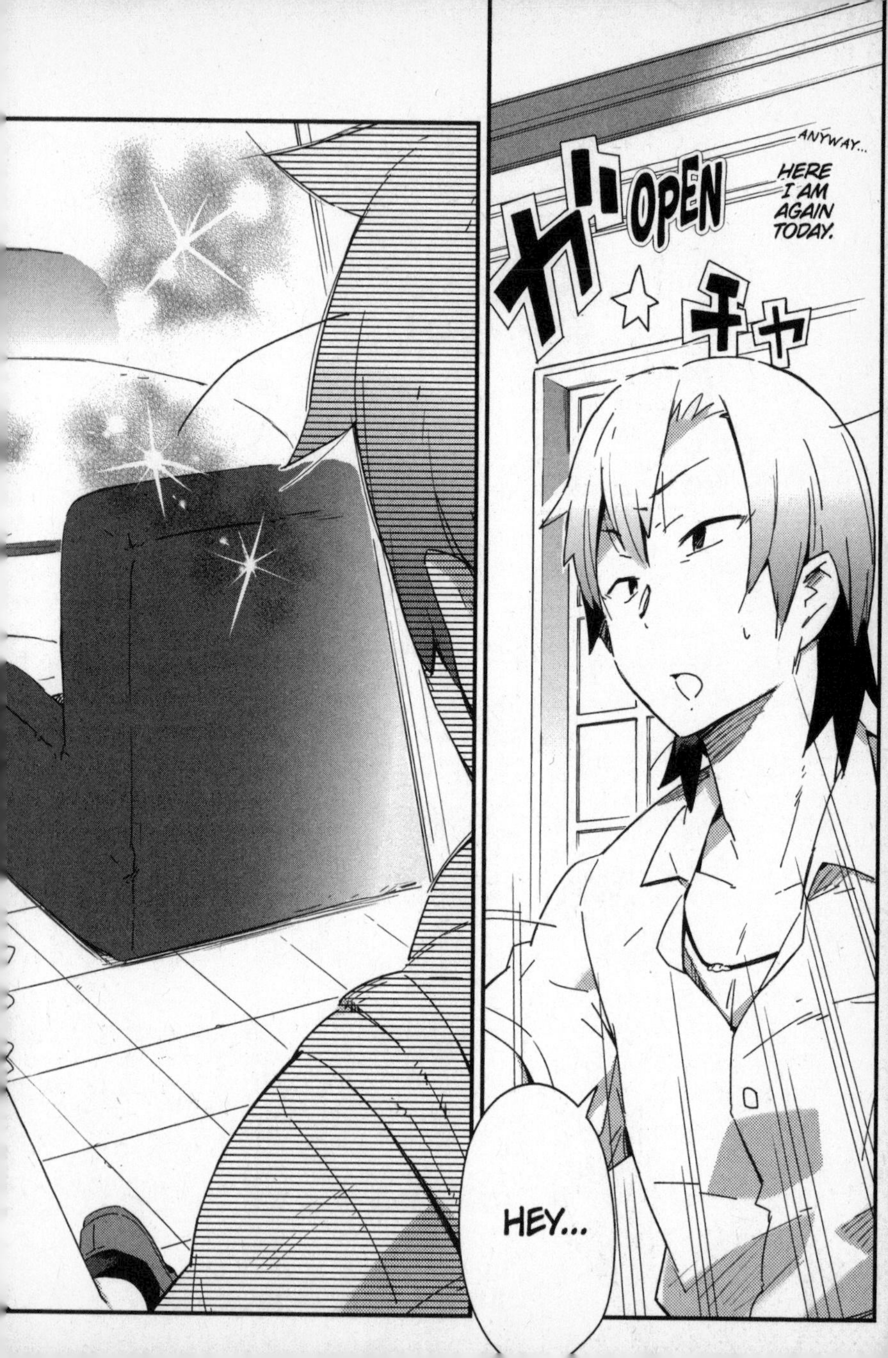
ANYWAY...
HERE I AM AGAIN TODAY.
ガ☆チャ
OPEN
HEY...

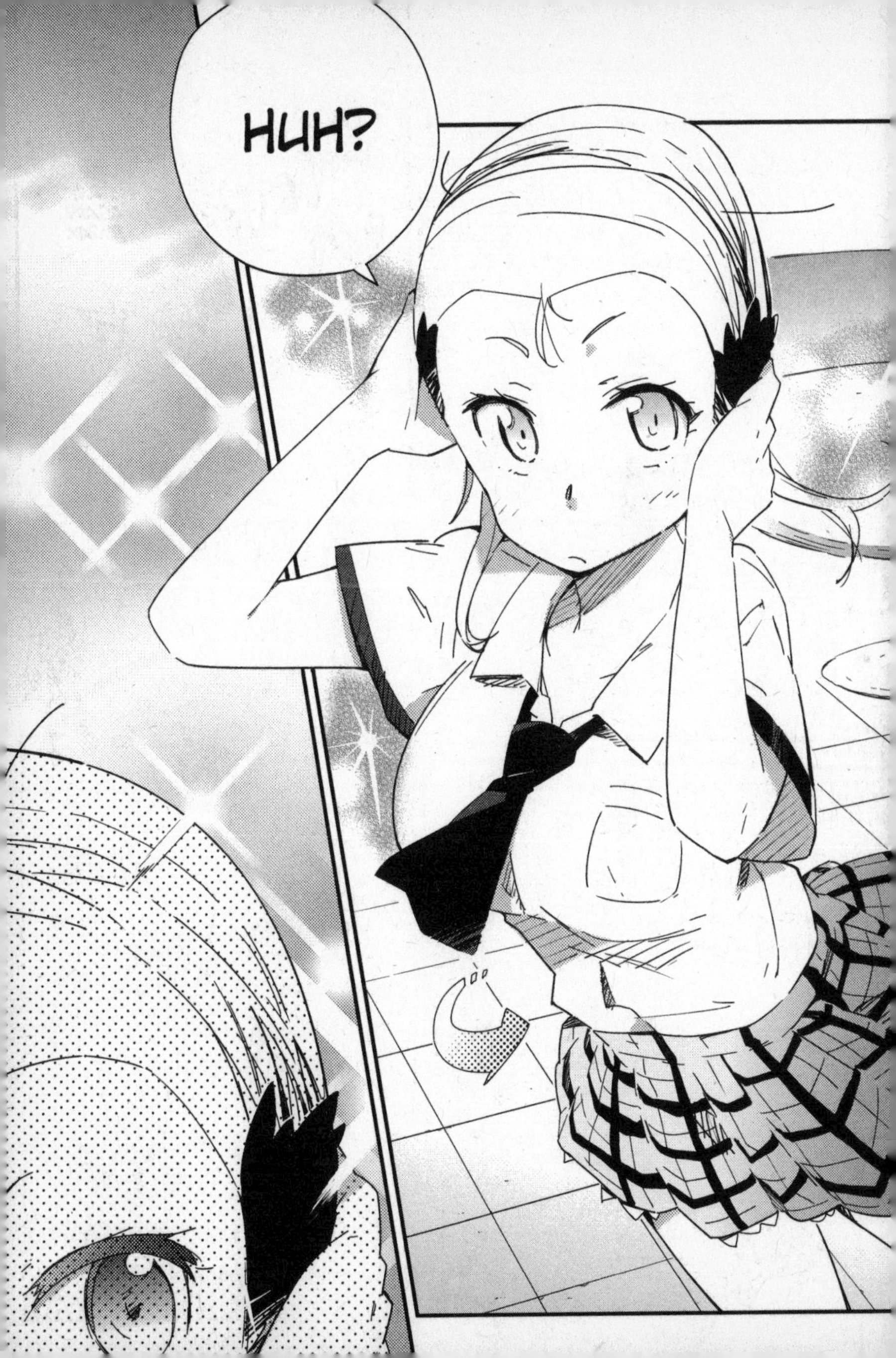
HUH?

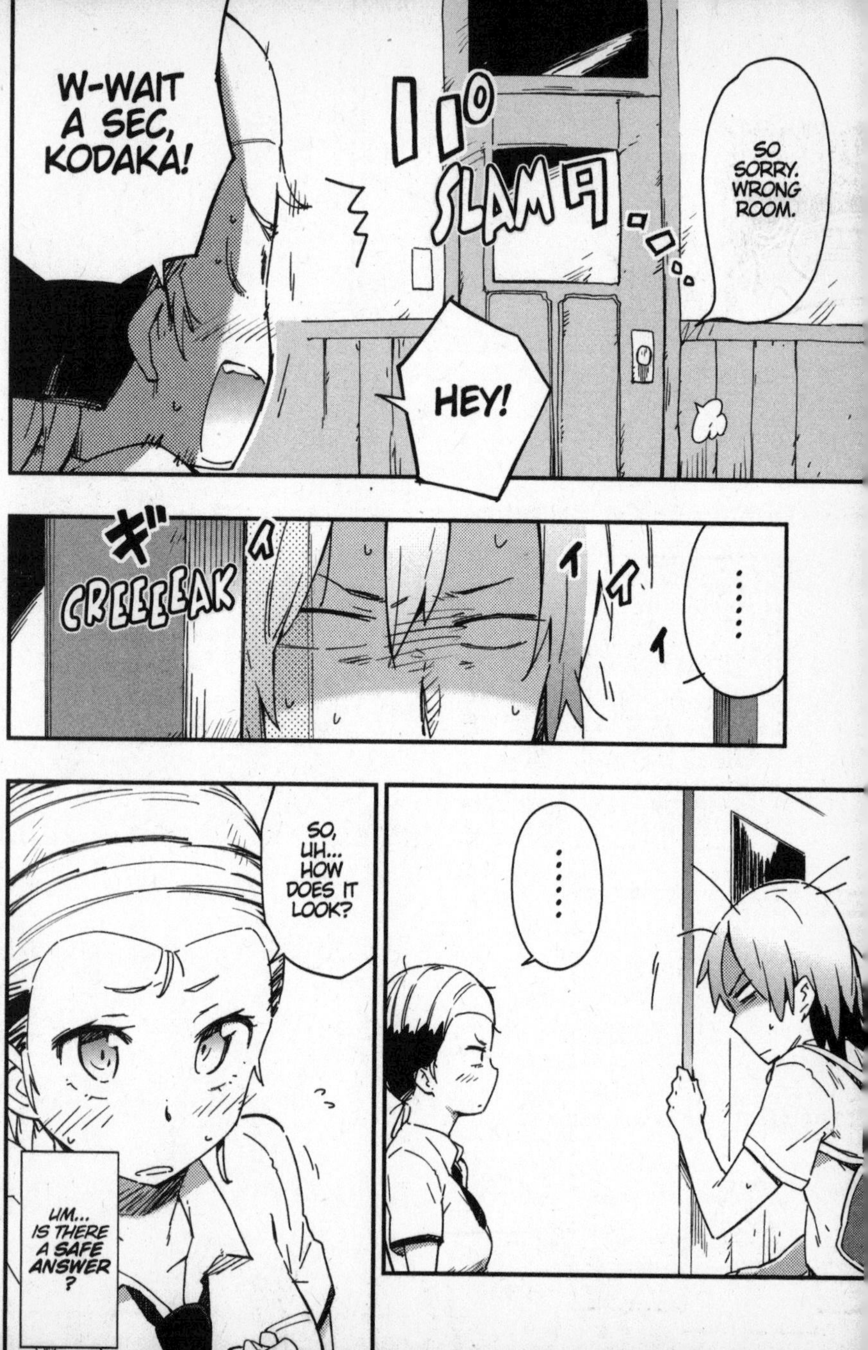
SO SORRY. WRONG ROOM.
SLAM
HEY!
W-WAIT A SEC, KODAKA!
……
CREEEEAK
……
SO, UH... HOW DOES IT LOOK?
UM... IS THERE A SAFE ANSWER?

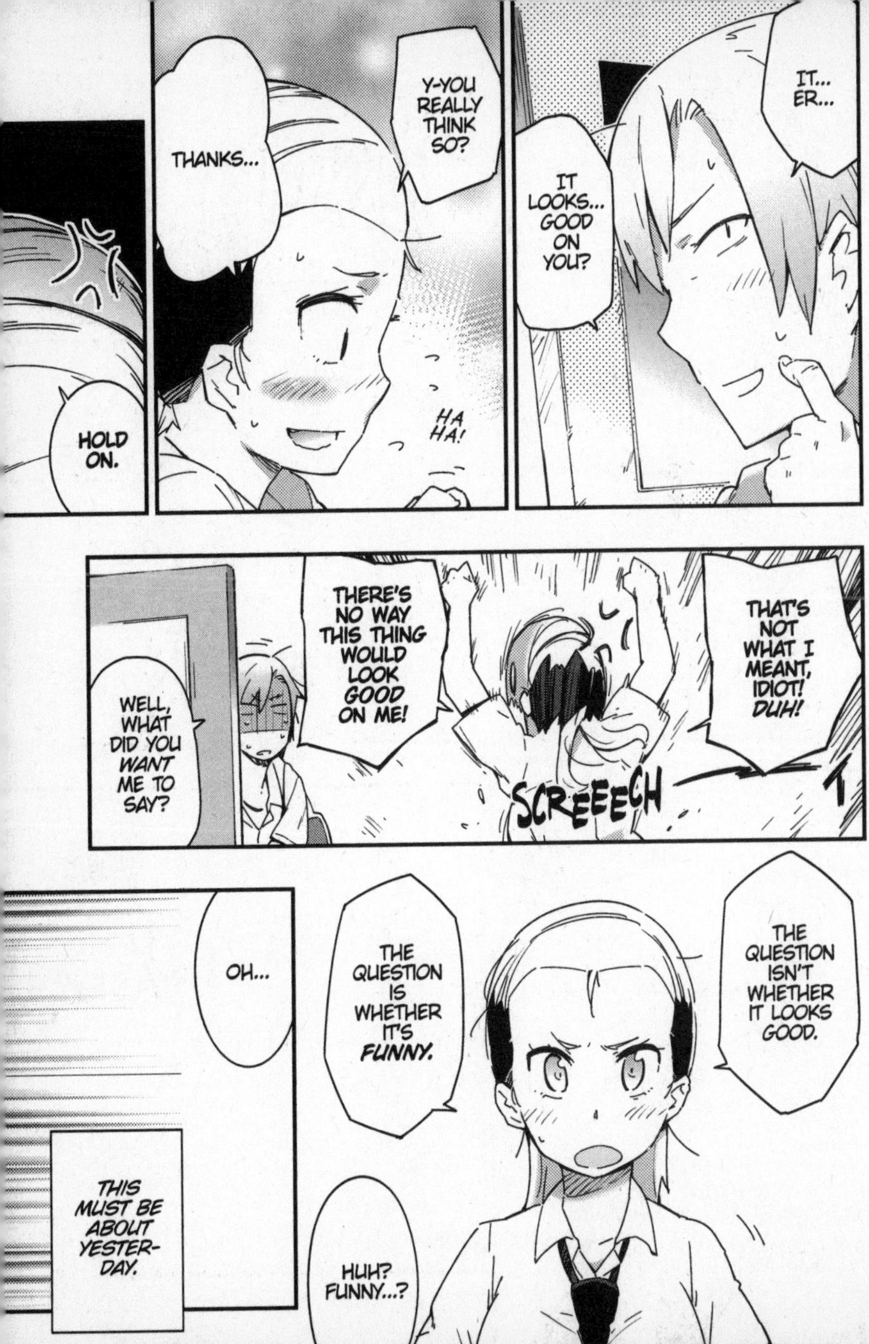
IT... ER...
IT LOOKS... GOOD ON YOU?
Y-YOU REALLY THINK SO?
THANKS...
HA HA!
HOLD ON.
THAT'S NOT WHAT I MEANT, IDIOT! *DUH!*
THERE'S NO WAY THIS THING WOULD LOOK *GOOD* ON ME!
SCREEECH
WELL, WHAT DID YOU *WANT* ME TO SAY?
THE QUESTION ISN'T WHETHER IT LOOKS GOOD.
THE QUESTION IS WHETHER IT'S *FUNNY.*
HUH? FUNNY...?
OH...
THIS MUST BE ABOUT YESTER-DAY.

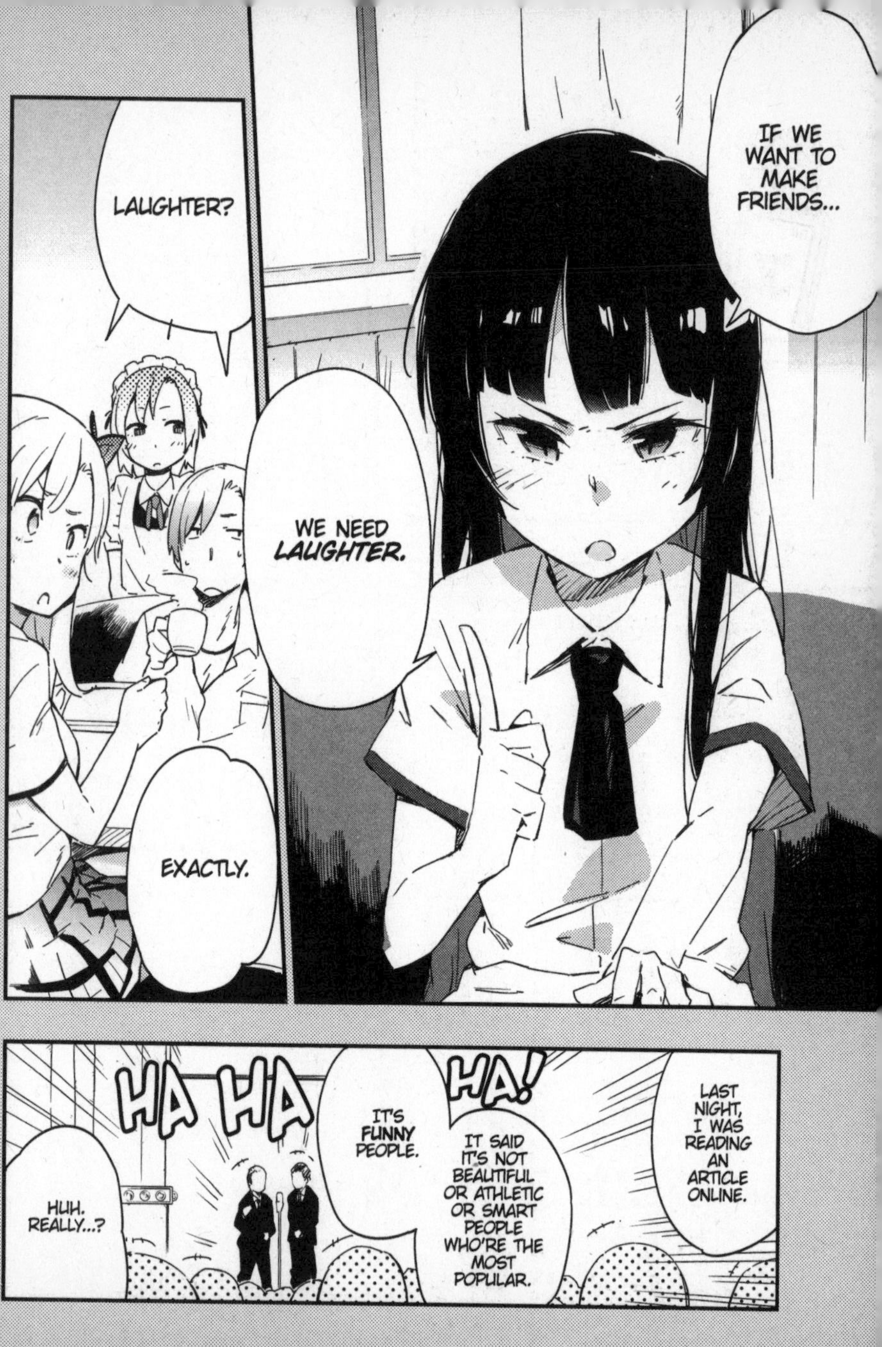
IF WE WANT TO MAKE FRIENDS...
WE NEED LAUGHTER.
LAUGHTER?
EXACTLY.
LAST NIGHT, I WAS READING AN ARTICLE ONLINE.
IT SAID IT'S NOT BEAUTIFUL OR ATHLETIC OR SMART PEOPLE WHO'RE THE MOST POPULAR.
IT'S FUNNY PEOPLE.
HA HA HA!
HUH. REALLY...?

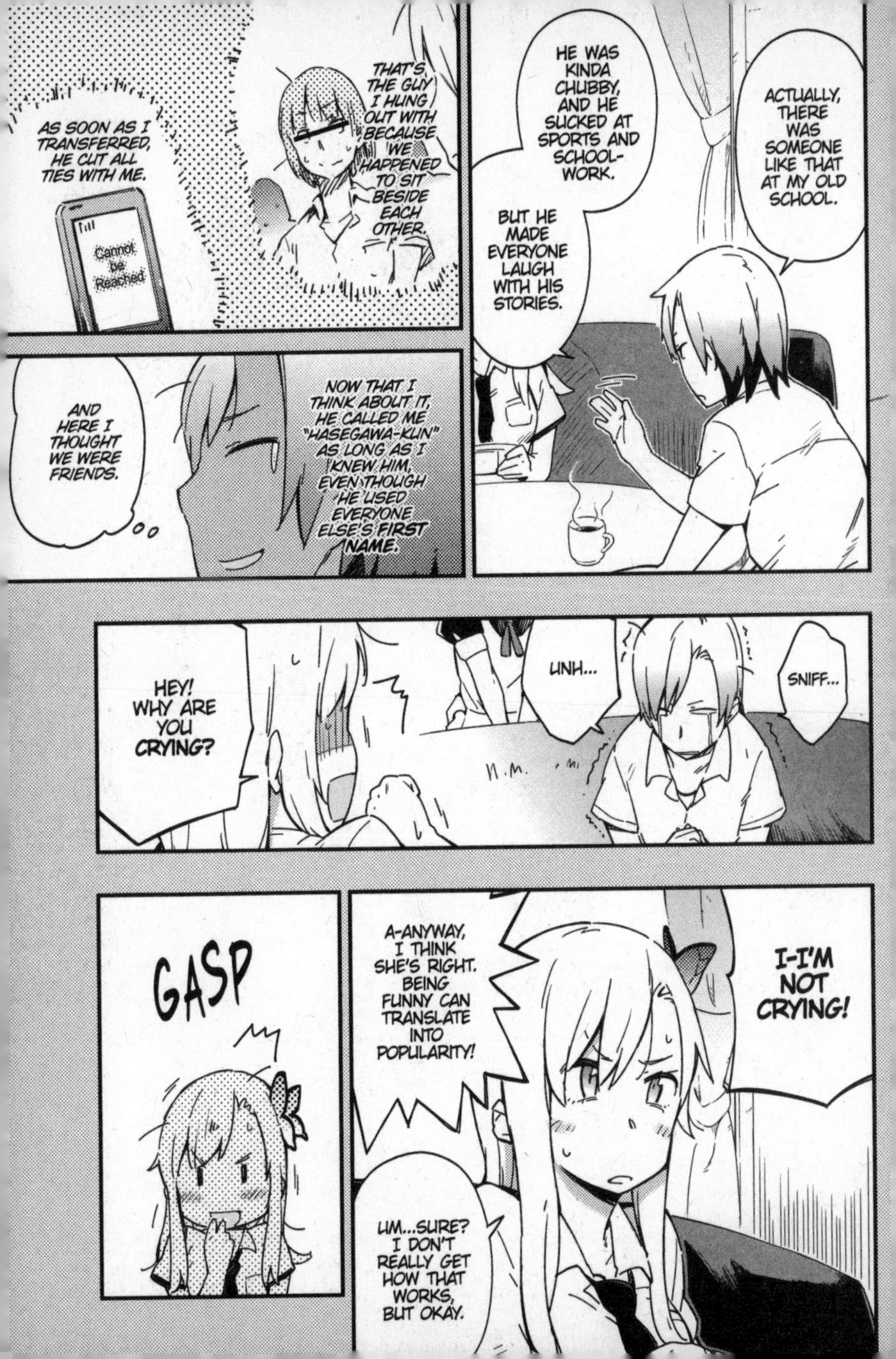
ACTUALLY, THERE WAS SOMEONE LIKE THAT AT MY OLD SCHOOL.
HE WAS KINDA CHUBBY, AND HE SUCKED AT SPORTS AND SCHOOL-WORK.
BUT HE MADE EVERYONE LAUGH WITH HIS STORIES.
THAT'S THE GUY I HUNG OUT WITH BECAUSE WE HAPPENED TO SIT BESIDE EACH OTHER.
AS SOON AS I TRANSFERRED, HE CUT ALL TIES WITH ME.
Cannot be Reached
NOW THAT I THINK ABOUT IT, HE CALLED ME "HASEGAWA-KUN" AS LONG AS I KNEW HIM, EVEN THOUGH HE USED EVERYONE ELSE'S FIRST NAME.
AND HERE I THOUGHT WE WERE FRIENDS.
SNIFF...
UNH...
HEY! WHY ARE YOU CRYING?
I-I'M NOT CRYING!
A-ANYWAY, I THINK SHE'S RIGHT. BEING FUNNY CAN TRANSLATE INTO POPULARITY!
UM...SURE? I DON'T REALLY GET HOW THAT WORKS, BUT OKAY.
GASP

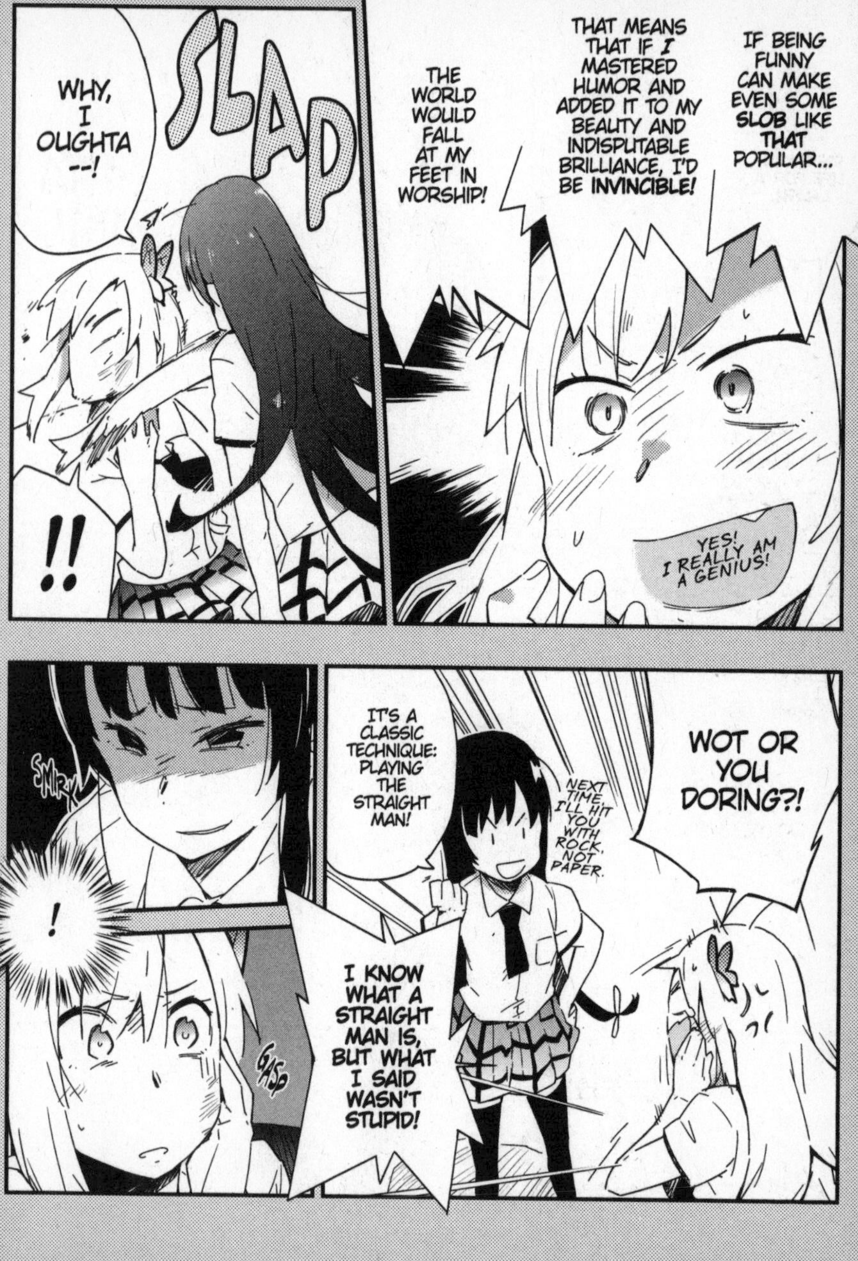
IF BEING FUNNY CAN MAKE EVEN SOME SLOB LIKE THAT POPULAR...
THAT MEANS THAT IF I MASTERED HUMOR AND ADDED IT TO MY BEAUTY AND INDISPUTABLE BRILLIANCE, I'D BE INVINCIBLE!
THE WORLD WOULD FALL AT MY FEET IN WORSHIP!
YES! I REALLY AM A GENIUS!
SLAP
WHY, I OUGHTA --!
!!
WOT OR YOU DORING?!
IT'S A CLASSIC TECHNIQUE: PLAYING THE STRAIGHT MAN!
NEXT TIME, I'LL HIT YOU WITH ROCK, NOT PAPER.
I KNOW WHAT A STRAIGHT MAN IS, BUT WHAT I SAID WASN'T STUPID!
SMIRK
!
GASP

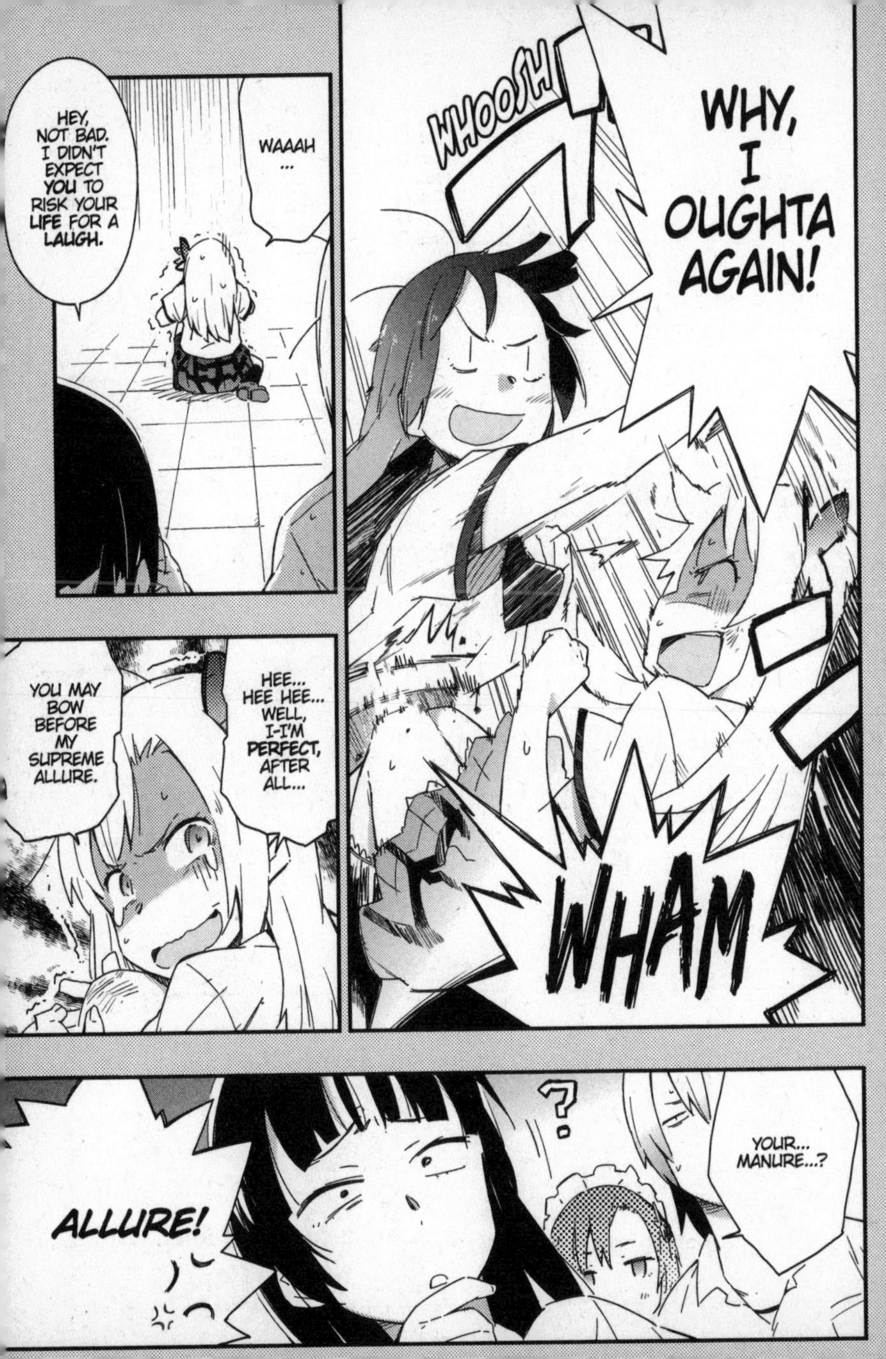
WHY, I OUGHTA AGAIN!
WHOOSH
WHAM
WAAAH ...
HEY, NOT BAD. I DIDN'T EXPECT YOU TO RISK YOUR LIFE FOR A LAUGH.
HEE... HEE HEE... WELL, I-I'M PERFECT, AFTER ALL...
YOU MAY BOW BEFORE MY SUPREME ALLURE.
YOUR... MANURE...?
?
ALLURE!

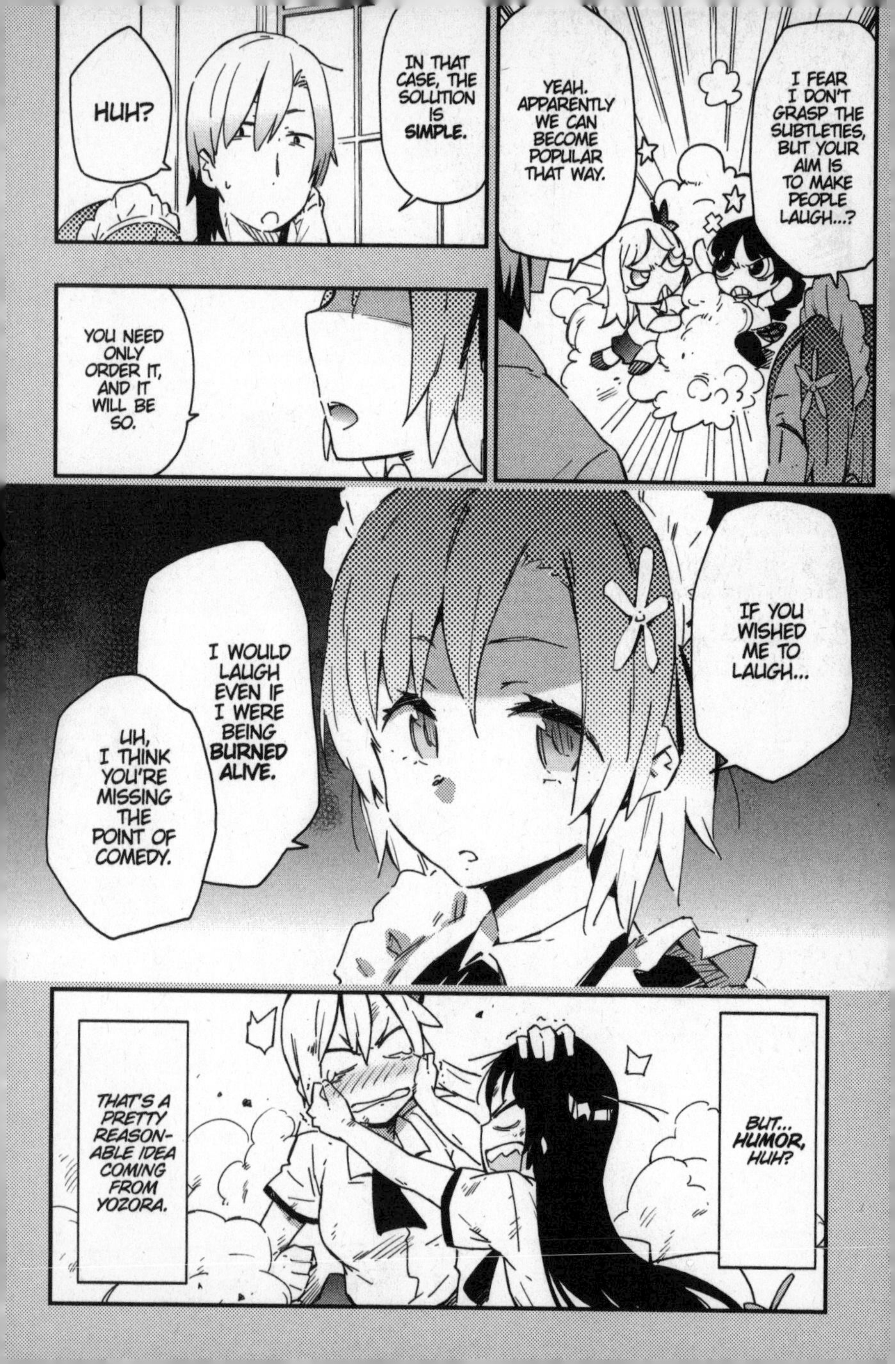
I FEAR I DON'T GRASP THE SUBTLETIES, BUT YOUR AIM IS TO MAKE PEOPLE LAUGH...?
YEAH. APPARENTLY WE CAN BECOME POPULAR THAT WAY.
IN THAT CASE, THE SOLUTION IS SIMPLE.
HUH?
YOU NEED ONLY ORDER IT, AND IT WILL BE SO.
IF YOU WISHED ME TO LAUGH...
I WOULD LAUGH EVEN IF I WERE BEING BURNED ALIVE.
UH, I THINK YOU'RE MISSING THE POINT OF COMEDY.
BUT... HUMOR, HUH?
THAT'S A PRETTY REASONABLE IDEA COMING FROM YOZORA.

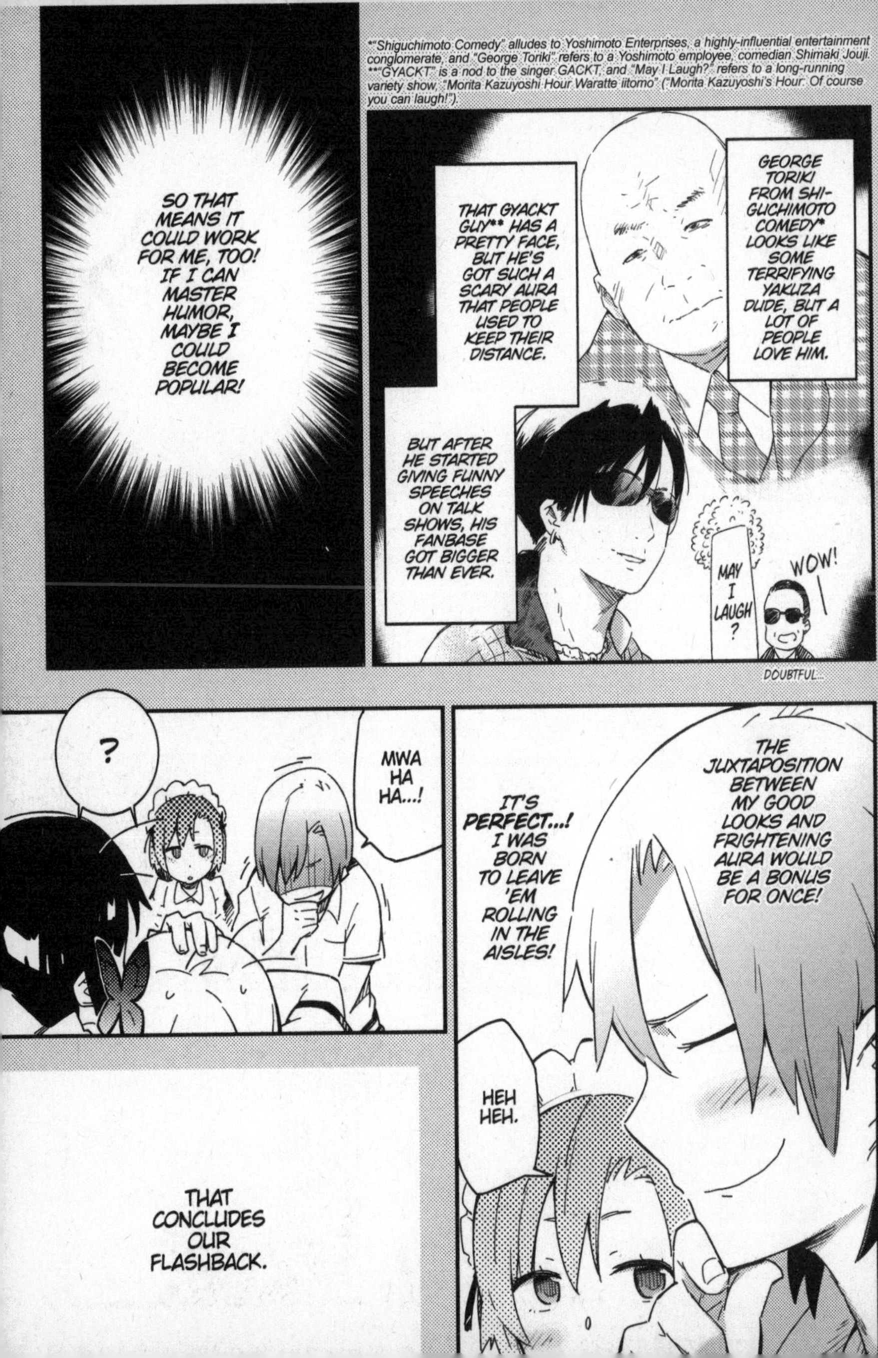
GEORGE TORIKI FROM SHI-GUCHIMOTO COMEDY* LOOKS LIKE SOME TERRIFYING YAKUZA DUDE, BUT A LOT OF PEOPLE LOVE HIM.
THAT GYACKT GUY** HAS A PRETTY FACE, BUT HE'S GOT SUCH A SCARY AURA THAT PEOPLE USED TO KEEP THEIR DISTANCE.
BUT AFTER HE STARTED GIVING FUNNY SPEECHES ON TALK SHOWS, HIS FANBASE GOT BIGGER THAN EVER.
WOW!
MAY I LAUGH?
DOUBTFUL...
SO THAT MEANS IT COULD WORK FOR ME, TOO! IF I CAN MASTER HUMOR, MAYBE I COULD BECOME POPULAR!
THE JUXTAPOSITION BETWEEN MY GOOD LOOKS AND FRIGHTENING AURA WOULD BE A BONUS FOR ONCE!
IT'S PERFECT...! I WAS BORN TO LEAVE 'EM ROLLING IN THE AISLES!
HEH HEH.
MWA HA HA...!
?
THAT CONCLUDES OUR FLASHBACK.

*"Shiguchimoto Comedy" alludes to Yoshimoto Enterprises, a highly-influential entertainment conglomerate, and "George Toriki" refers to a Yoshimoto employee, comedian Shimaki Jouji.
**"GYACKT" is a nod to the singer GACKT, and "May I Laugh?" refers to a long-running variety show, "Morita Kazuyoshi Hour Waratte iitomo" ("Morita Kazuyoshi's Hour: Of course you can laugh!").

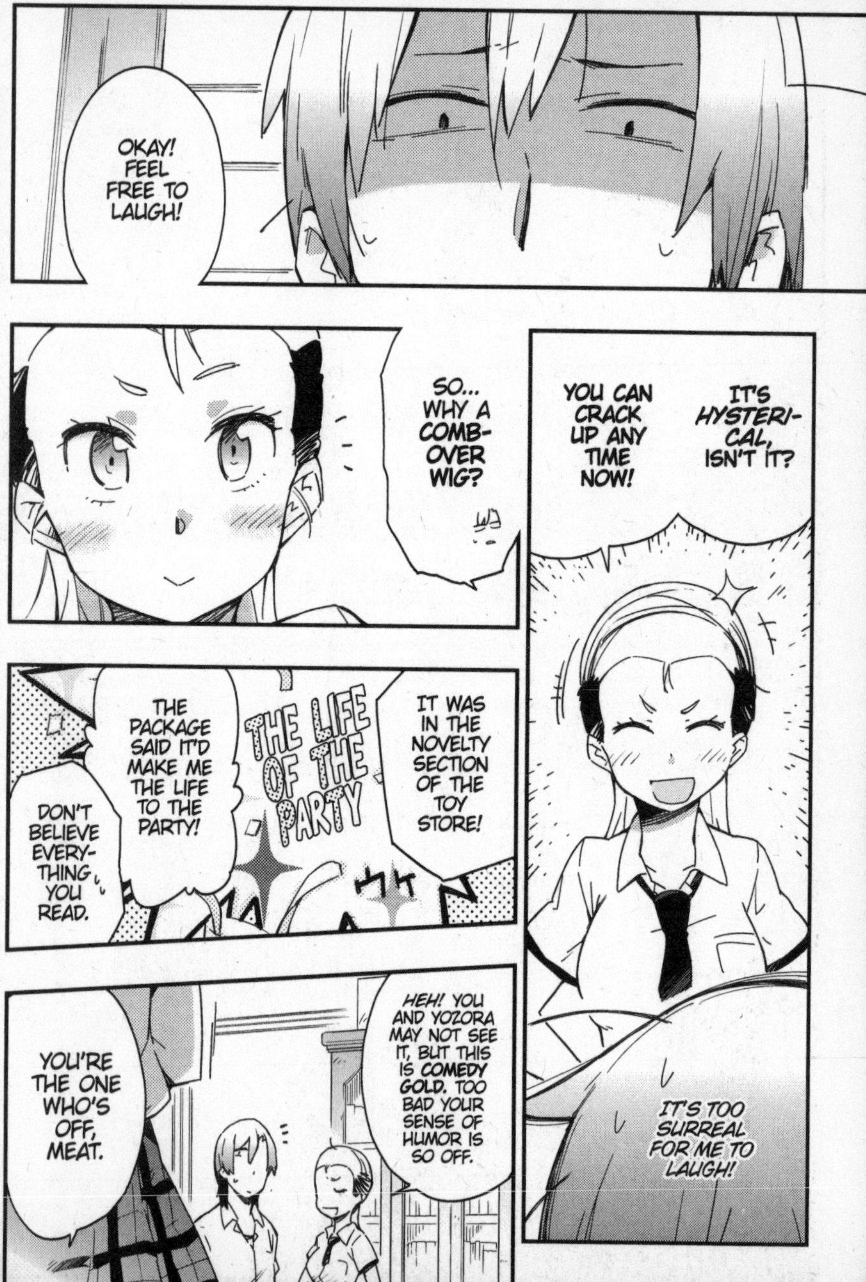
OKAY! FEEL FREE TO LAUGH!
IT'S HYSTERICAL, ISN'T IT?
YOU CAN CRACK UP ANY TIME NOW!
IT'S TOO SURREAL FOR ME TO LAUGH!
SO... WHY A COMB-OVER WIG?
IT WAS IN THE NOVELTY SECTION OF THE TOY STORE!
THE LIFE OF THE PARTY
THE PACKAGE SAID IT'D MAKE ME THE LIFE TO THE PARTY!
DON'T BELIEVE EVERYTHING YOU READ.
HEH! YOU AND YOZORA MAY NOT SEE IT, BUT THIS IS COMEDY GOLD. TOO BAD YOUR SENSE OF HUMOR IS SO OFF.
YOU'RE THE ONE WHO'S OFF, MEAT.

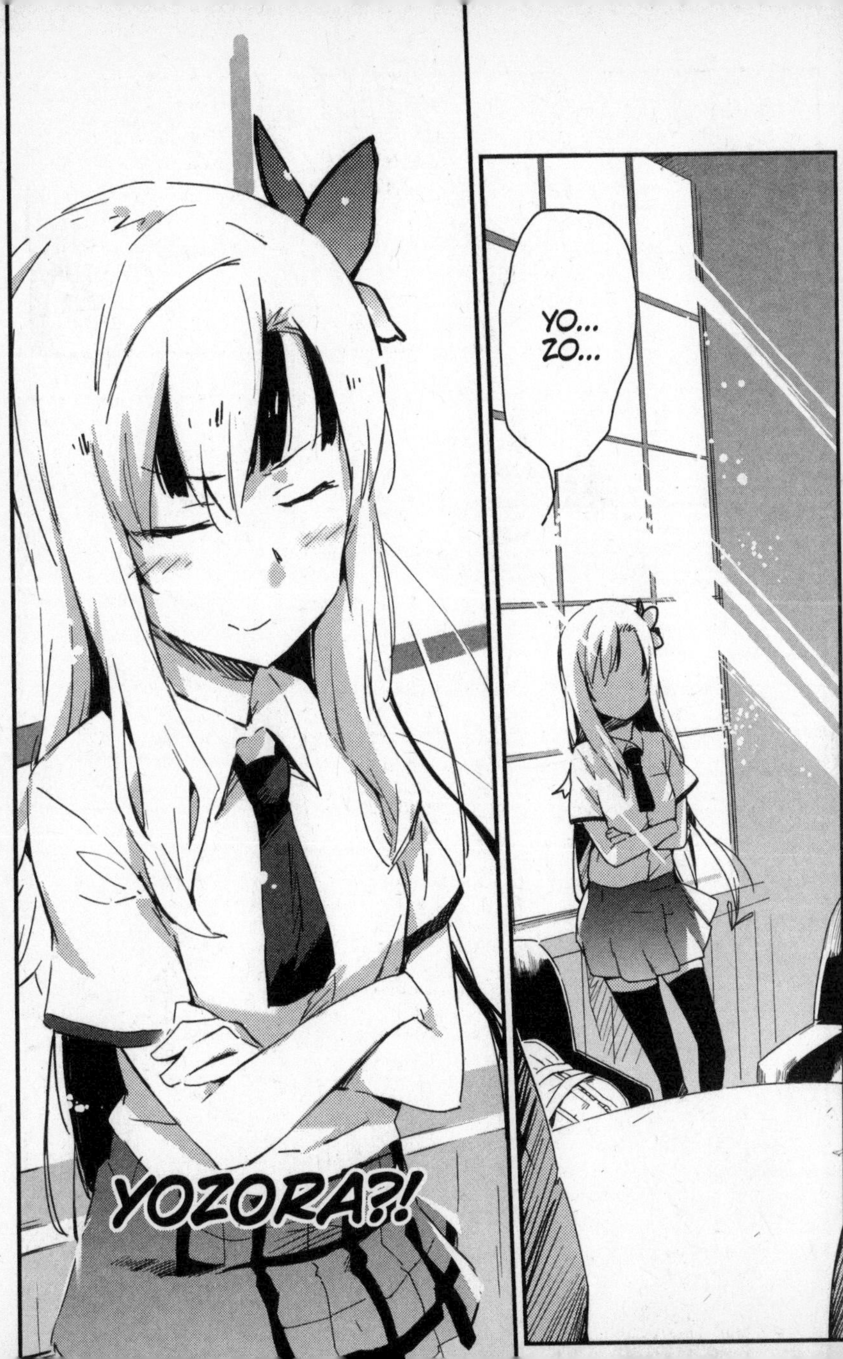
YO... ZO...
YOZORA?!

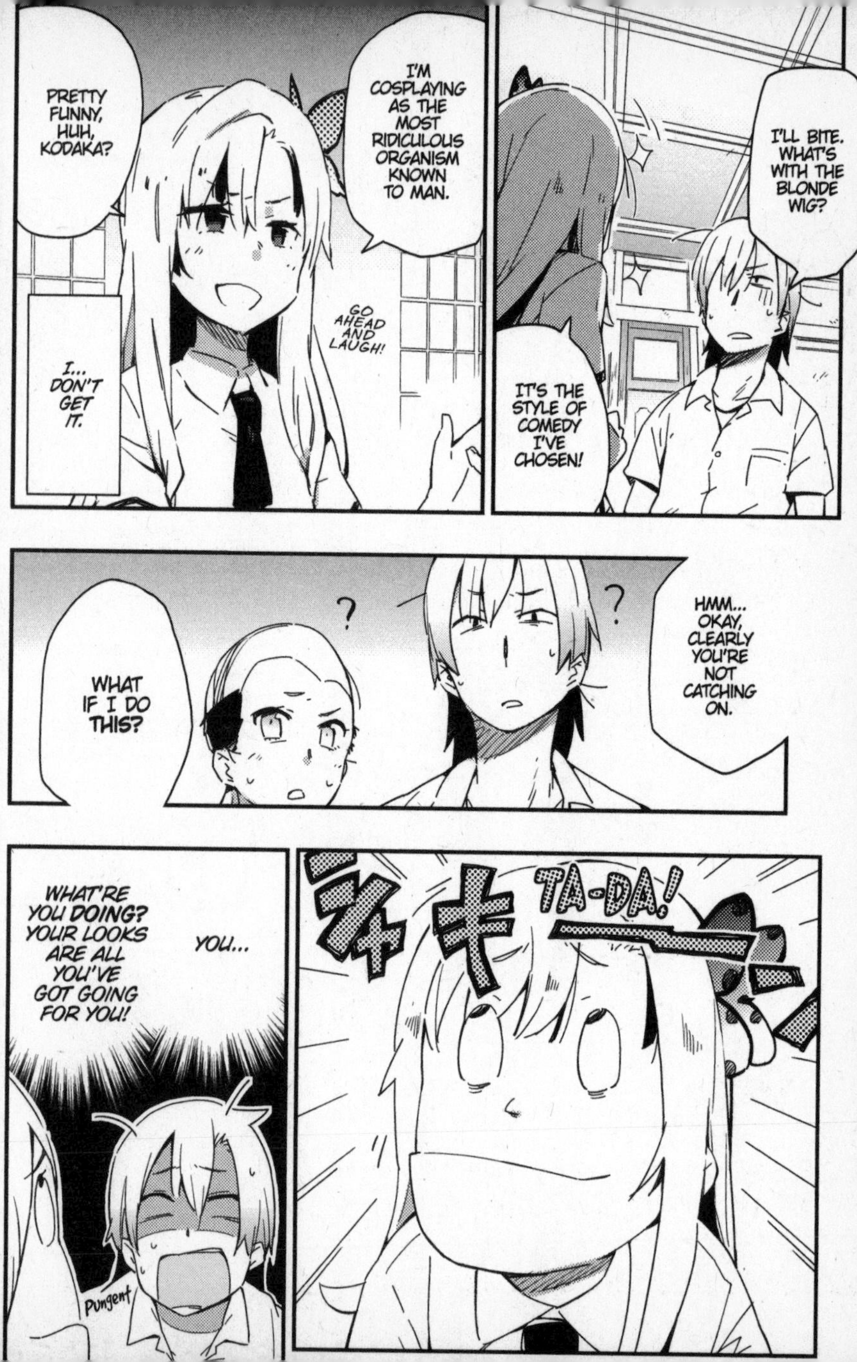

I'LL BITE. WHAT'S WITH THE BLONDE WIG?
IT'S THE STYLE OF COMEDY I'VE CHOSEN!
I'M COSPLAYING AS THE MOST RIDICULOUS ORGANISM KNOWN TO MAN.
PRETTY FUNNY, HUH, KODAKA?
GO AHEAD AND LAUGH!
I... DON'T GET IT.
HMM... OKAY, CLEARLY YOU'RE NOT CATCHING ON.
WHAT IF I DO THIS?
TA-DA!
YOU...
WHAT'RE YOU DOING? YOUR LOOKS ARE ALL YOU'VE GOT GOING FOR YOU!
Pungent

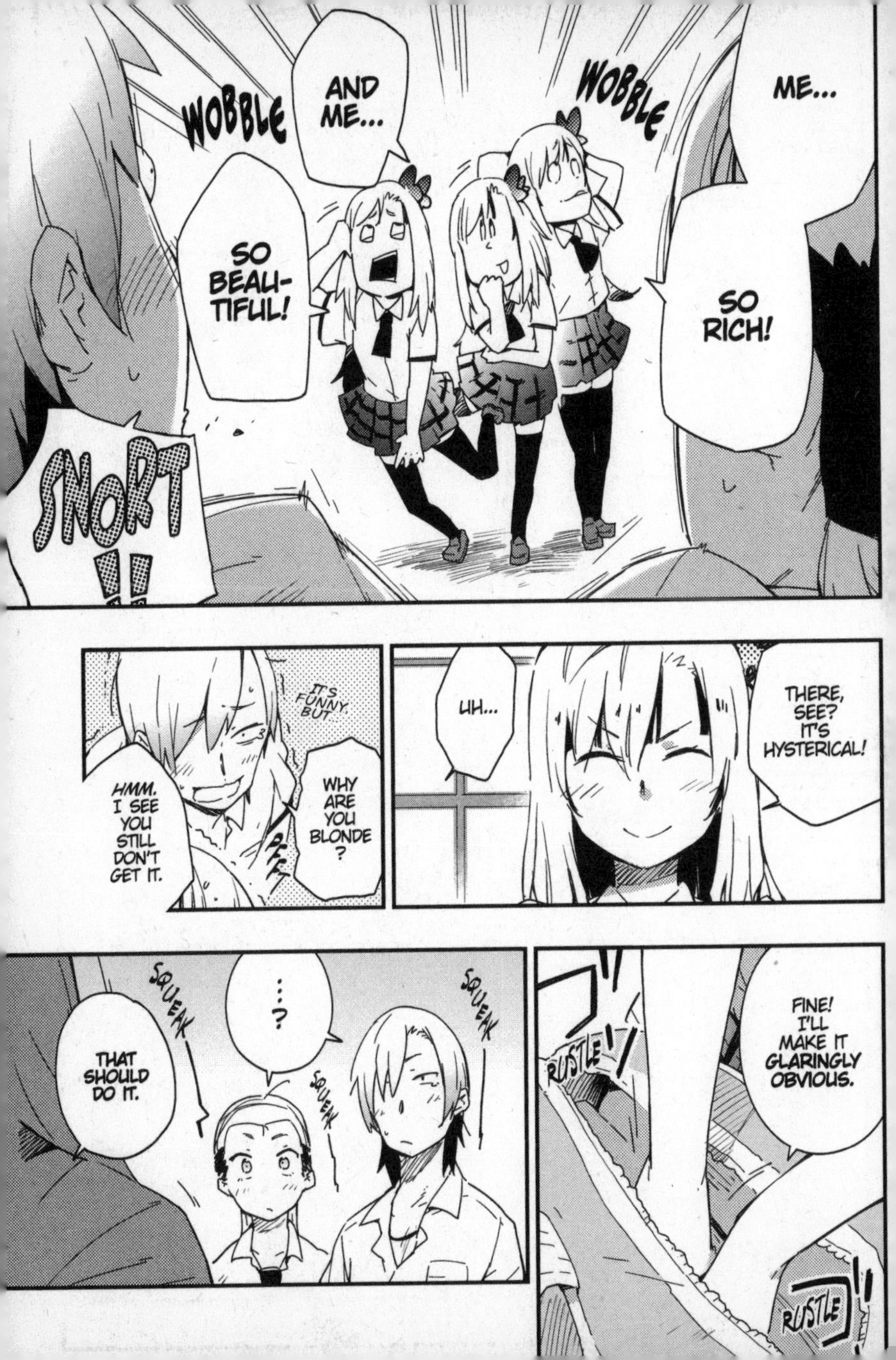
ME...
WOBBLE
AND ME...
WOBBLE
SO RICH!
SO BEAUTIFUL!
SNORT!!
THERE, SEE? IT'S HYSTERICAL!
UH...
IT'S FUNNY, BUT
WHY ARE YOU BLONDE?
HMM. I SEE YOU STILL DON'T GET IT.
FINE! I'LL MAKE IT GLARINGLY OBVIOUS.
RUSTLE!
RUSTLE!
SQUEAK
...?
SQUEAK
SQUEAK
THAT SHOULD DO IT.

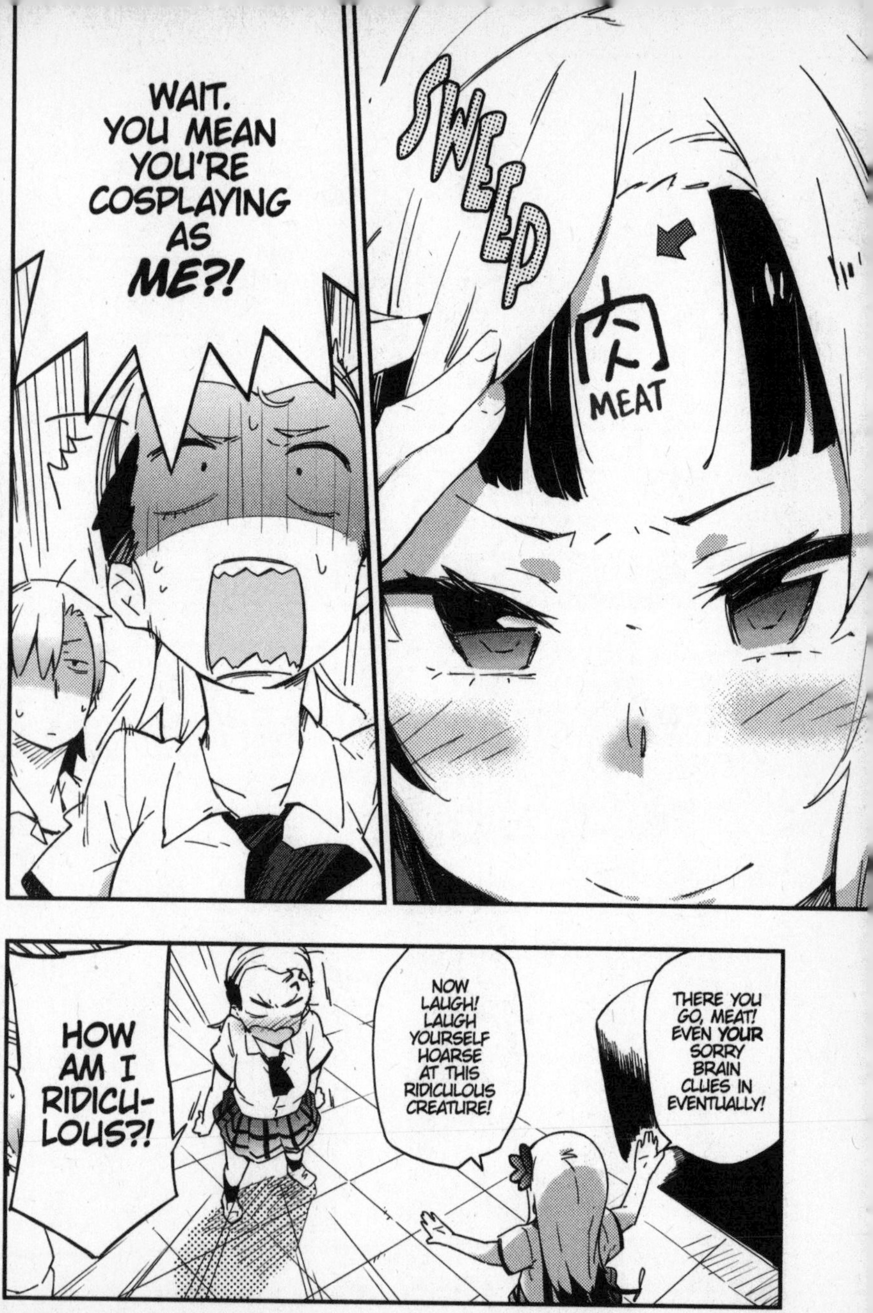
SWEEP
肉
MEAT
WAIT. YOU MEAN YOU'RE COSPLAYING AS ME?!
THERE YOU GO, MEAT! EVEN YOUR SORRY BRAIN CLUES IN EVENTUALLY!
NOW LAUGH! LAUGH YOURSELF HOARSE AT THIS RIDICULOUS CREATURE!
HOW AM I RIDICU-LOUS?!

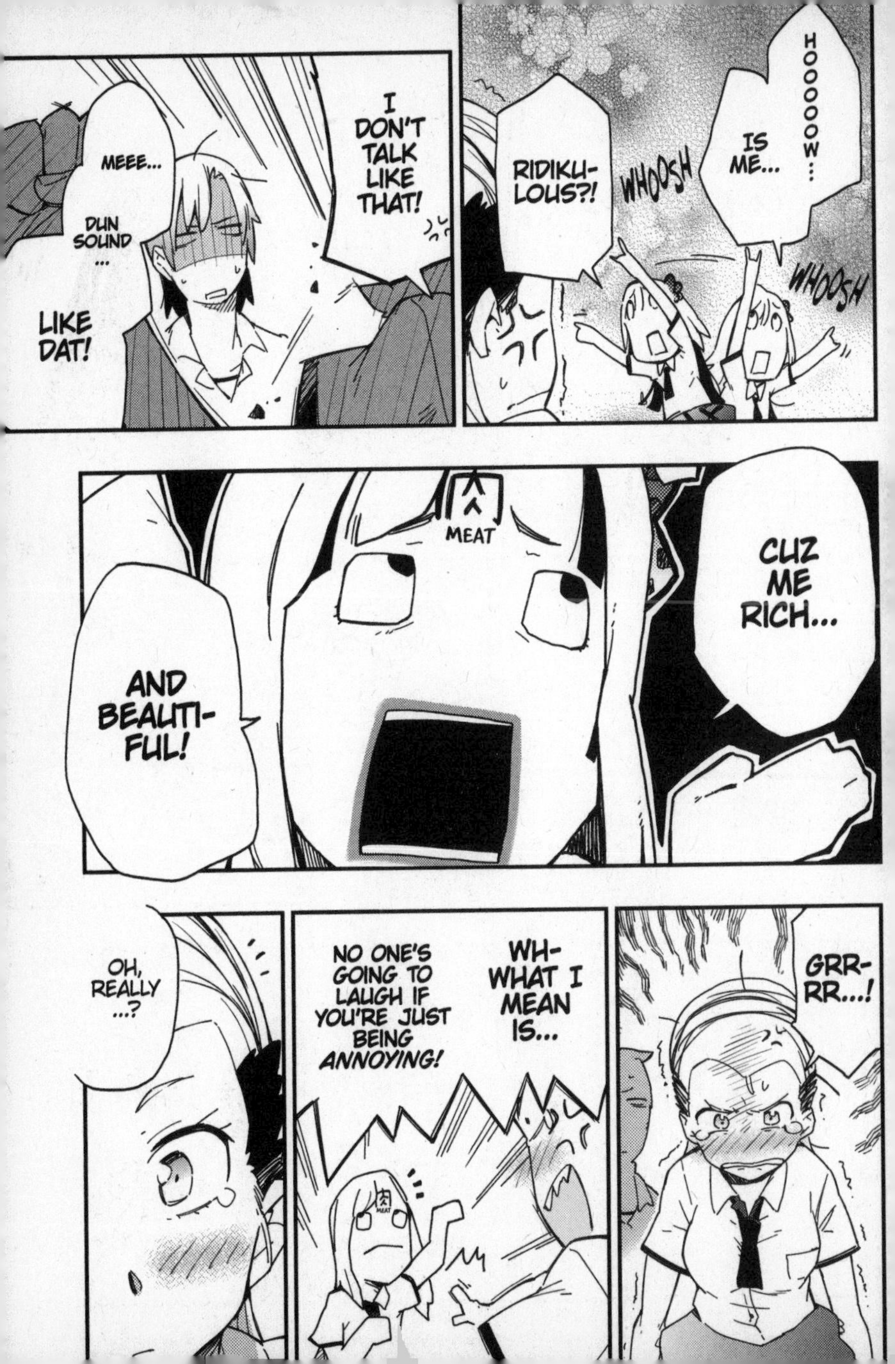
HOOOOOW...
IS ME...
RIDIKU-LOUS?!
WHOOSH
WHOOSH
I DON'T TALK LIKE THAT!
MEEE...
DUN SOUND ...
LIKE DAT!
CUZ ME RICH...
MEAT
AND BEAUTI-FUL!
GRRR-RR...!
WH-WHAT I MEAN IS...
NO ONE'S GOING TO LAUGH IF YOU'RE JUST BEING ANNOYING!
MEAT
OH, REALLY ...?

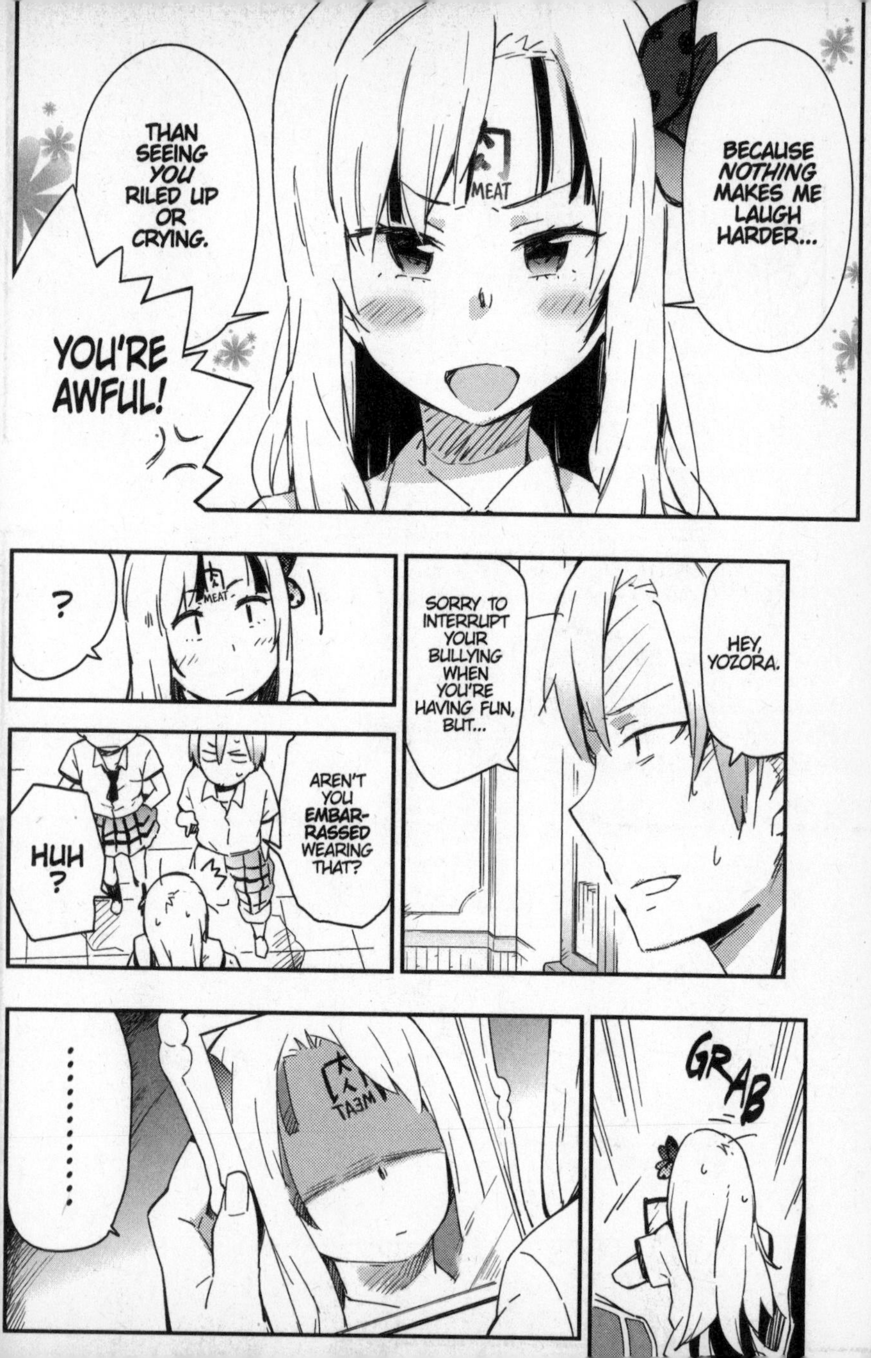
BECAUSE NOTHING MAKES ME LAUGH HARDER...
MEAT
THAN SEEING YOU RILED UP OR CRYING.
YOU'RE AWFUL!
HEY, YOZORA.
SORRY TO INTERRUPT YOUR BULLYING WHEN YOU'RE HAVING FUN, BUT...
MEAT
?
AREN'T YOU EMBARRASSED WEARING THAT?
HUH?
GRAB
......

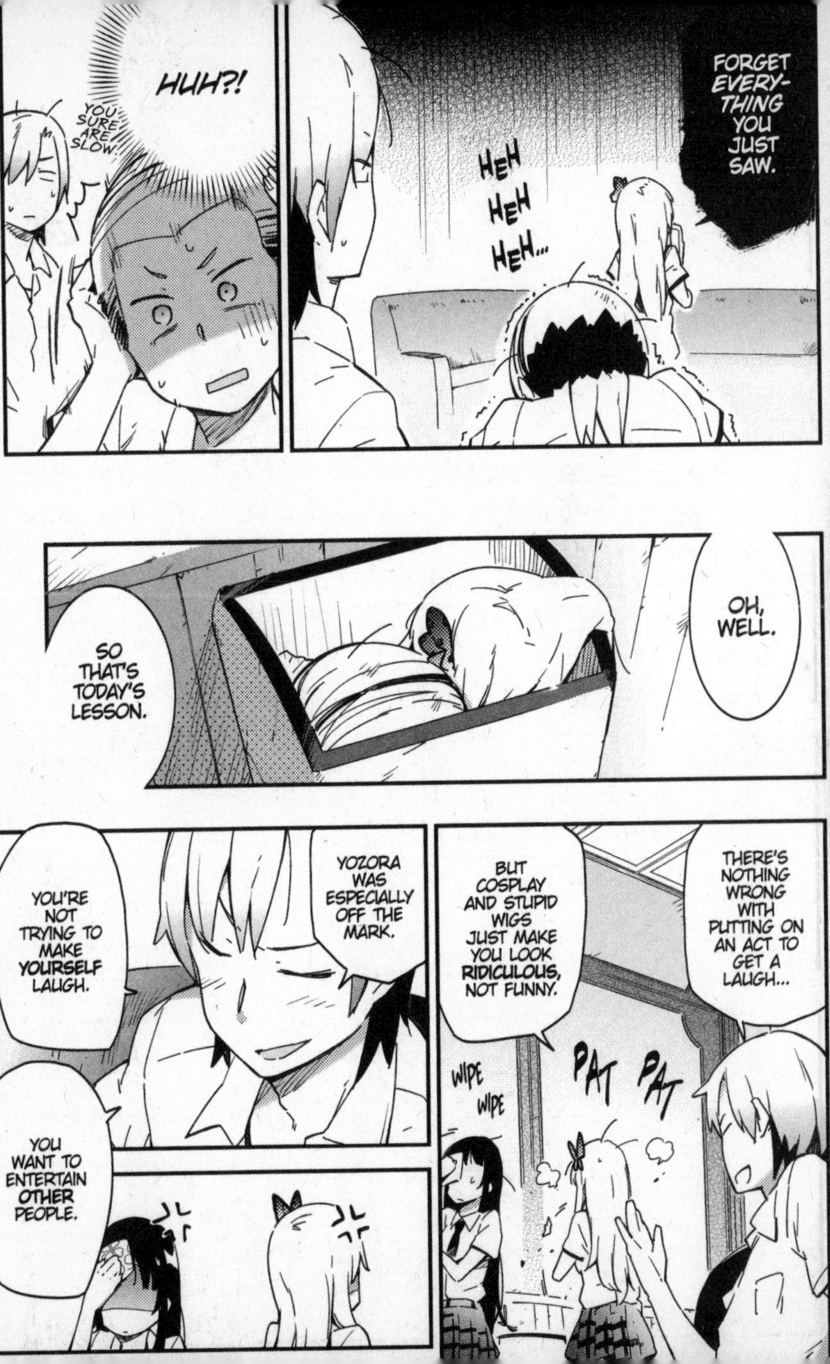
FORGET EVERYTHING YOU JUST SAW.
HEH HEH HEH...
HUH?!
YOU SURE ARE SLOW.
OH, WELL.
SO THAT'S TODAY'S LESSON.
THERE'S NOTHING WRONG WITH PUTTING ON AN ACT TO GET A LAUGH...
BUT COSPLAY AND STUPID WIGS JUST MAKE YOU LOOK RIDICULOUS, NOT FUNNY.
PAT PAT
WIPE WIPE
YOZORA WAS ESPECIALLY OFF THE MARK.
YOU'RE NOT TRYING TO MAKE YOURSELF LAUGH.
YOU WANT TO ENTERTAIN OTHER PEOPLE.

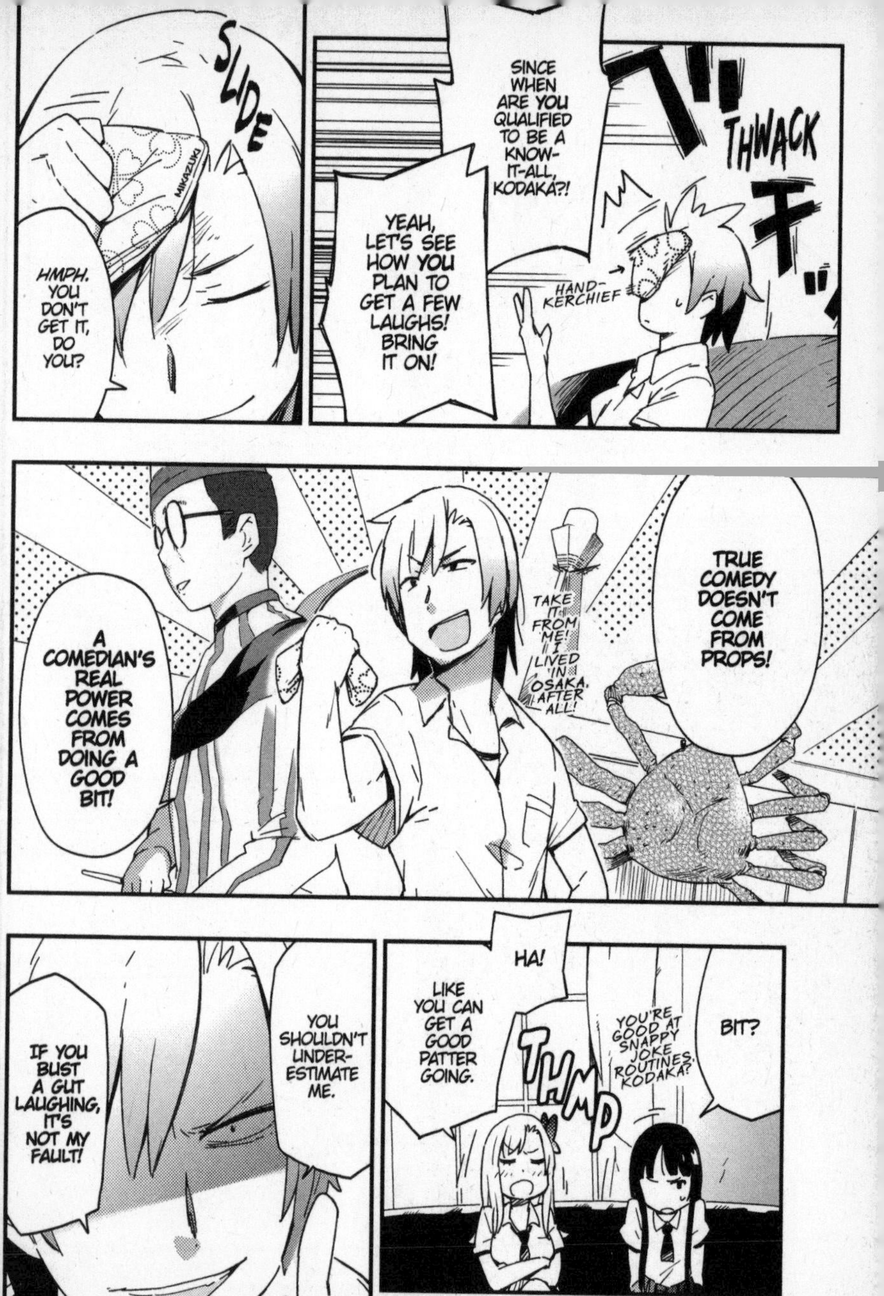
SINCE WHEN ARE YOU QUALIFIED TO BE A KNOW-IT-ALL, KODAKA?!
THWACK
YEAH, LET'S SEE HOW YOU PLAN TO GET A FEW LAUGHS! BRING IT ON!
HAND-KERCHIEF
SLIDE
MIKAZUKI
HMPH. YOU DON'T GET IT, DO YOU?
TRUE COMEDY DOESN'T COME FROM PROPS!
TAKE IT FROM ME! I LIVED IN OSAKA, AFTER ALL!
A COMEDIAN'S REAL POWER COMES FROM DOING A GOOD BIT!
BIT?
YOU'RE GOOD AT SNAPPY JOKE ROUTINES, KODAKA?
HA!
LIKE YOU CAN GET A GOOD PATTER GOING.
THMP
YOU SHOULDN'T UNDER-ESTIMATE ME.
IF YOU BUST A GUT LAUGHING, IT'S NOT MY FAULT!

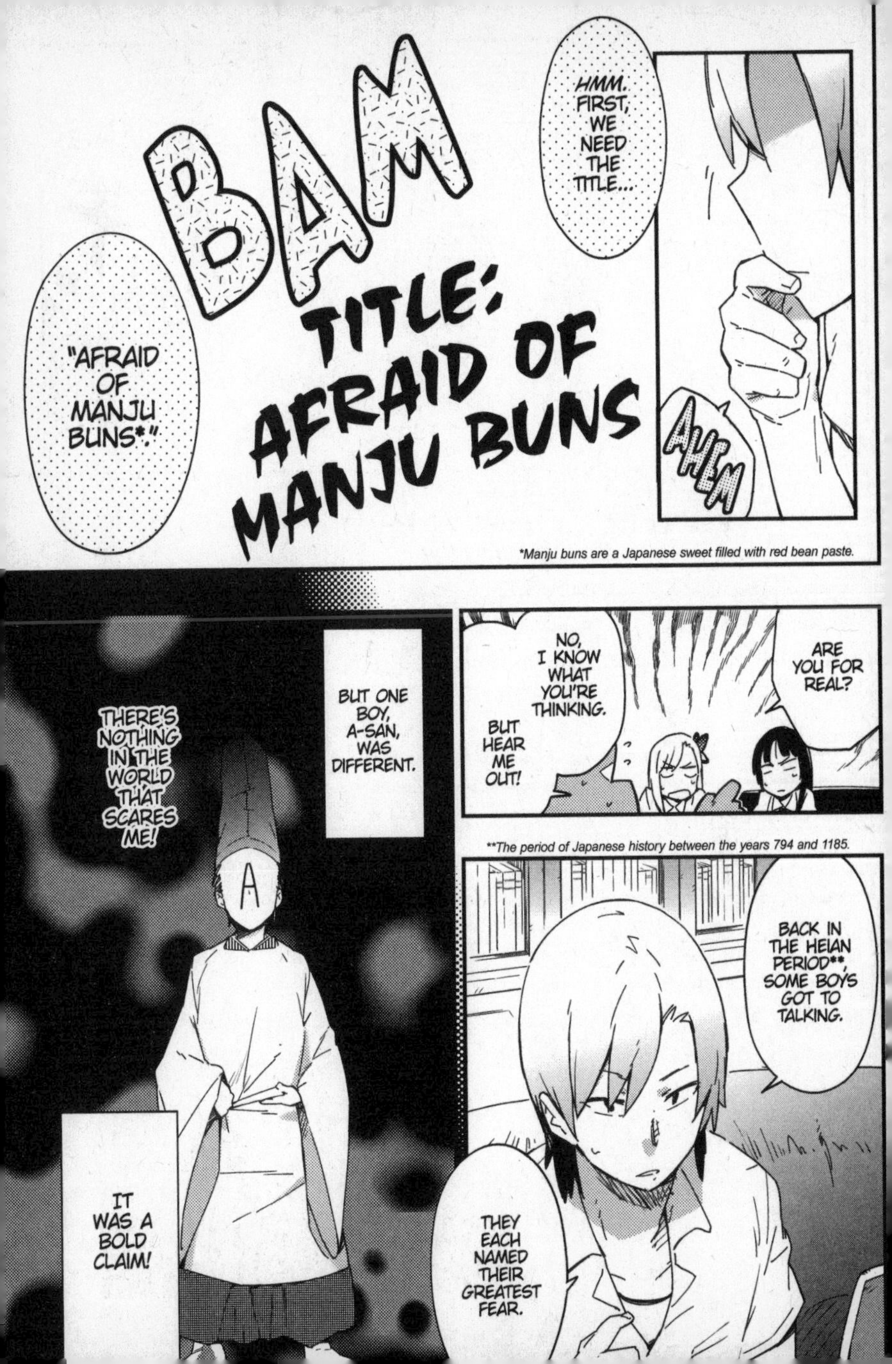
HMM. FIRST, WE NEED THE TITLE...
AHEM
BAM
TITLE: AFRAID OF MANJU BUNS
"AFRAID OF MANJU BUNS*."
ARE YOU FOR REAL?
NO, I KNOW WHAT YOU'RE THINKING.
BUT HEAR ME OUT!
BACK IN THE HEIAN PERIOD**, SOME BOYS GOT TO TALKING.
THEY EACH NAMED THEIR GREATEST FEAR.
BUT ONE BOY, A-SAN, WAS DIFFERENT.
THERE'S NOTHING IN THE WORLD THAT SCARES ME!
A
IT WAS A BOLD CLAIM!

*Manju buns are a Japanese sweet filled with red bean paste.

**The period of Japanese history between the years 794 and 1185.

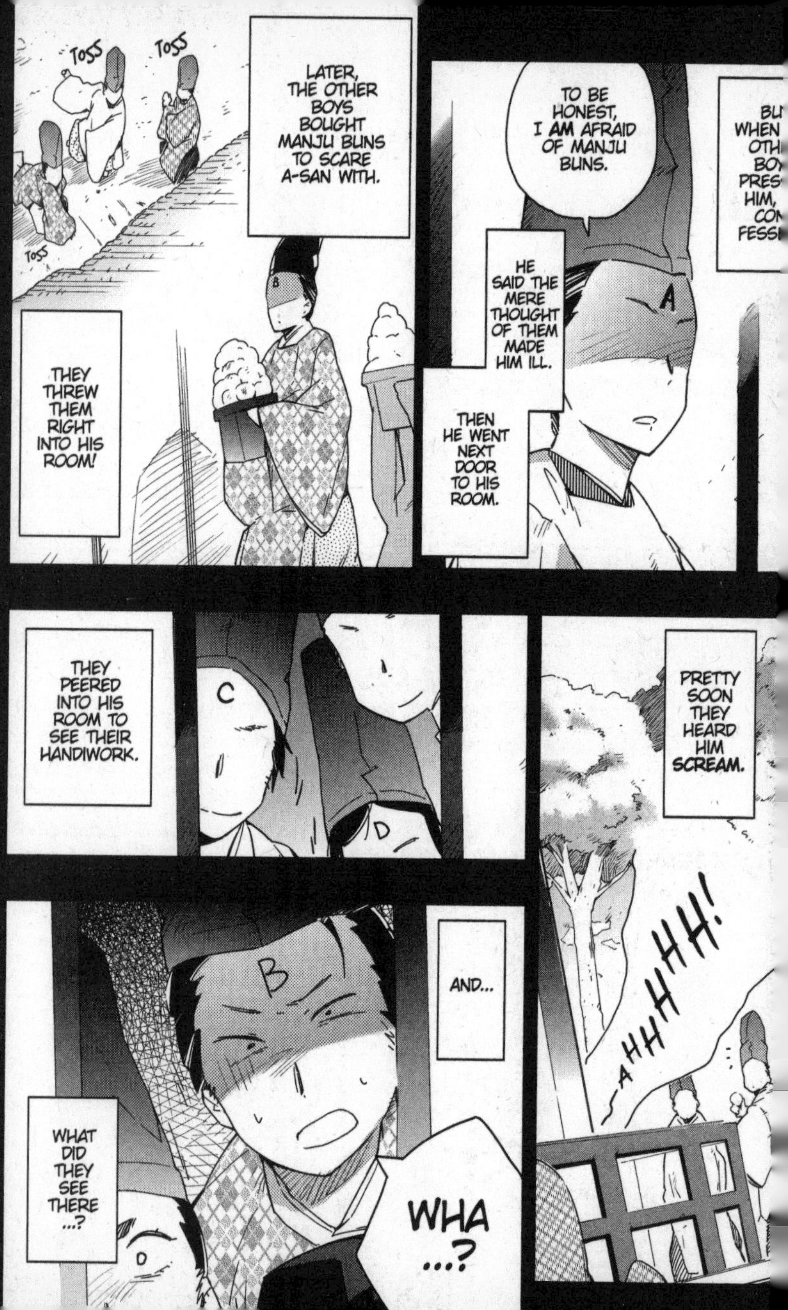
BU
WHEN
OTH
BOY
PRES
HIM,
CON
FESS
TO BE HONEST, I AM AFRAID OF MANJU BUNS.
HE SAID THE MERE THOUGHT OF THEM MADE HIM ILL.
THEN HE WENT NEXT DOOR TO HIS ROOM.
LATER, THE OTHER BOYS BOUGHT MANJU BUNS TO SCARE A-SAN WITH.
TOSS
TOSS
TOSS
THEY THREW THEM RIGHT INTO HIS ROOM!
PRETTY SOON THEY HEARD HIM SCREAM.
AHHHHH!
THEY PEERED INTO HIS ROOM TO SEE THEIR HANDIWORK.
AND...
WHAT DID THEY SEE THERE ...?
WHA ...?

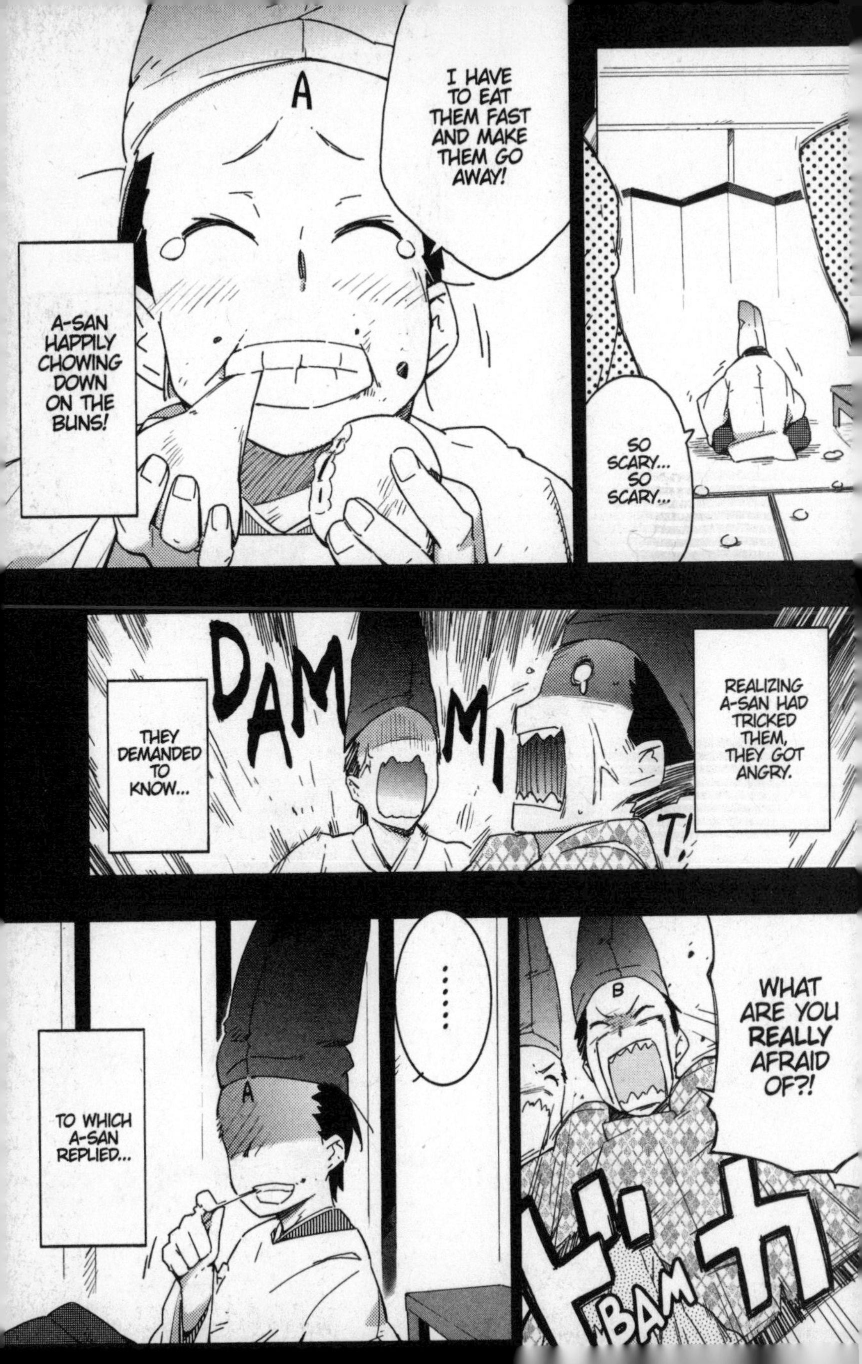
SO SCARY... SO SCARY...
I HAVE TO EAT THEM FAST AND MAKE THEM GO AWAY!
A-SAN HAPPILY CHOWING DOWN ON THE BUNS!
REALIZING A-SAN HAD TRICKED THEM, THEY GOT ANGRY.
DAMMIT!
THEY DEMANDED TO KNOW...
WHAT ARE YOU REALLY AFRAID OF?!
BAM
......
TO WHICH A-SAN REPLIED...

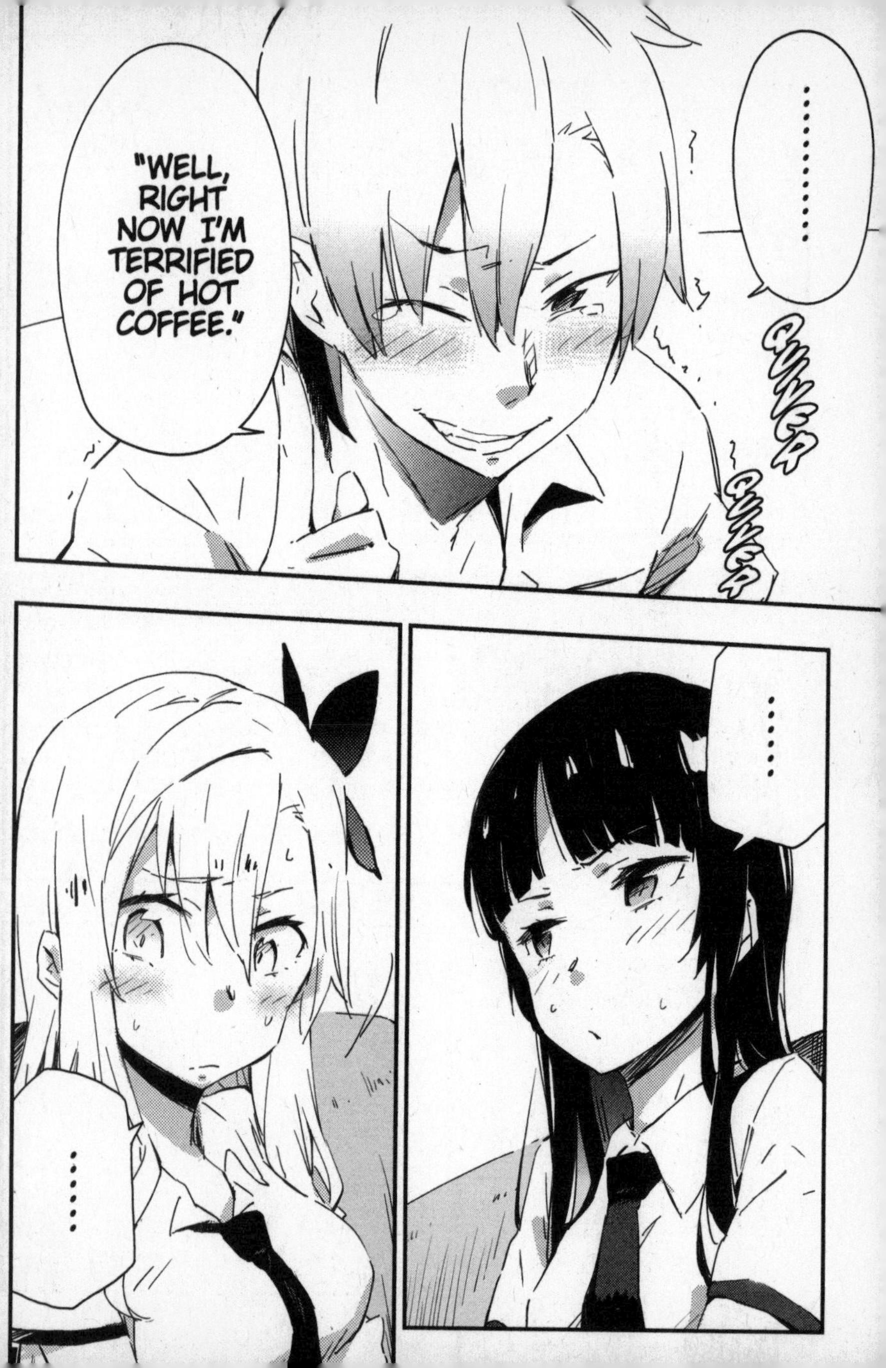
......
"WELL, RIGHT NOW I'M TERRIFIED OF HOT COFFEE."
QUIVER
QUIVER
......
......

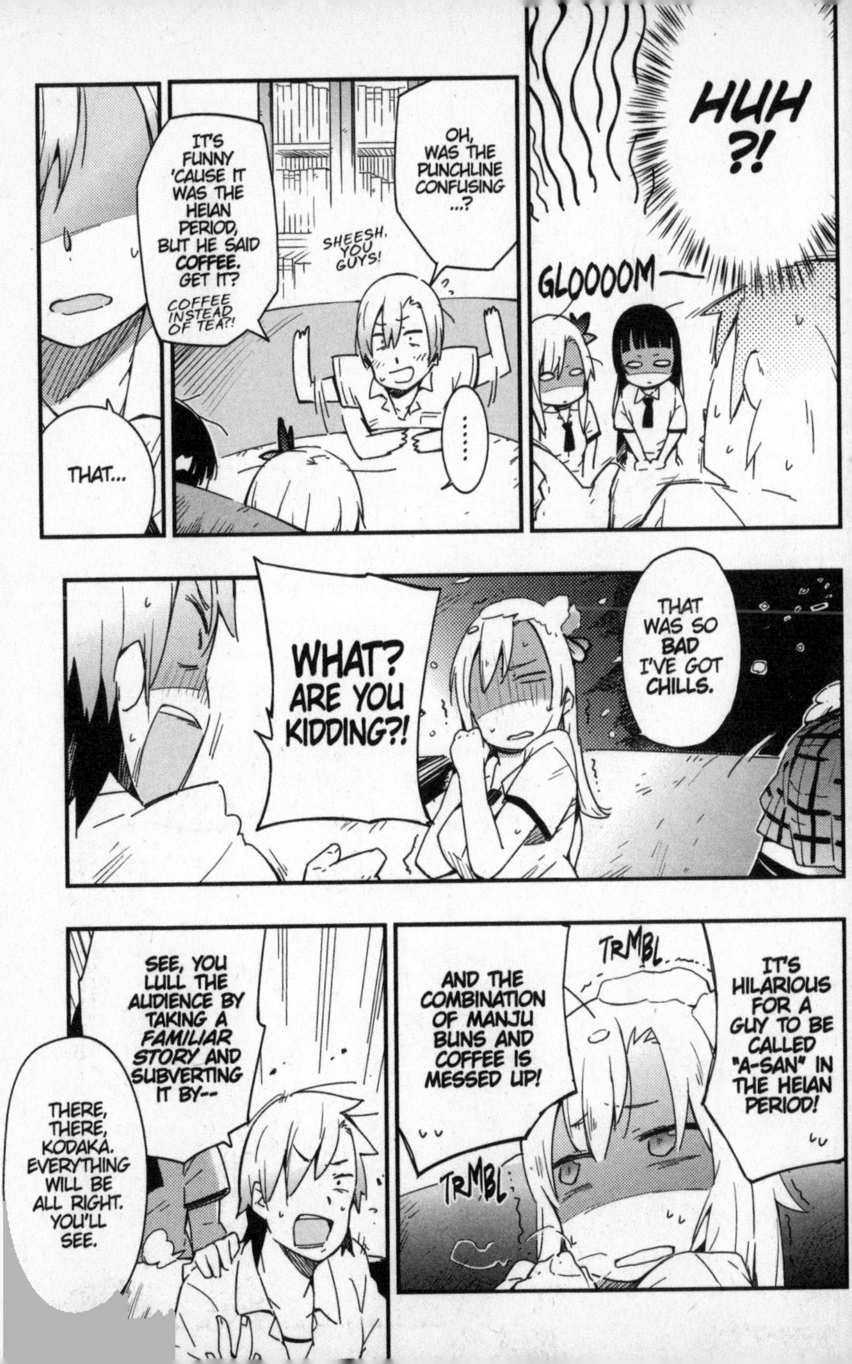
HUH ?!
GLOOOOM—
OH, WAS THE PUNCHLINE CONFUSING ...?
SHEESH, YOU GUYS!
......
IT'S FUNNY 'CAUSE IT WAS THE HEIAN PERIOD, BUT HE SAID COFFEE. GET IT?
COFFEE INSTEAD OF TEA?!
THAT...
THAT WAS SO BAD I'VE GOT CHILLS.
WHAT? ARE YOU KIDDING?!
IT'S HILARIOUS FOR A GUY TO BE CALLED "A-SAN" IN THE HEIAN PERIOD!
TRMBL...
AND THE COMBINATION OF MANJU BUNS AND COFFEE IS MESSED UP!
TRMBL
SEE, YOU LULL THE AUDIENCE BY TAKING A FAMILIAR STORY AND SUBVERTING IT BY--
THERE, THERE, KODAKA. EVERYTHING WILL BE ALL RIGHT. YOU'LL SEE.

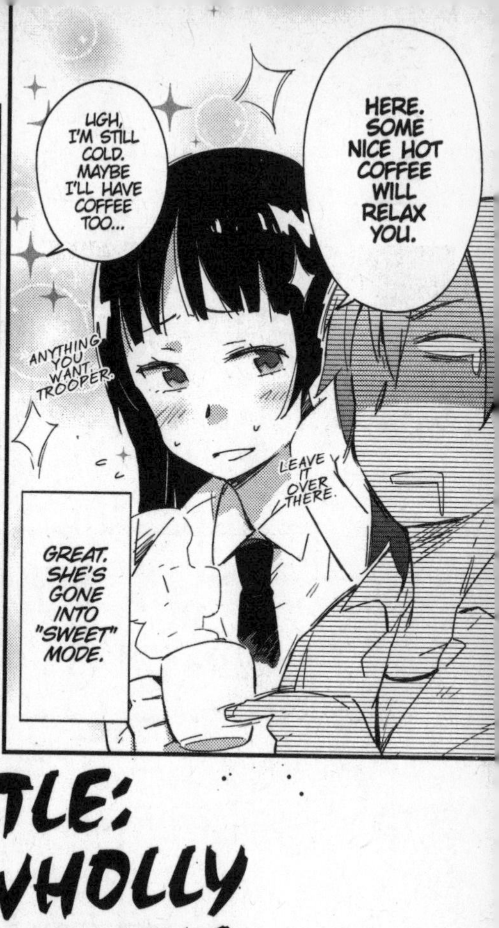
HERE. SOME NICE HOT COFFEE WILL RELAX YOU.
UGH, I'M STILL COLD. MAYBE I'LL HAVE COFFEE TOO...
ANYTHING YOU WANT, TROOPER.
LEAVE IT OVER THERE.
GREAT. SHE'S GONE INTO "SWEET" MODE.
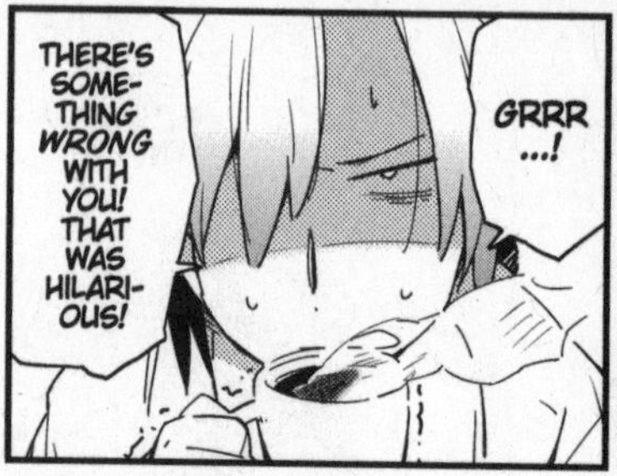
GRRR...!
THERE'S SOMETHING WRONG WITH YOU! THAT WAS HILARIOUS!
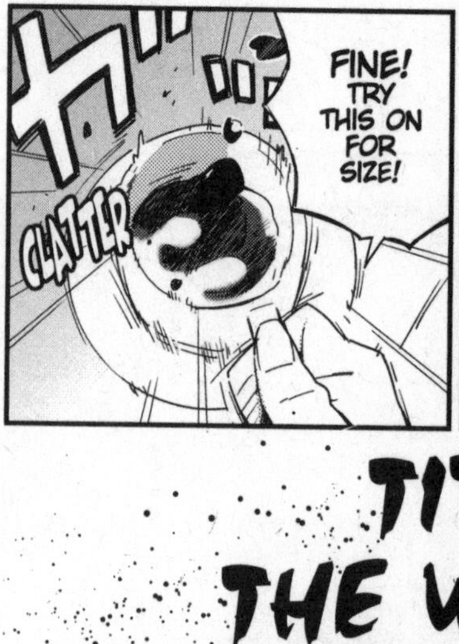
FINE! TRY THIS ON FOR SIZE!
CLATTER

TITLE: THE WHOLLY TERRIFYING SHUMAI INCIDENT

*Shumai are a type of pork-filled Chinese dumpling.

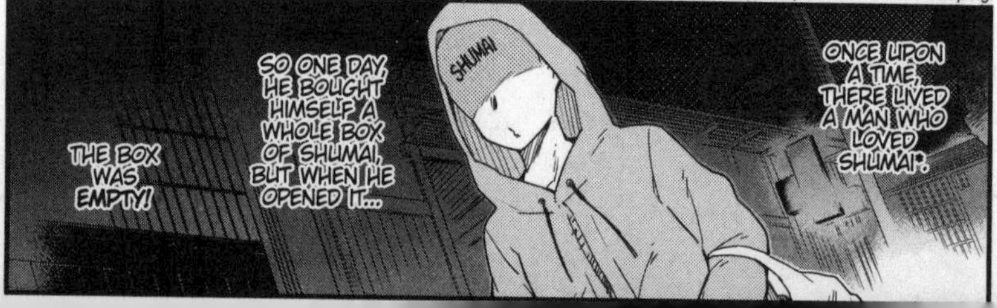
ONCE UPON A TIME, THERE LIVED A MAN WHO LOVED SHUMAI*.
SHUMAI
SO ONE DAY, HE BOUGHT HIMSELF A WHOLE BOX OF SHUMAI, BUT WHEN HE OPENED IT...
THE BOX WAS EMPTY!

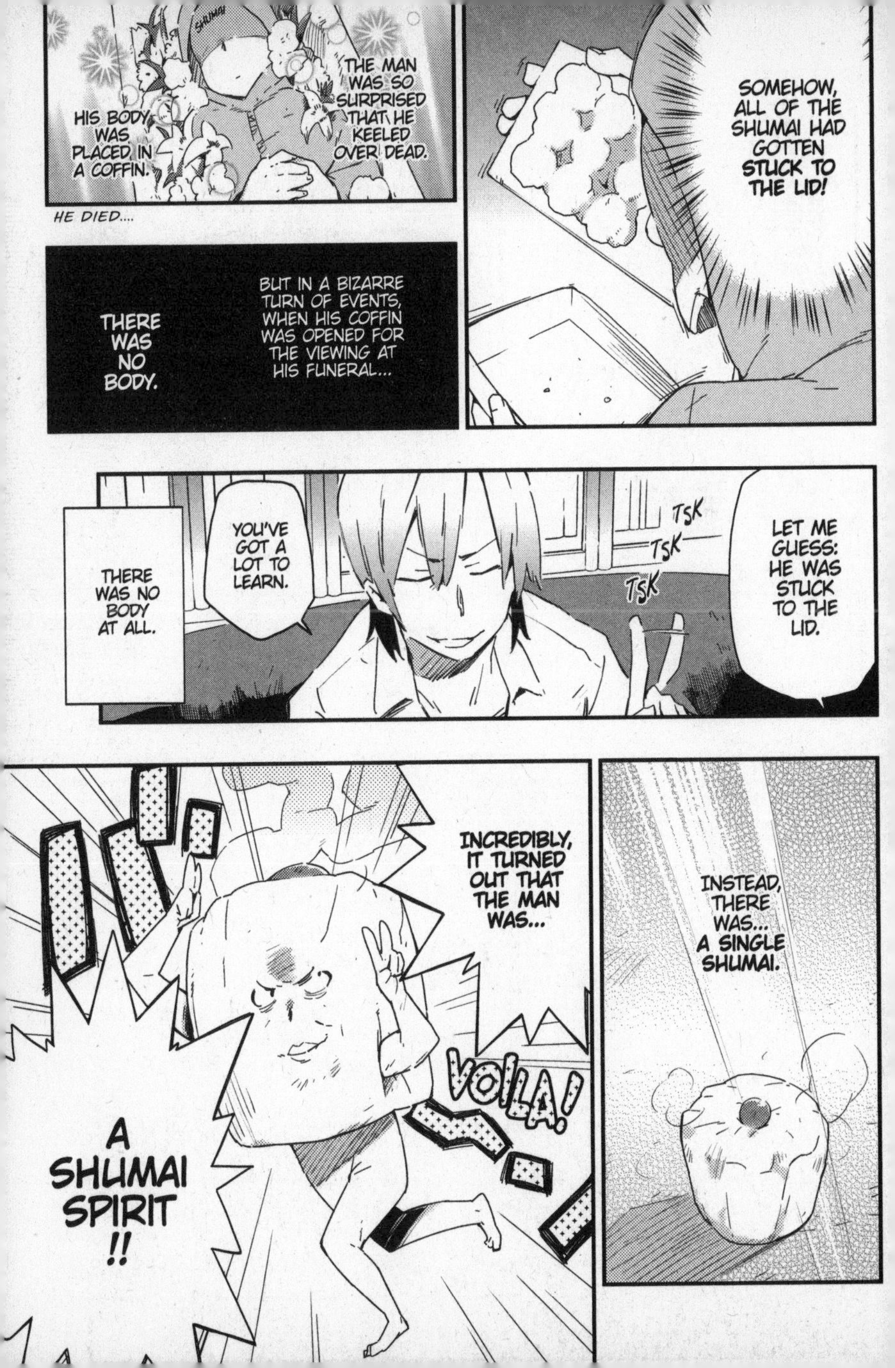
SOMEHOW, ALL OF THE SHUMAI HAD GOTTEN STUCK TO THE LID!
SHUMAI
THE MAN WAS SO SURPRISED THAT HE KEELED OVER DEAD.
HIS BODY WAS PLACED IN A COFFIN.
HE DIED....
BUT IN A BIZARRE TURN OF EVENTS, WHEN HIS COFFIN WAS OPENED FOR THE VIEWING AT HIS FUNERAL...
THERE WAS NO BODY.
LET ME GUESS: HE WAS STUCK TO THE LID.
TSK
TSK
TSK
YOU'VE GOT A LOT TO LEARN.
THERE WAS NO BODY AT ALL.
INSTEAD, THERE WAS... A SINGLE SHUMAI.
INCREDIBLY, IT TURNED OUT THAT THE MAN WAS...
VOILA!
A SHUMAI SPIRIT !!

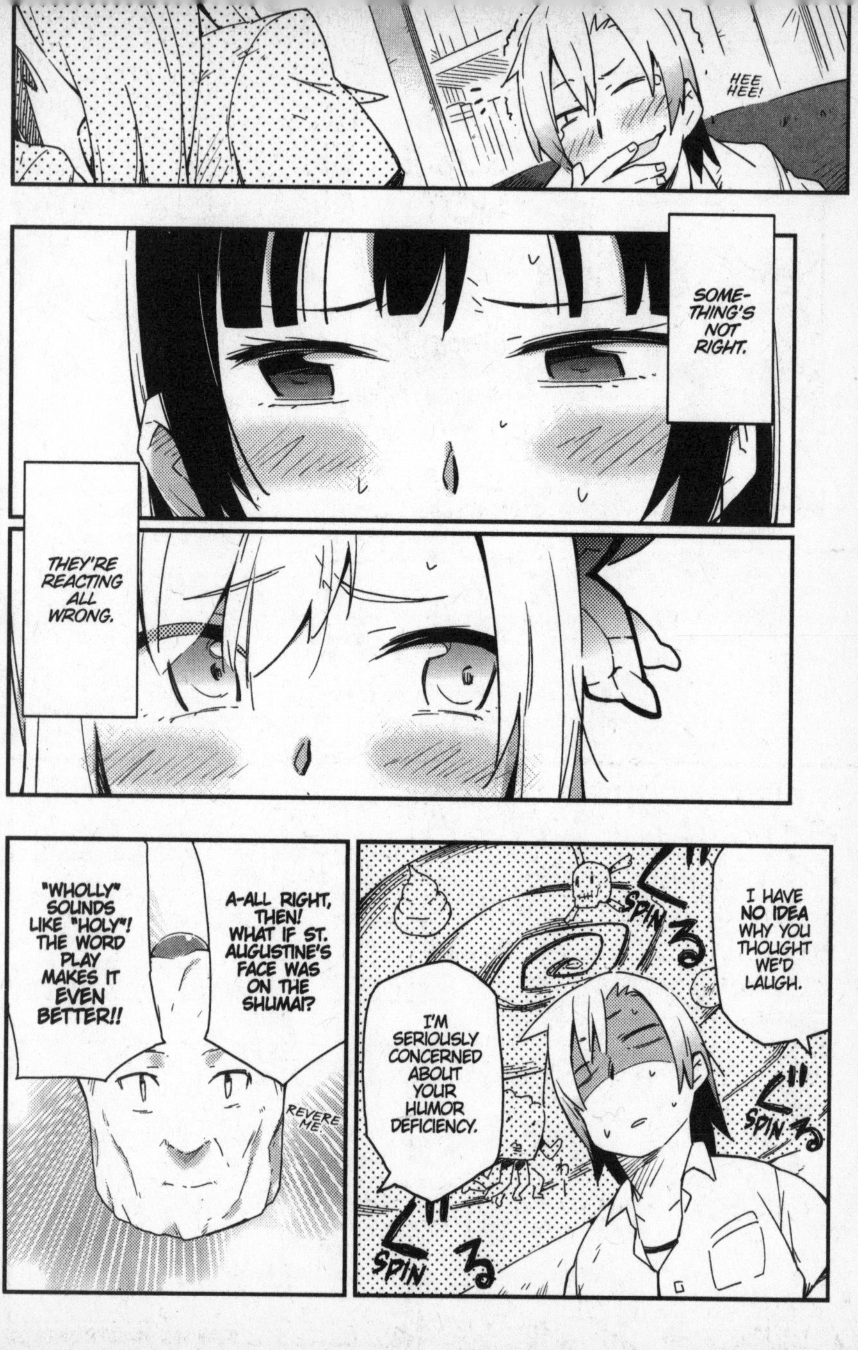
HEE HEE!
SOME-THING'S NOT RIGHT.
THEY'RE REACTING ALL WRONG.
I HAVE NO IDEA WHY YOU THOUGHT WE'D LAUGH.
SPIN
SPIN
I'M SERIOUSLY CONCERNED ABOUT YOUR HUMOR DEFICIENCY.
SPIN
A-ALL RIGHT, THEN! WHAT IF ST. AUGUSTINE'S FACE WAS ON THE SHUMAI?
"WHOLLY" SOUNDS LIKE "HOLY"! THE WORD PLAY MAKES IT EVEN BETTER!!
REVERE ME.

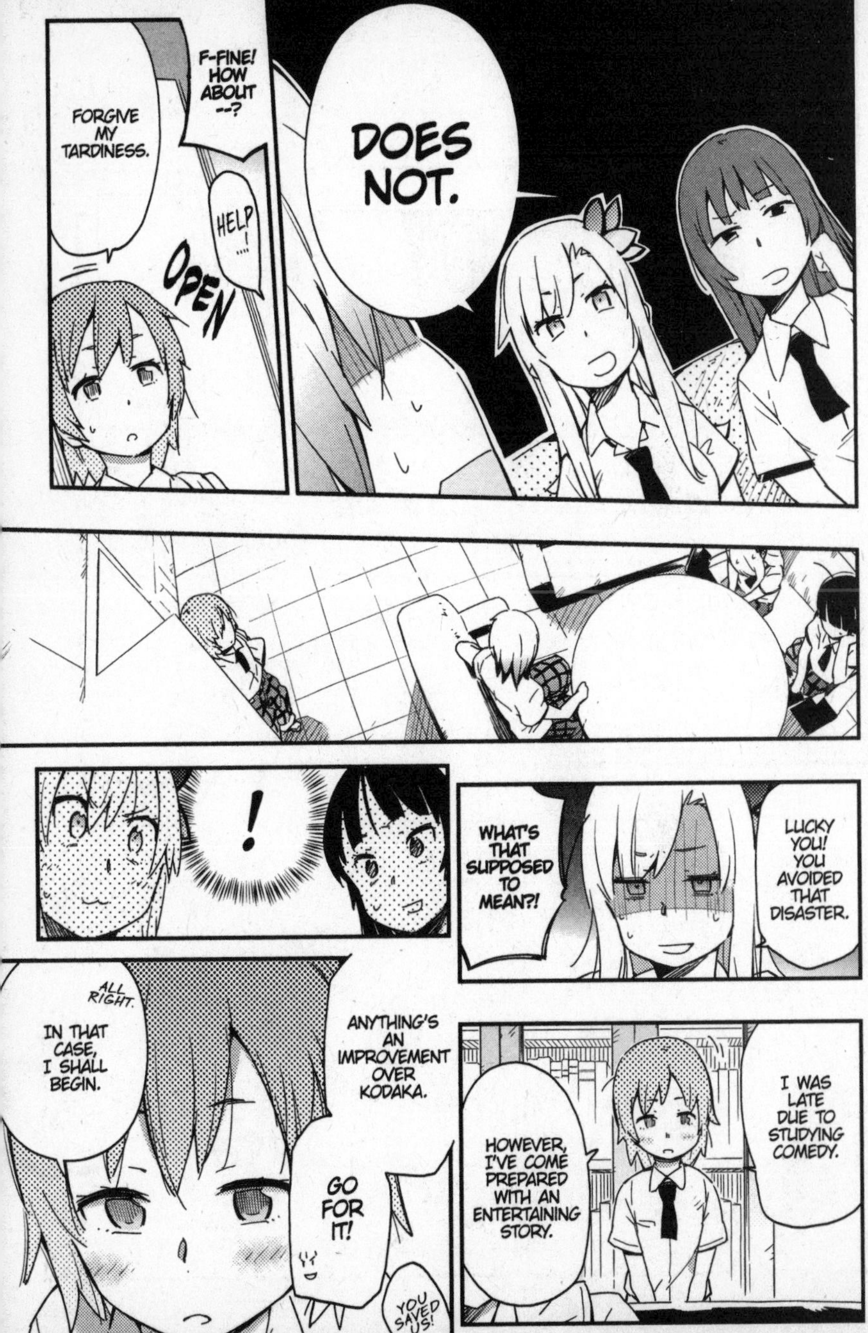
DOES NOT.
F-FINE! HOW ABOUT --?
FORGIVE MY TARDINESS.
HELP...!
OPEN
LUCKY YOU! YOU AVOIDED THAT DISASTER.
WHAT'S THAT SUPPOSED TO MEAN?!
!
I WAS LATE DUE TO STUDYING COMEDY.
HOWEVER, I'VE COME PREPARED WITH AN ENTERTAINING STORY.
ANYTHING'S AN IMPROVEMENT OVER KODAKA.
ALL RIGHT.
IN THAT CASE, I SHALL BEGIN.
GO FOR IT!
YOU SAVED US!

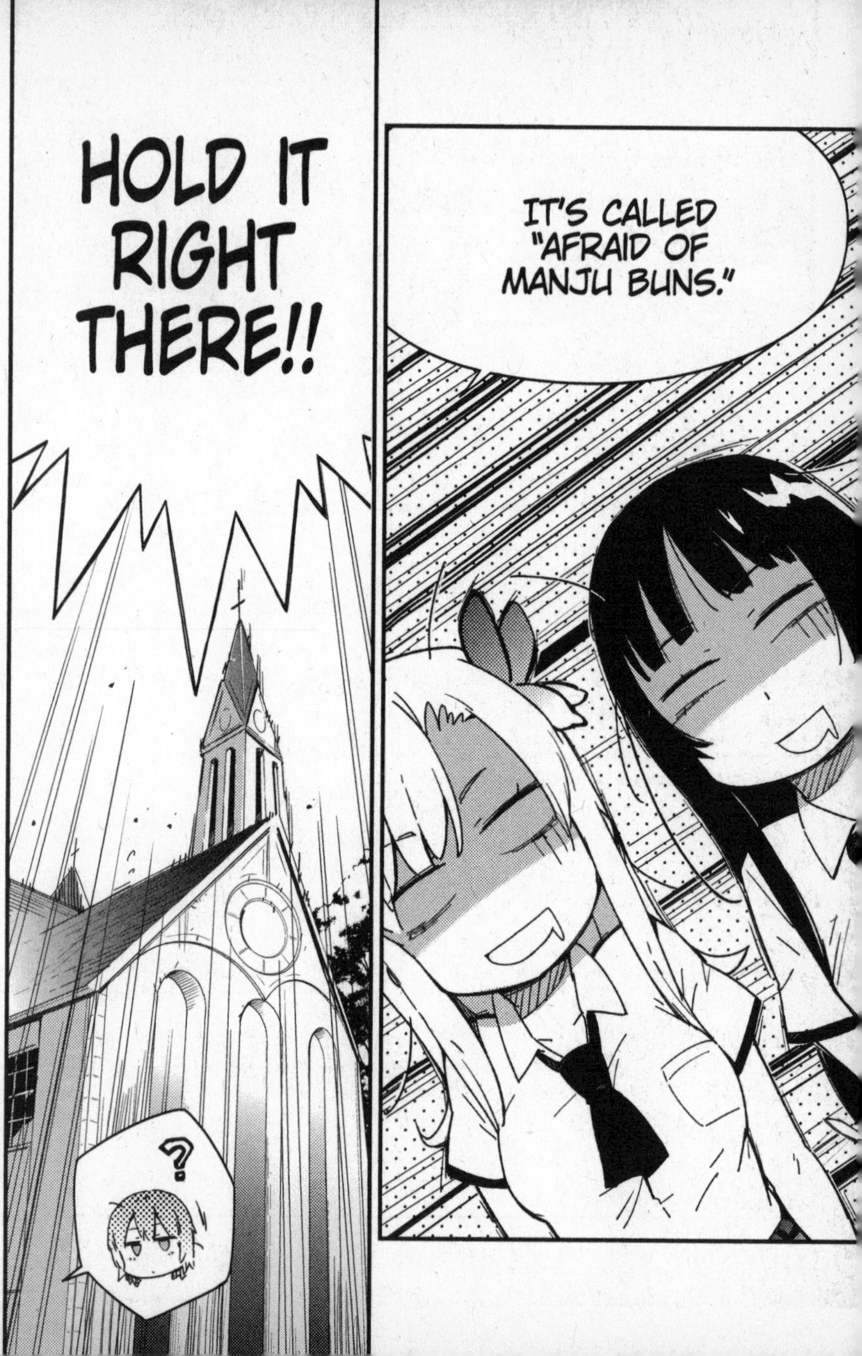
IT'S CALLED "AFRAID OF MANJU BUNS."
HOLD IT RIGHT THERE!!
?

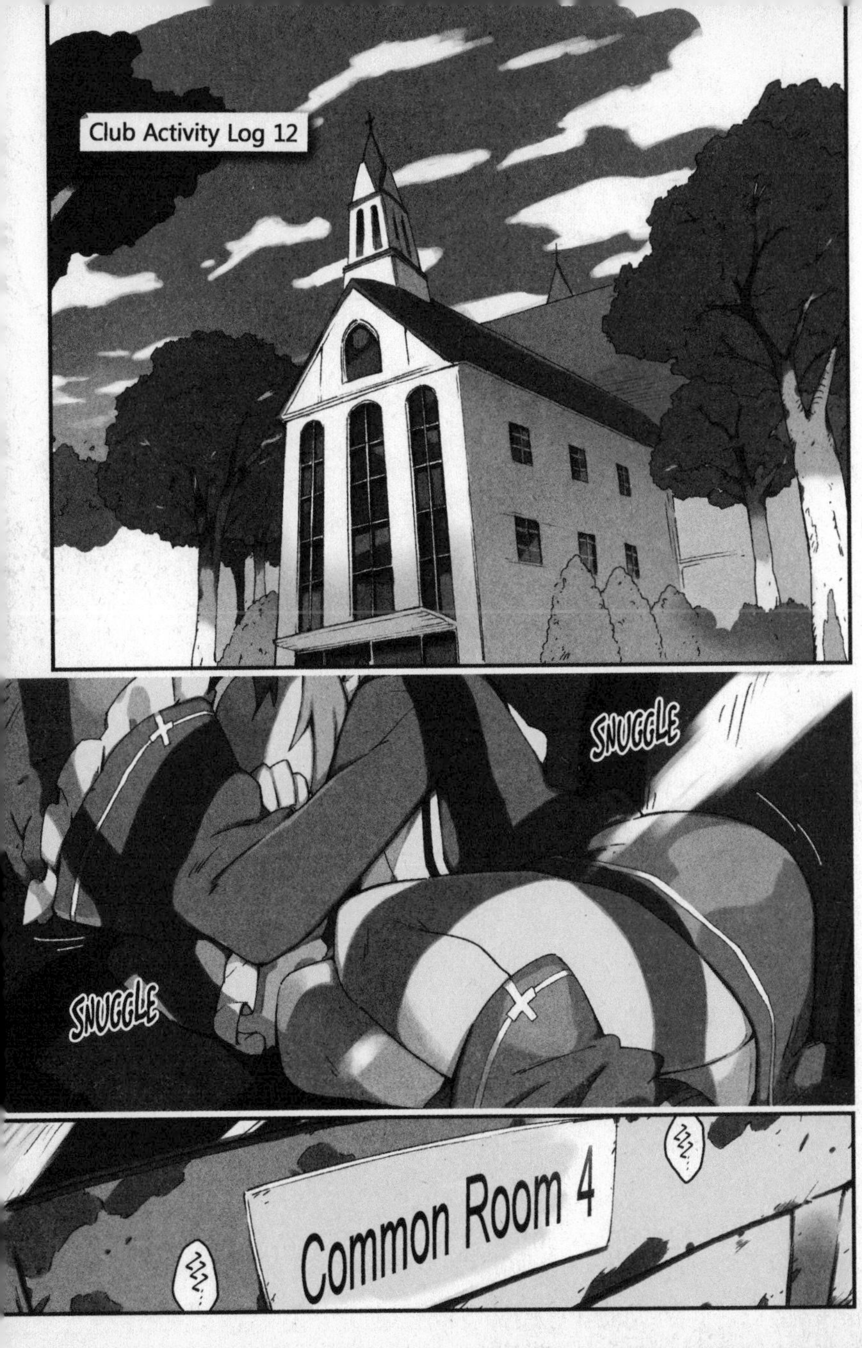
Club Activity Log 12
SNUGGLE
SNUGGLE
Common Room 4

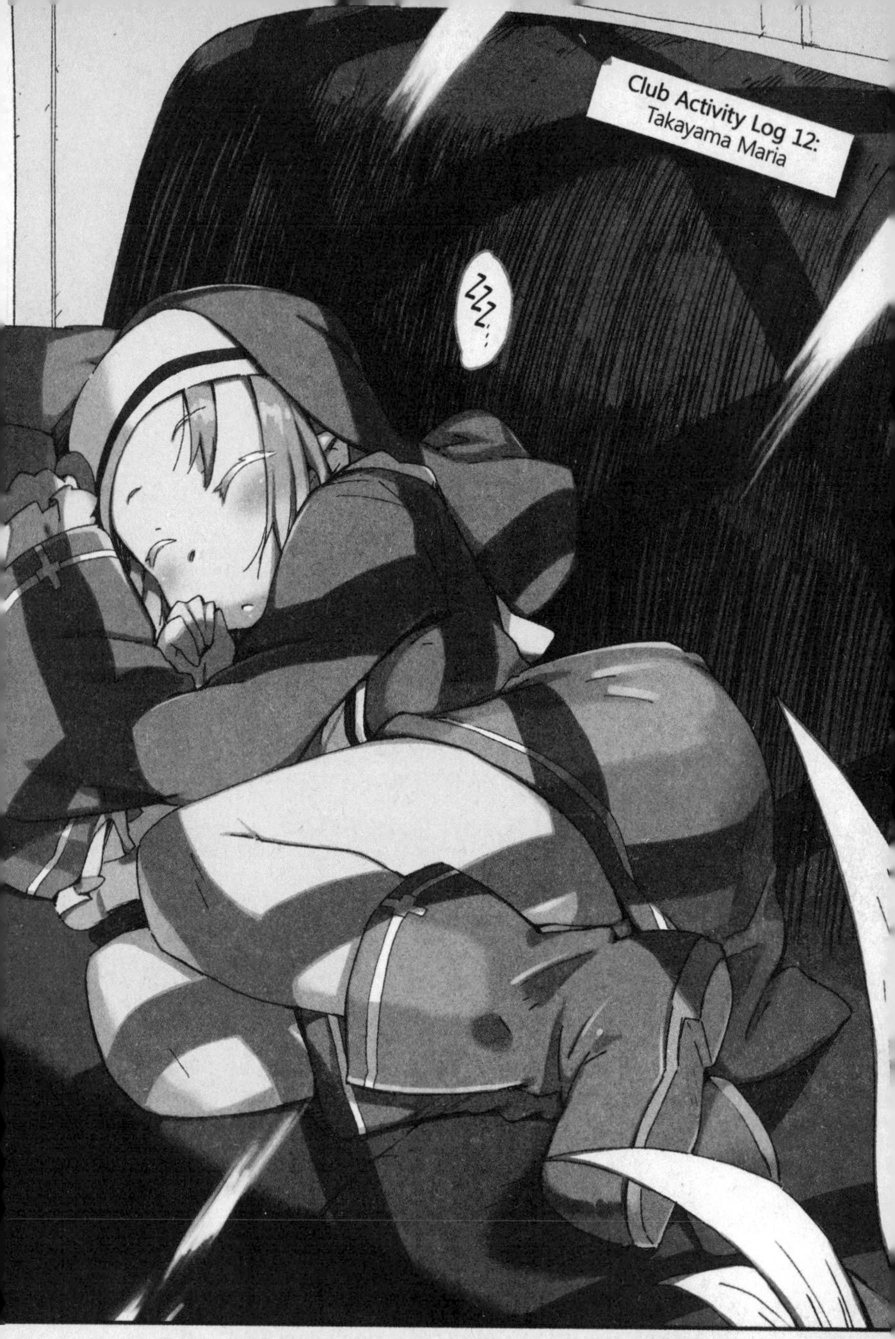
Club Activity Log 12:
Takayama Maria
ZZZ...

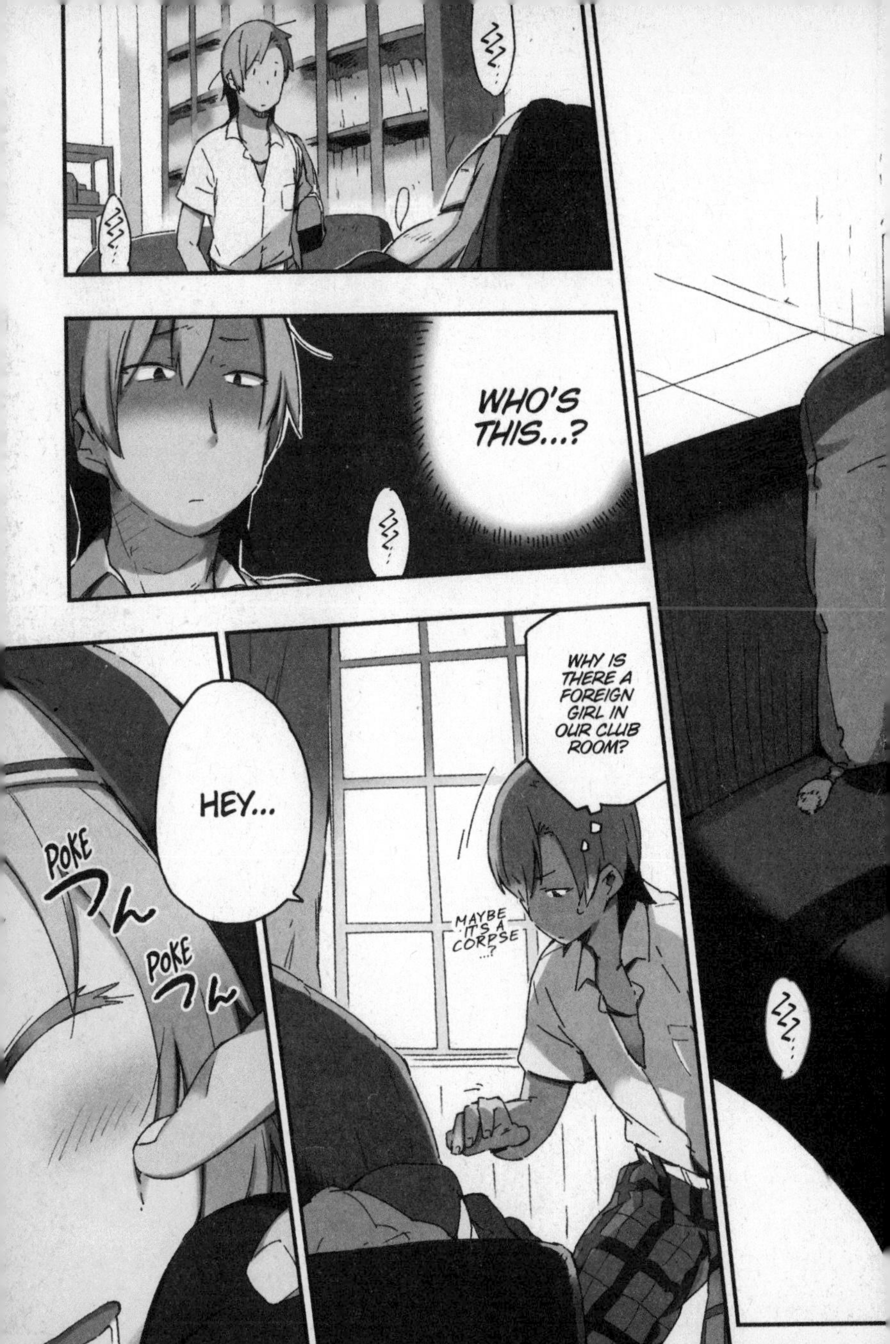
ZZZ...
ZZZ...
ZZZ...
WHO'S THIS...?
ZZZ...
WHY IS THERE A FOREIGN GIRL IN OUR CLUB ROOM?
MAYBE IT'S A CORPSE ...?
HEY...
POKE つん
POKE つん

Haganai

I don't have many friends

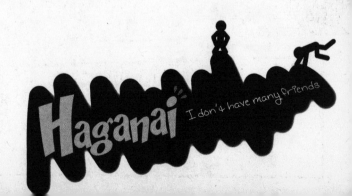

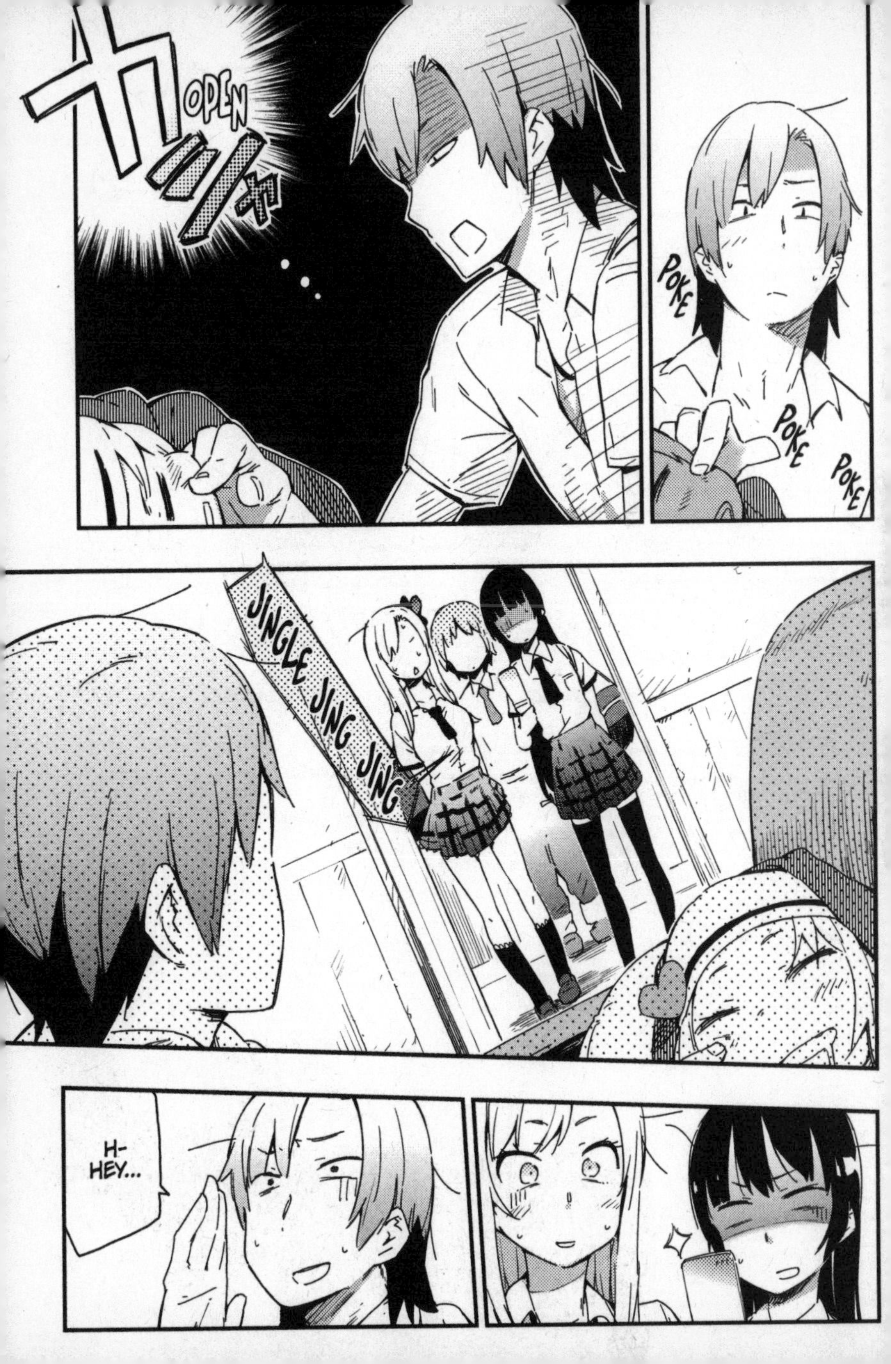
POKE
POKE
POKE
OPEN
...
JINGLE JING JING
H-HEY...

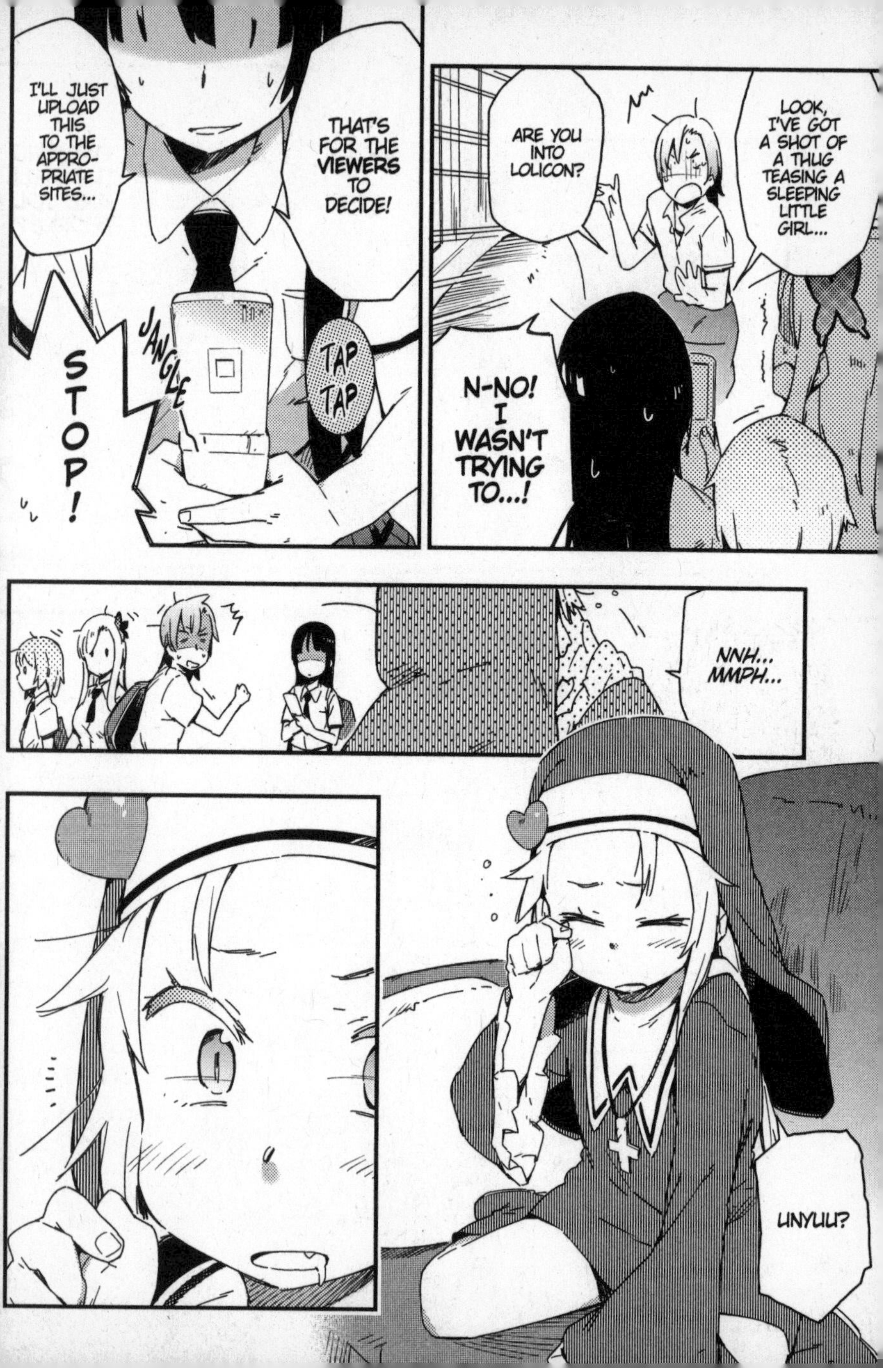
LOOK, I'VE GOT A SHOT OF A THUG TEASING A SLEEPING LITTLE GIRL...
ARE YOU INTO LOLICON?
N-NO! I WASN'T TRYING TO...!
THAT'S FOR THE VIEWERS TO DECIDE!
I'LL JUST UPLOAD THIS TO THE APPROPRIATE SITES...
TAP TAP
JANGLE
STOP!
NNH... MMPH...
UNYUU?

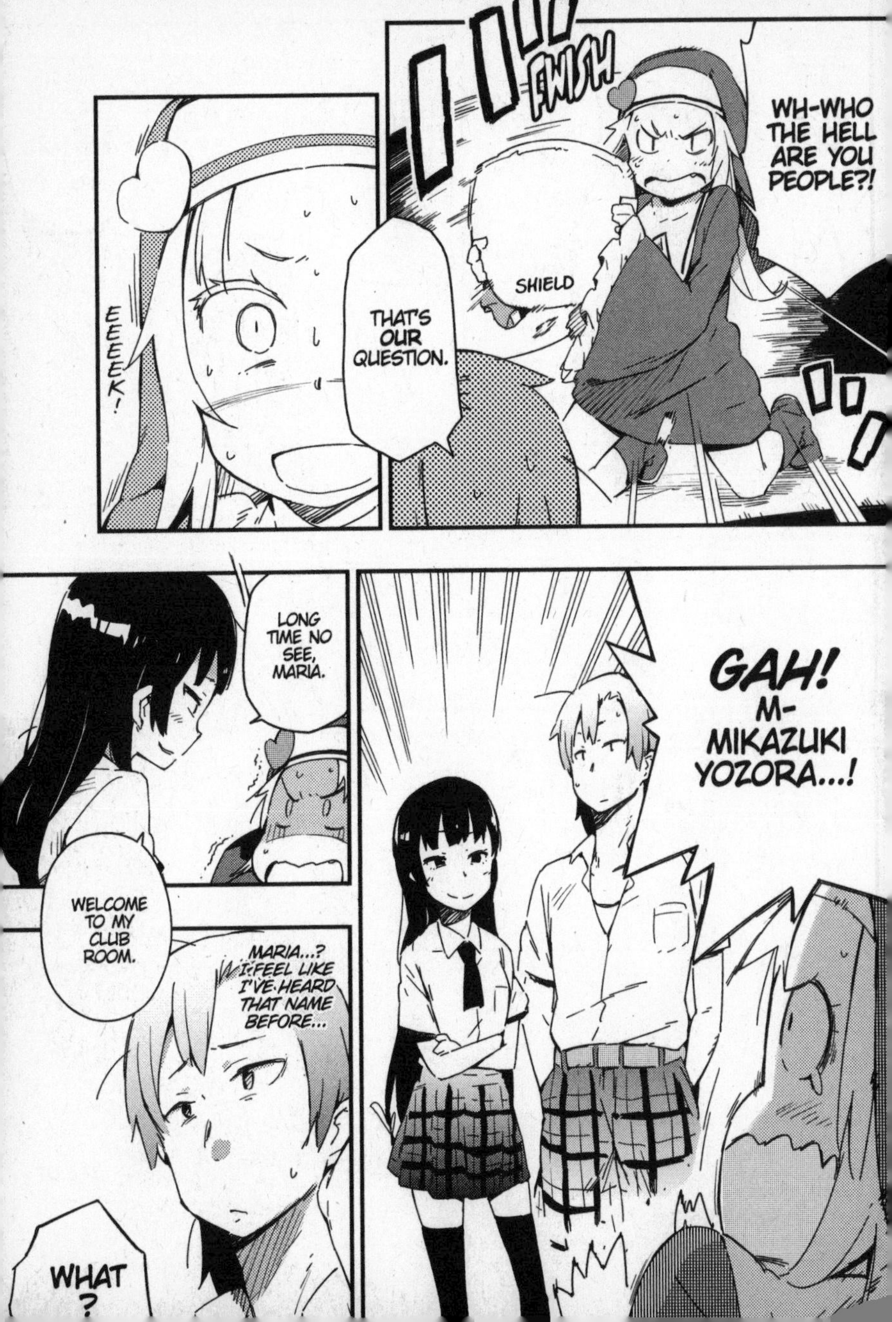
FWISH
WH-WHO THE HELL ARE YOU PEOPLE?!
SHIELD
THAT'S OUR QUESTION.
EEEEEK!
GAH! M-MIKAZUKI YOZORA...!
LONG TIME NO SEE, MARIA.
WELCOME TO MY CLUB ROOM.
MARIA...? I FEEL LIKE I'VE HEARD THAT NAME BEFORE...
WHAT?

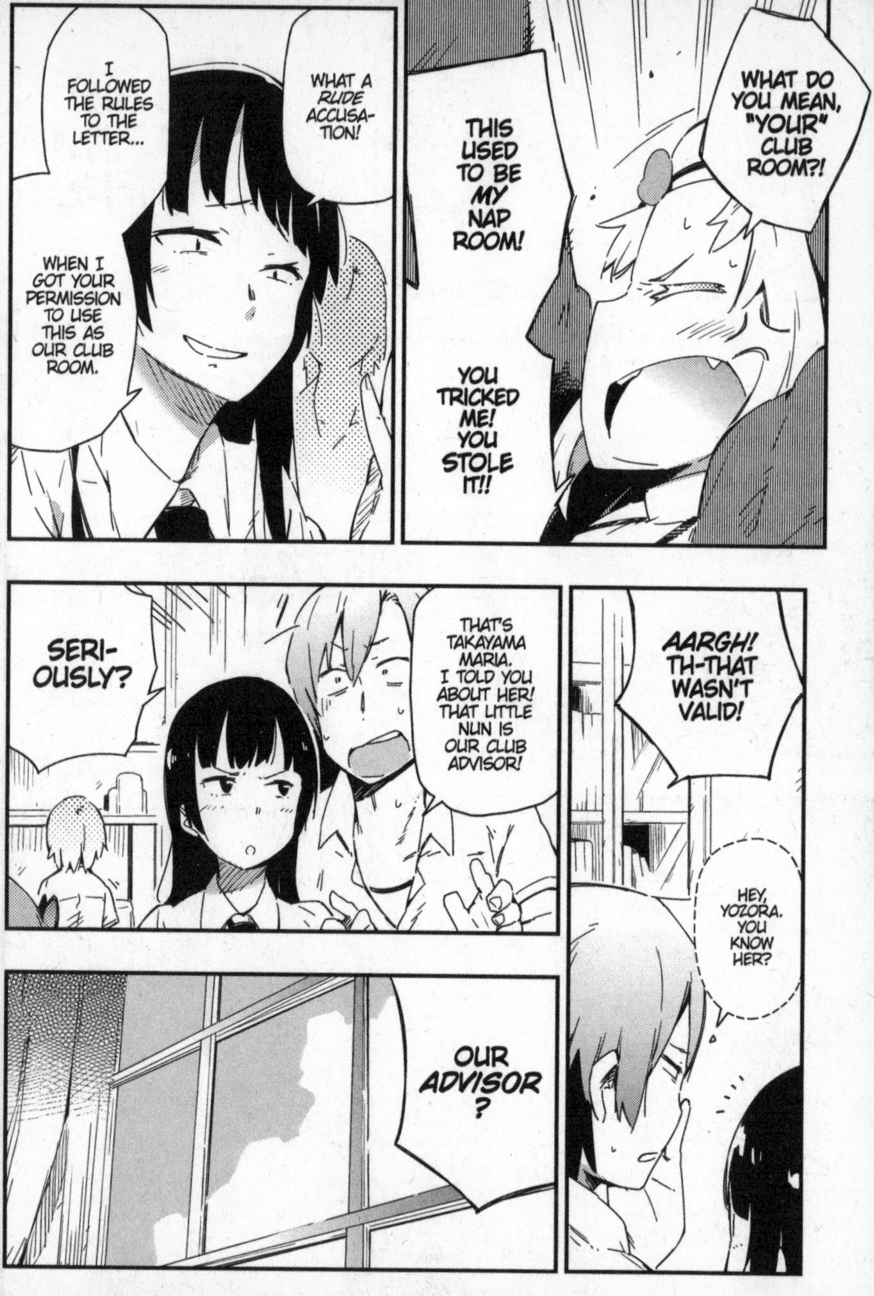
WHAT DO YOU MEAN, "YOUR" CLUB ROOM?!
THIS USED TO BE MY NAP ROOM!
YOU TRICKED ME! YOU STOLE IT!!
WHAT A RUDE ACCUSATION!
I FOLLOWED THE RULES TO THE LETTER...
WHEN I GOT YOUR PERMISSION TO USE THIS AS OUR CLUB ROOM.
AARGH! TH-THAT WASN'T VALID!
HEY, YOZORA. YOU KNOW HER?
THAT'S TAKAYAMA MARIA. I TOLD YOU ABOUT HER! THAT LITTLE NUN IS OUR CLUB ADVISOR!
SERI-OUSLY?
OUR ADVISOR?

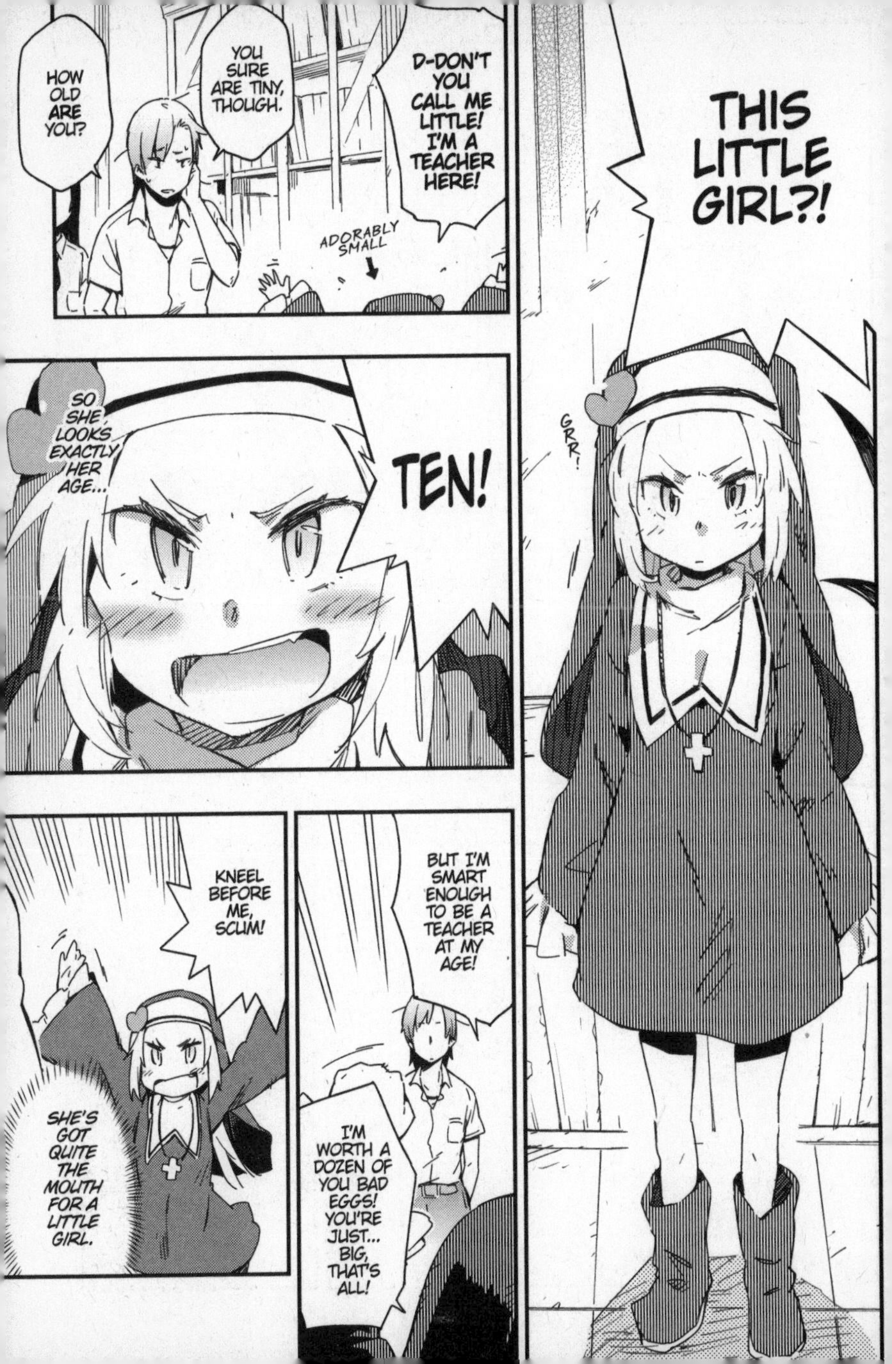
THIS LITTLE GIRL?!
GRR!
D-DON'T YOU CALL ME LITTLE! I'M A TEACHER HERE!
ADORABLY SMALL
YOU SURE ARE TINY, THOUGH.
HOW OLD ARE YOU?
TEN!
SO SHE LOOKS EXACTLY HER AGE...
BUT I'M SMART ENOUGH TO BE A TEACHER AT MY AGE!
I'M WORTH A DOZEN OF YOU BAD EGGS! YOU'RE JUST... BIG, THAT'S ALL!
KNEEL BEFORE ME, SCUM!
SHE'S GOT QUITE THE MOUTH FOR A LITTLE GIRL.

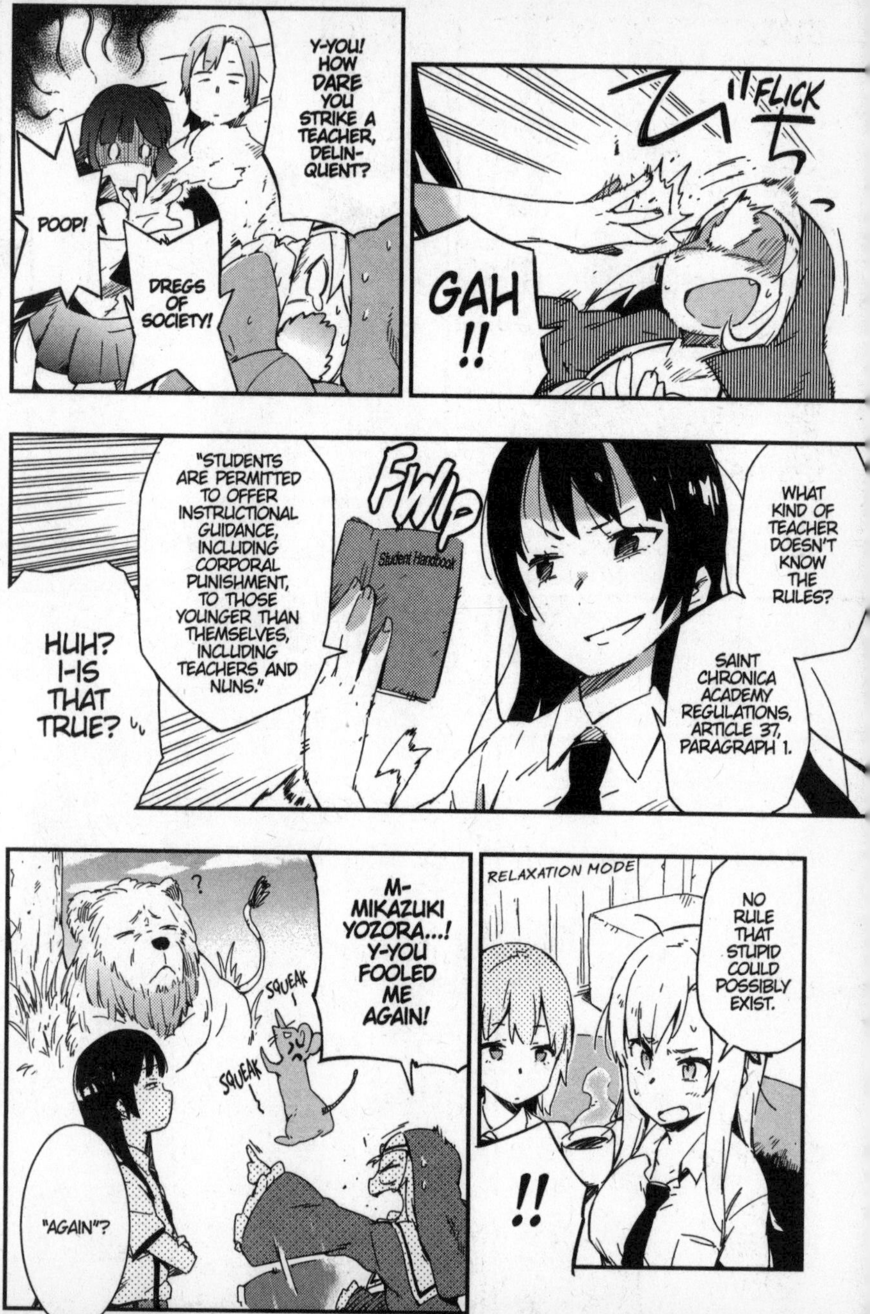
FLICK
GAH !!
Y-YOU! HOW DARE YOU STRIKE A TEACHER, DELINQUENT?
POOP!
DREGS OF SOCIETY!
WHAT KIND OF TEACHER DOESN'T KNOW THE RULES?
SAINT CHRONICA ACADEMY REGULATIONS, ARTICLE 37, PARAGRAPH 1.
FWIP
Student Handbook
"STUDENTS ARE PERMITTED TO OFFER INSTRUCTIONAL GUIDANCE, INCLUDING CORPORAL PUNISHMENT, TO THOSE YOUNGER THAN THEMSELVES, INCLUDING TEACHERS AND NUNS."
HUH? I-IS THAT TRUE?
RELAXATION MODE
NO RULE THAT STUPID COULD POSSIBLY EXIST.
!!
?
M-MIKAZUKI YOZORA...! Y-YOU FOOLED ME AGAIN!
SQUEAK
SQUEAK
"AGAIN"?

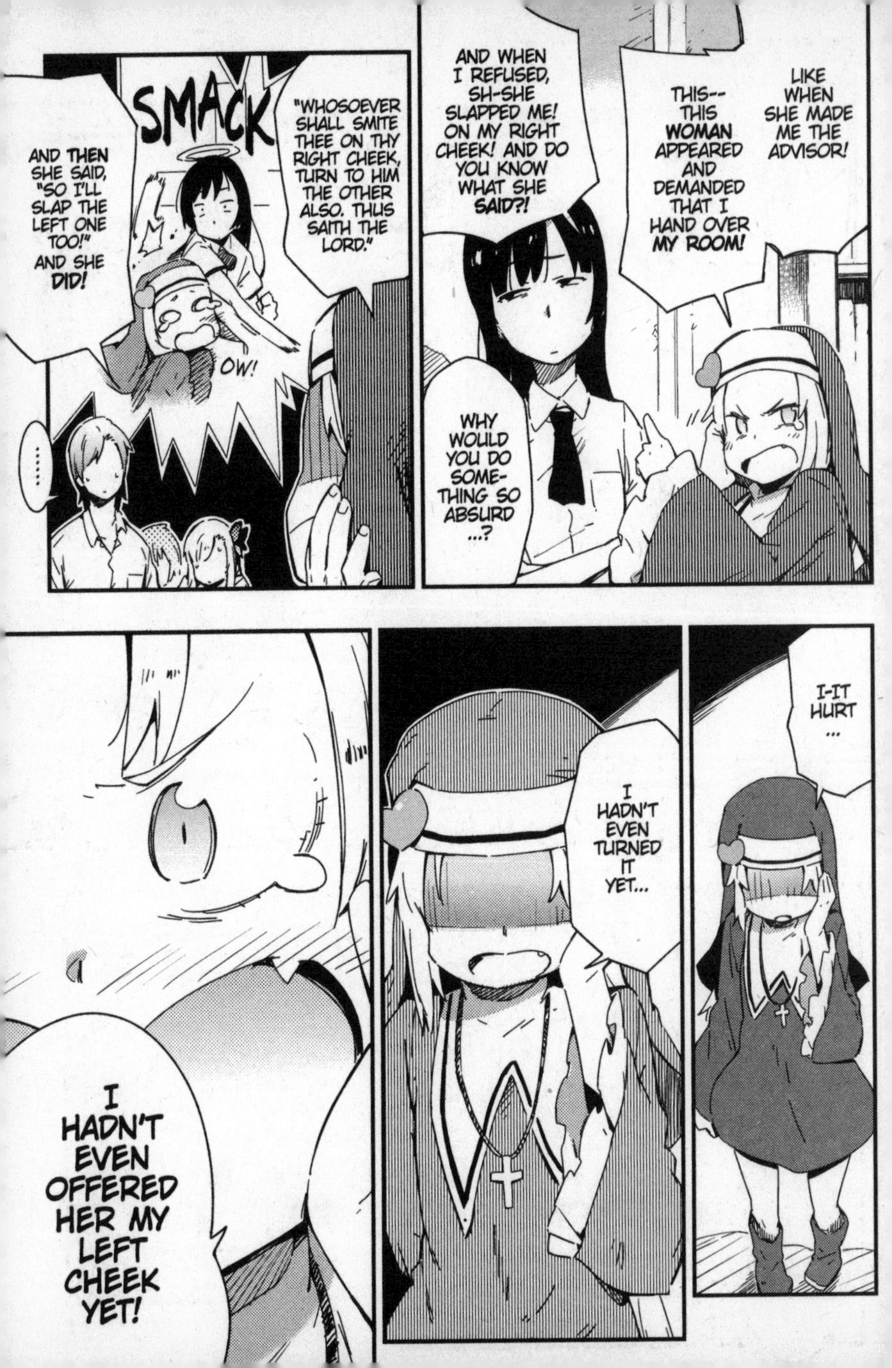

LIKE WHEN SHE MADE ME THE ADVISOR!
THIS-- THIS WOMAN APPEARED AND DEMANDED THAT I HAND OVER MY ROOM!
AND WHEN I REFUSED, SH-SHE SLAPPED ME! ON MY RIGHT CHEEK! AND DO YOU KNOW WHAT SHE SAID?!
WHY WOULD YOU DO SOME-THING SO ABSURD ...?
"WHOSOEVER SHALL SMITE THEE ON THY RIGHT CHEEK, TURN TO HIM THE OTHER ALSO. THUS SAITH THE LORD."
SMACK
AND THEN SHE SAID, "SO I'LL SLAP THE LEFT ONE TOO!" AND SHE DID!
OW!
......
I-IT HURT ...
I HADN'T EVEN TURNED IT YET...
I HADN'T EVEN OFFERED HER MY LEFT CHEEK YET!

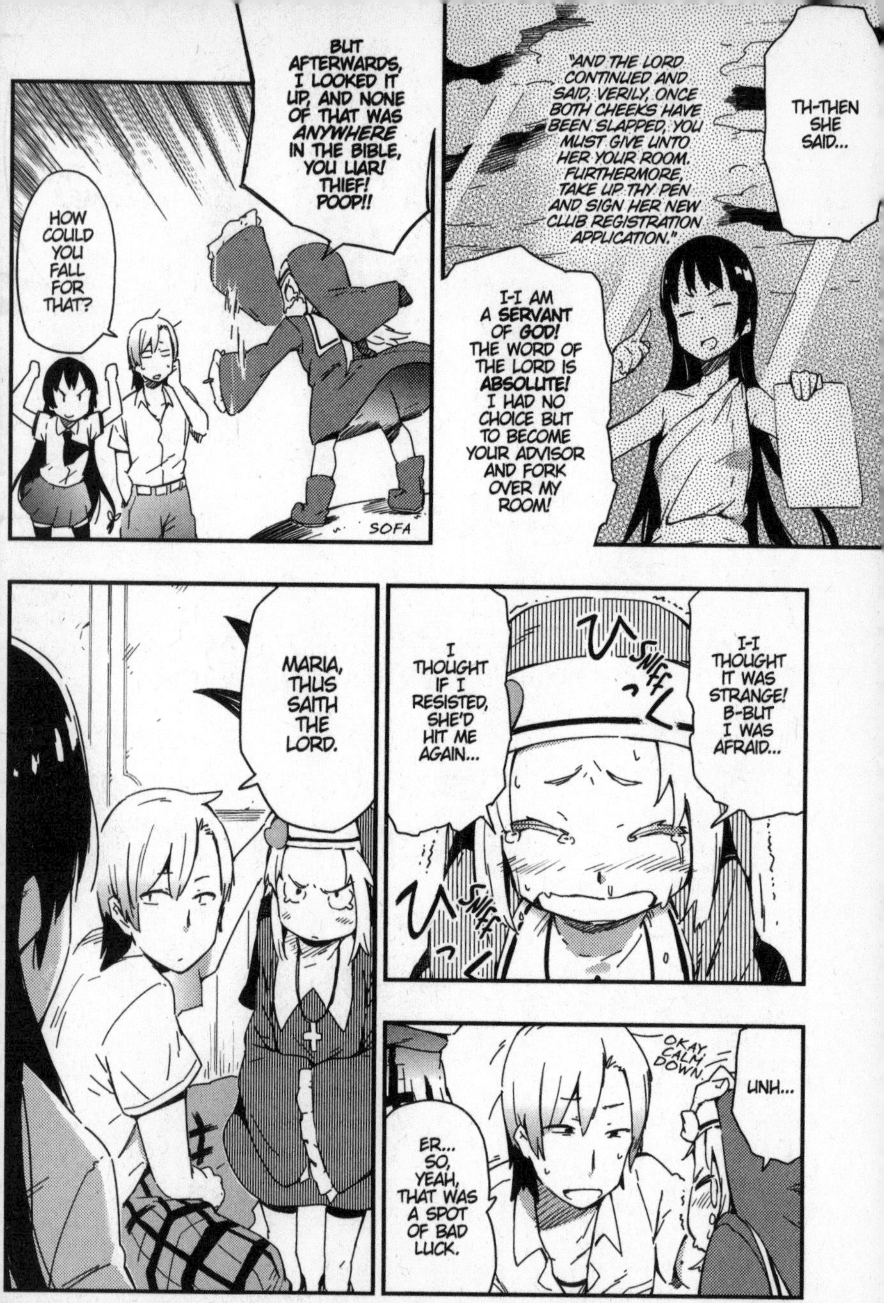
TH-THEN SHE SAID...
"AND THE LORD CONTINUED AND SAID, VERILY, ONCE BOTH CHEEKS HAVE BEEN SLAPPED, YOU MUST GIVE UNTO HER YOUR ROOM. FURTHERMORE, TAKE UP THY PEN AND SIGN HER NEW CLUB REGISTRATION APPLICATION."
I-I AM A SERVANT OF GOD! THE WORD OF THE LORD IS ABSOLUTE! I HAD NO CHOICE BUT TO BECOME YOUR ADVISOR AND FORK OVER MY ROOM!
BUT AFTERWARDS, I LOOKED IT UP, AND NONE OF THAT WAS ANYWHERE IN THE BIBLE, YOU LIAR! THIEF! POOP!!
HOW COULD YOU FALL FOR THAT?
SOFA
I-I THOUGHT IT WAS STRANGE! B-BUT I WAS AFRAID...
SNIFF
I THOUGHT IF I RESISTED, SHE'D HIT ME AGAIN...
SNIFF
UNH...
OKAY, CALM DOWN.
ER... SO, YEAH, THAT WAS A SPOT OF BAD LUCK.
MARIA, THUS SAITH THE LORD.

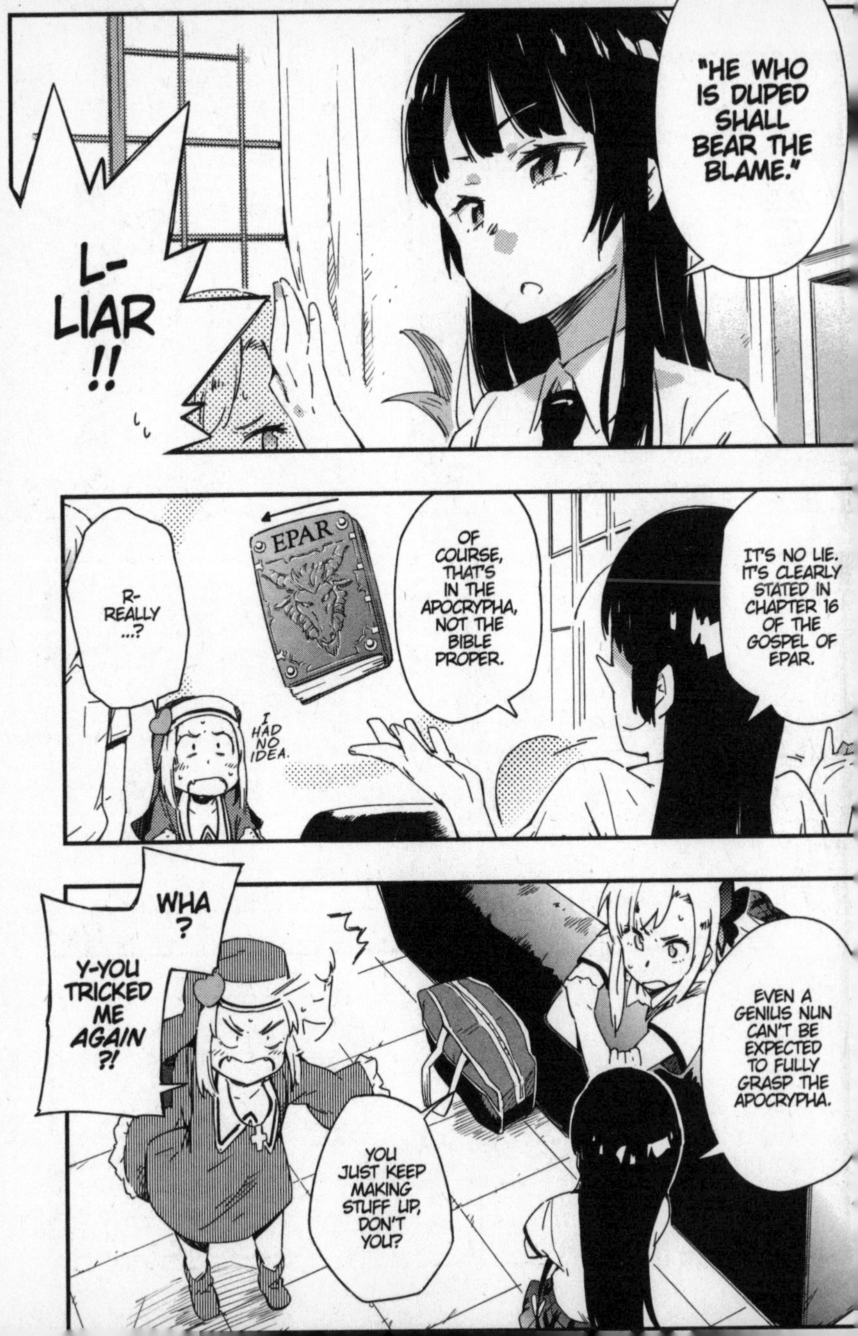
"HE WHO IS DUPED SHALL BEAR THE BLAME."
L-LIAR!!
IT'S NO LIE. IT'S CLEARLY STATED IN CHAPTER 16 OF THE GOSPEL OF EPAR.
OF COURSE, THAT'S IN THE APOCRYPHA, NOT THE BIBLE PROPER.
EPAR
R-REALLY ...?
I HAD NO IDEA.
EVEN A GENIUS NUN CAN'T BE EXPECTED TO FULLY GRASP THE APOCRYPHA.
WHA?
Y-YOU TRICKED ME AGAIN?!
YOU JUST KEEP MAKING STUFF UP, DON'T YOU?

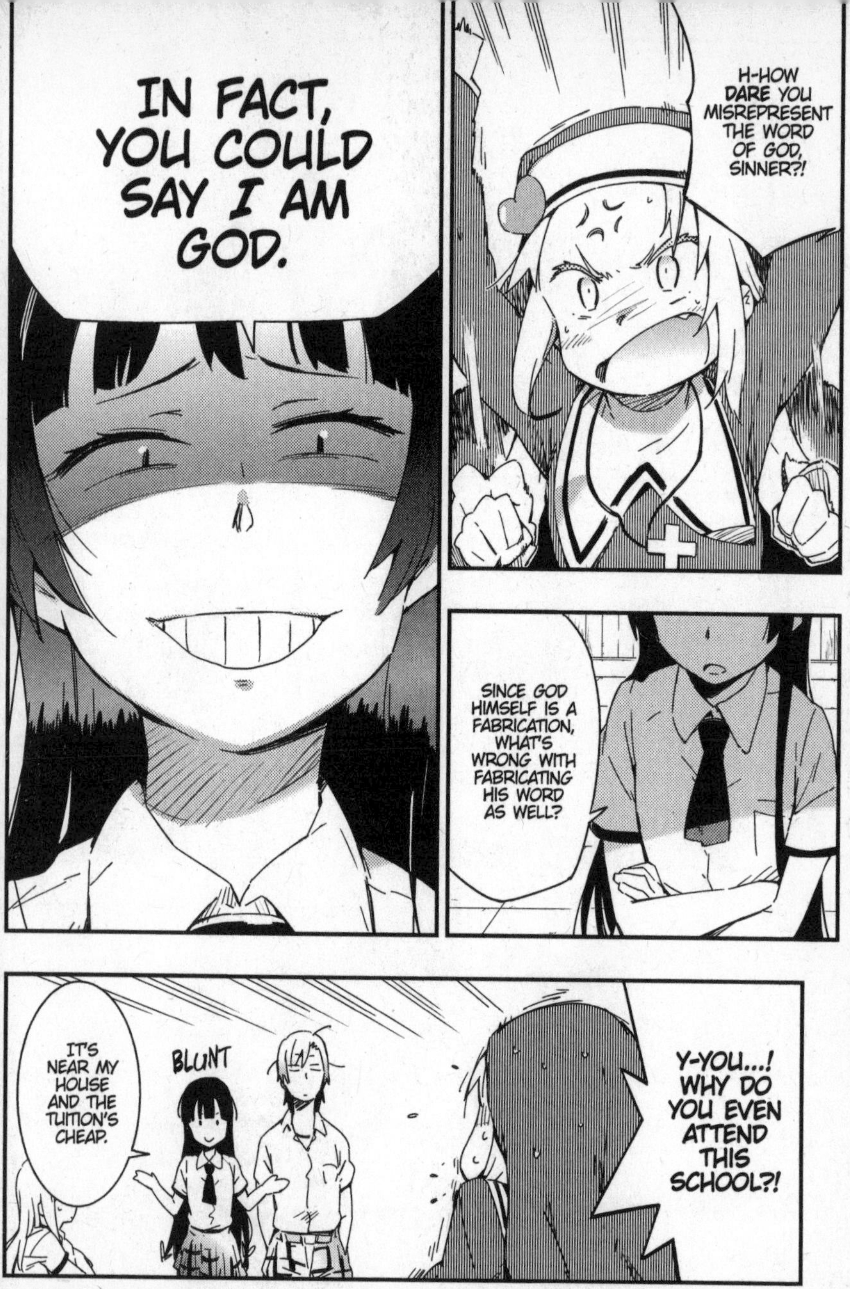

H-HOW DARE YOU MISREPRESENT THE WORD OF GOD, SINNER?!
SINCE GOD HIMSELF IS A FABRICATION, WHAT'S WRONG WITH FABRICATING HIS WORD AS WELL?
IN FACT, YOU COULD SAY I AM GOD.
Y-YOU...! WHY DO YOU EVEN ATTEND THIS SCHOOL?!
BLUNT
IT'S NEAR MY HOUSE AND THE TUITION'S CHEAP.

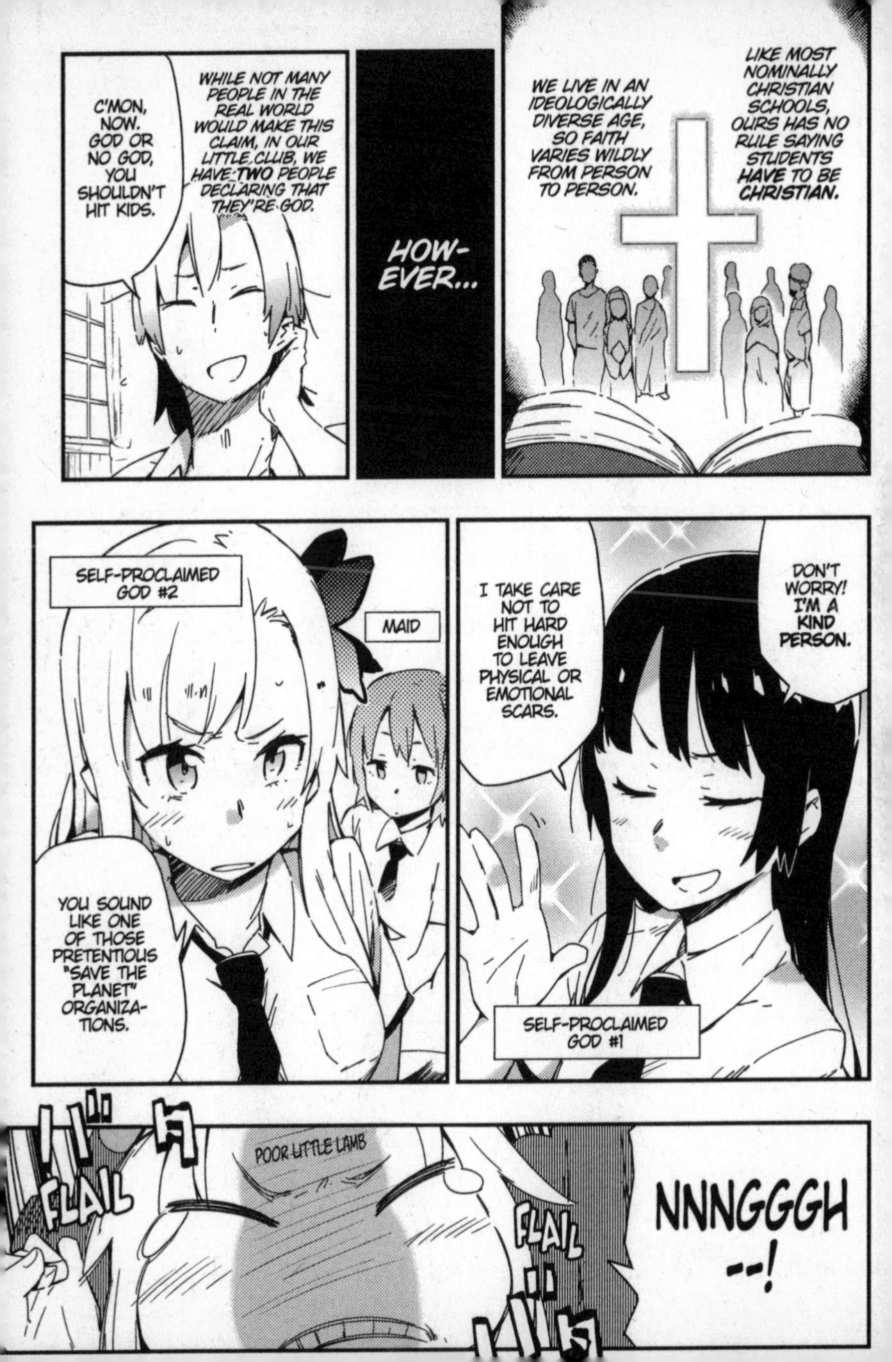
LIKE MOST NOMINALLY CHRISTIAN SCHOOLS, OURS HAS NO RULE SAYING STUDENTS **HAVE TO BE CHRISTIAN.**
WE LIVE IN AN IDEOLOGICALLY DIVERSE AGE, SO FAITH VARIES WILDLY FROM PERSON TO PERSON.
HOW-EVER...
WHILE NOT MANY PEOPLE IN THE REAL WORLD WOULD MAKE THIS CLAIM, IN OUR LITTLE CLUB, WE HAVE **TWO** PEOPLE DECLARING THAT THEY'RE GOD.
C'MON, NOW. GOD OR NO GOD, YOU SHOULDN'T HIT KIDS.
DON'T WORRY! I'M A KIND PERSON.
I TAKE CARE NOT TO HIT HARD ENOUGH TO LEAVE PHYSICAL OR EMOTIONAL SCARS.
SELF-PROCLAIMED GOD #1
SELF-PROCLAIMED GOD #2
MAID
YOU SOUND LIKE ONE OF THOSE PRETENTIOUS "SAVE THE PLANET" ORGANIZA-TIONS.
NNNGGGH--!
FLAIL
POOR LITTLE LAMB
FLAIL

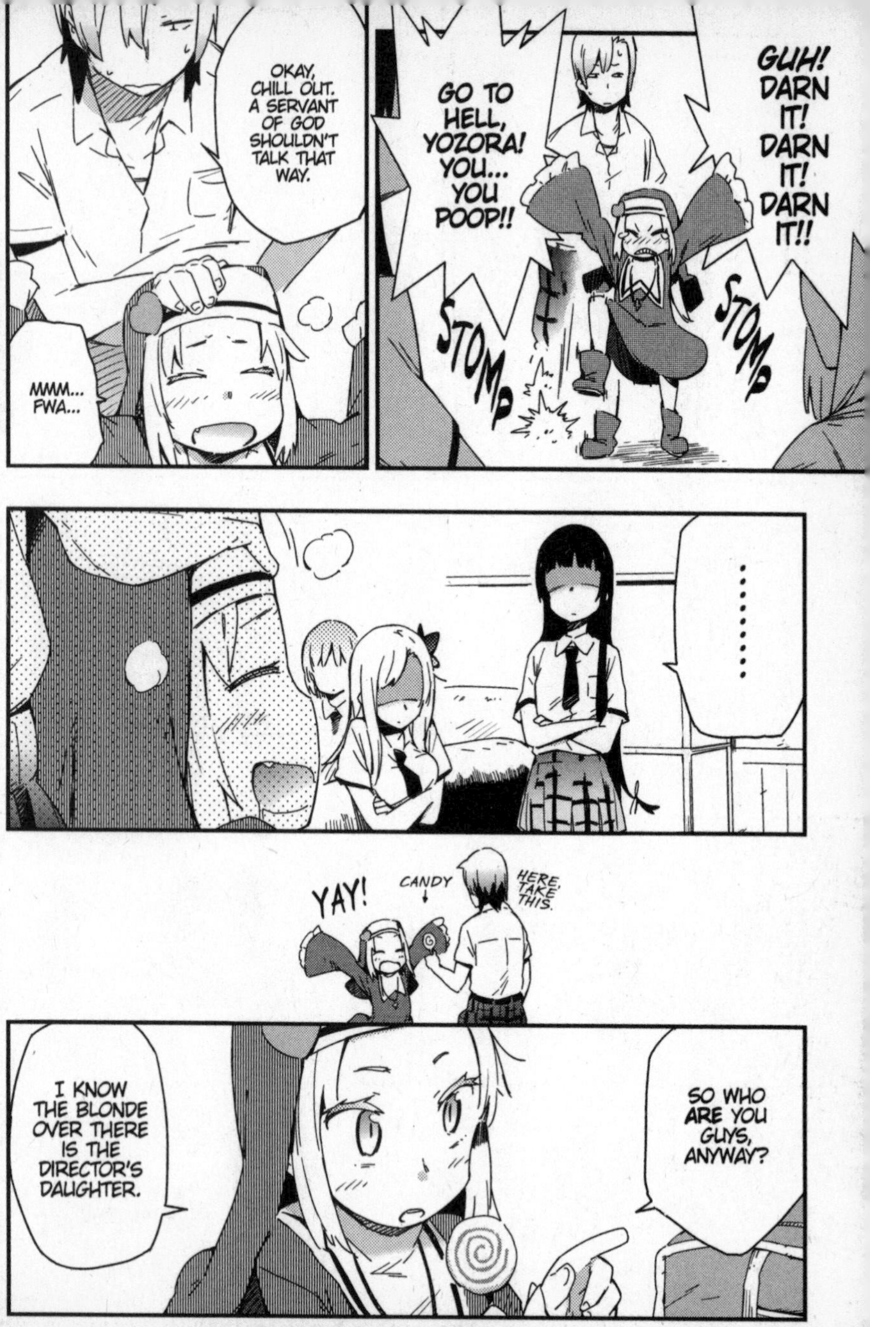
GUH! DARN IT! DARN IT! DARN IT!!
GO TO HELL, YOZORA! YOU... YOU POOP!!
STOMP
STOMP
OKAY, CHILL OUT. A SERVANT OF GOD SHOULDN'T TALK THAT WAY.
MMM... FWA...
......
HERE, TAKE THIS.
CANDY
YAY!
SO WHO ARE YOU GUYS, ANYWAY?
I KNOW THE BLONDE OVER THERE IS THE DIRECTOR'S DAUGHTER.

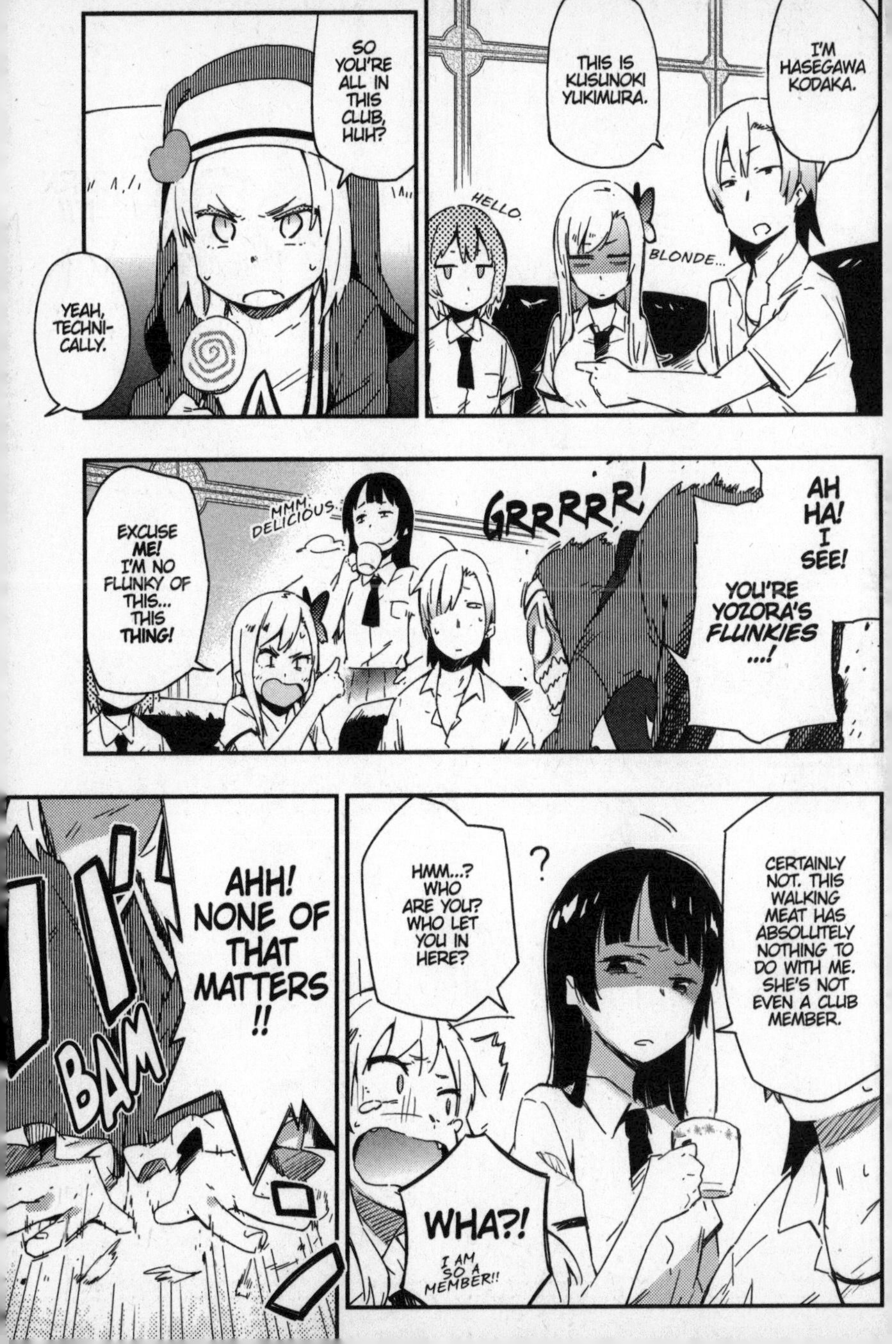
I'M HASEGAWA KODAKA.
THIS IS KUSUNOKI YUKIMURA.
HELLO.
BLONDE...
SO YOU'RE ALL IN THIS CLUB, HUH?
YEAH, TECHNICALLY.
AH HA! I SEE!
YOU'RE YOZORA'S FLUNKIES ...!
GRRRRR!
MMM, DELICIOUS...
EXCUSE ME! I'M NO FLUNKY OF THIS... THIS THING!
CERTAINLY NOT. THIS WALKING MEAT HAS ABSOLUTELY NOTHING TO DO WITH ME. SHE'S NOT EVEN A CLUB MEMBER.
?
HMM...? WHO ARE YOU? WHO LET YOU IN HERE?
WHA?!
I AM SO A MEMBER!!
AHH! NONE OF THAT MATTERS!!
BAM

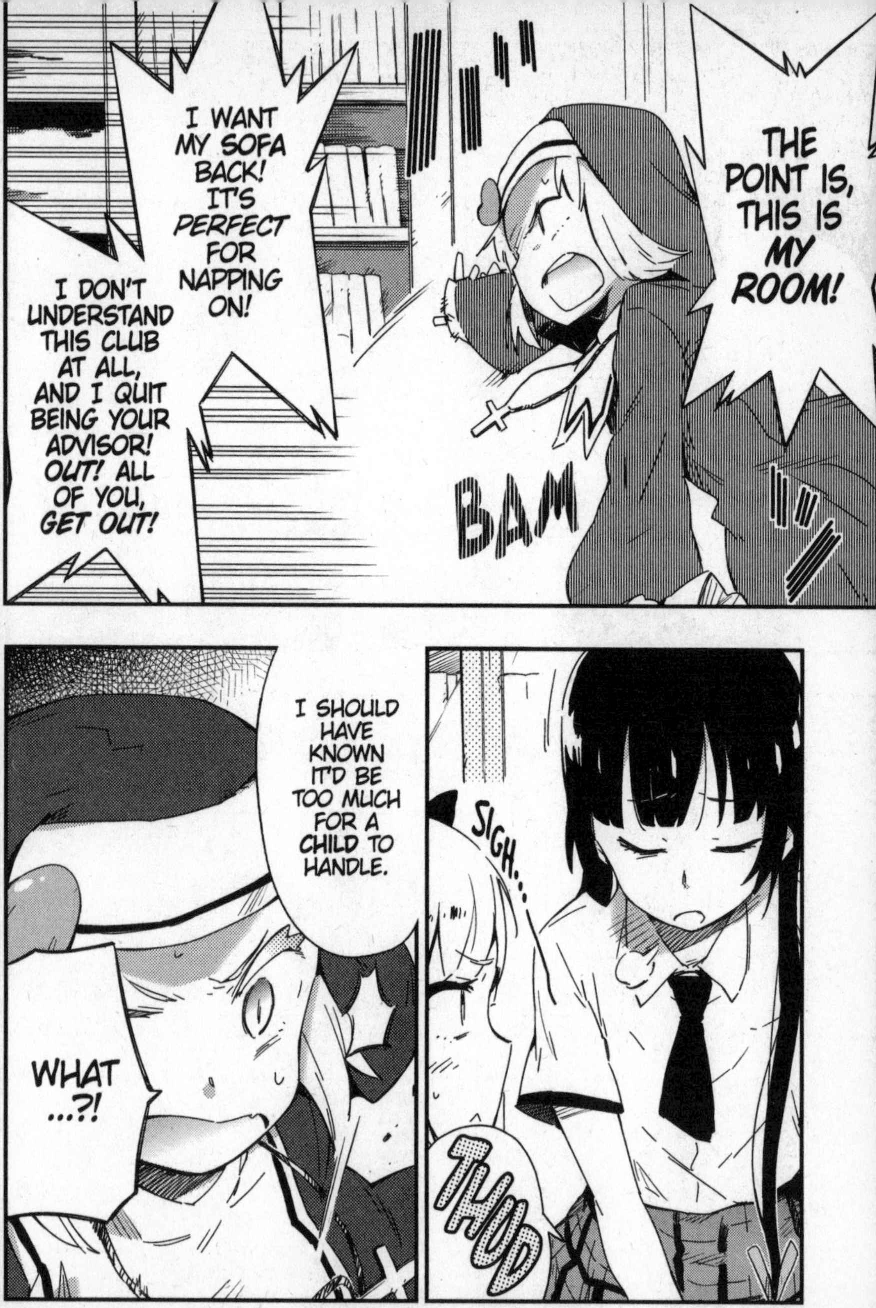

THE POINT IS, THIS IS MY ROOM!
I WANT MY SOFA BACK! IT'S PERFECT FOR NAPPING ON!
I DON'T UNDERSTAND THIS CLUB AT ALL, AND I QUIT BEING YOUR ADVISOR! OUT! ALL OF YOU, GET OUT!
BAM
SIGH...
I SHOULD HAVE KNOWN IT'D BE TOO MUCH FOR A CHILD TO HANDLE.
THUD
WHAT ...?!

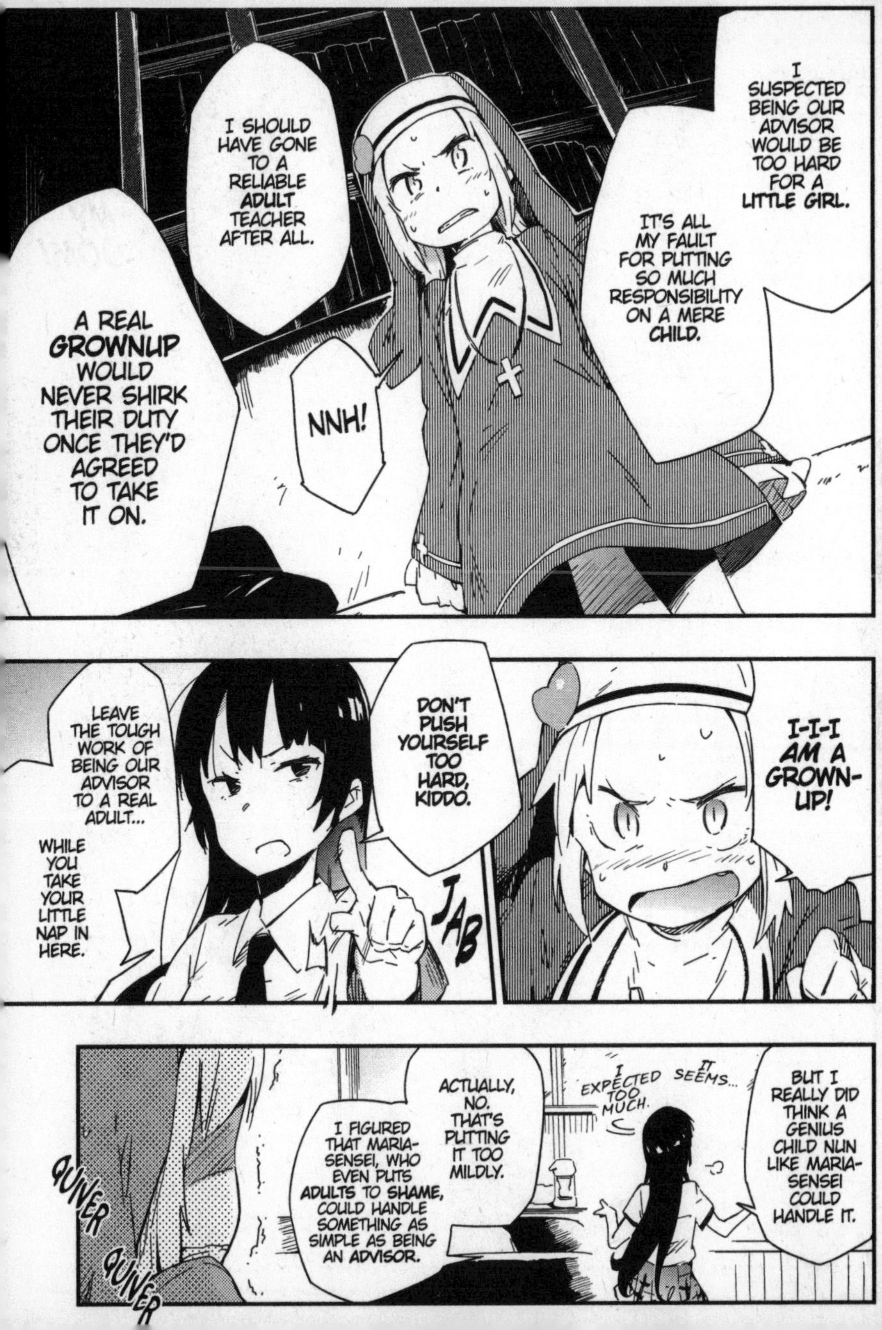
I SUSPECTED BEING OUR ADVISOR WOULD BE TOO HARD FOR A LITTLE GIRL.
IT'S ALL MY FAULT FOR PUTTING SO MUCH RESPONSIBILITY ON A MERE CHILD.
I SHOULD HAVE GONE TO A RELIABLE ADULT TEACHER AFTER ALL.
NNH!
A REAL GROWNUP WOULD NEVER SHIRK THEIR DUTY ONCE THEY'D AGREED TO TAKE IT ON.
I-I-I AM A GROWN-UP!
DON'T PUSH YOURSELF TOO HARD, KIDDO.
JAB
LEAVE THE TOUGH WORK OF BEING OUR ADVISOR TO A REAL ADULT...
WHILE YOU TAKE YOUR LITTLE NAP IN HERE.
BUT I REALLY DID THINK A GENIUS CHILD NUN LIKE MARIA-SENSEI COULD HANDLE IT.
IT SEEMS... I EXPECTED TOO MUCH.
ACTUALLY, NO. THAT'S PUTTING IT TOO MILDLY.
I FIGURED THAT MARIA-SENSEI, WHO EVEN PUTS ADULTS TO SHAME, COULD HANDLE SOMETHING AS SIMPLE AS BEING AN ADVISOR.
QUIVER QUIVER

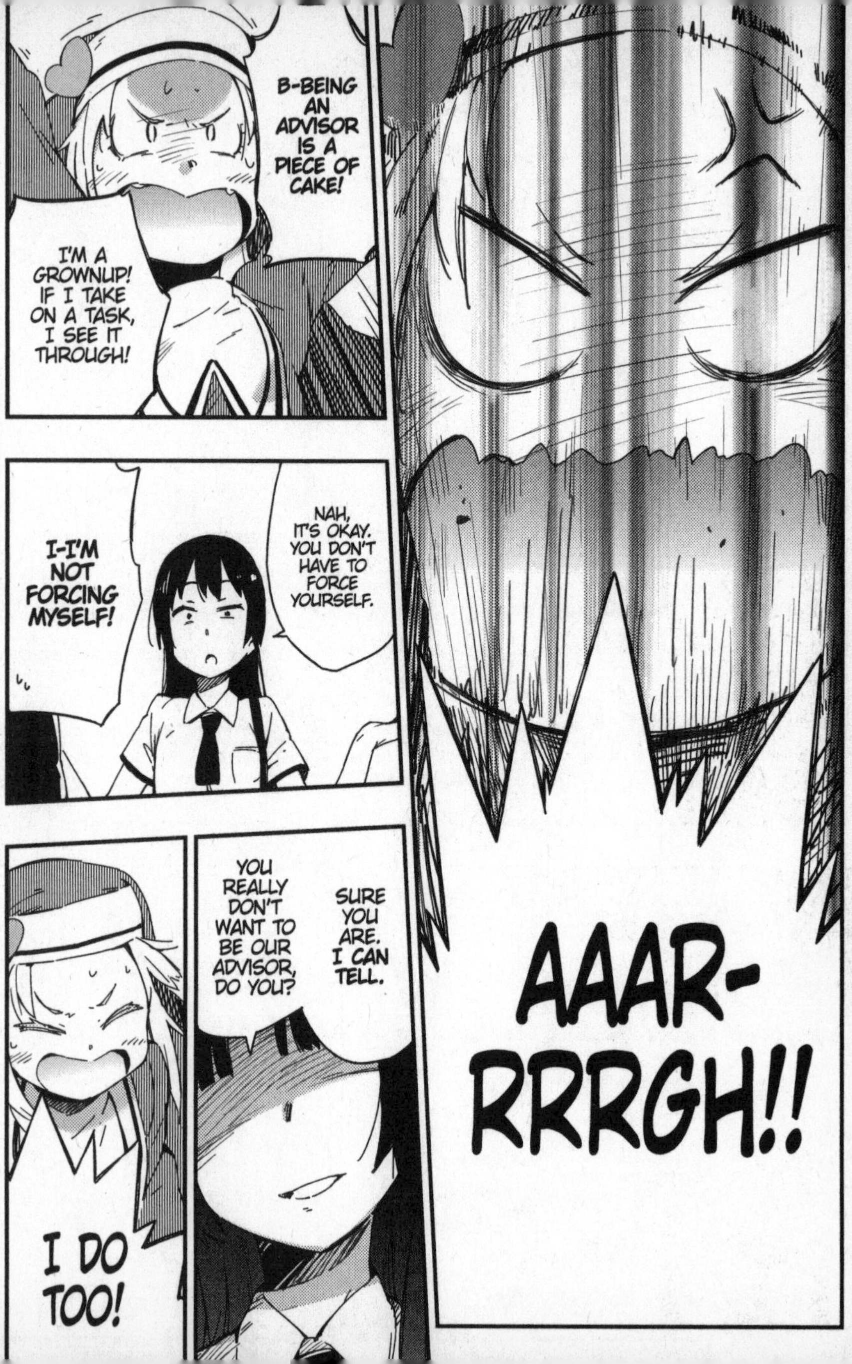
AAAR-RRRGH!!
B-BEING AN ADVISOR IS A PIECE OF CAKE!
I'M A GROWNUP! IF I TAKE ON A TASK, I SEE IT THROUGH!
NAH, IT'S OKAY. YOU DON'T HAVE TO FORCE YOURSELF.
I-I'M NOT FORCING MYSELF!
SURE YOU ARE. I CAN TELL.
YOU REALLY DON'T WANT TO BE OUR ADVISOR, DO YOU?
I DO TOO!

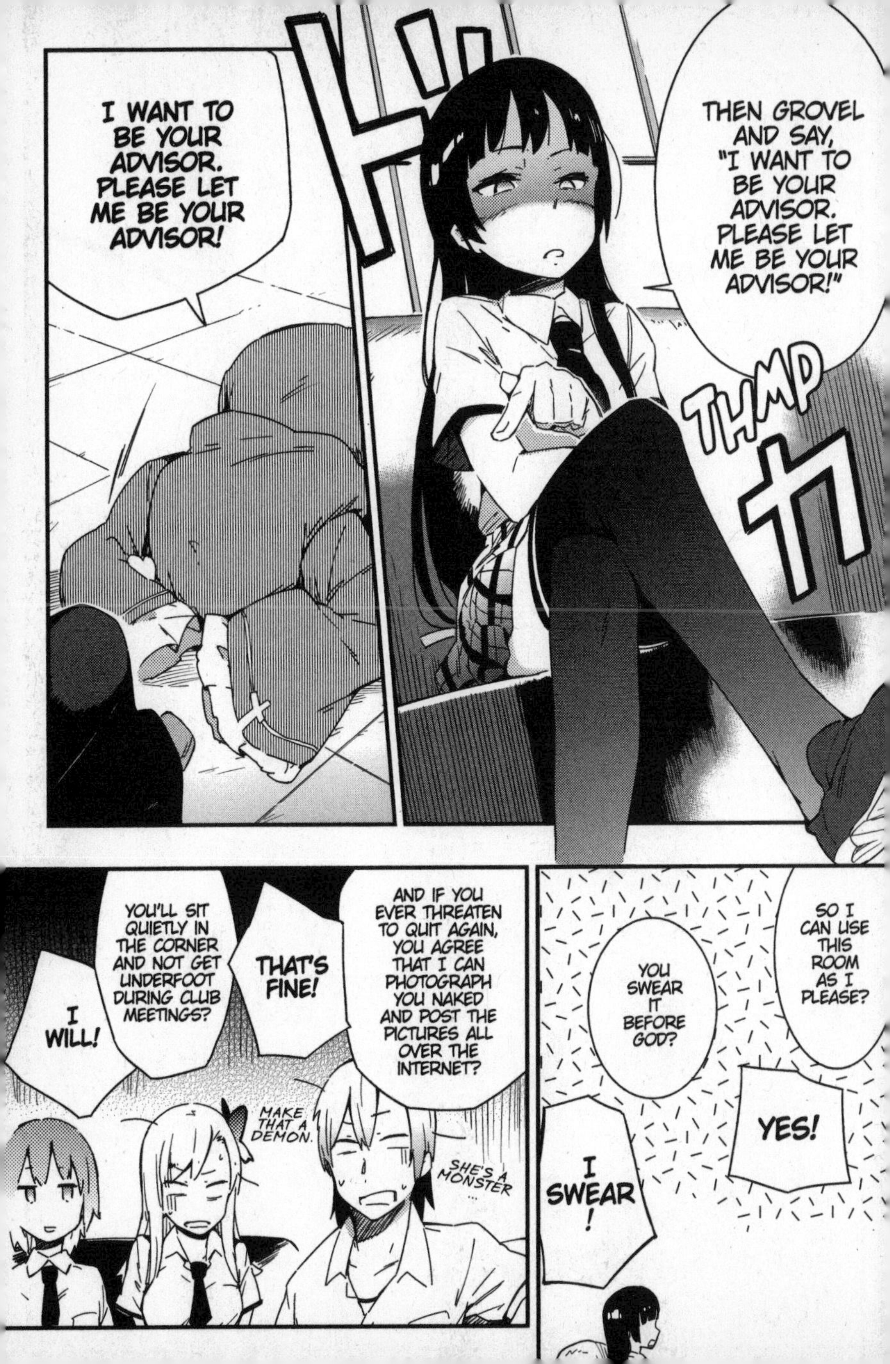
THEN GROVEL AND SAY, "I WANT TO BE YOUR ADVISOR. PLEASE LET ME BE YOUR ADVISOR!"
THMP
I WANT TO BE YOUR ADVISOR. PLEASE LET ME BE YOUR ADVISOR!
SO I CAN USE THIS ROOM AS I PLEASE?
YES!
YOU SWEAR IT BEFORE GOD?
I SWEAR!
AND IF YOU EVER THREATEN TO QUIT AGAIN, YOU AGREE THAT I CAN PHOTOGRAPH YOU NAKED AND POST THE PICTURES ALL OVER THE INTERNET?
THAT'S FINE!
YOU'LL SIT QUIETLY IN THE CORNER AND NOT GET UNDERFOOT DURING CLUB MEETINGS?
I WILL!
SHE'S A MONSTER...
MAKE THAT A DEMON.

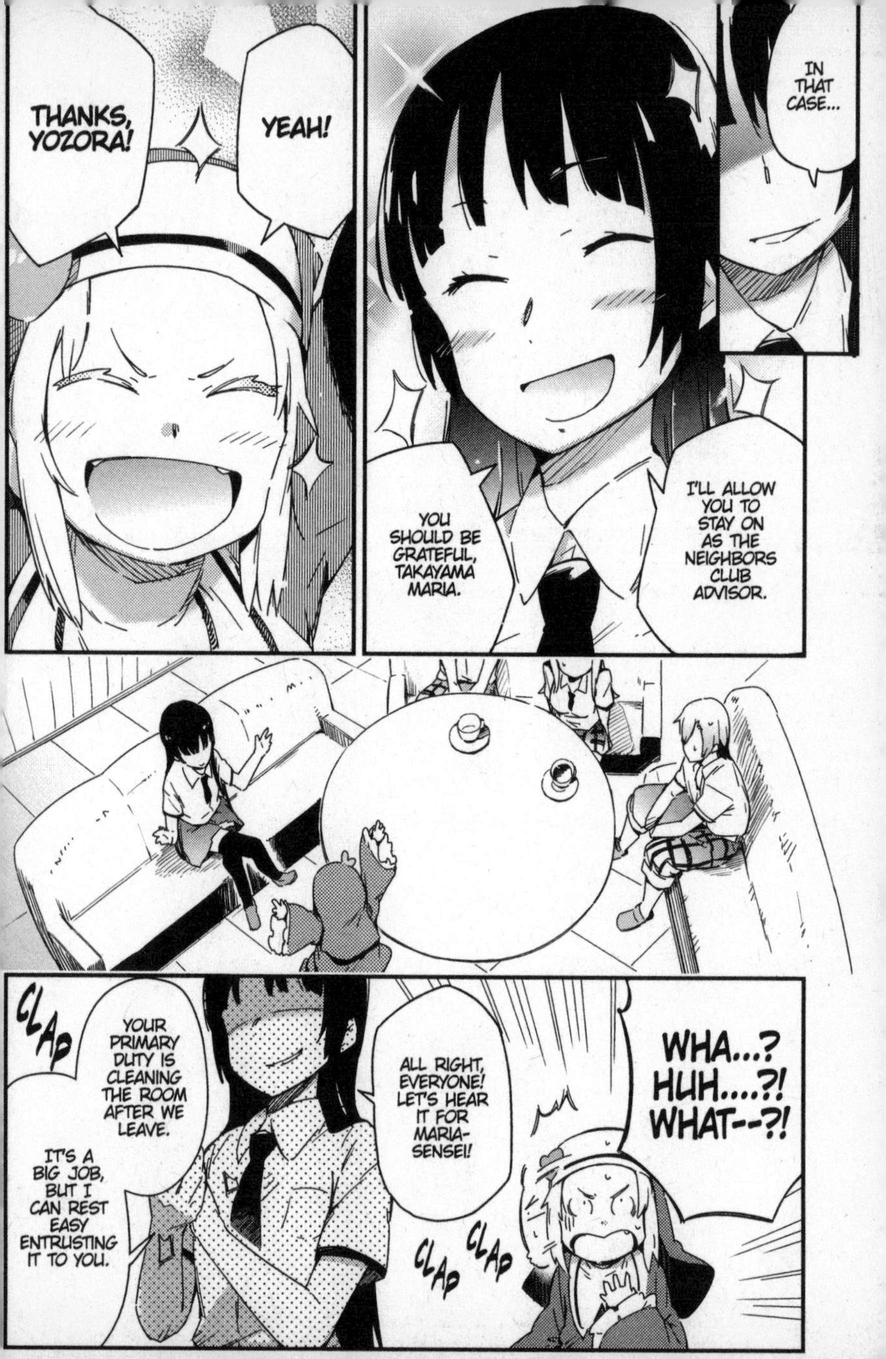
IN THAT CASE...
I'LL ALLOW YOU TO STAY ON AS THE NEIGHBORS CLUB ADVISOR.
YOU SHOULD BE GRATEFUL, TAKAYAMA MARIA.
YEAH!
THANKS, YOZORA!
WHA...? HUH....?! WHAT--?!
ALL RIGHT, EVERYONE! LET'S HEAR IT FOR MARIA-SENSEI!
CLAP
CLAP
YOUR PRIMARY DUTY IS CLEANING THE ROOM AFTER WE LEAVE.
IT'S A BIG JOB, BUT I CAN REST EASY ENTRUSTING IT TO YOU.
CLAP

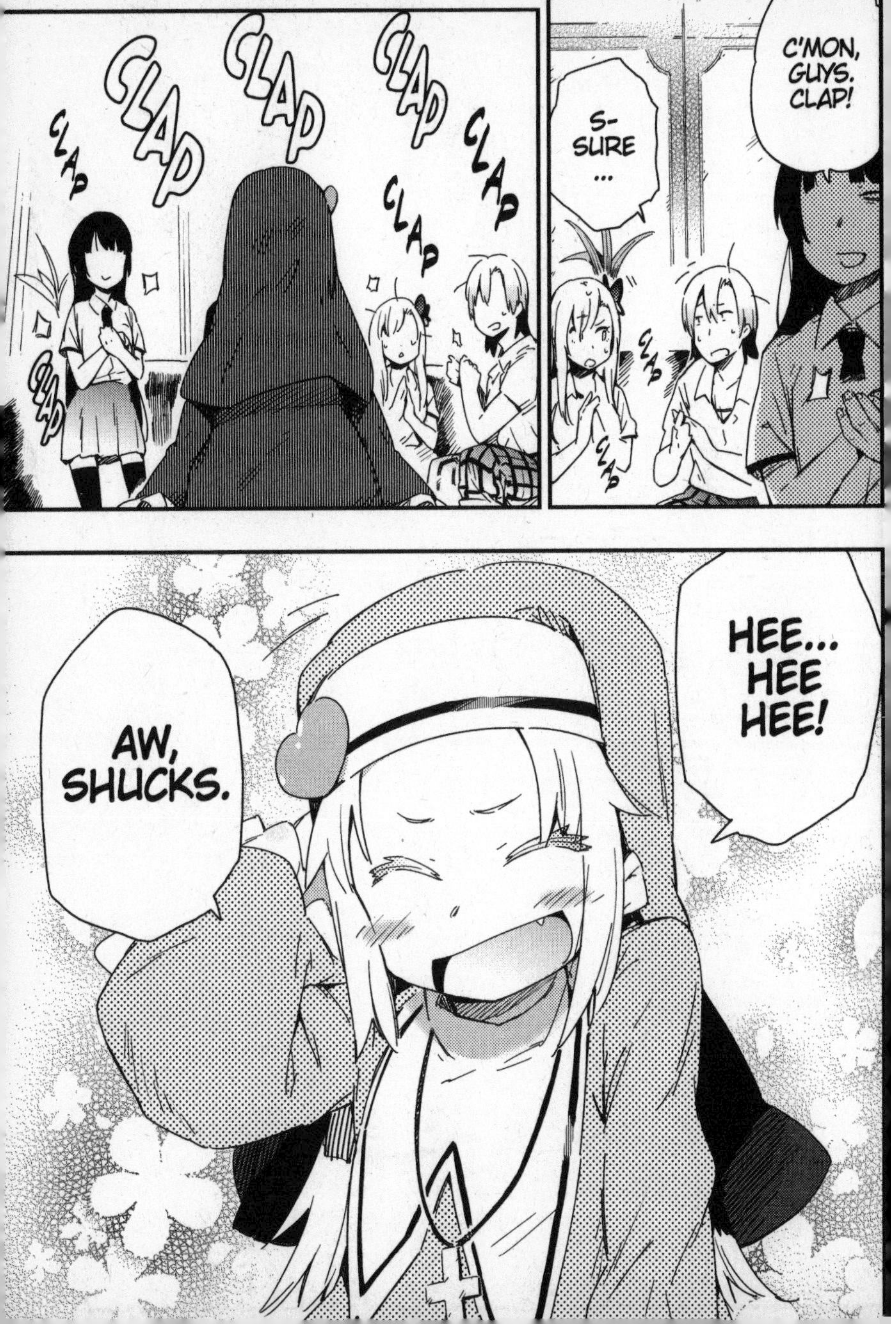
C'MON, GUYS. CLAP!
S- SURE ...
CLAP
CLAP
CLAP
CLAP
CLAP
CLAP
CLAP
CLAP
CLAP
HEE... HEE HEE!
AW, SHUCKS.

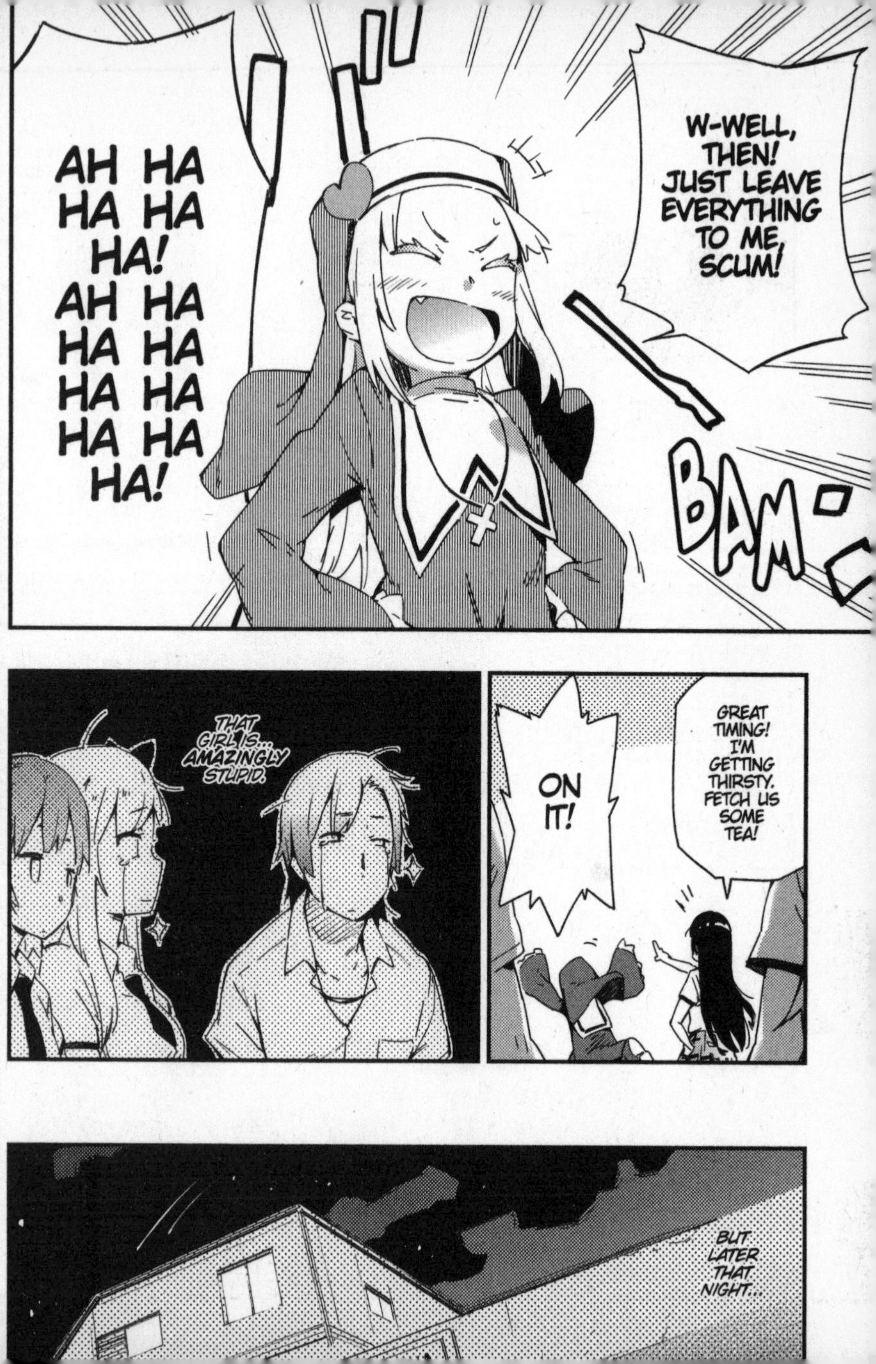
W-WELL, THEN! JUST LEAVE EVERYTHING TO ME, SCUM!
BAM
AH HA HA HA HA! AH HA HA HA HA HA HA HA HA!
GREAT TIMING! I'M GETTING THIRSTY. FETCH US SOME TEA!
ON IT!
THAT GIRL IS... AMAZINGLY STUPID.
BUT LATER THAT NIGHT...

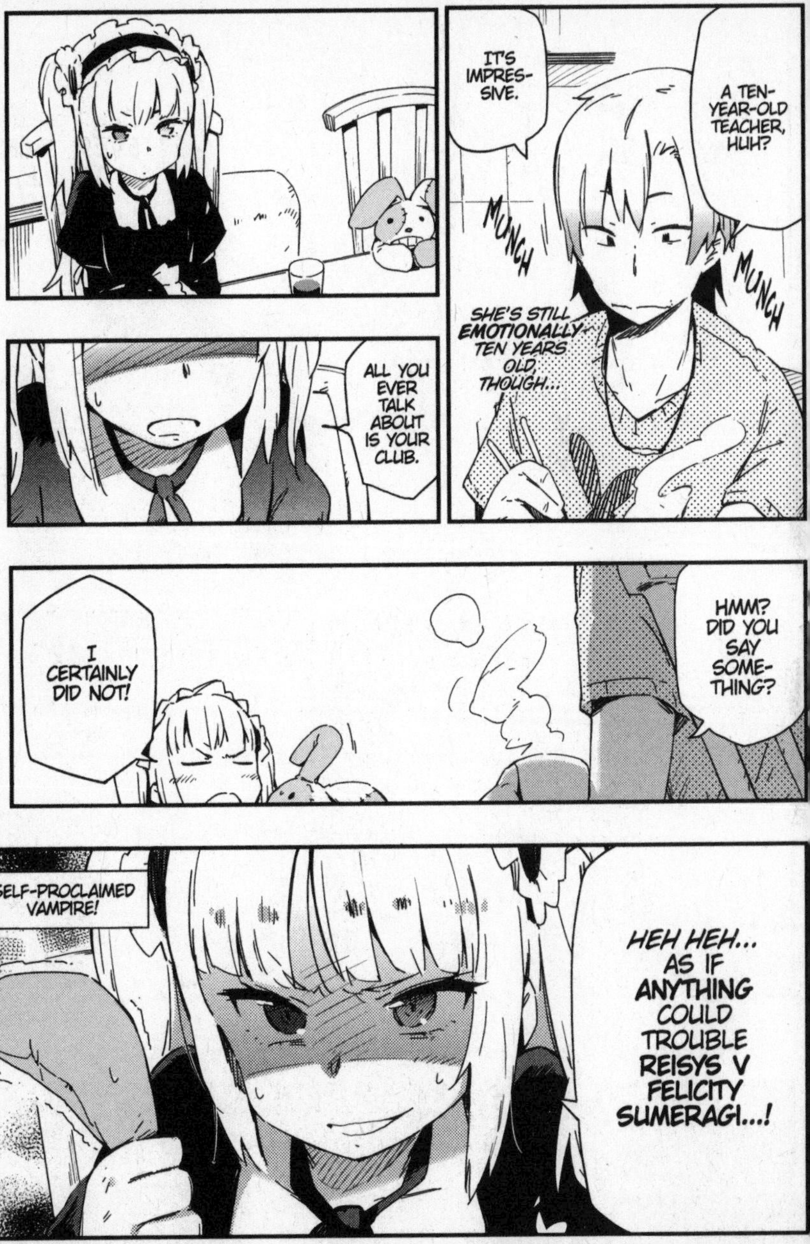
A TEN-YEAR-OLD TEACHER, HUH?
IT'S IMPRESSIVE.
MUNCH
MUNCH
SHE'S STILL EMOTIONALLY TEN YEARS OLD, THOUGH...
ALL YOU EVER TALK ABOUT IS YOUR CLUB.
HMM? DID YOU SAY SOMETHING?
I CERTAINLY DID NOT!
HEH HEH... AS IF ANYTHING COULD TROUBLE REISYS V FELICITY SUMERAGI...!
SELF-PROCLAIMED VAMPIRE!

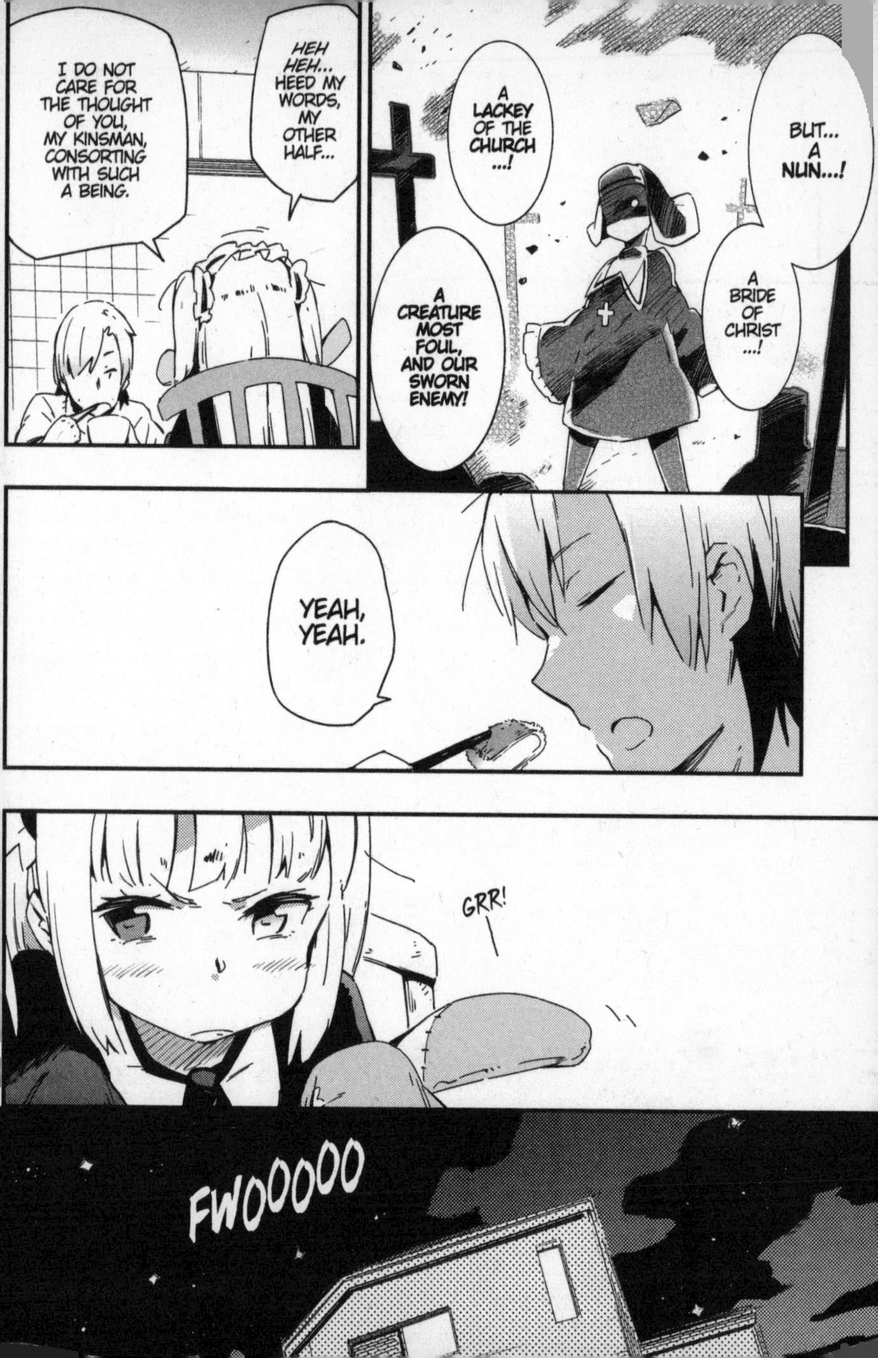
BUT... A NUN...!
A LACKEY OF THE CHURCH ...!
A BRIDE OF CHRIST ...!
A CREATURE MOST FOUL, AND OUR SWORN ENEMY!
HEH HEH... HEED MY WORDS, MY OTHER HALF...
I DO NOT CARE FOR THE THOUGHT OF YOU, MY KINSMAN, CONSORTING WITH SUCH A BEING.
YEAH, YEAH.
GRR!
FWOOOOO

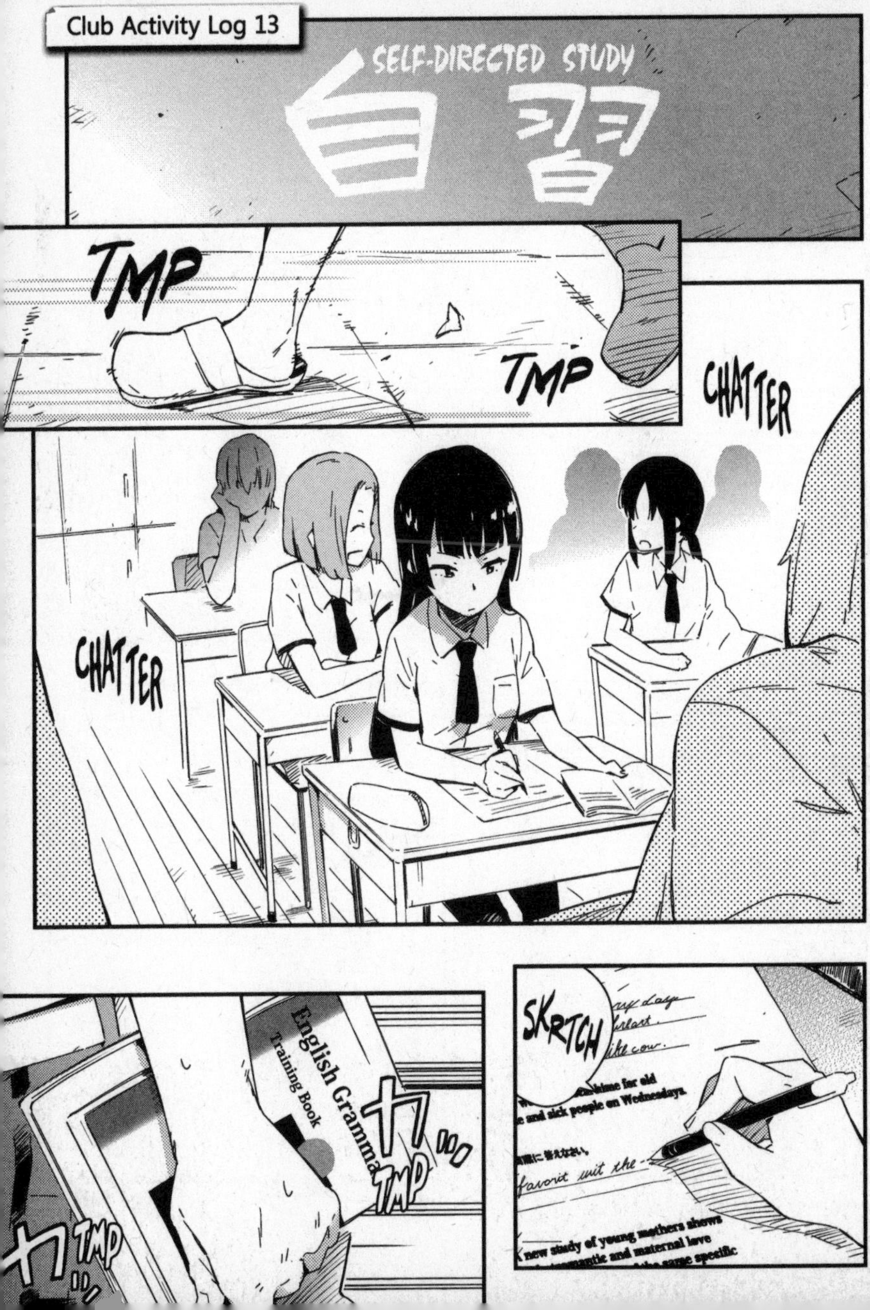

Club Activity Log 13
SELF-DIRECTED STUDY
自習
TMP
TMP
CHATTER
CHATTER
SKRTCH
ike cow.
e and sick people on Wednesdays.
favorit wit the-
new study of young mothers shows
and maternal love
English Grammar
Training Book
TMP
TMP

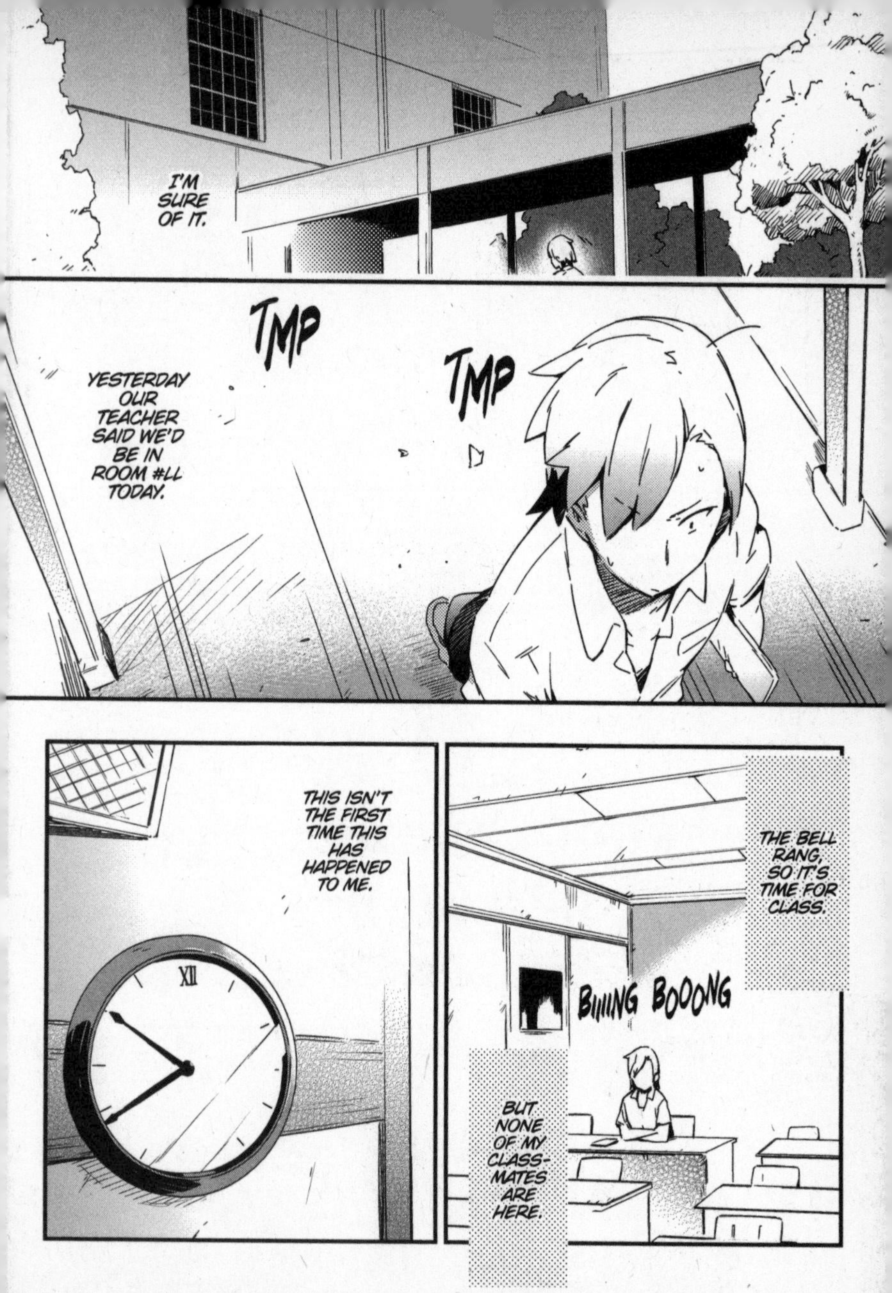
I'M SURE OF IT.
TMP
TMP
YESTERDAY OUR TEACHER SAID WE'D BE IN ROOM #11 TODAY.
THE BELL RANG, SO IT'S TIME FOR CLASS.
BIIIING BOOONG
BUT NONE OF MY CLASS-MATES ARE HERE.
THIS ISN'T THE FIRST TIME THIS HAS HAPPENED TO ME.

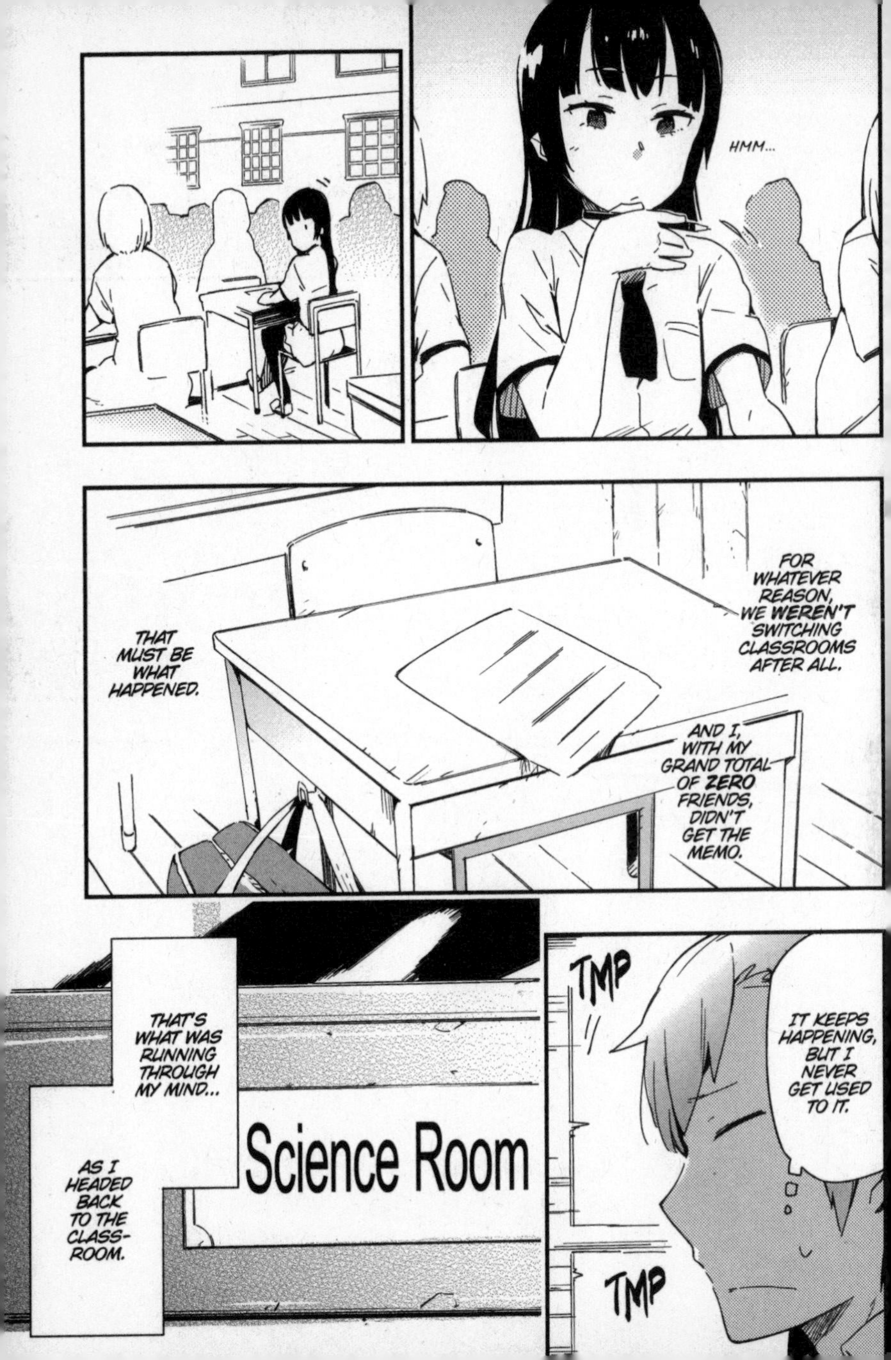
HMM...
FOR WHATEVER REASON, WE WEREN'T SWITCHING CLASSROOMS AFTER ALL.
AND I, WITH MY GRAND TOTAL OF ZERO FRIENDS, DIDN'T GET THE MEMO.
THAT MUST BE WHAT HAPPENED.
TMP
IT KEEPS HAPPENING, BUT I NEVER GET USED TO IT.
TMP
THAT'S WHAT WAS RUNNING THROUGH MY MIND...
AS I HEADED BACK TO THE CLASS-ROOM.
Science Room

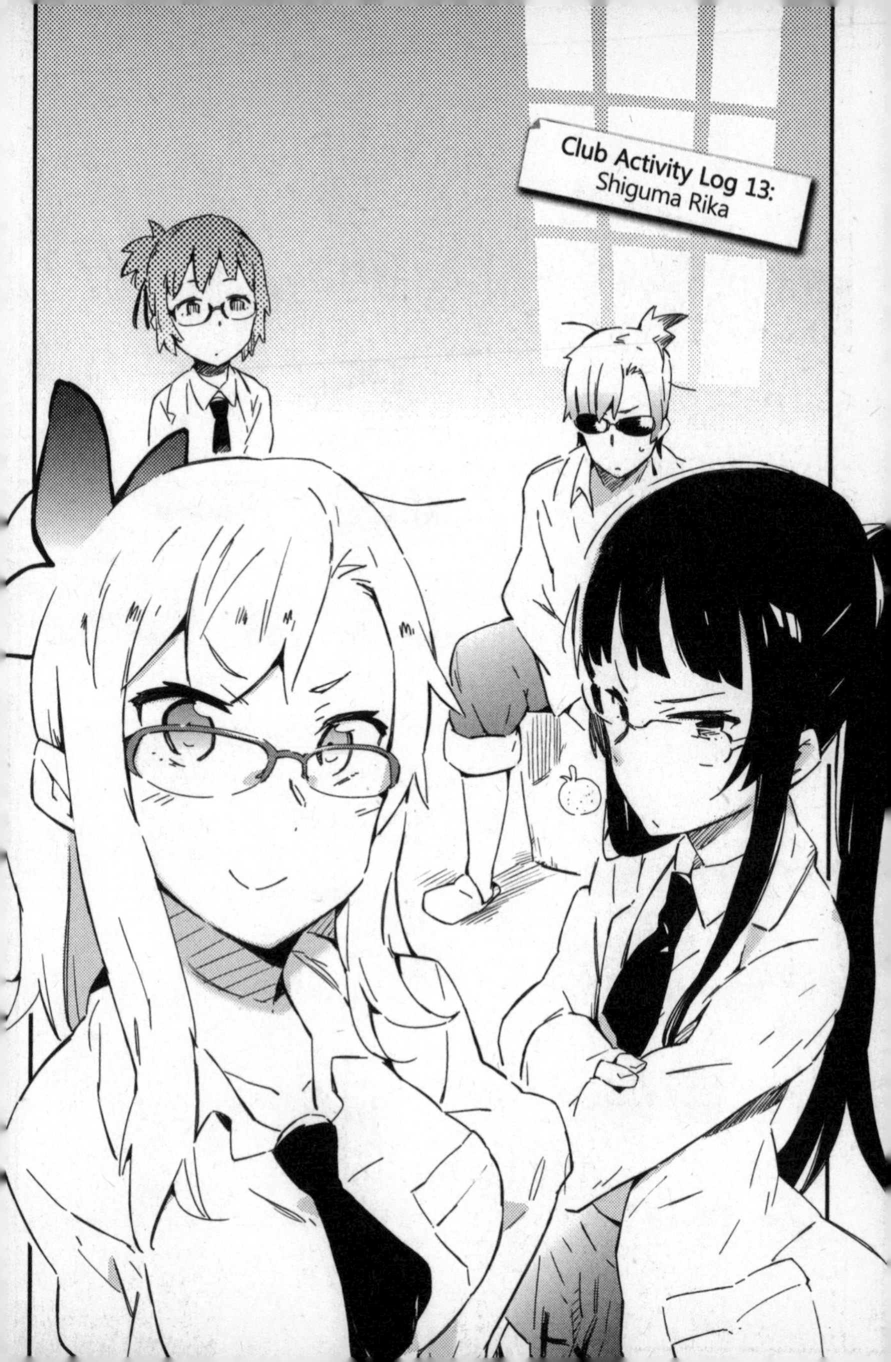
Club Activity Log 13:
Shiguma Rika

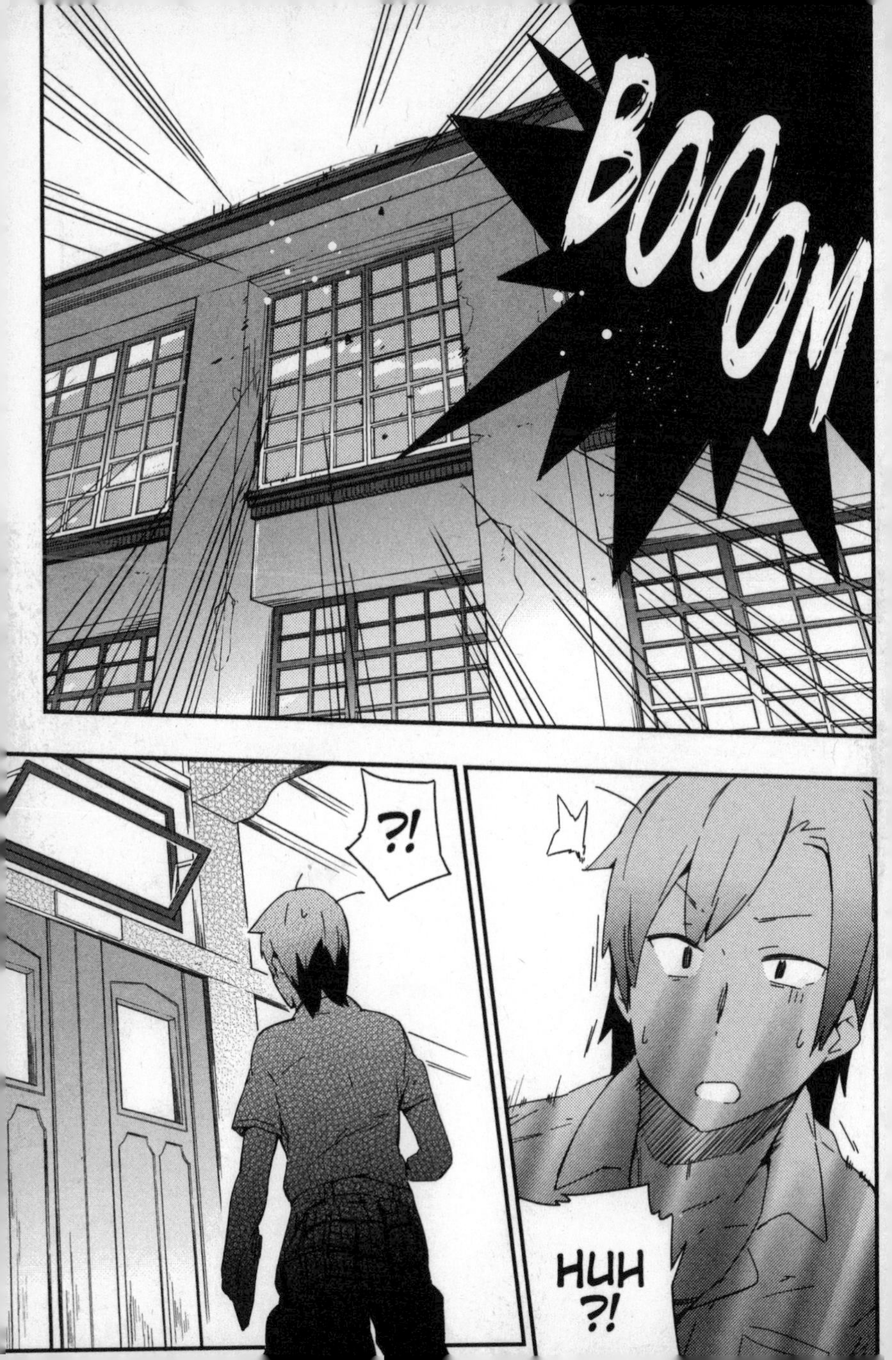
BOOOM
HUH ?!
?!

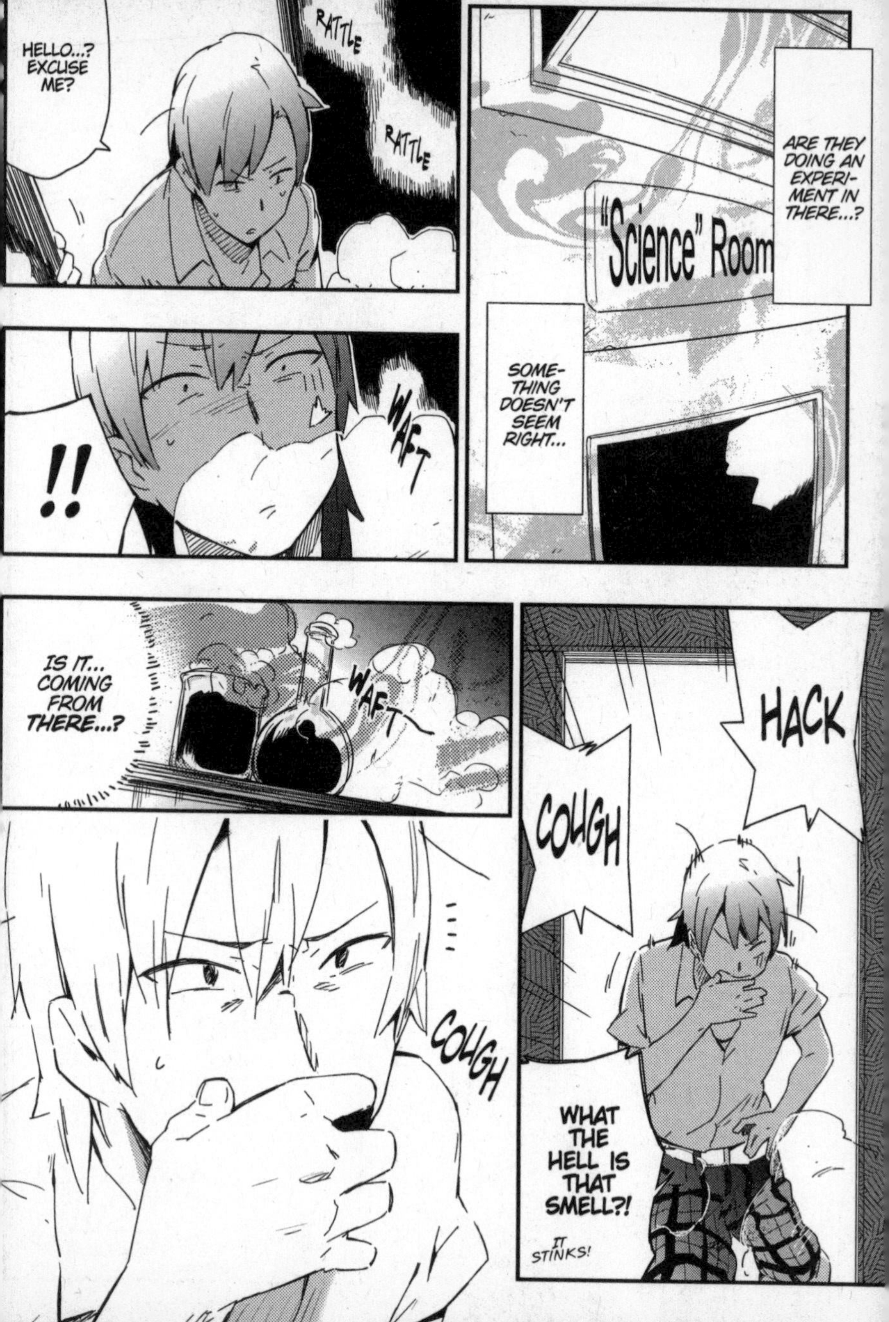
ARE THEY DOING AN EXPERIMENT IN THERE...?
"Science" Room
SOMETHING DOESN'T SEEM RIGHT...
RATTLE
RATTLE
HELLO...? EXCUSE ME?
WAFT
!!
HACK
COUGH
WHAT THE HELL IS THAT SMELL?!
IT STINKS!
WAFT
IS IT... COMING FROM THERE...?
COUGH
...

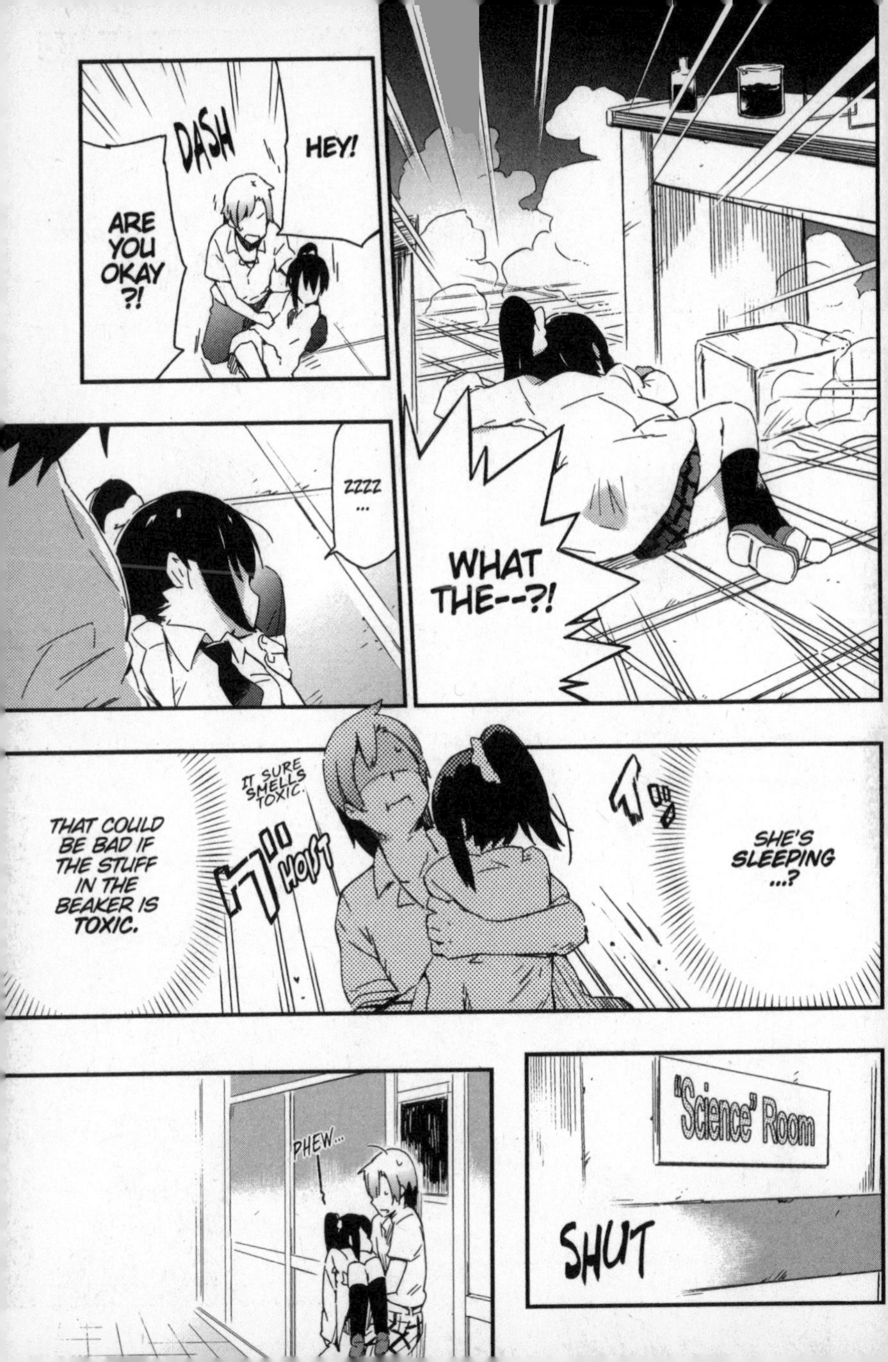
WHAT THE--?!
HEY!
DASH
ARE YOU OKAY?!
ZZZZ...
SHE'S SLEEPING...?
IT SURE SMELLS TOXIC.
HOIST
THAT COULD BE BAD IF THE STUFF IN THE BEAKER IS TOXIC.
"Science" Room
SHUT
PHEW...

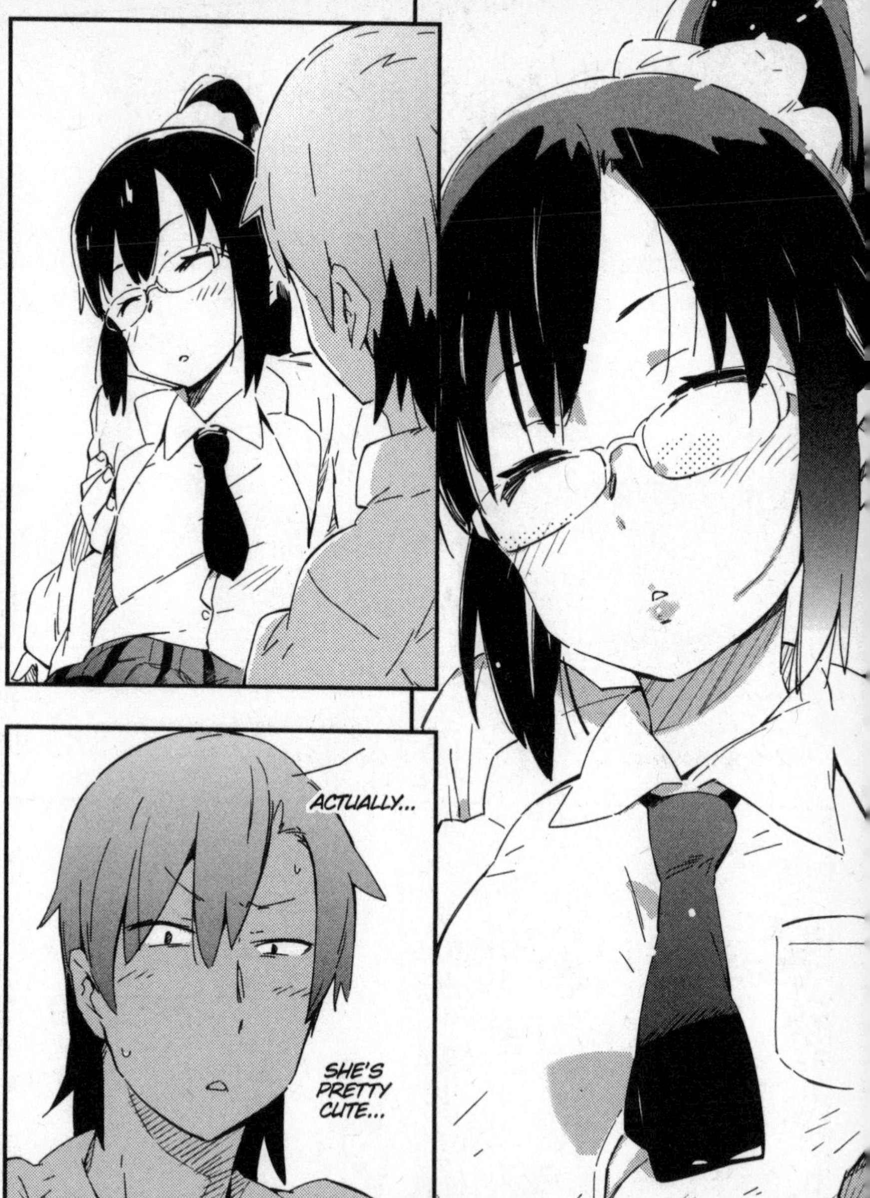
ACTUALLY...
SHE'S PRETTY CUTE...

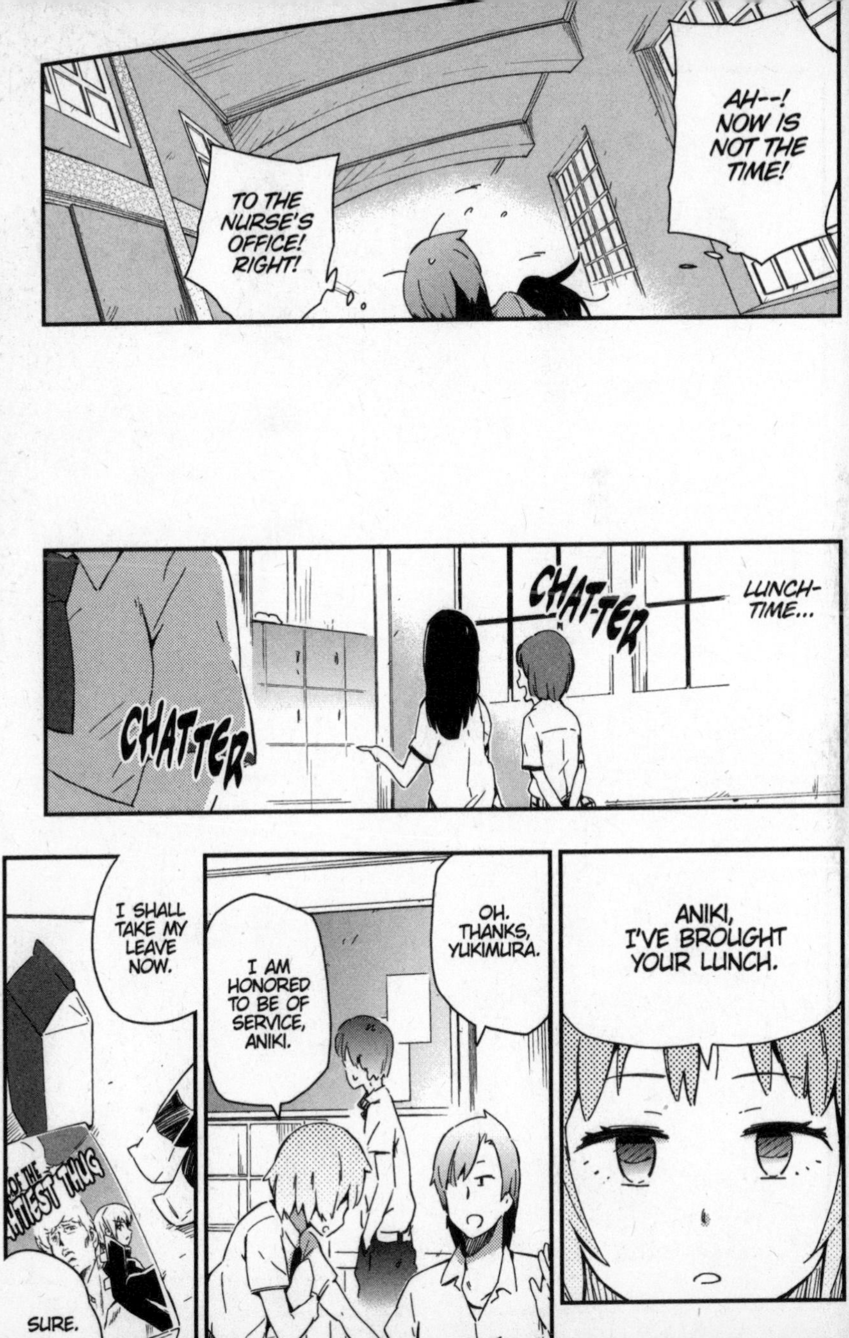
AH--! NOW IS NOT THE TIME!
TO THE NURSE'S OFFICE! RIGHT!
LUNCH-TIME...
CHAT-TER
CHATTER
ANIKI, I'VE BROUGHT YOUR LUNCH.
OH. THANKS, YUKIMURA.
I AM HONORED TO BE OF SERVICE, ANIKI.
I SHALL TAKE MY LEAVE NOW.
SURE.

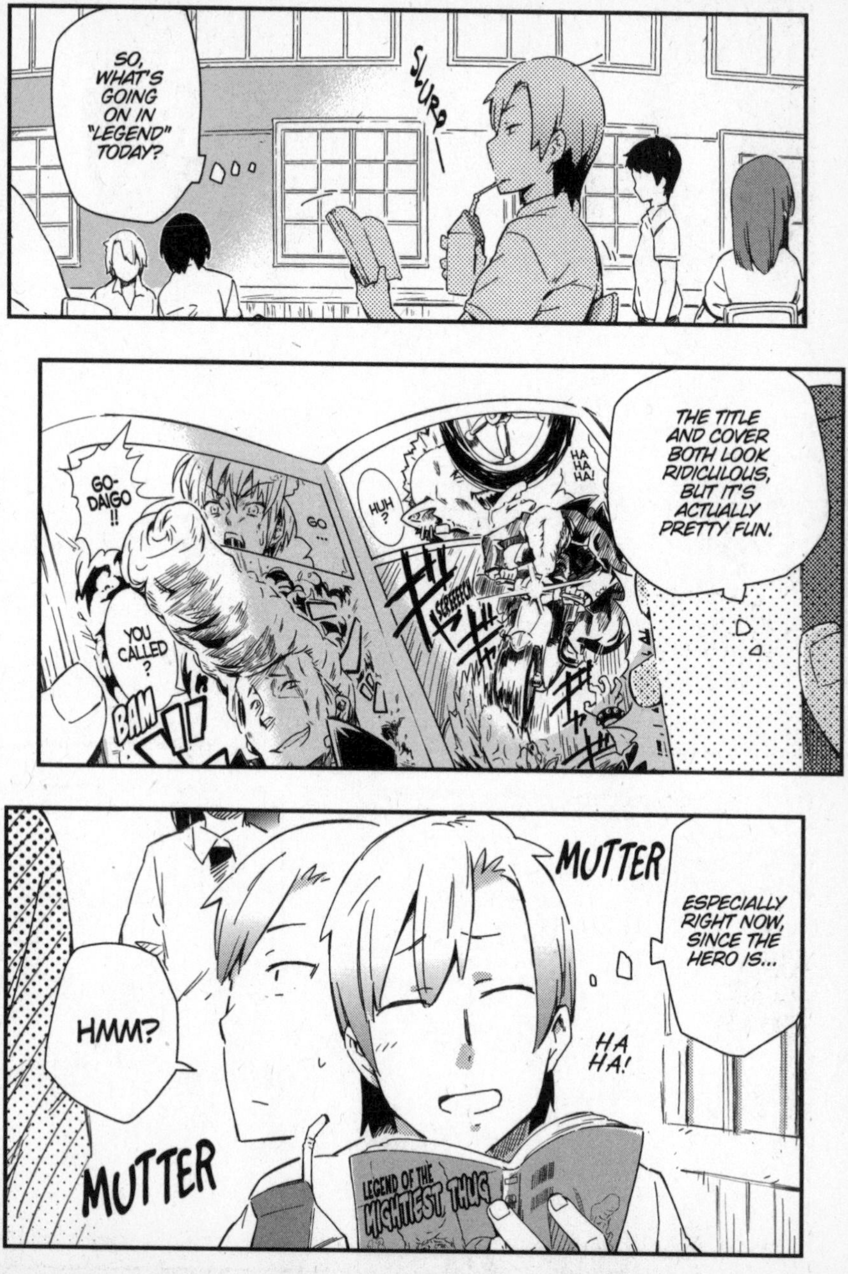
SLURP
SO, WHAT'S GOING ON IN "LEGEND" TODAY?
THE TITLE AND COVER BOTH LOOK RIDICULOUS, BUT IT'S ACTUALLY PRETTY FUN.
HA HA HA!
HUH?
SCREEEECH
GO...
GO-DAIGO!!
YOU CALLED?
BAM
ESPECIALLY RIGHT NOW, SINCE THE HERO IS...
MUTTER
HA HA!
HMM?
MUTTER
LEGEND OF THE MIGHTIEST THUG

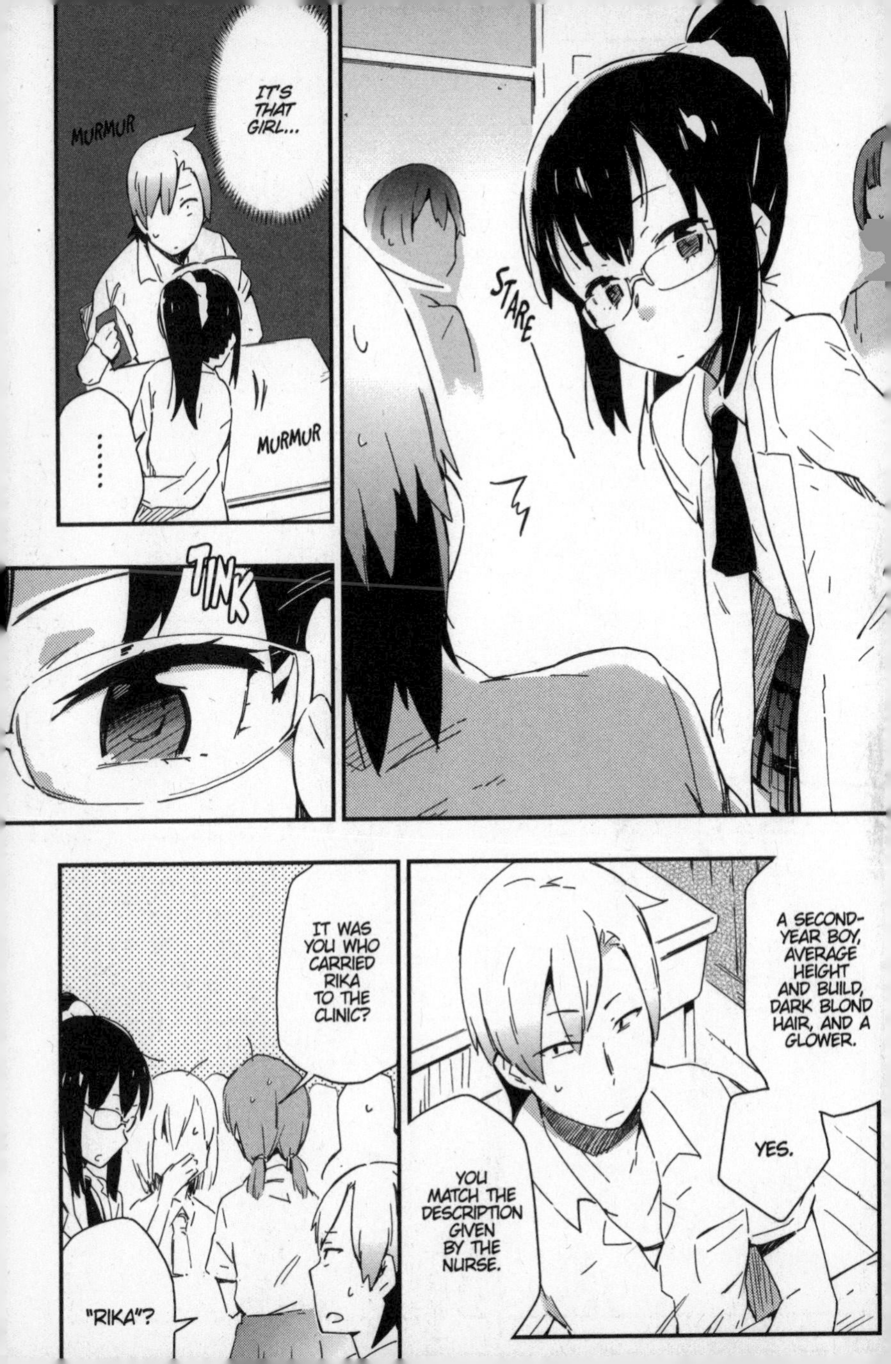
STARE
IT'S THAT GIRL...
MURMUR
MURMUR
......
TINK
A SECOND-YEAR BOY, AVERAGE HEIGHT AND BUILD, DARK BLOND HAIR, AND A GLOWER.
YES.
YOU MATCH THE DESCRIPTION GIVEN BY THE NURSE.
IT WAS YOU WHO CARRIED RIKA TO THE CLINIC?
"RIKA"?

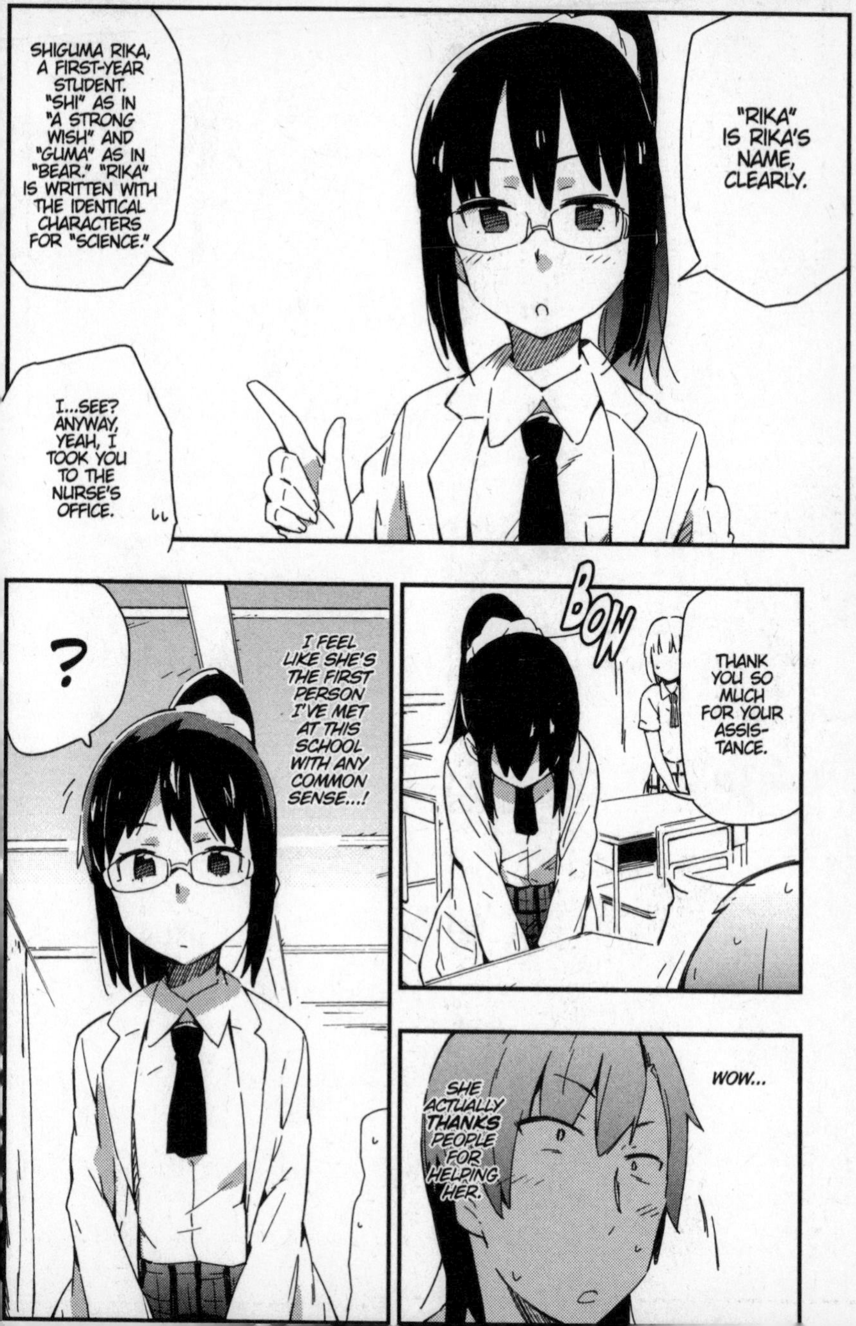
"RIKA" IS RIKA'S NAME, CLEARLY.
SHIGUMA RIKA, A FIRST-YEAR STUDENT. "SHI" AS IN "A STRONG WISH" AND "GUMA" AS IN "BEAR." "RIKA" IS WRITTEN WITH THE IDENTICAL CHARACTERS FOR "SCIENCE."
I...SEE? ANYWAY, YEAH, I TOOK YOU TO THE NURSE'S OFFICE.
BOW
THANK YOU SO MUCH FOR YOUR ASSIS-TANCE.
WOW...
SHE ACTUALLY THANKS PEOPLE FOR HELPING HER.
?
I FEEL LIKE SHE'S THE FIRST PERSON I'VE MET AT THIS SCHOOL WITH ANY COMMON SENSE...!

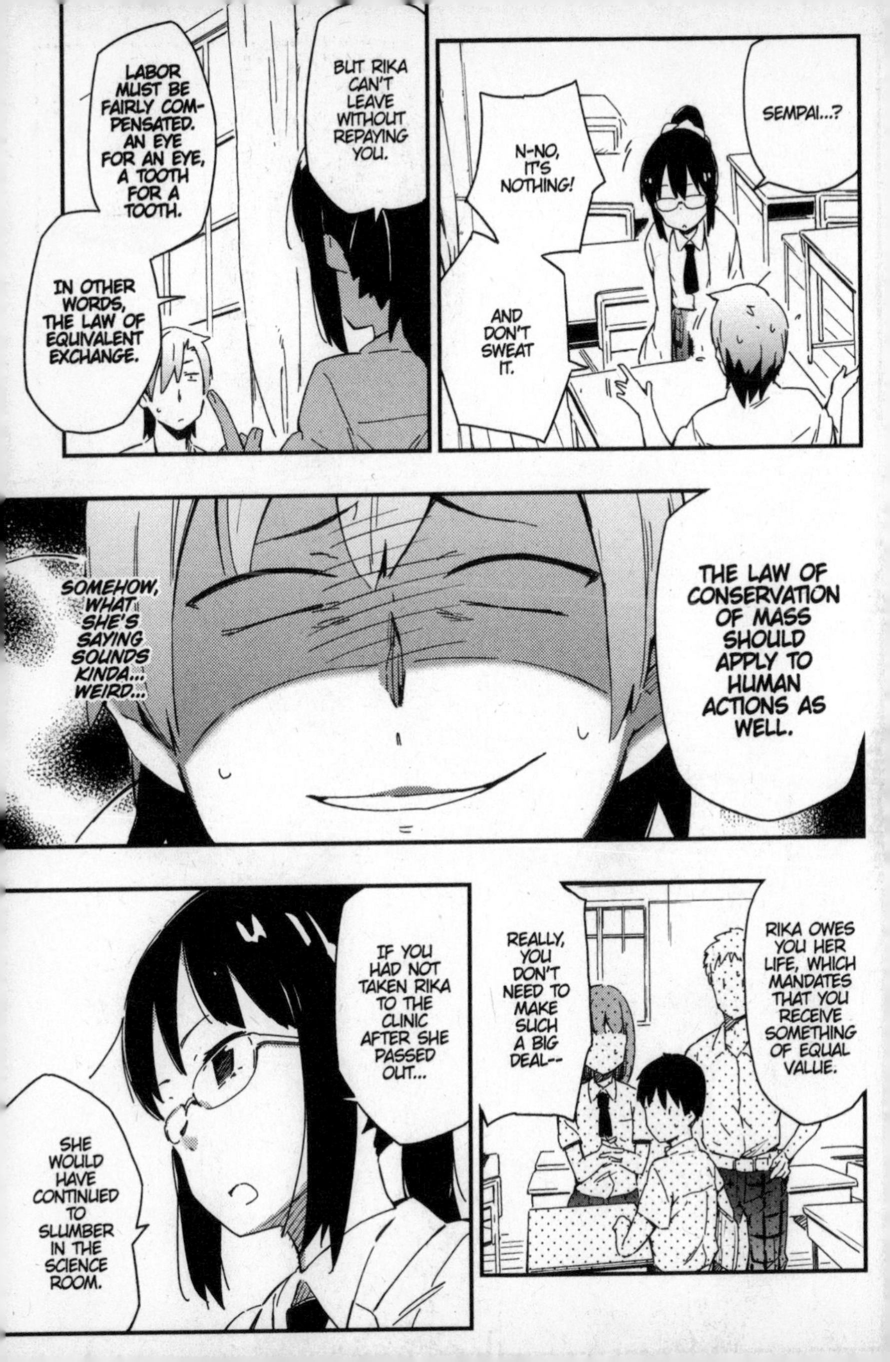
SEMPAI...?
N-NO, IT'S NOTHING!
AND DON'T SWEAT IT.
BUT RIKA CAN'T LEAVE WITHOUT REPAYING YOU.
LABOR MUST BE FAIRLY COMPENSATED. AN EYE FOR AN EYE, A TOOTH FOR A TOOTH.
IN OTHER WORDS, THE LAW OF EQUIVALENT EXCHANGE.
THE LAW OF CONSERVATION OF MASS SHOULD APPLY TO HUMAN ACTIONS AS WELL.
SOMEHOW, WHAT SHE'S SAYING SOUNDS KINDA... WEIRD...
RIKA OWES YOU HER LIFE, WHICH MANDATES THAT YOU RECEIVE SOMETHING OF EQUAL VALUE.
REALLY, YOU DON'T NEED TO MAKE SUCH A BIG DEAL--
IF YOU HAD NOT TAKEN RIKA TO THE CLINIC AFTER SHE PASSED OUT...
SHE WOULD HAVE CONTINUED TO SLUMBER IN THE SCIENCE ROOM.

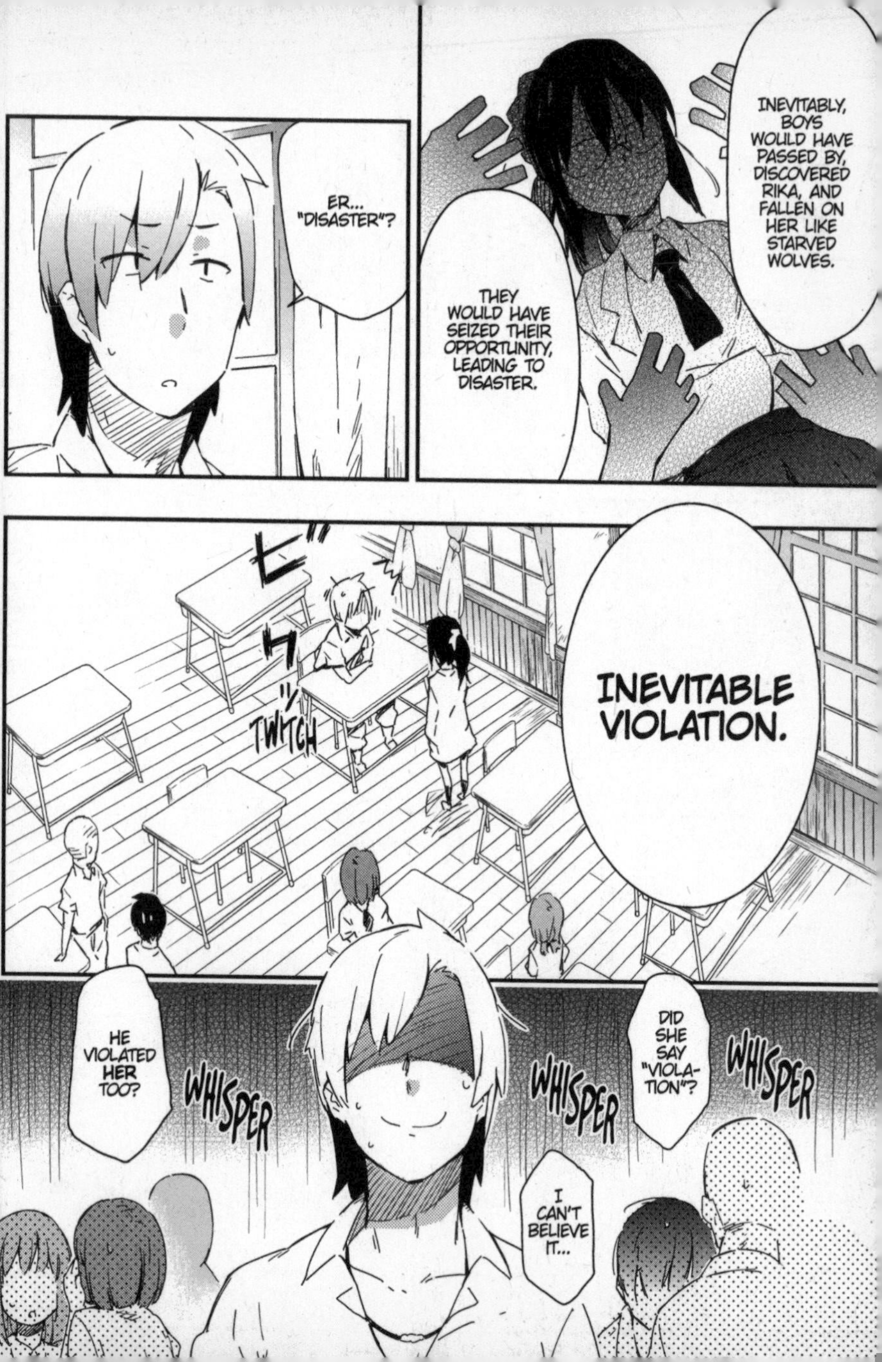
INEVITABLY, BOYS WOULD HAVE PASSED BY, DISCOVERED RIKA, AND FALLEN ON HER LIKE STARVED WOLVES.
THEY WOULD HAVE SEIZED THEIR OPPORTUNITY, LEADING TO DISASTER.
ER... "DISASTER"?
INEVITABLE VIOLATION.
TWITCH
WHISPER
DID SHE SAY "VIOLA-TION"?
WHISPER
I CAN'T BELIEVE IT...
HE VIOLATED HER TOO?
WHISPER

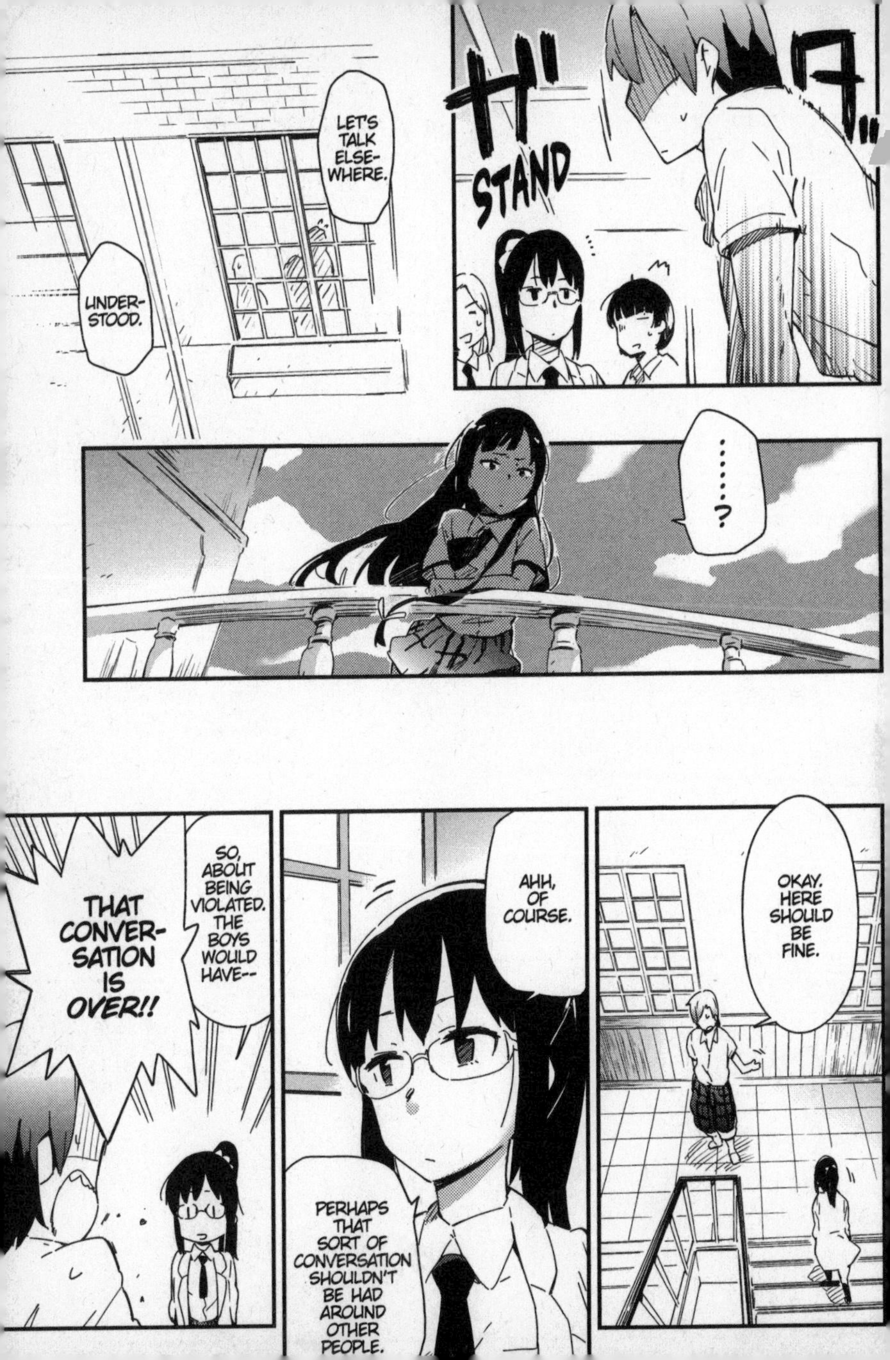
STAND
LET'S TALK ELSE-WHERE.
UNDER-STOOD.
......?
OKAY. HERE SHOULD BE FINE.
AHH, OF COURSE.
PERHAPS THAT SORT OF CONVERSATION SHOULDN'T BE HAD AROUND OTHER PEOPLE.
SO, ABOUT BEING VIOLATED. THE BOYS WOULD HAVE--
THAT CONVER-SATION IS OVER!!

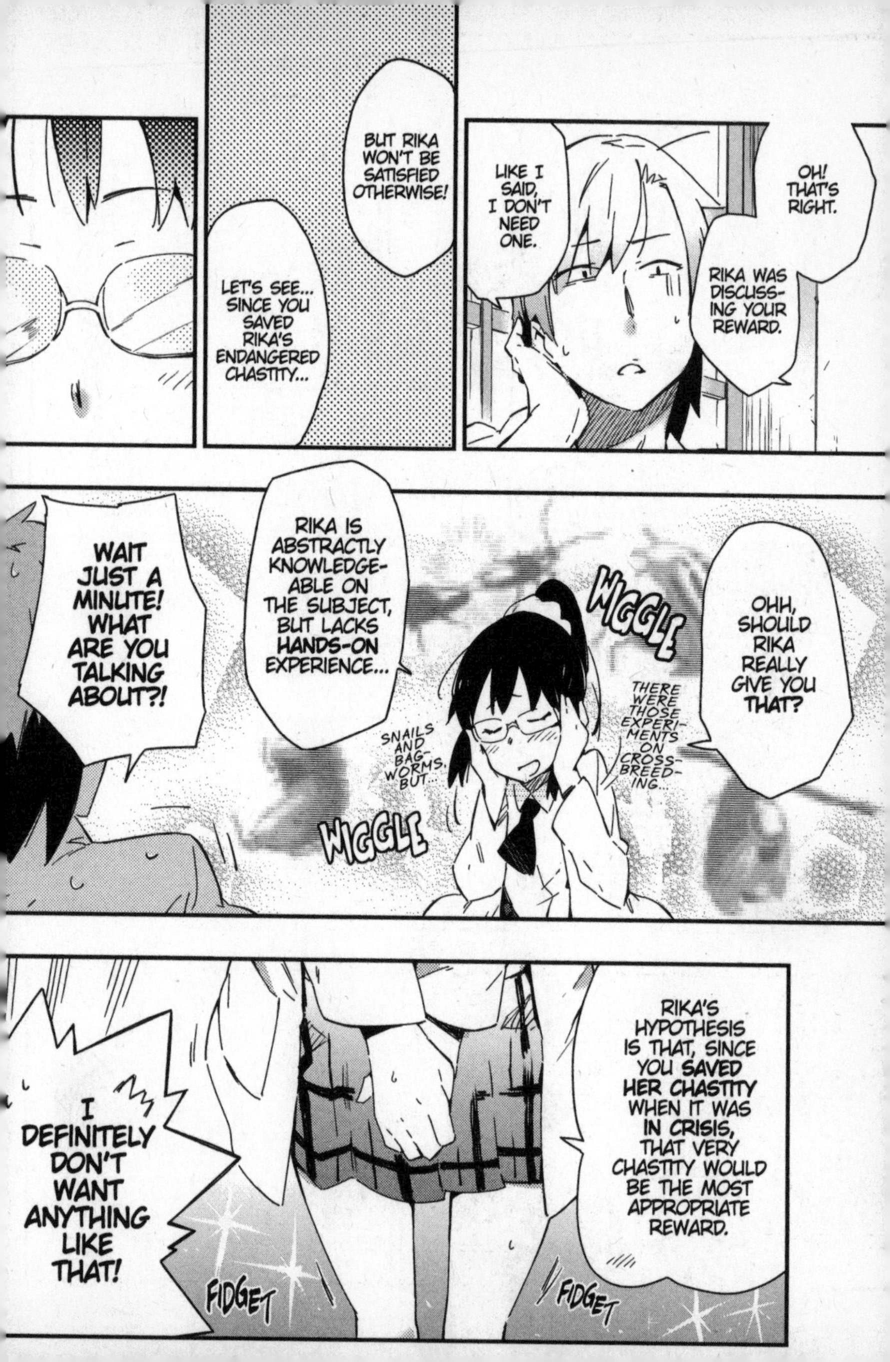
OH! THAT'S RIGHT.
RIKA WAS DISCUSS-ING YOUR REWARD.
LIKE I SAID, I DON'T NEED ONE.
BUT RIKA WON'T BE SATISFIED OTHERWISE!
LET'S SEE... SINCE YOU SAVED RIKA'S ENDANGERED CHASTITY...
OHH, SHOULD RIKA REALLY GIVE YOU THAT?
WIGGLE
THERE WERE THOSE EXPERI-MENTS ON CROSS-BREED-ING...
SNAILS AND BAG-WORMS, BUT...
RIKA IS ABSTRACTLY KNOWLEDGE-ABLE ON THE SUBJECT, BUT LACKS HANDS-ON EXPERIENCE...
WIGGLE
WAIT JUST A MINUTE! WHAT ARE YOU TALKING ABOUT?!
RIKA'S HYPOTHESIS IS THAT, SINCE YOU SAVED HER CHASTITY WHEN IT WAS IN CRISIS, THAT VERY CHASTITY WOULD BE THE MOST APPROPRIATE REWARD.
FIDGET
FIDGET
I DEFINITELY DON'T WANT ANYTHING LIKE THAT!

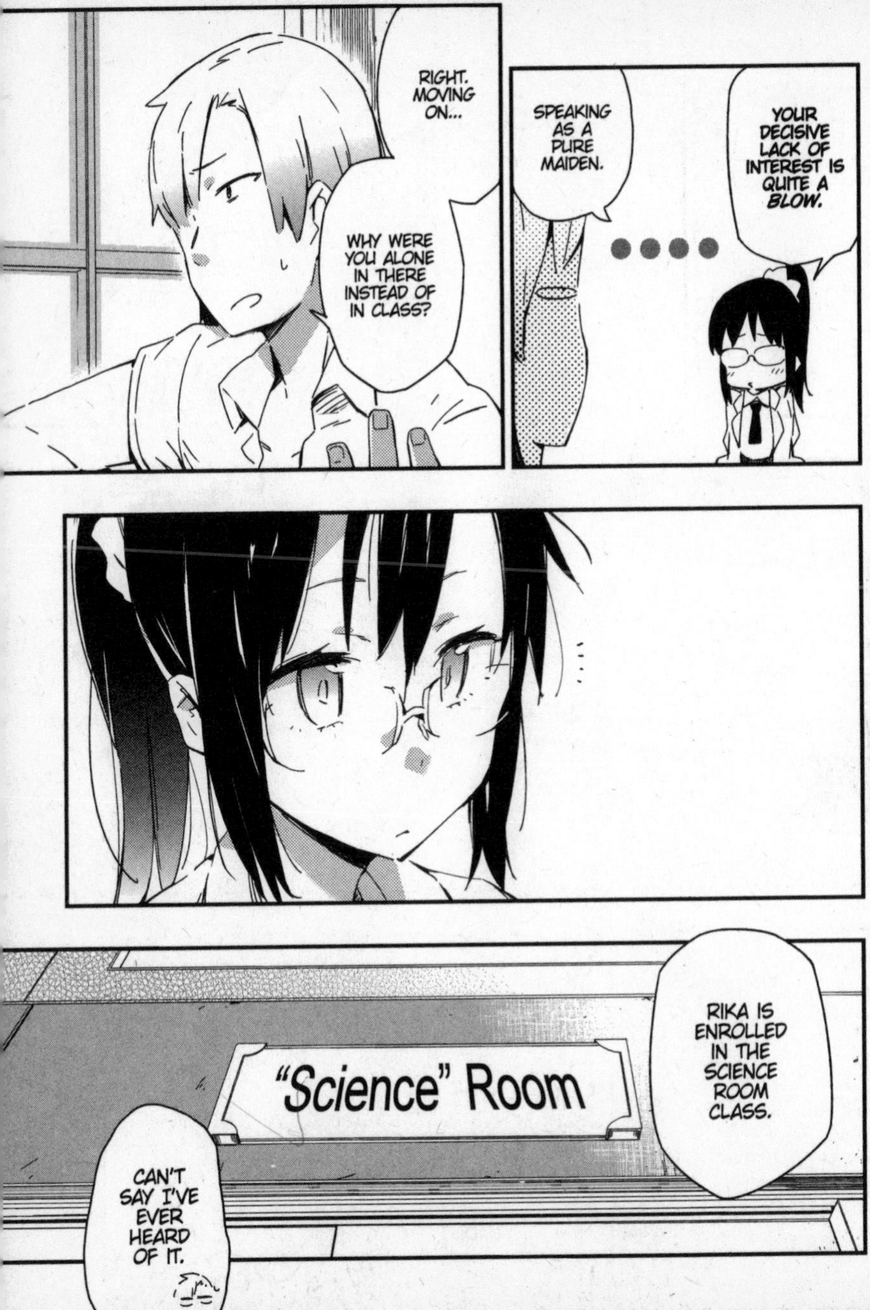
YOUR DECISIVE LACK OF INTEREST IS QUITE A *BLOW.*
SPEAKING AS A PURE MAIDEN.
RIGHT. MOVING ON...
WHY WERE YOU ALONE IN THERE INSTEAD OF IN CLASS?
RIKA IS ENROLLED IN THE SCIENCE ROOM CLASS.
"Science" Room
CAN'T SAY I'VE EVER HEARD OF IT.

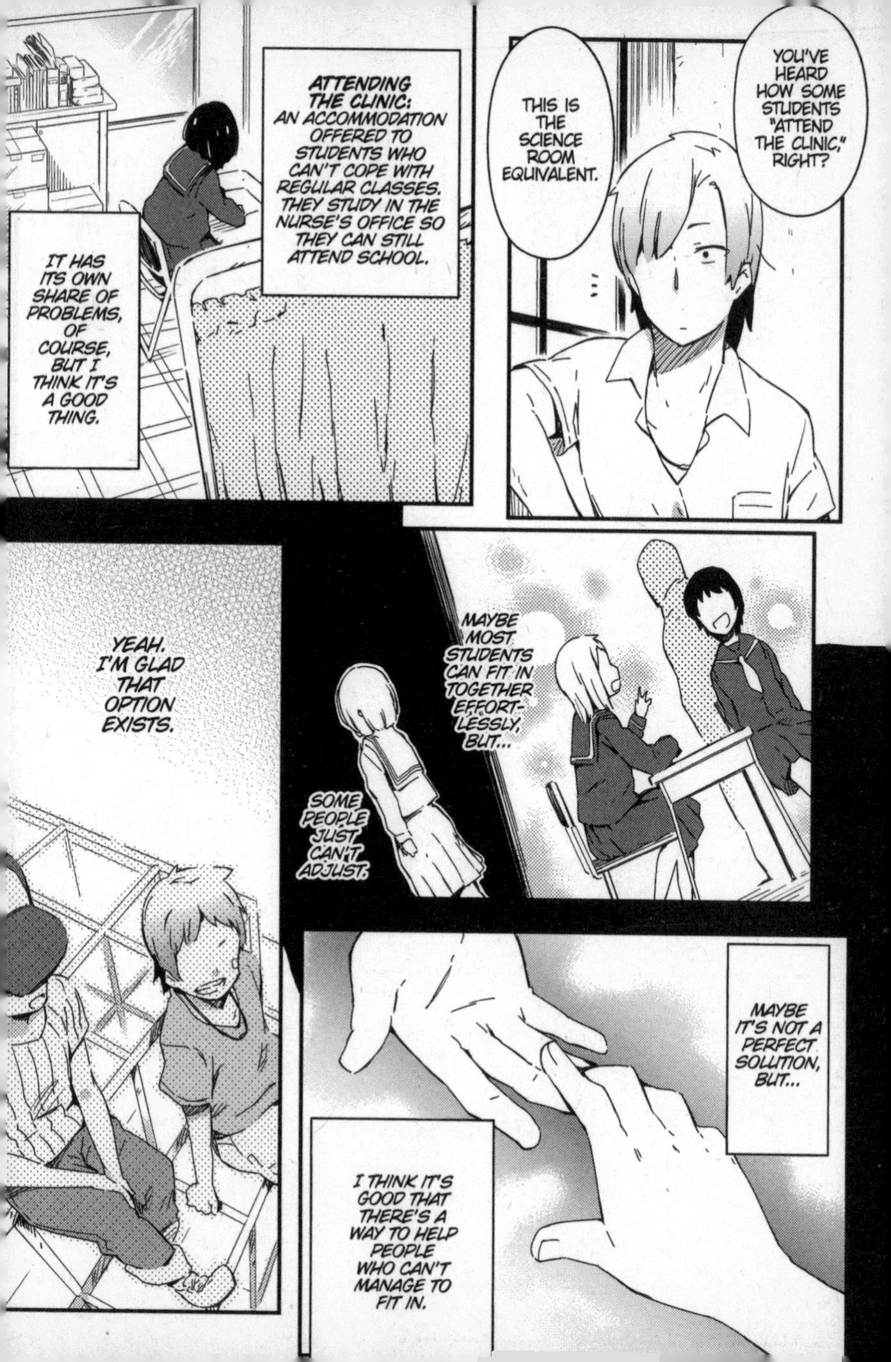

YOU'VE HEARD HOW SOME STUDENTS "ATTEND THE CLINIC," RIGHT?
THIS IS THE SCIENCE ROOM EQUIVALENT.
ATTENDING THE CLINIC: AN ACCOMMODATION OFFERED TO STUDENTS WHO CAN'T COPE WITH REGULAR CLASSES. THEY STUDY IN THE NURSE'S OFFICE SO THEY CAN STILL ATTEND SCHOOL.
IT HAS ITS OWN SHARE OF PROBLEMS, OF COURSE, BUT I THINK IT'S A GOOD THING.
MAYBE MOST STUDENTS CAN FIT IN TOGETHER EFFORTLESSLY, BUT...
SOME PEOPLE JUST CAN'T ADJUST.
MAYBE IT'S NOT A PERFECT SOLUTION, BUT...
I THINK IT'S GOOD THAT THERE'S A WAY TO HELP PEOPLE WHO CAN'T MANAGE TO FIT IN.
YEAH. I'M GLAD THAT OPTION EXISTS.

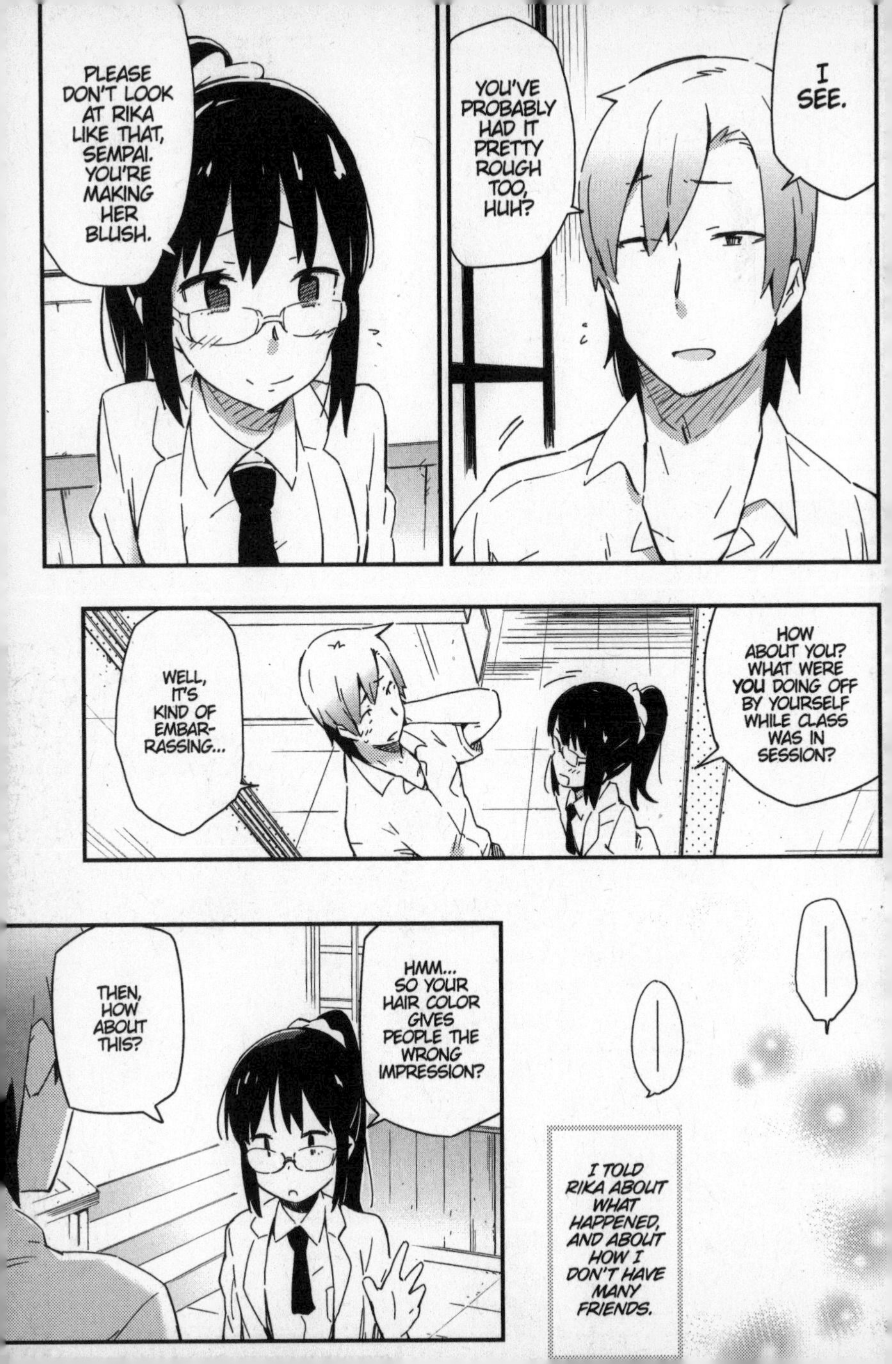
I SEE.
YOU'VE PROBABLY HAD IT PRETTY ROUGH TOO, HUH?
PLEASE DON'T LOOK AT RIKA LIKE THAT, SEMPAI. YOU'RE MAKING HER BLUSH.
HOW ABOUT YOU? WHAT WERE YOU DOING OFF BY YOURSELF WHILE CLASS WAS IN SESSION?
WELL, IT'S KIND OF EMBARRASSING...
I TOLD RIKA ABOUT WHAT HAPPENED, AND ABOUT HOW I DON'T HAVE MANY FRIENDS.
HMM... SO YOUR HAIR COLOR GIVES PEOPLE THE WRONG IMPRESSION?
THEN, HOW ABOUT THIS?

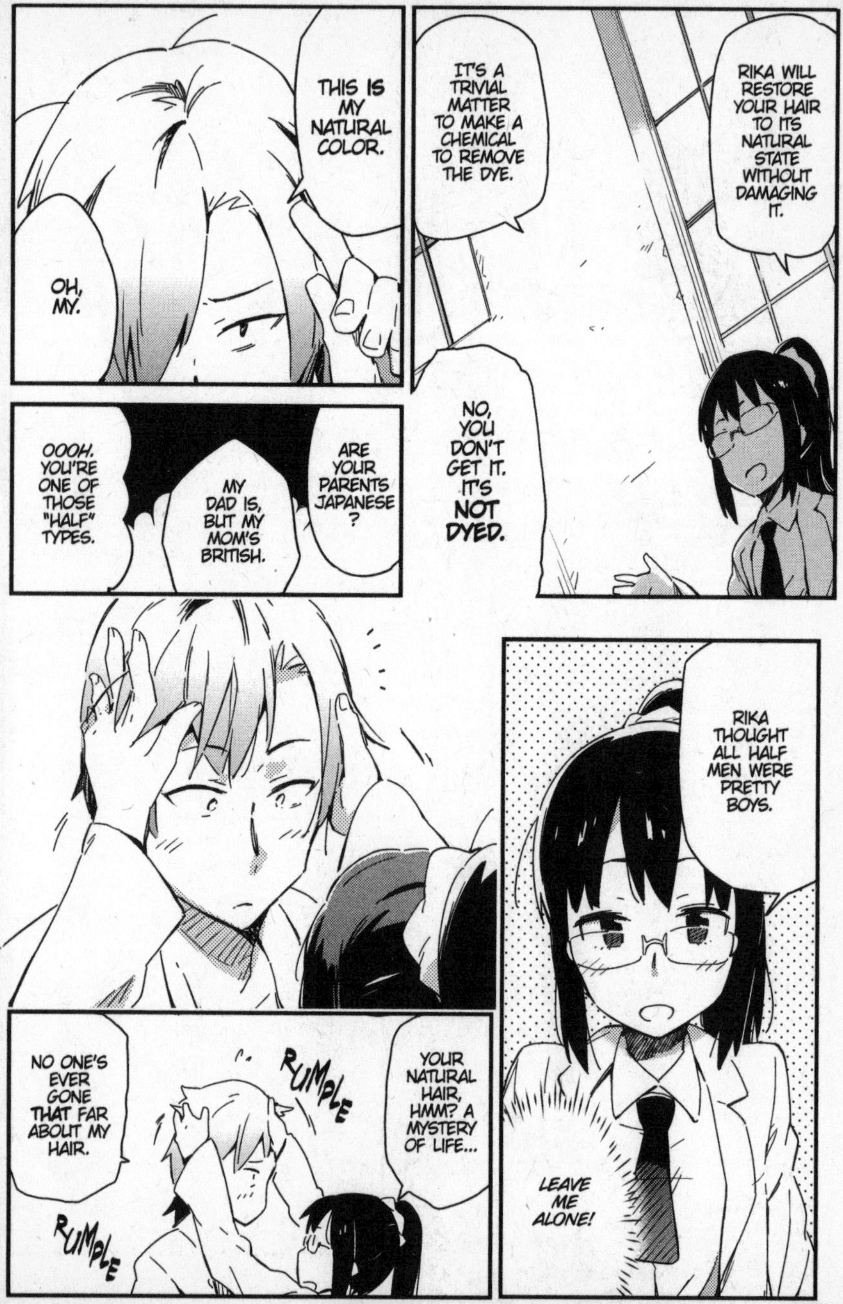
RIKA WILL RESTORE YOUR HAIR TO ITS NATURAL STATE WITHOUT DAMAGING IT.
IT'S A TRIVIAL MATTER TO MAKE A CHEMICAL TO REMOVE THE DYE.
NO, YOU DON'T GET IT. IT'S NOT DYED.
THIS IS MY NATURAL COLOR.
OH, MY.
ARE YOUR PARENTS JAPANESE?
MY DAD IS, BUT MY MOM'S BRITISH.
OOOH. YOU'RE ONE OF THOSE "HALF" TYPES.
RIKA THOUGHT ALL HALF MEN WERE PRETTY BOYS.
LEAVE ME ALONE!
YOUR NATURAL HAIR, HMM? A MYSTERY OF LIFE...
RUMPLE
NO ONE'S EVER GONE THAT FAR ABOUT MY HAIR.
RUMPLE

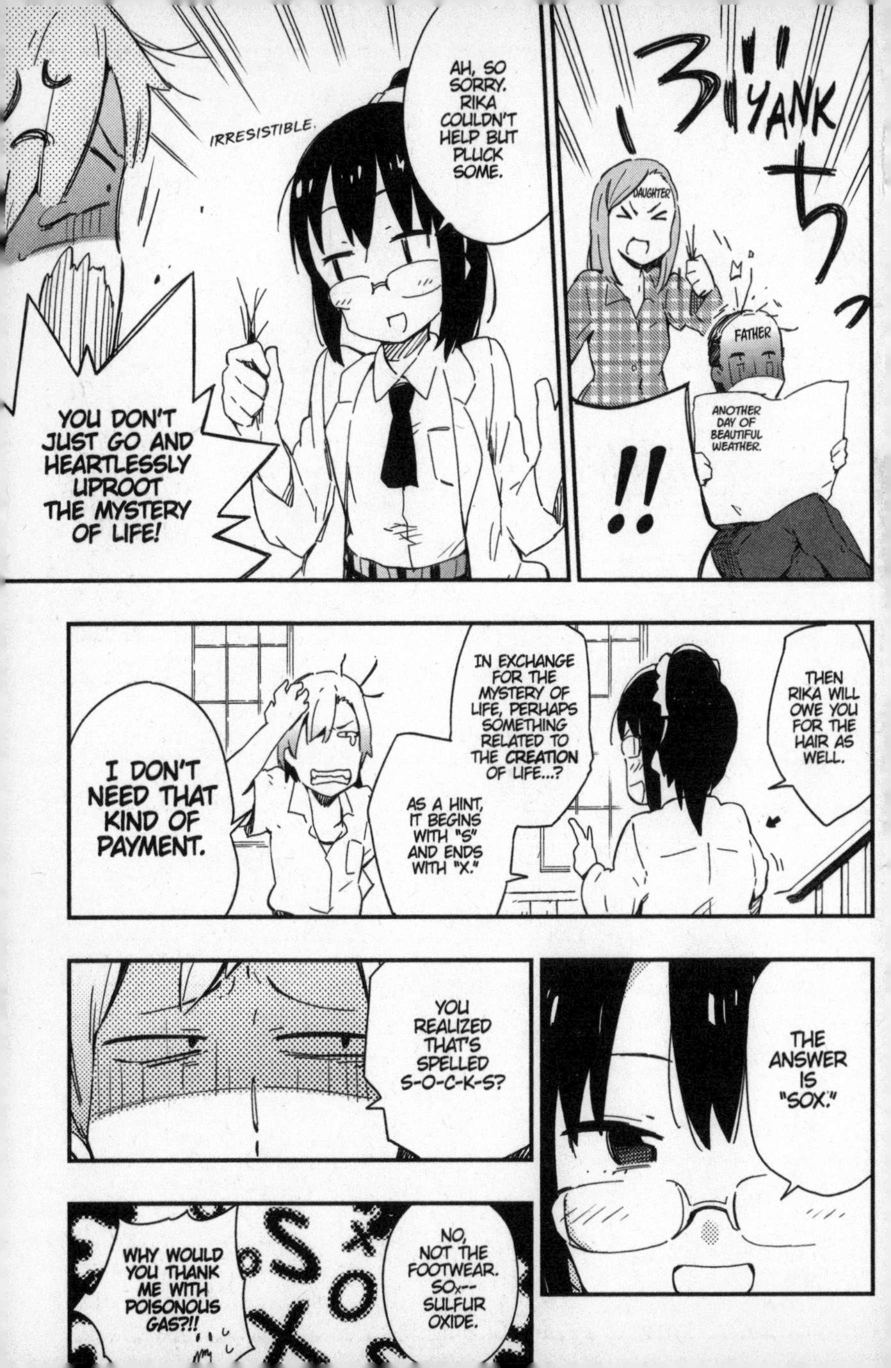
YANK
DAUGHTER
FATHER
ANOTHER DAY OF BEAUTIFUL WEATHER.
!!
AH, SO SORRY. RIKA COULDN'T HELP BUT PLUCK SOME.
IRRESISTIBLE.
YOU DON'T JUST GO AND HEARTLESSLY UPROOT THE MYSTERY OF LIFE!
THEN RIKA WILL OWE YOU FOR THE HAIR AS WELL.
IN EXCHANGE FOR THE MYSTERY OF LIFE, PERHAPS SOMETHING RELATED TO THE CREATION OF LIFE...?
AS A HINT, IT BEGINS WITH "S" AND ENDS WITH "X."
I DON'T NEED THAT KIND OF PAYMENT.
THE ANSWER IS "SOX."
YOU REALIZED THAT'S SPELLED S-O-C-K-S?
NO, NOT THE FOOTWEAR. SOx-- SULFUR OXIDE.
WHY WOULD YOU THANK ME WITH POISONOUS GAS?!!

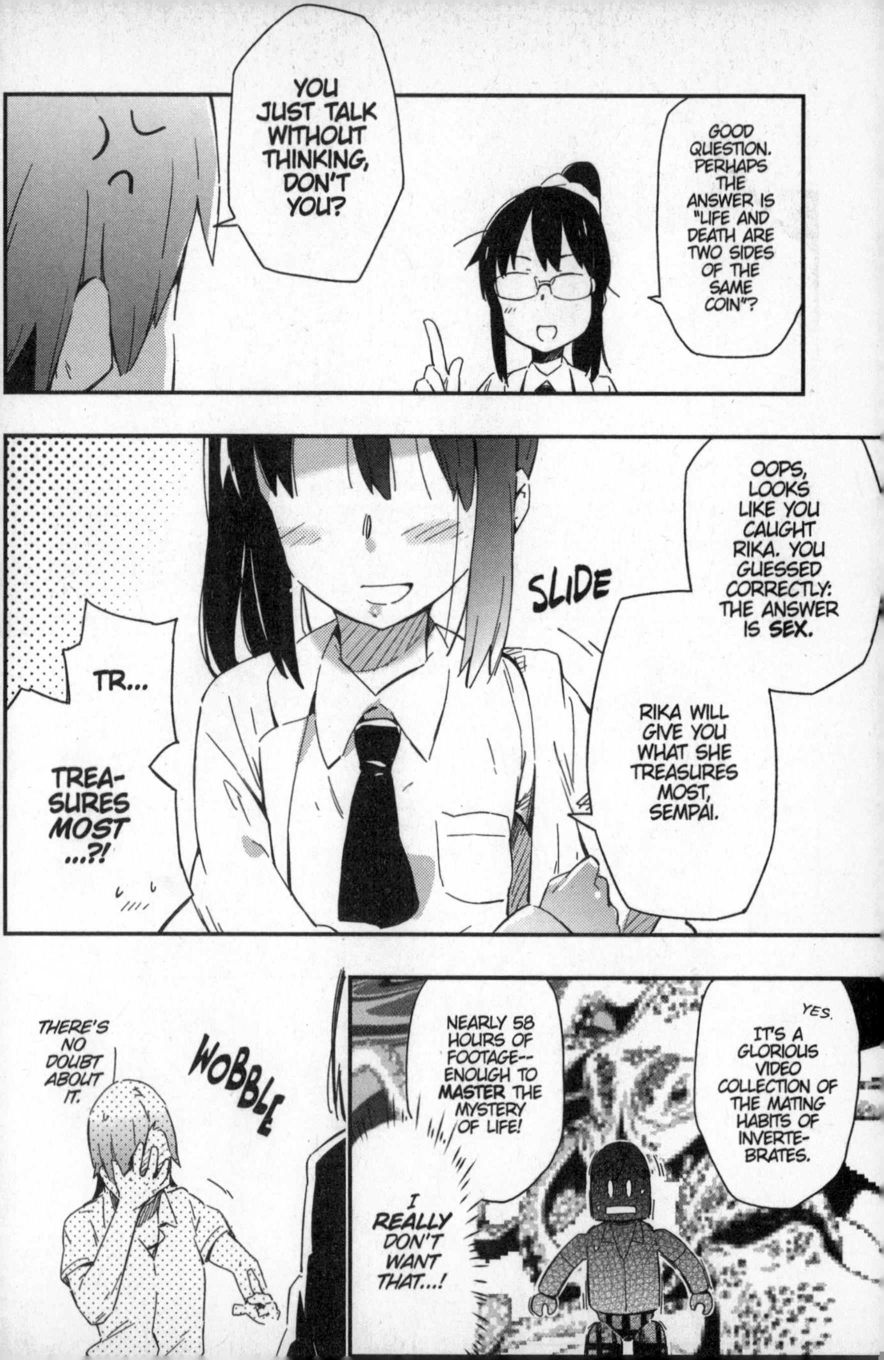
GOOD QUESTION. PERHAPS THE ANSWER IS "LIFE AND DEATH ARE TWO SIDES OF THE SAME COIN"?
YOU JUST TALK WITHOUT THINKING, DON'T YOU?
OOPS, LOOKS LIKE YOU CAUGHT RIKA. YOU GUESSED CORRECTLY: THE ANSWER IS SEX.
SLIDE
RIKA WILL GIVE YOU WHAT SHE TREASURES MOST, SEMPAI.
TR...
TREA-SURES MOST ...?!
YES.
IT'S A GLORIOUS VIDEO COLLECTION OF THE MATING HABITS OF INVERTE-BRATES.
NEARLY 58 HOURS OF FOOTAGE--ENOUGH TO MASTER THE MYSTERY OF LIFE!
I REALLY DON'T WANT THAT...!
WOBBLE
THERE'S NO DOUBT ABOUT IT.

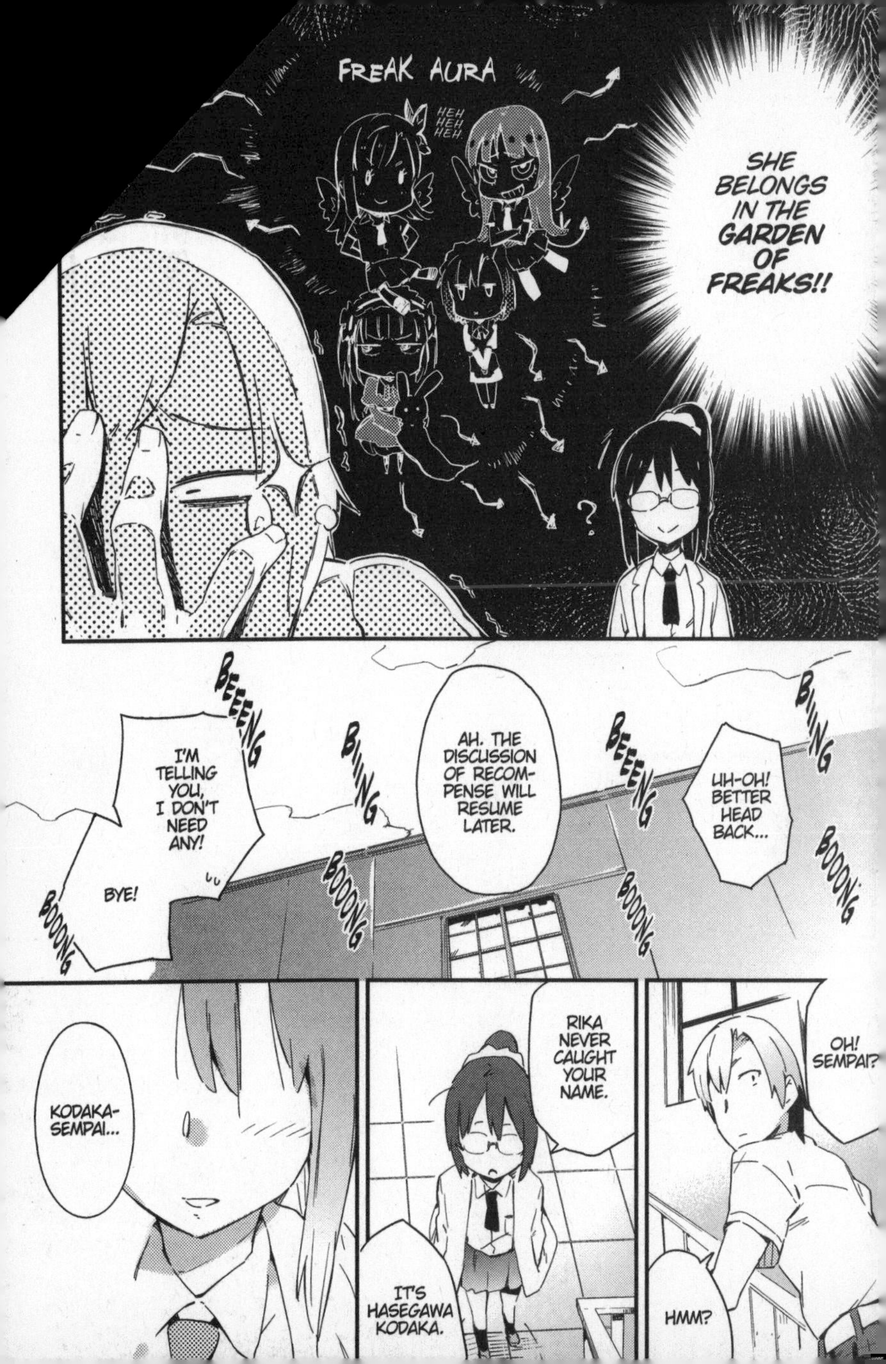
SHE BELONGS IN THE GARDEN OF FREAKS!!
FREAK AURA
HEH HEH HEH.
BIIING
UH-OH! BETTER HEAD BACK...
BOOONG
BEEENG
BOOONG
AH. THE DISCUSSION OF RECOMPENSE WILL RESUME LATER.
BIIING
BOOONG
BEEENG
I'M TELLING YOU, I DON'T NEED ANY!
BYE!
BOOONG
OH! SEMPAI?
HMM?
RIKA NEVER CAUGHT YOUR NAME.
IT'S HASEGAWA KODAKA.
KODAKA-SEMPAI...

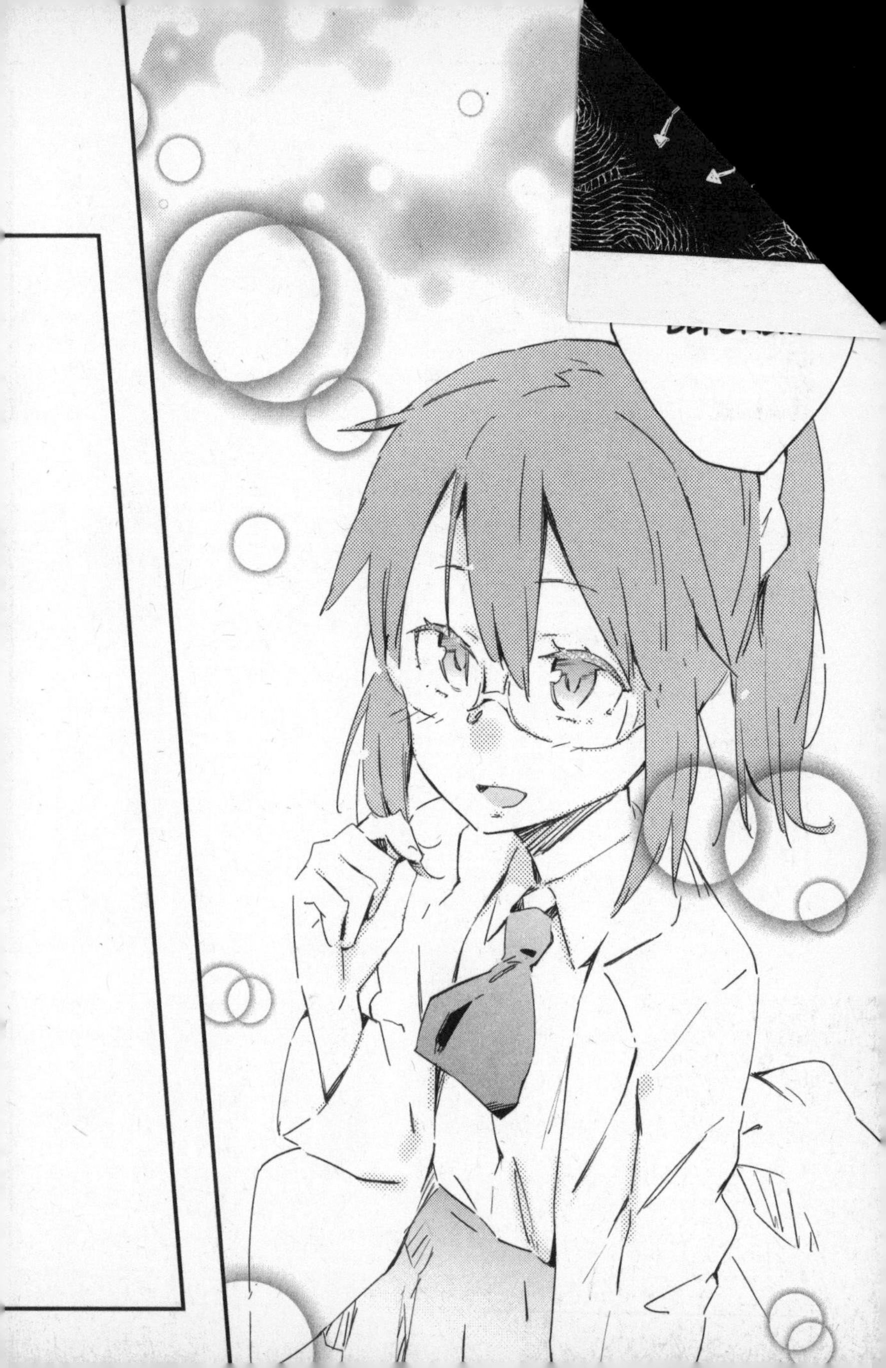

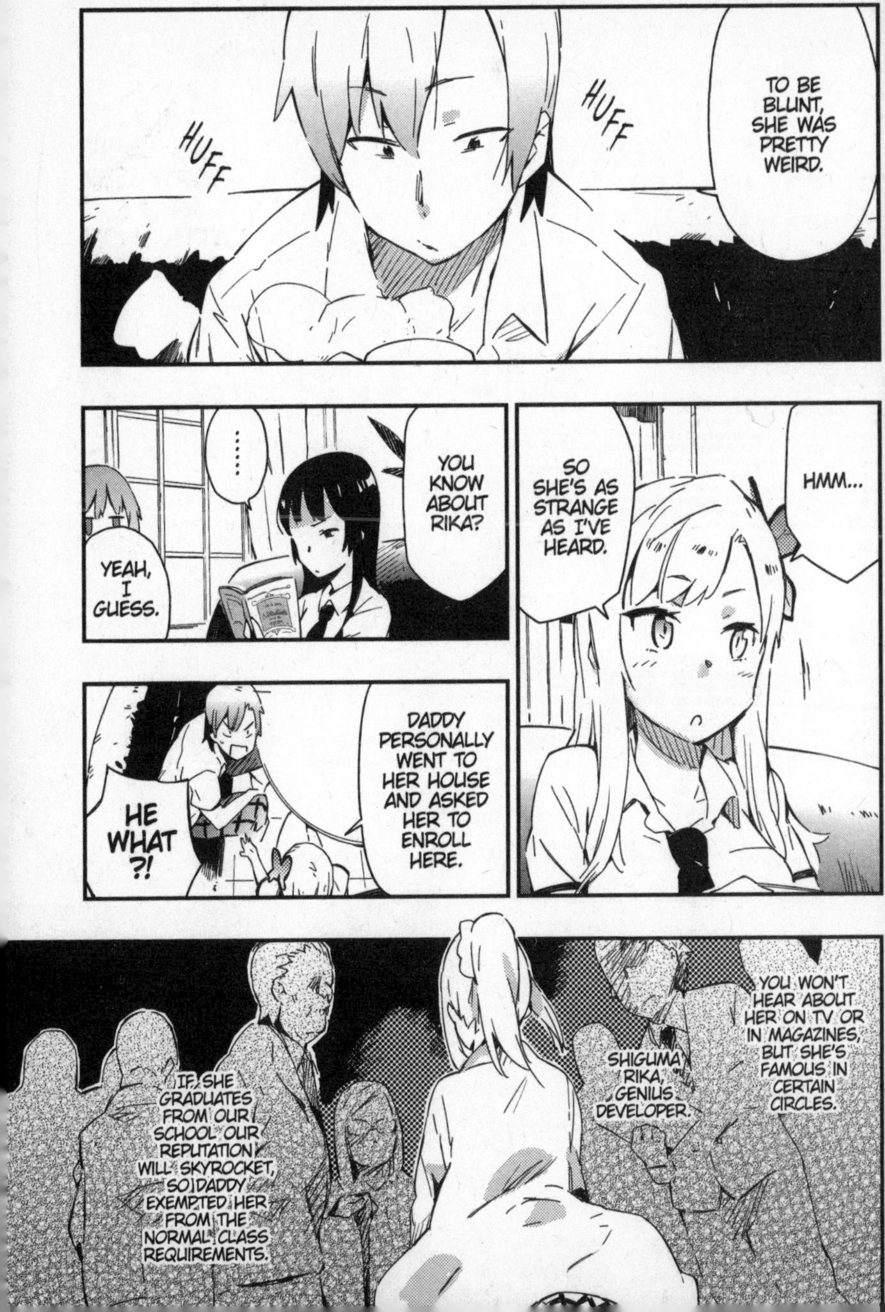
TO BE BLUNT, SHE WAS PRETTY WEIRD.
HUFF
HUFF
HMM...
SO SHE'S AS STRANGE AS I'VE HEARD.
YOU KNOW ABOUT RIKA?
......
YEAH, I GUESS.
DADDY PERSONALLY WENT TO HER HOUSE AND ASKED HER TO ENROLL HERE.
HE WHAT?!
YOU WON'T HEAR ABOUT HER ON TV OR IN MAGAZINES, BUT SHE'S FAMOUS IN CERTAIN CIRCLES.
SHIGUMA RIKA, GENIUS DEVELOPER.
IF SHE GRADUATES FROM OUR SCHOOL OUR REPUTATION WILL SKYROCKET, SO DADDY EXEMPTED HER FROM THE NORMAL CLASS REQUIREMENTS.

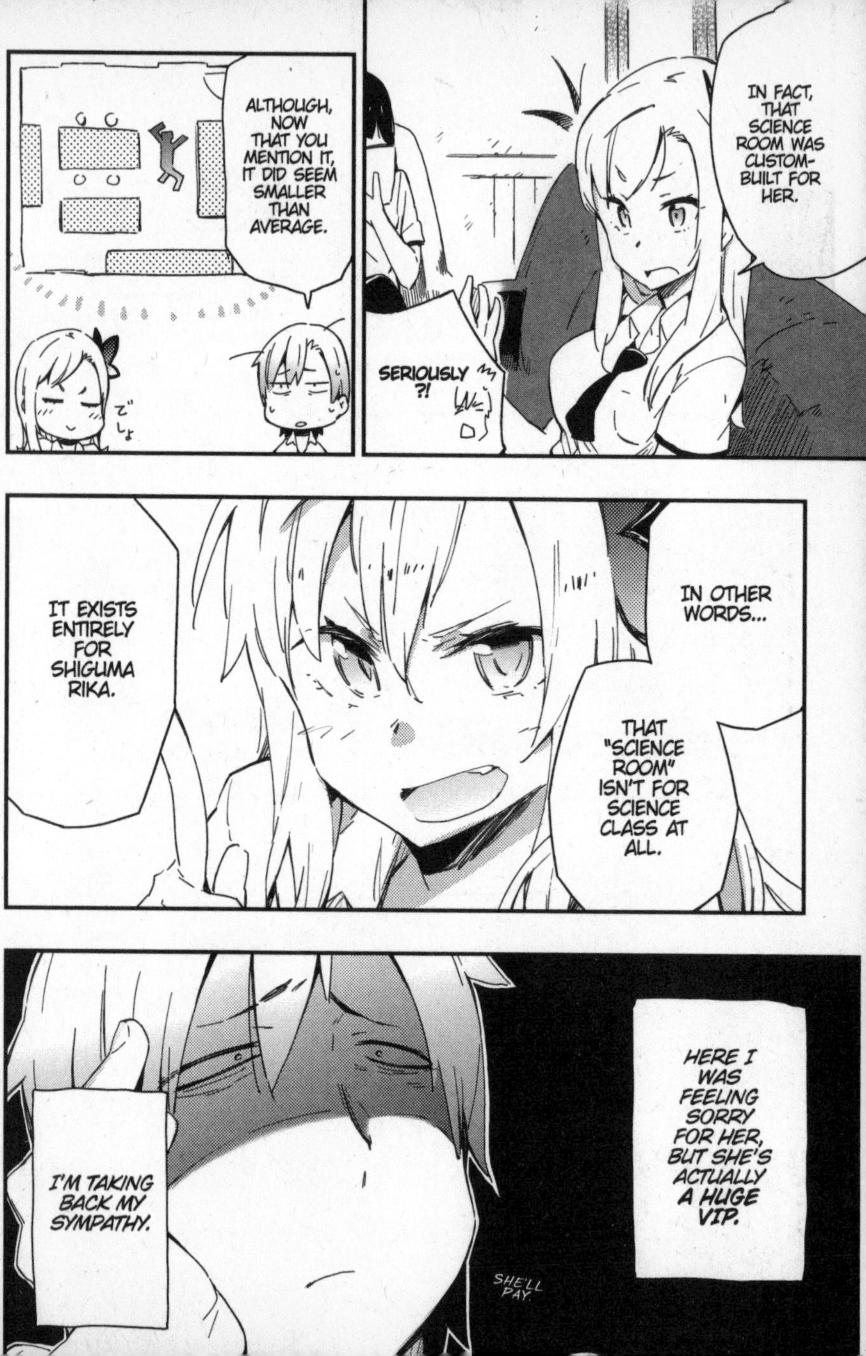
IN FACT, THAT SCIENCE ROOM WAS CUSTOM-BUILT FOR HER.
SERIOUSLY ?!
ALTHOUGH, NOW THAT YOU MENTION IT, IT DID SEEM SMALLER THAN AVERAGE.
でしょ
IN OTHER WORDS...
THAT "SCIENCE ROOM" ISN'T FOR SCIENCE CLASS AT ALL.
IT EXISTS ENTIRELY FOR SHIGUMA RIKA.
HERE I WAS FEELING SORRY FOR HER, BUT SHE'S ACTUALLY A HUGE VIP.
SHE'LL PAY.
I'M TAKING BACK MY SYMPATHY.

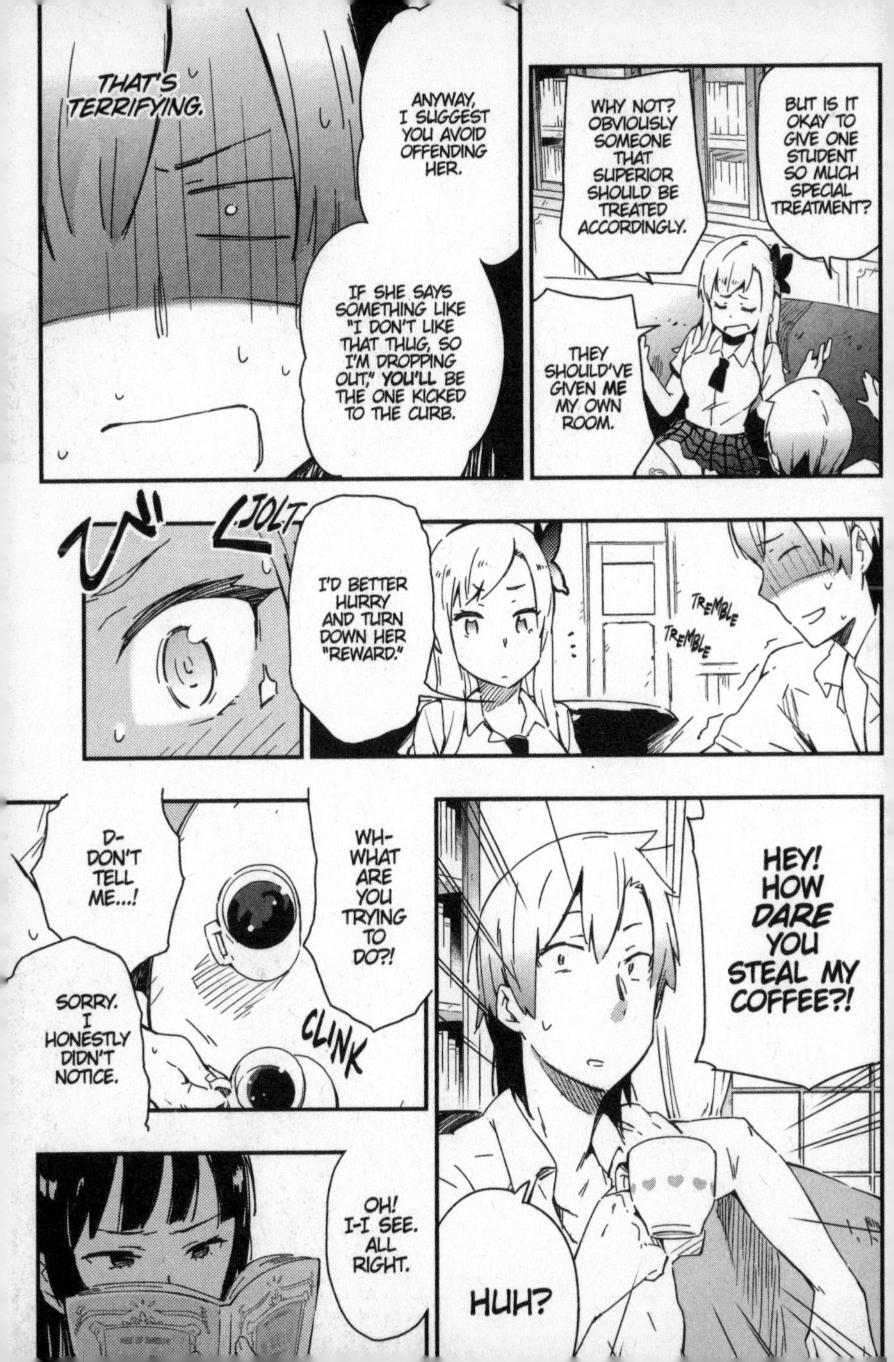
BUT IS IT OKAY TO GIVE ONE STUDENT SO MUCH SPECIAL TREATMENT?
WHY NOT? OBVIOUSLY SOMEONE THAT SUPERIOR SHOULD BE TREATED ACCORDINGLY.
THEY SHOULD'VE GIVEN ME MY OWN ROOM.
ANYWAY, I SUGGEST YOU AVOID OFFENDING HER.
IF SHE SAYS SOMETHING LIKE "I DON'T LIKE THAT THUG, SO I'M DROPPING OUT," YOU'LL BE THE ONE KICKED TO THE CURB.
THAT'S TERRIFYING.
TREMBLE TREMBLE
I'D BETTER HURRY AND TURN DOWN HER "REWARD."
JOLT
HEY! HOW DARE YOU STEAL MY COFFEE?!
HUH?
WH-WHAT ARE YOU TRYING TO DO?!
D-DON'T TELL ME...!
CLINK
SORRY. I HONESTLY DIDN'T NOTICE.
OH! I-I SEE. ALL RIGHT.

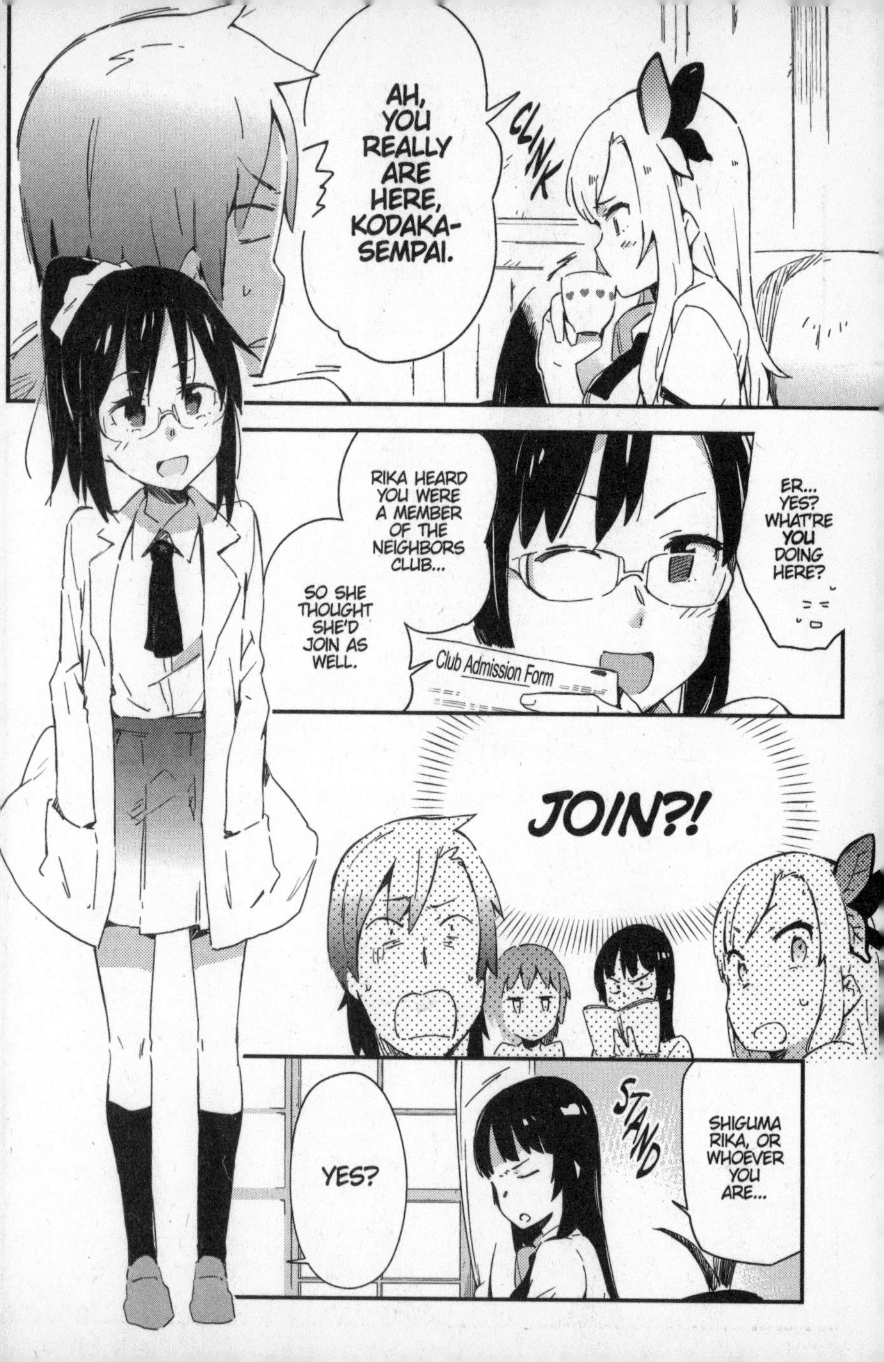
CLINK
AH, YOU REALLY ARE HERE, KODAKA-SEMPAI.
ER... YES? WHAT'RE YOU DOING HERE?
RIKA HEARD YOU WERE A MEMBER OF THE NEIGHBORS CLUB...
SO SHE THOUGHT SHE'D JOIN AS WELL.
Club Admission Form
JOIN?!
SHIGUMA RIKA, OR WHOEVER YOU ARE...
STAND
YES?

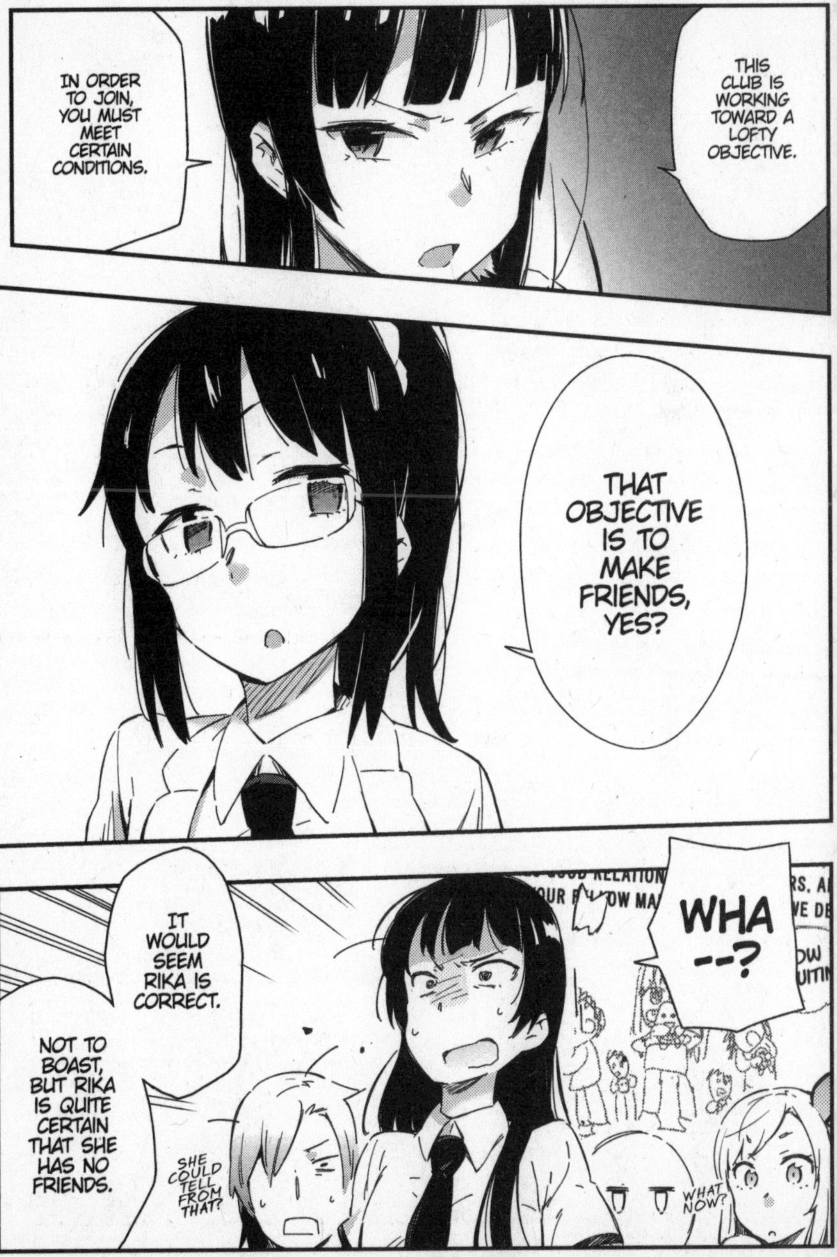
THIS CLUB IS WORKING TOWARD A LOFTY OBJECTIVE.
IN ORDER TO JOIN, YOU MUST MEET CERTAIN CONDITIONS.
THAT OBJECTIVE IS TO MAKE FRIENDS, YES?
WHA--?
IT WOULD SEEM RIKA IS CORRECT.
NOT TO BOAST, BUT RIKA IS QUITE CERTAIN THAT SHE HAS NO FRIENDS.
WHAT NOW?
SHE COULD TELL FROM THAT?

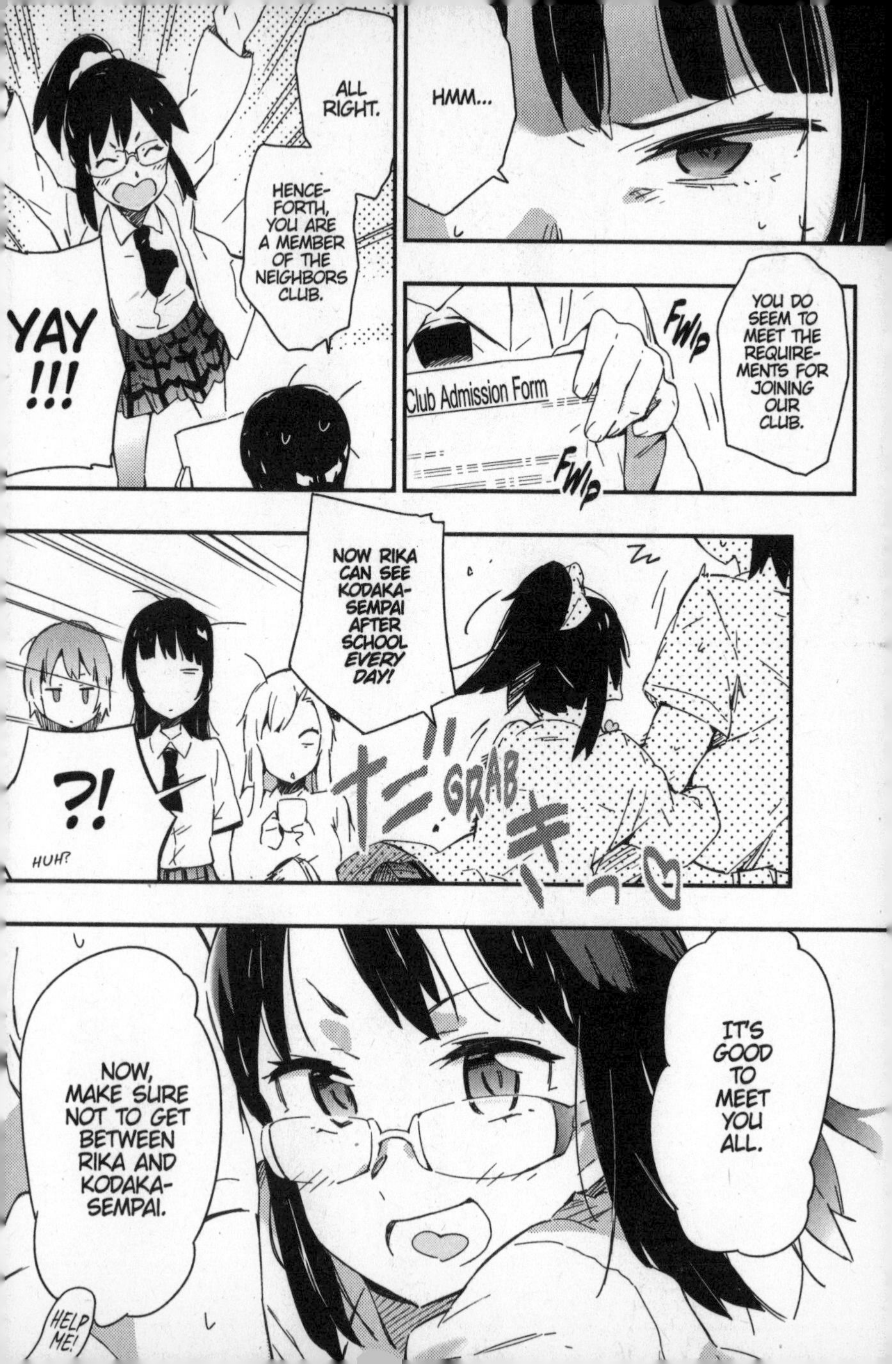
HMM...
YOU DO SEEM TO MEET THE REQUIREMENTS FOR JOINING OUR CLUB.
FWIP
Club Admission Form
FWIP
ALL RIGHT.
HENCEFORTH, YOU ARE A MEMBER OF THE NEIGHBORS CLUB.
YAY!!!
NOW RIKA CAN SEE KODAKA-SEMPAI AFTER SCHOOL EVERY DAY!
GRAB
?!
HUH?
IT'S GOOD TO MEET YOU ALL.
NOW, MAKE SURE NOT TO GET BETWEEN RIKA AND KODAKA-SEMPAI.
HELP ME!

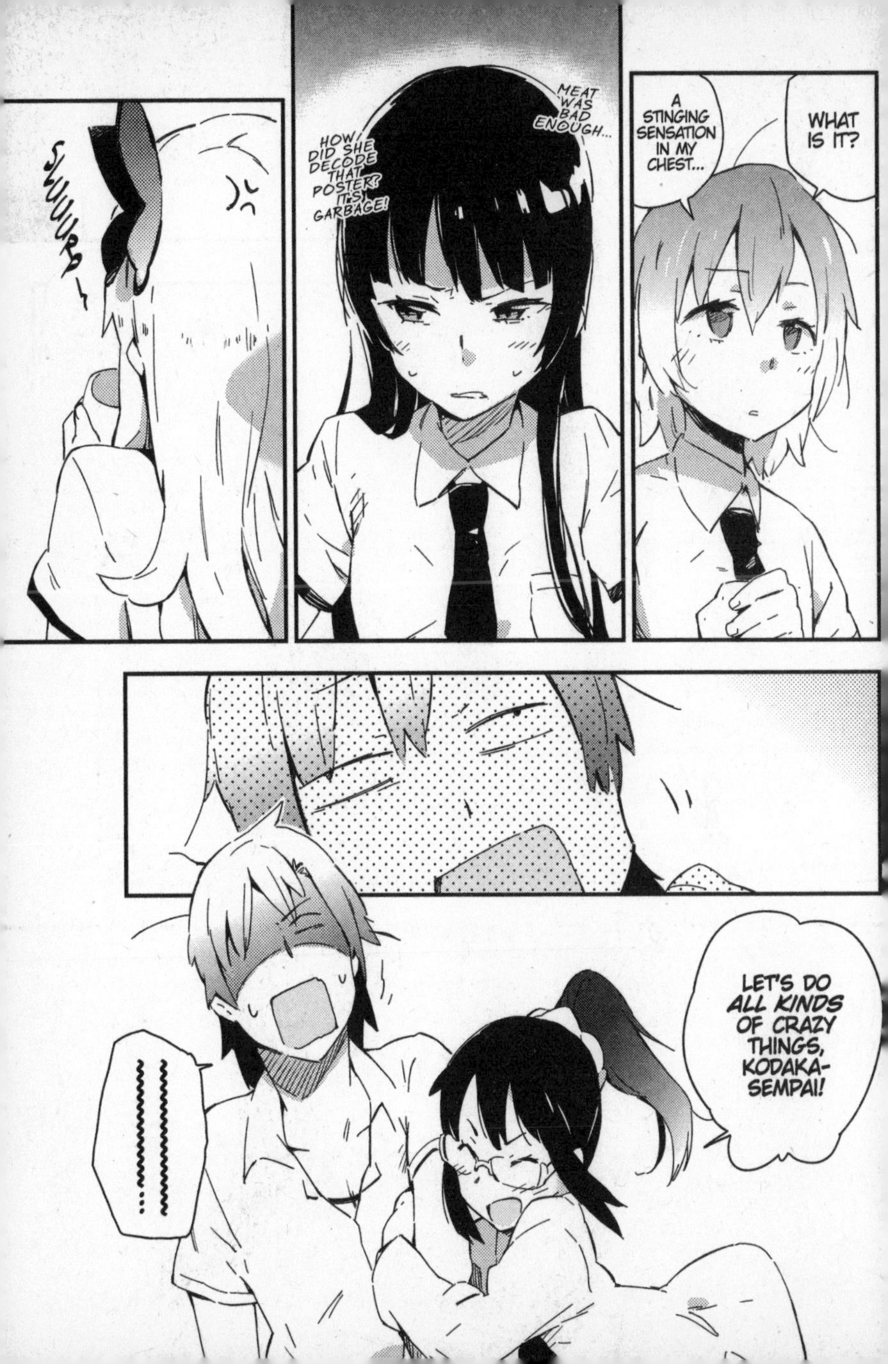
WHAT IS IT?
A STINGING SENSATION IN MY CHEST...
MEAT WAS BAD ENOUGH...
HOW DID SHE DECODE THAT POSTER? IT'S GARBAGE!
SLUUURP
LET'S DO ALL KINDS OF CRAZY THINGS, KODAKA-SEMPAI!
......

SHIGUMA RIKA (志熊 理科): "Rika" is a common Japanese name, but rarely written with the characters for "science." In this case, they're interchangeable. Her last name, "Shiguma," is a play on the Japanese pronunciation of the Greek letter "sigma (Σ)."

Haganai I don't have many friends

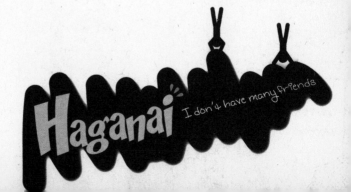

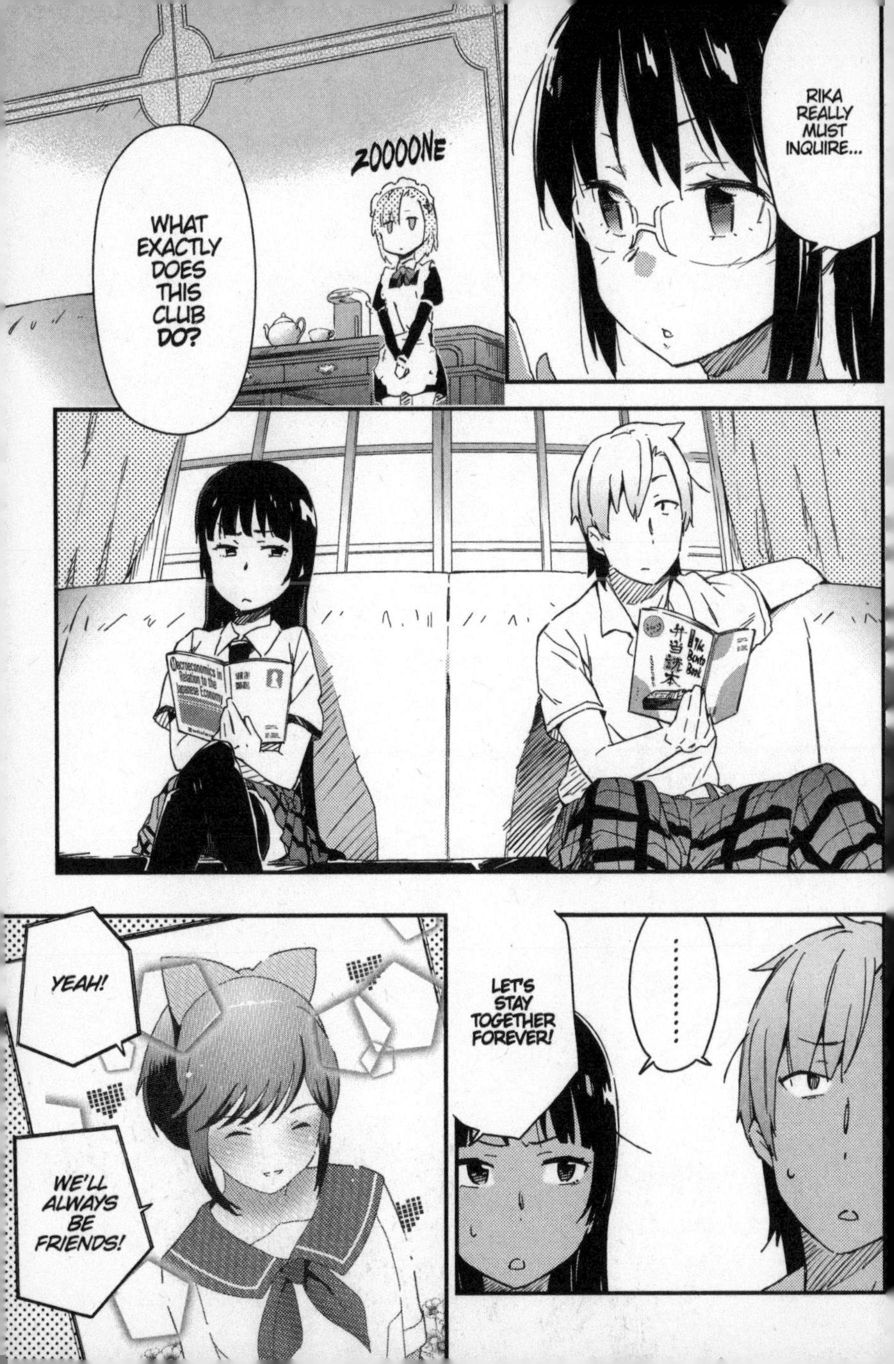
RIKA REALLY MUST INQUIRE...
ZOOOONE
WHAT EXACTLY DOES THIS CLUB DO?
弁当読本
The Bento Book
Macroeconomics in Relation to the Japanese Economy
......
LET'S STAY TOGETHER FOREVER!
YEAH!
WE'LL ALWAYS BE FRIENDS!

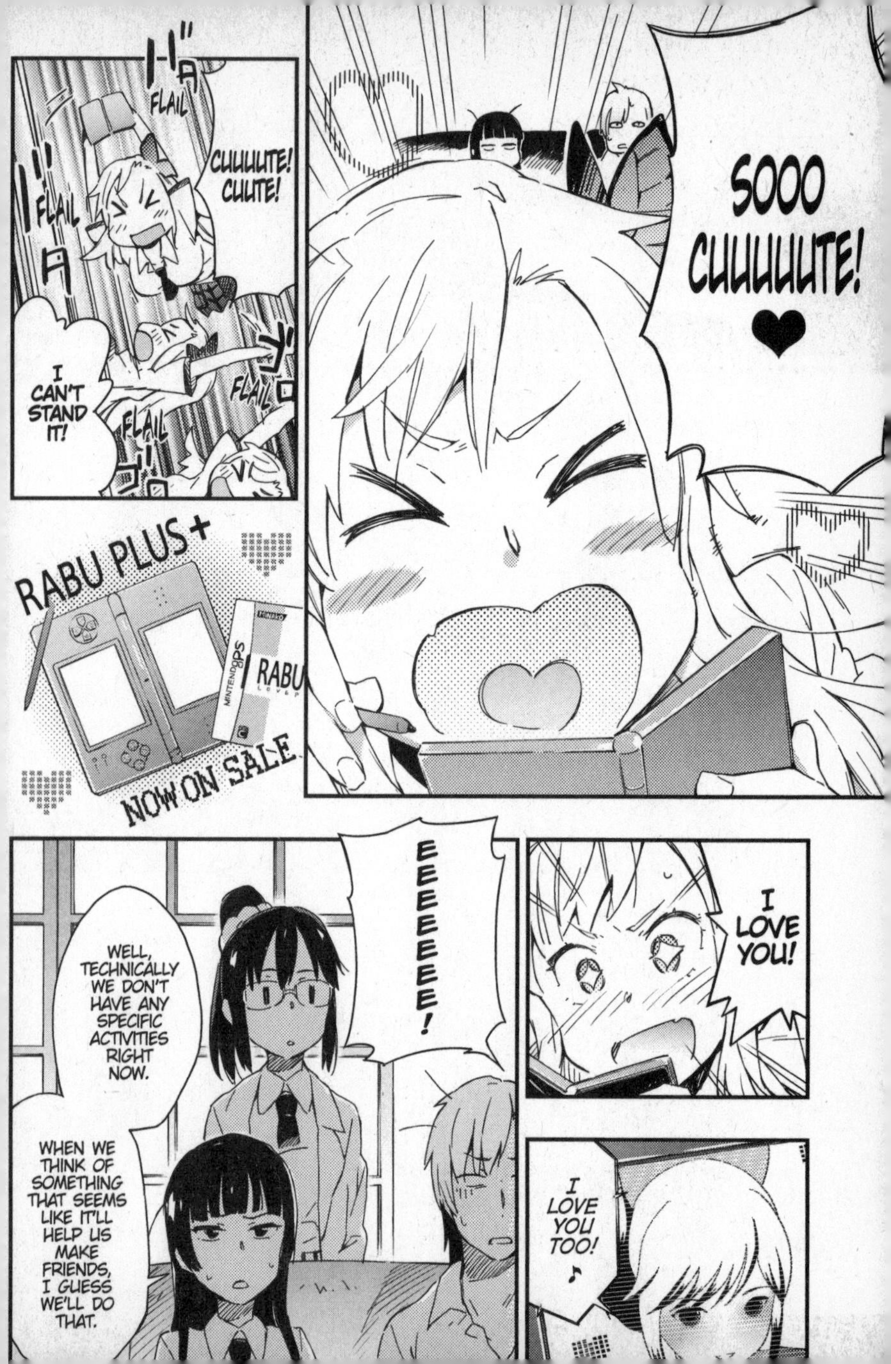
SOOO CUUUUUTE! ♥
FLAIL
FLAIL
CUUUUTE! CUUTE!
FLAIL
FLAIL
I CAN'T STAND IT!
RABU PLUS+
NINTENDO DPS
RABU
NOW ON SALE
I LOVE YOU!
I LOVE YOU TOO! ♪
EEEEEEEE!
WELL, TECHNICALLY WE DON'T HAVE ANY SPECIFIC ACTIVITIES RIGHT NOW.
WHEN WE THINK OF SOMETHING THAT SEEMS LIKE IT'LL HELP US MAKE FRIENDS, I GUESS WE'LL DO THAT.

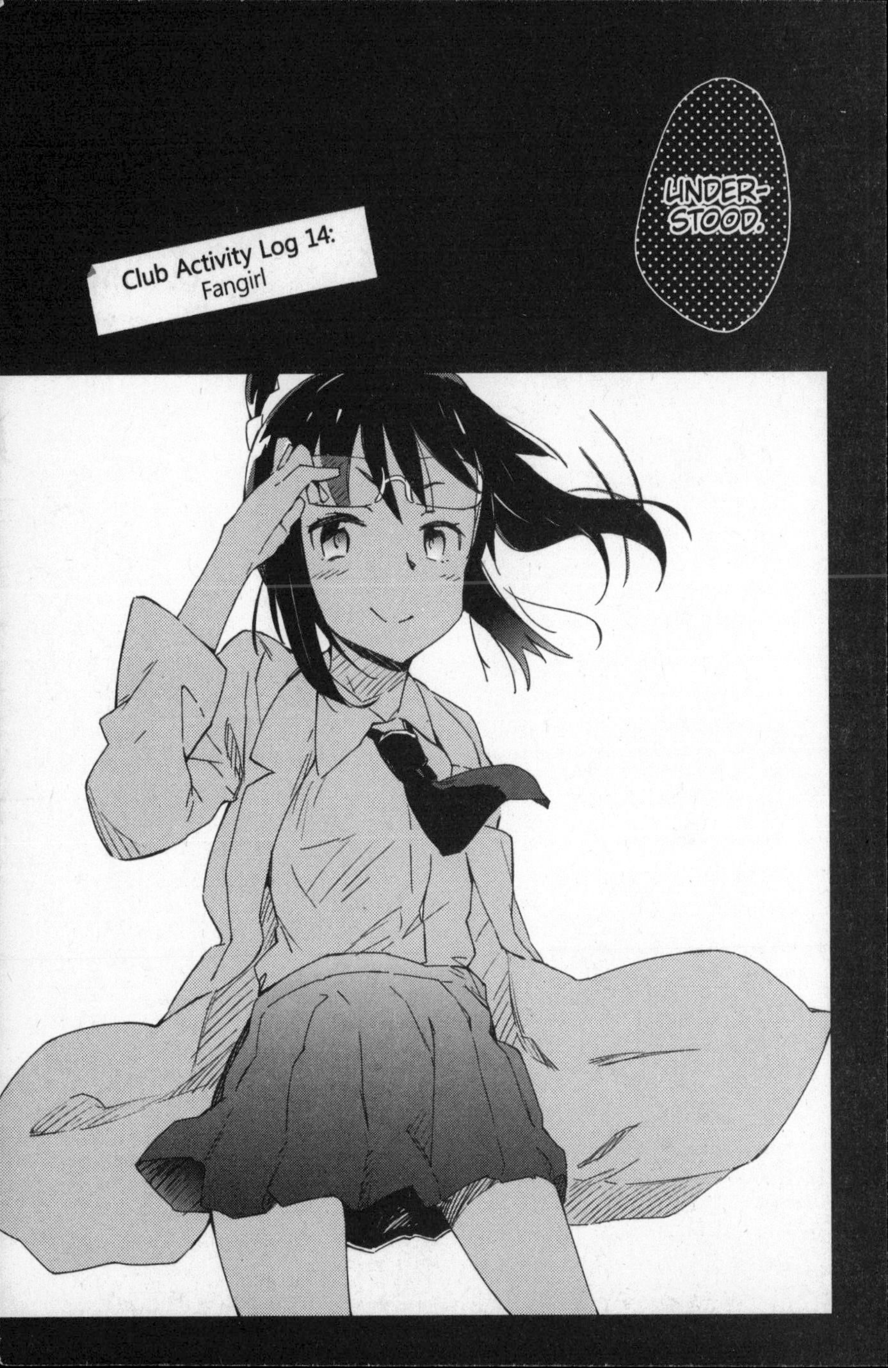
UNDER-STOOD.
Club Activity Log 14:
Fangirl

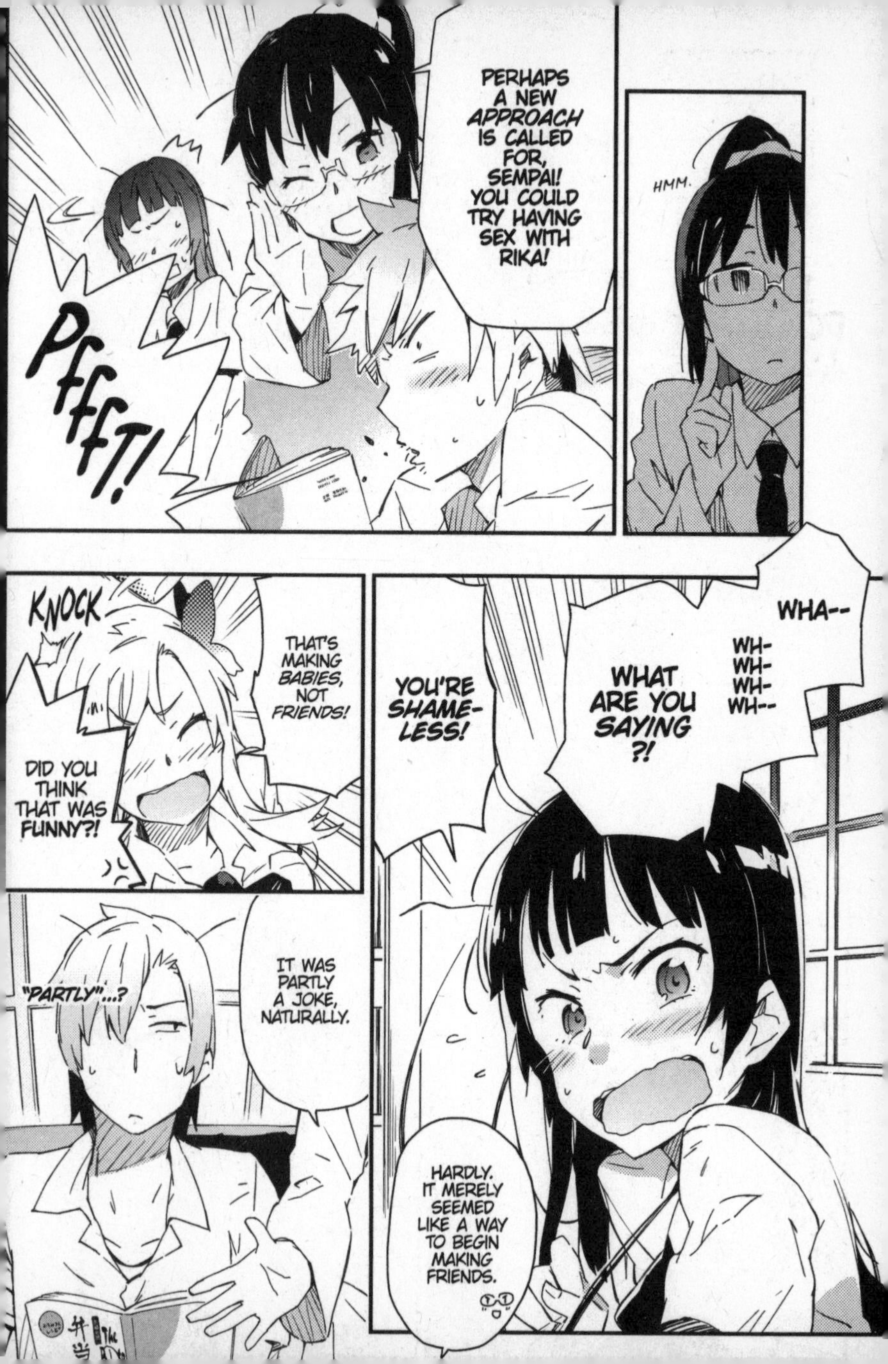
HMM.
PERHAPS A NEW APPROACH IS CALLED FOR, SEMPAI! YOU COULD TRY HAVING SEX WITH RIKA!
PFFFT!!
WHA--
WH- WH- WH- WH--
WHAT ARE YOU SAYING?!
YOU'RE SHAME-LESS!
HARDLY. IT MERELY SEEMED LIKE A WAY TO BEGIN MAKING FRIENDS.
THAT'S MAKING BABIES, NOT FRIENDS!
KNOCK
DID YOU THINK THAT WAS FUNNY?!
IT WAS PARTLY A JOKE, NATURALLY.
"PARTLY"...?

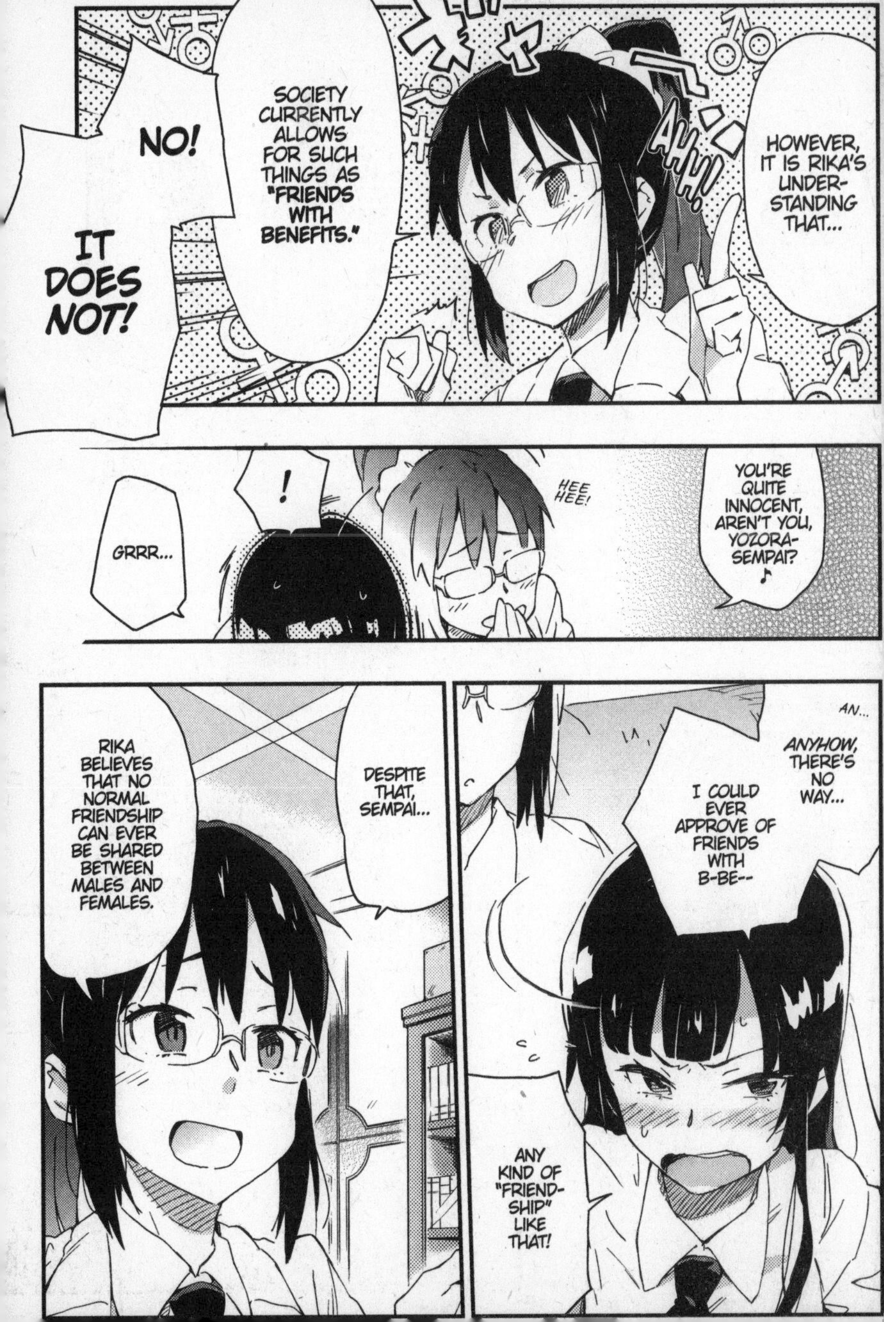
HOWEVER, IT IS RIKA'S UNDER-STANDING THAT...
AHH!
SOCIETY CURRENTLY ALLOWS FOR SUCH THINGS AS "FRIENDS WITH BENEFITS."
NO!
IT DOES NOT!
YOU'RE QUITE INNOCENT, AREN'T YOU, YOZORA-SEMPAI? ♪
HEE HEE!
!
GRRR...
AN...
ANYHOW, THERE'S NO WAY...
I COULD EVER APPROVE OF FRIENDS WITH B-BE--
ANY KIND OF "FRIEND-SHIP" LIKE THAT!
DESPITE THAT, SEMPAI...
RIKA BELIEVES THAT NO NORMAL FRIENDSHIP CAN EVER BE SHARED BETWEEN MALES AND FEMALES.

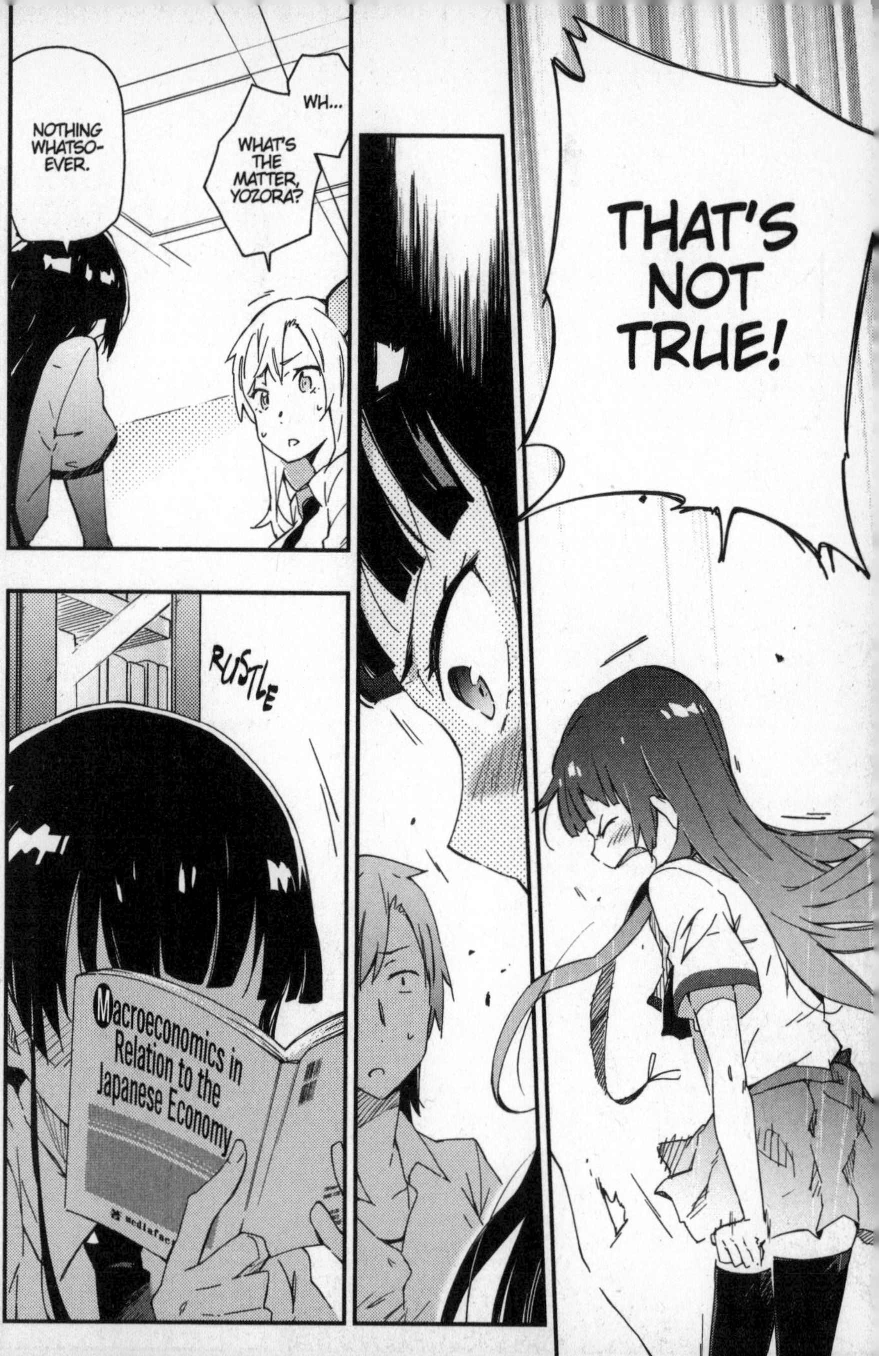
THAT'S NOT TRUE!
WH...
WHAT'S THE MATTER, YOZORA?
NOTHING WHATSO-EVER.
RUSTLE
Macroeconomics in Relation to the Japanese Economy

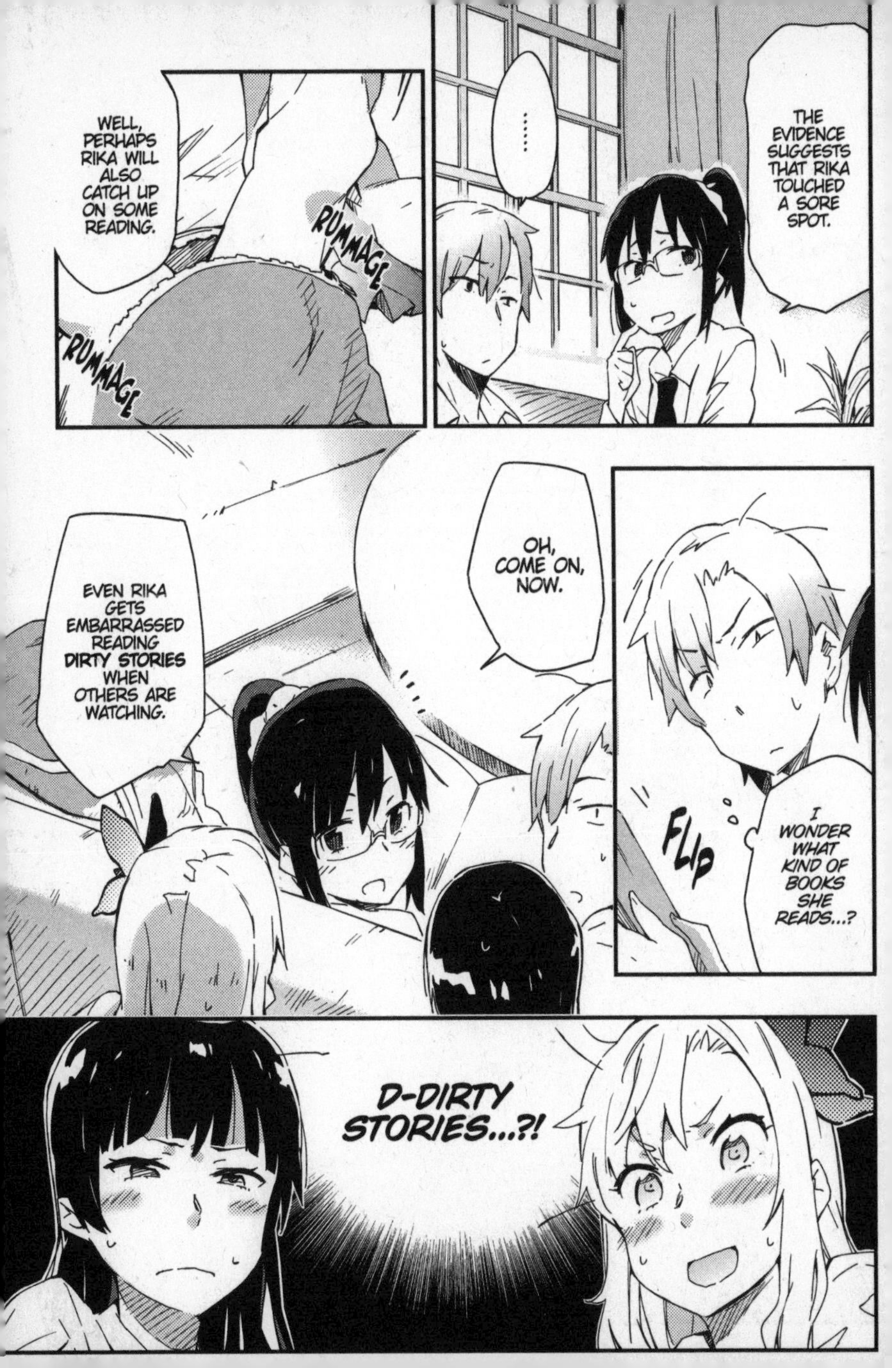

THE EVIDENCE SUGGESTS THAT RIKA TOUCHED A SORE SPOT.
......
WELL, PERHAPS RIKA WILL ALSO CATCH UP ON SOME READING.
RUMMAGE
RUMMAGE
I WONDER WHAT KIND OF BOOKS SHE READS...?
FLIP
OH, COME ON, NOW.
EVEN RIKA GETS EMBARRASSED READING DIRTY STORIES WHEN OTHERS ARE WATCHING.
D-DIRTY STORIES...?!

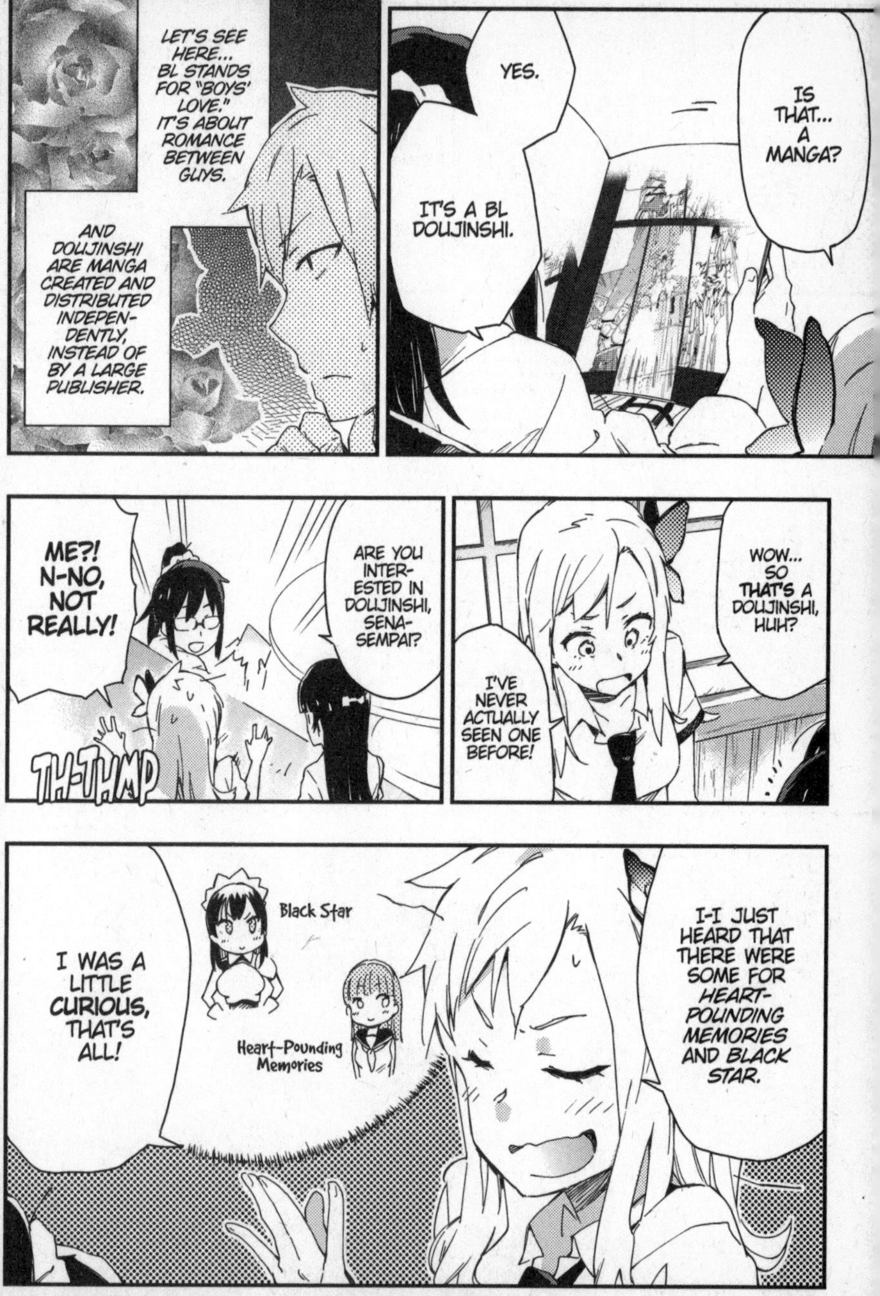
IS THAT... A MANGA?
YES.
IT'S A BL DOUJINSHI.
LET'S SEE HERE... BL STANDS FOR "BOYS' LOVE." IT'S ABOUT ROMANCE BETWEEN GUYS.
AND DOUJINSHI ARE MANGA CREATED AND DISTRIBUTED INDEPEN-DENTLY, INSTEAD OF BY A LARGE PUBLISHER.
WOW... SO THAT'S A DOUJINSHI, HUH?
I'VE NEVER ACTUALLY SEEN ONE BEFORE!
ARE YOU INTER-ESTED IN DOUJINSHI, SENA-SEMPAI?
ME?! N-NO, NOT REALLY!
TH-THMP
I-I JUST HEARD THAT THERE WERE SOME FOR HEART-POUNDING MEMORIES AND BLACK STAR.
Black Star
Heart-Pounding Memories
I WAS A LITTLE CURIOUS, THAT'S ALL!

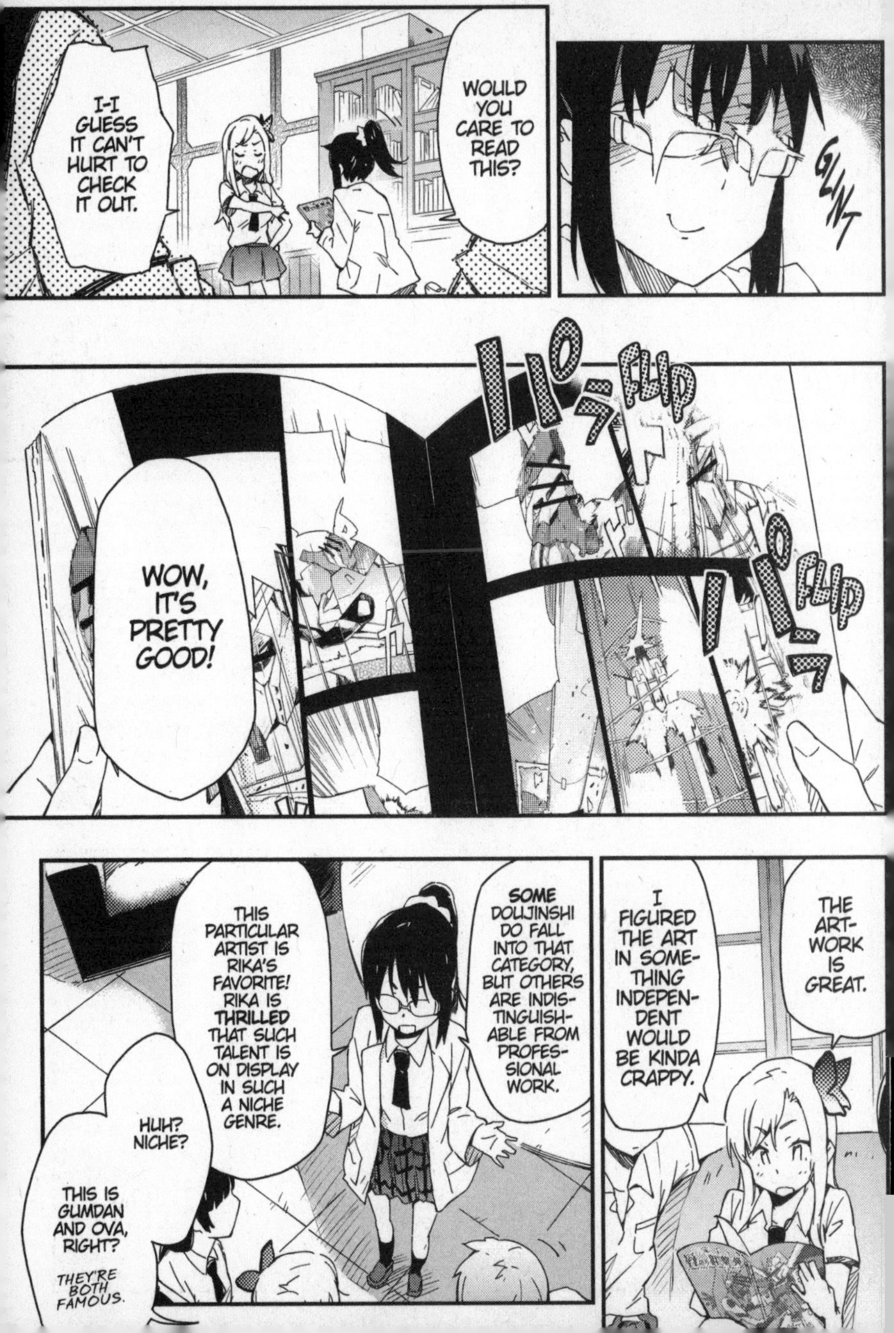
GLINT
WOULD YOU CARE TO READ THIS?
I-I GUESS IT CAN'T HURT TO CHECK IT OUT.
パラ FLIP
パラ FLIP
WOW, IT'S PRETTY GOOD!
THE ARTWORK IS GREAT.
I FIGURED THE ART IN SOMETHING INDEPENDENT WOULD BE KINDA CRAPPY.
SOME DOUJINSHI DO FALL INTO THAT CATEGORY, BUT OTHERS ARE INDISTINGUISHABLE FROM PROFESSIONAL WORK.
THIS PARTICULAR ARTIST IS RIKA'S FAVORITE! RIKA IS THRILLED THAT SUCH TALENT IS ON DISPLAY IN SUCH A NICHE GENRE.
HUH? NICHE?
THIS IS GUMDAN AND OVA, RIGHT?
THEY'RE BOTH FAMOUS.

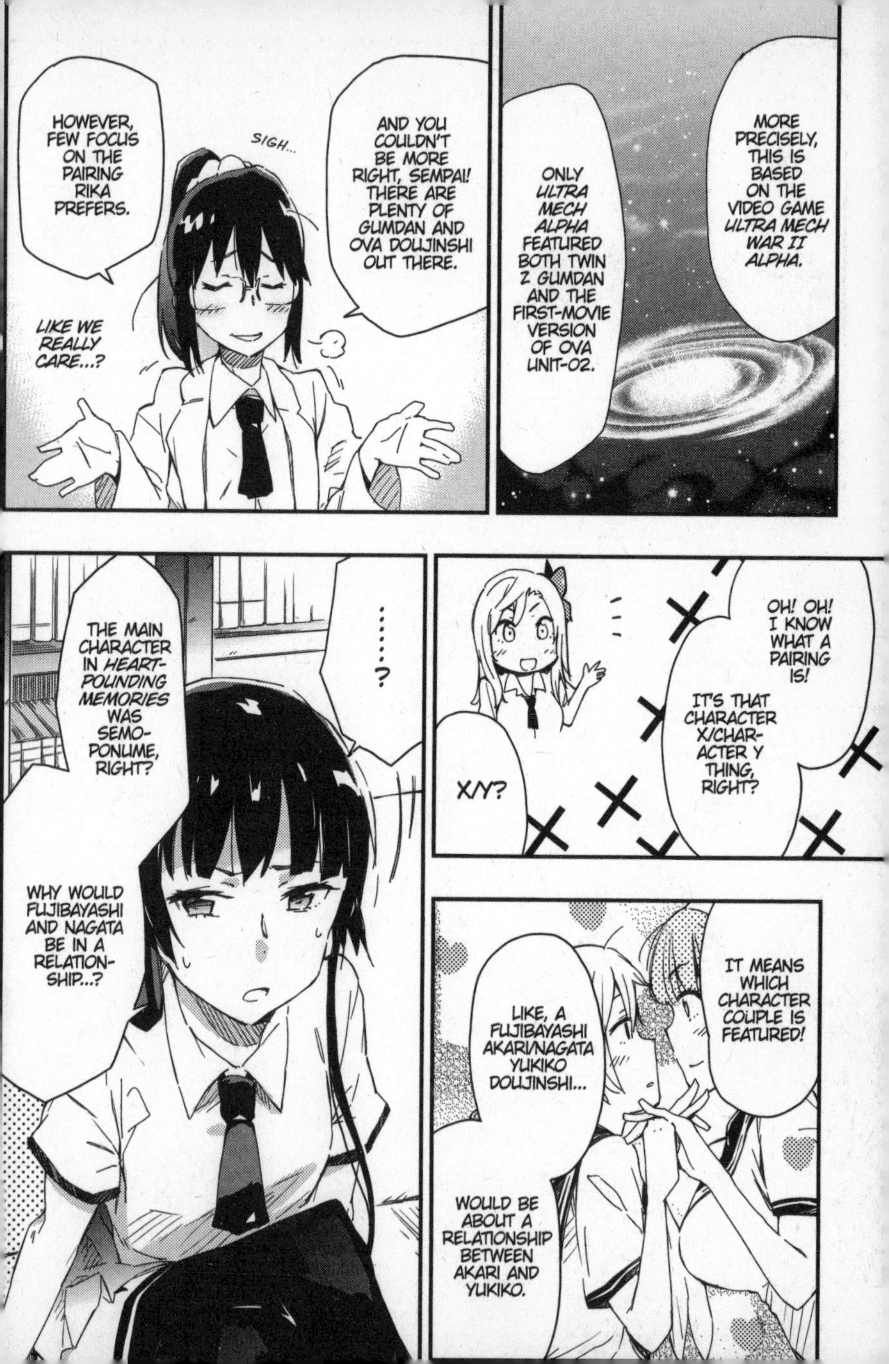
MORE PRECISELY, THIS IS BASED ON THE VIDEO GAME *ULTRA MECH WAR II ALPHA.*
ONLY *ULTRA MECH ALPHA* FEATURED BOTH TWIN Z GUMDAN AND THE FIRST-MOVIE VERSION OF OVA UNIT-02.
AND YOU COULDN'T BE MORE RIGHT, SEMPAI! THERE ARE PLENTY OF GUMDAN AND OVA DOUJINSHI OUT THERE.
SIGH...
HOWEVER, FEW FOCUS ON THE PAIRING RIKA PREFERS.
LIKE WE REALLY CARE...?
OH! OH! I KNOW WHAT A PAIRING IS!
IT'S THAT CHARACTER X/CHARACTER Y THING, RIGHT?
X/Y?
IT MEANS WHICH CHARACTER COUPLE IS FEATURED!
LIKE, A FUJIBAYASHI AKARI/NAGATA YUKIKO DOUJINSHI...
WOULD BE ABOUT A RELATIONSHIP BETWEEN AKARI AND YUKIKO.
......?
THE MAIN CHARACTER IN *HEART-POUNDING MEMORIES* WAS SEMO-PONUME, RIGHT?
WHY WOULD FUJIBAYASHI AND NAGATA BE IN A RELATIONSHIP...?

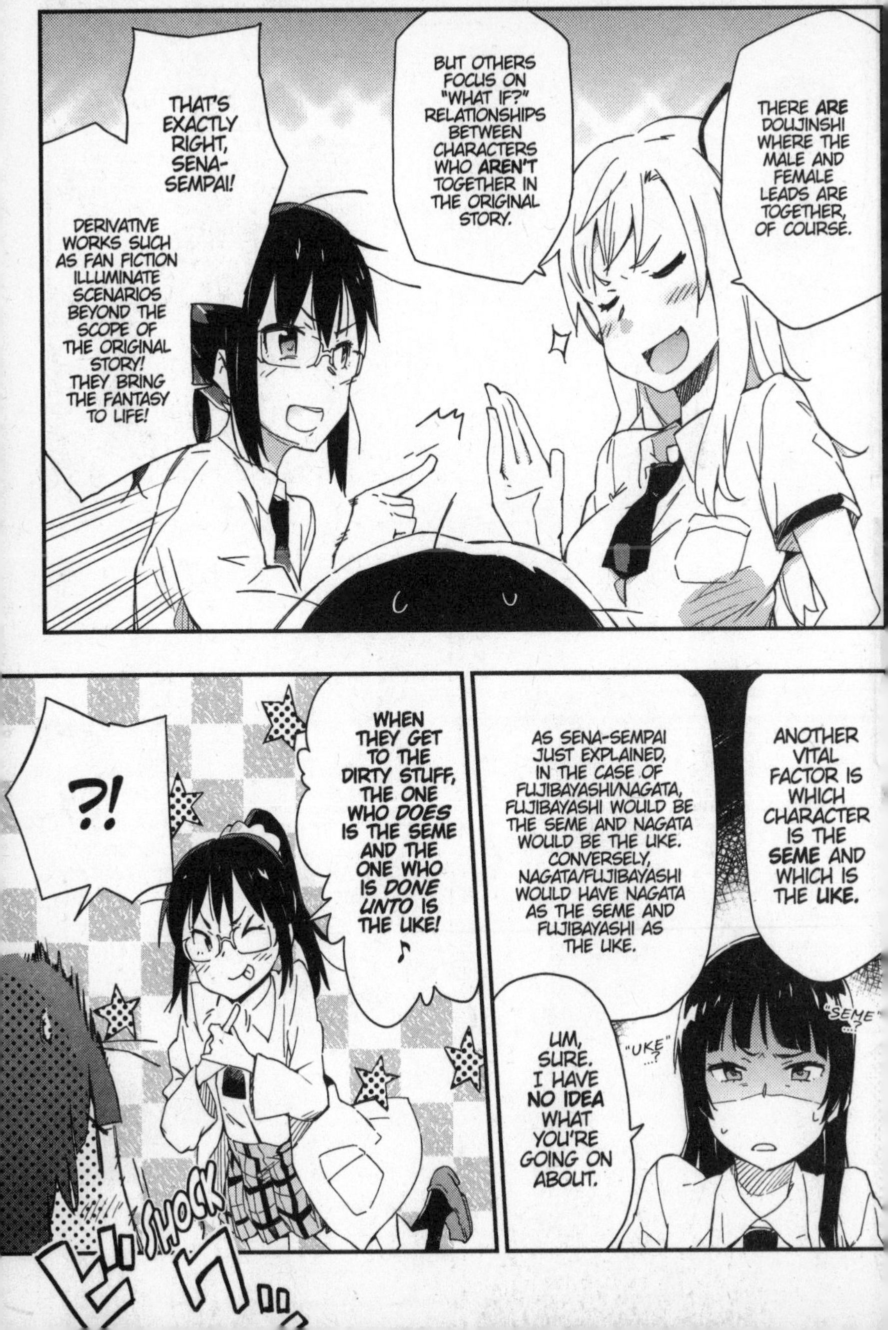
THERE **ARE** DOUJINSHI WHERE THE MALE AND FEMALE LEADS ARE TOGETHER, OF COURSE.
BUT OTHERS FOCUS ON "WHAT IF?" RELATIONSHIPS BETWEEN CHARACTERS WHO **AREN'T** TOGETHER IN THE ORIGINAL STORY.
THAT'S EXACTLY RIGHT, SENA-SEMPAI!
DERIVATIVE WORKS SUCH AS FAN FICTION ILLUMINATE SCENARIOS BEYOND THE SCOPE OF THE ORIGINAL STORY! THEY BRING THE FANTASY TO LIFE!
ANOTHER VITAL FACTOR IS WHICH CHARACTER IS THE **SEME** AND WHICH IS THE **UKE.**
AS SENA-SEMPAI JUST EXPLAINED, IN THE CASE OF FUJIBAYASHI/NAGATA, FUJIBAYASHI WOULD BE THE SEME AND NAGATA WOULD BE THE UKE. CONVERSELY, NAGATA/FUJIBAYASHI WOULD HAVE NAGATA AS THE SEME AND FUJIBAYASHI AS THE UKE.
"SEME"?
"UKE"...?
UM, SURE. I HAVE **NO IDEA** WHAT YOU'RE GOING ON ABOUT.
WHEN THEY GET TO THE DIRTY STUFF, THE ONE WHO *DOES* IS THE SEME AND THE ONE WHO IS *DONE UNTO* IS THE UKE! ♪
?!
SHOCK

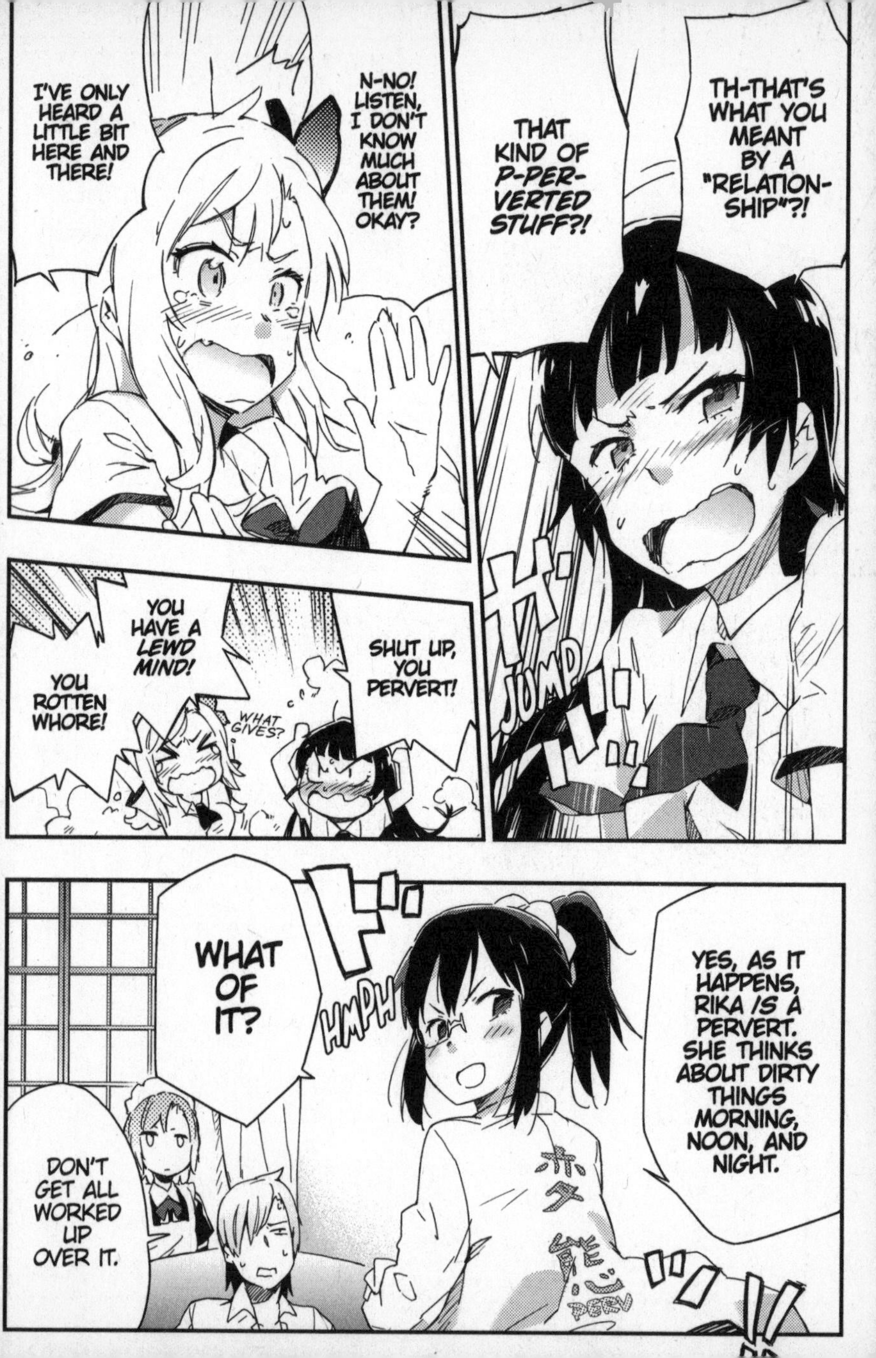
TH-THAT'S WHAT YOU MEANT BY A "RELATIONSHIP"?!
THAT KIND OF P-PERVERTED STUFF?!
JUMP
N-NO! LISTEN, I DON'T KNOW MUCH ABOUT THEM! OKAY?
I'VE ONLY HEARD A LITTLE BIT HERE AND THERE!
SHUT UP, YOU PERVERT!
WHAT GIVES?
YOU HAVE A LEWD MIND!
YOU ROTTEN WHORE!
YES, AS IT HAPPENS, RIKA IS A PERVERT. SHE THINKS ABOUT DIRTY THINGS MORNING, NOON, AND NIGHT.
HMPH
WHAT OF IT?
DON'T GET ALL WORKED UP OVER IT.

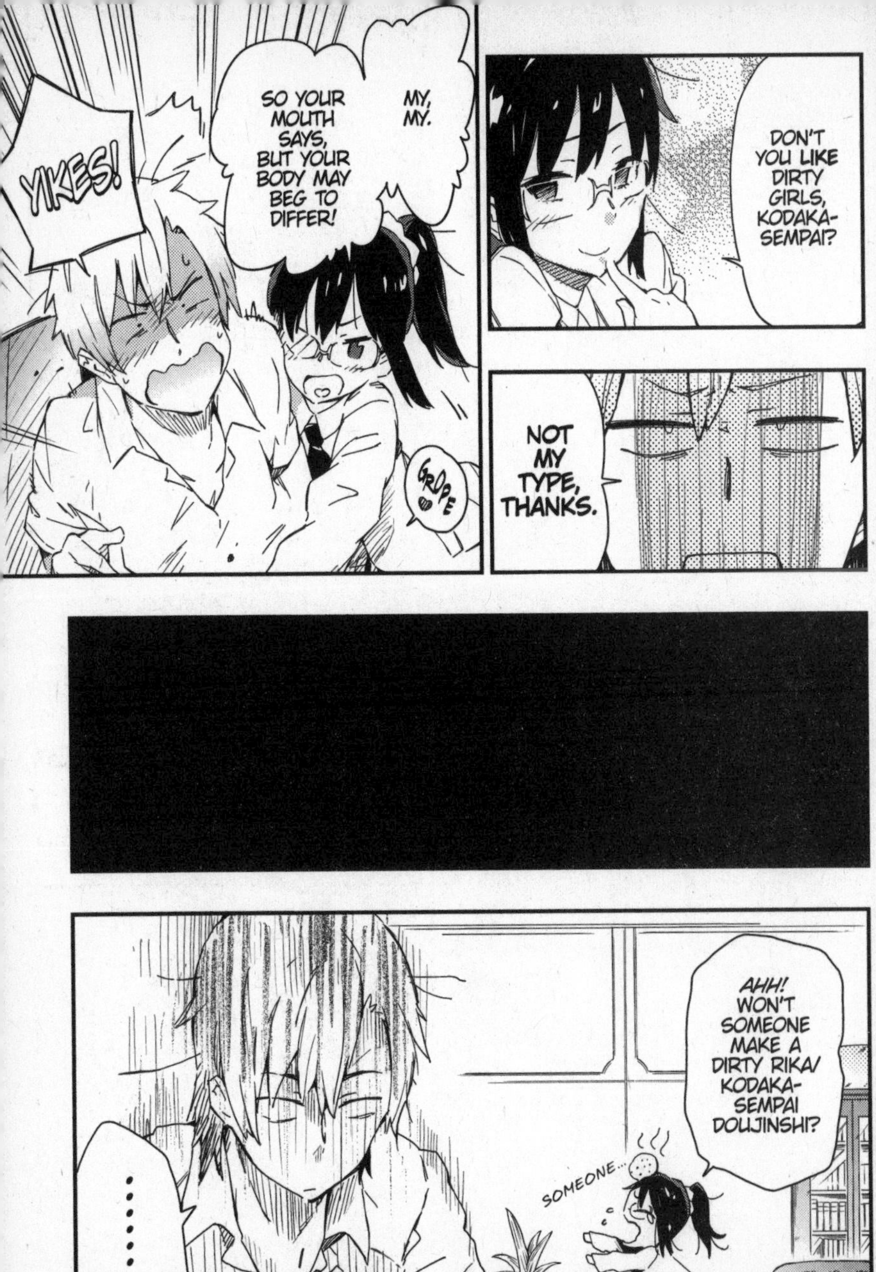
DON'T YOU LIKE DIRTY GIRLS, KODAKA-SEMPAI?
NOT MY TYPE, THANKS.
MY, MY.
SO YOUR MOUTH SAYS, BUT YOUR BODY MAY BEG TO DIFFER!
YIKES!
GROPE
AHH! WON'T SOMEONE MAKE A DIRTY RIKA/ KODAKA-SEMPAI DOUJINSHI?
SOMEONE...
......

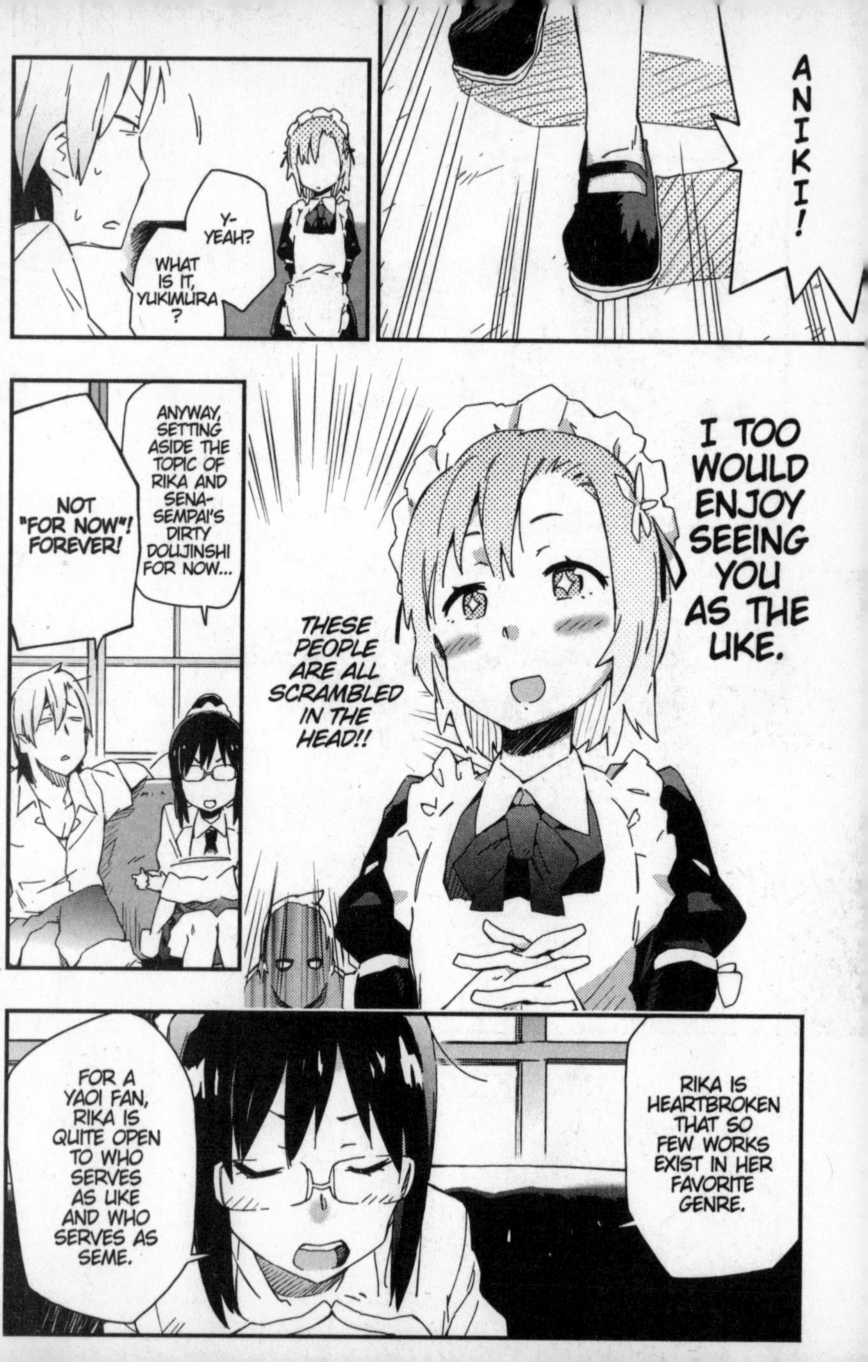
ANIKI!
Y-YEAH?
WHAT IS IT, YUKIMURA?
I TOO WOULD ENJOY SEEING YOU AS THE UKE.
THESE PEOPLE ARE ALL SCRAMBLED IN THE HEAD!!
ANYWAY, SETTING ASIDE THE TOPIC OF RIKA AND SENA-SEMPAI'S DIRTY DOUJINSHI FOR NOW...
NOT "FOR NOW"! FOREVER!
RIKA IS HEARTBROKEN THAT SO FEW WORKS EXIST IN HER FAVORITE GENRE.
FOR A YAOI FAN, RIKA IS QUITE OPEN TO WHO SERVES AS UKE AND WHO SERVES AS SEME.

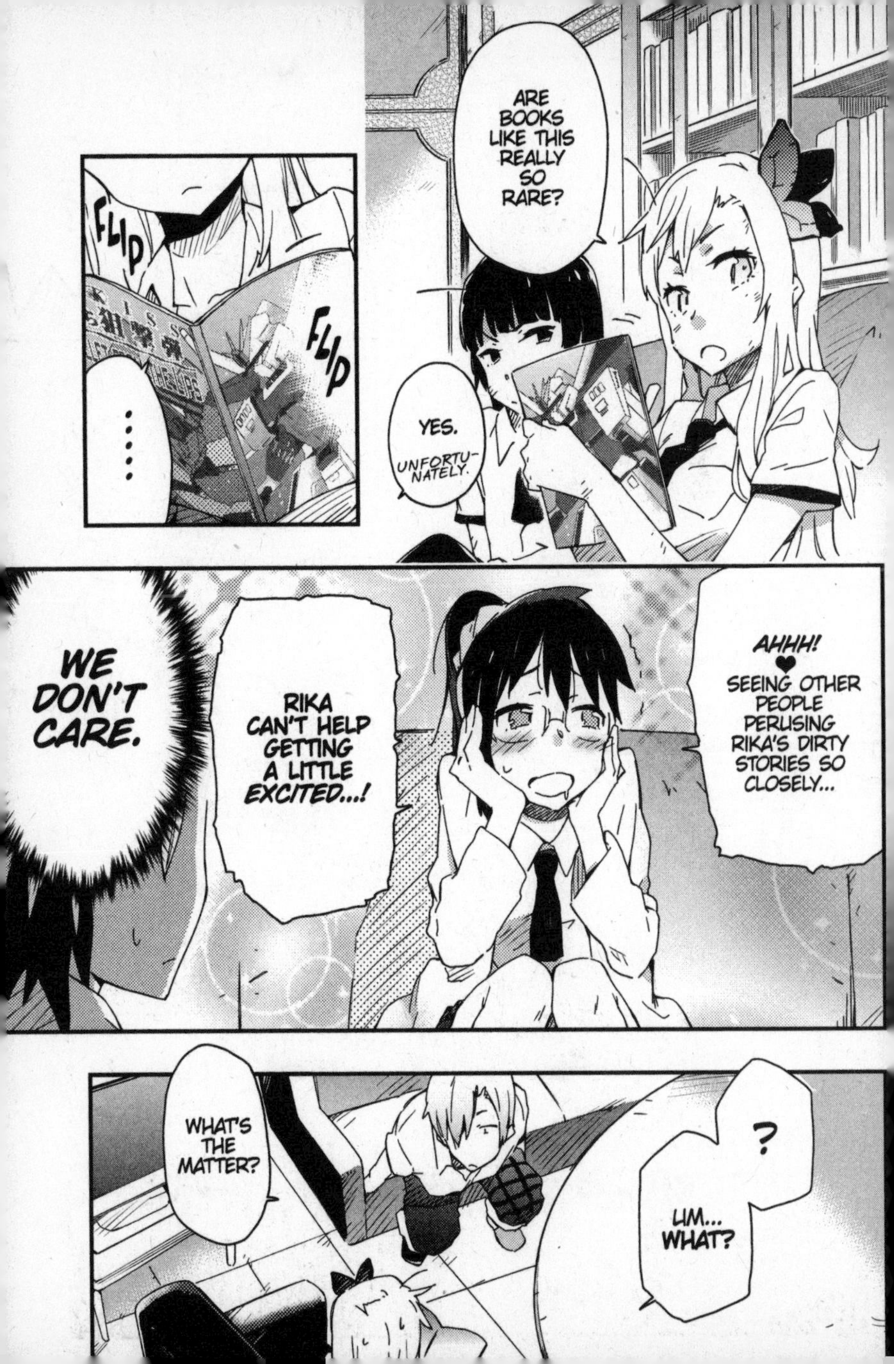
ARE BOOKS LIKE THIS REALLY SO RARE?
YES.
UNFORTUNATELY.
FLIP
FLIP
.....
AHHH! ❤ SEEING OTHER PEOPLE PERUSING RIKA'S DIRTY STORIES SO CLOSELY...
RIKA CAN'T HELP GETTING A LITTLE EXCITED...!
WE DON'T CARE.
WHAT'S THE MATTER?
? UM... WHAT?

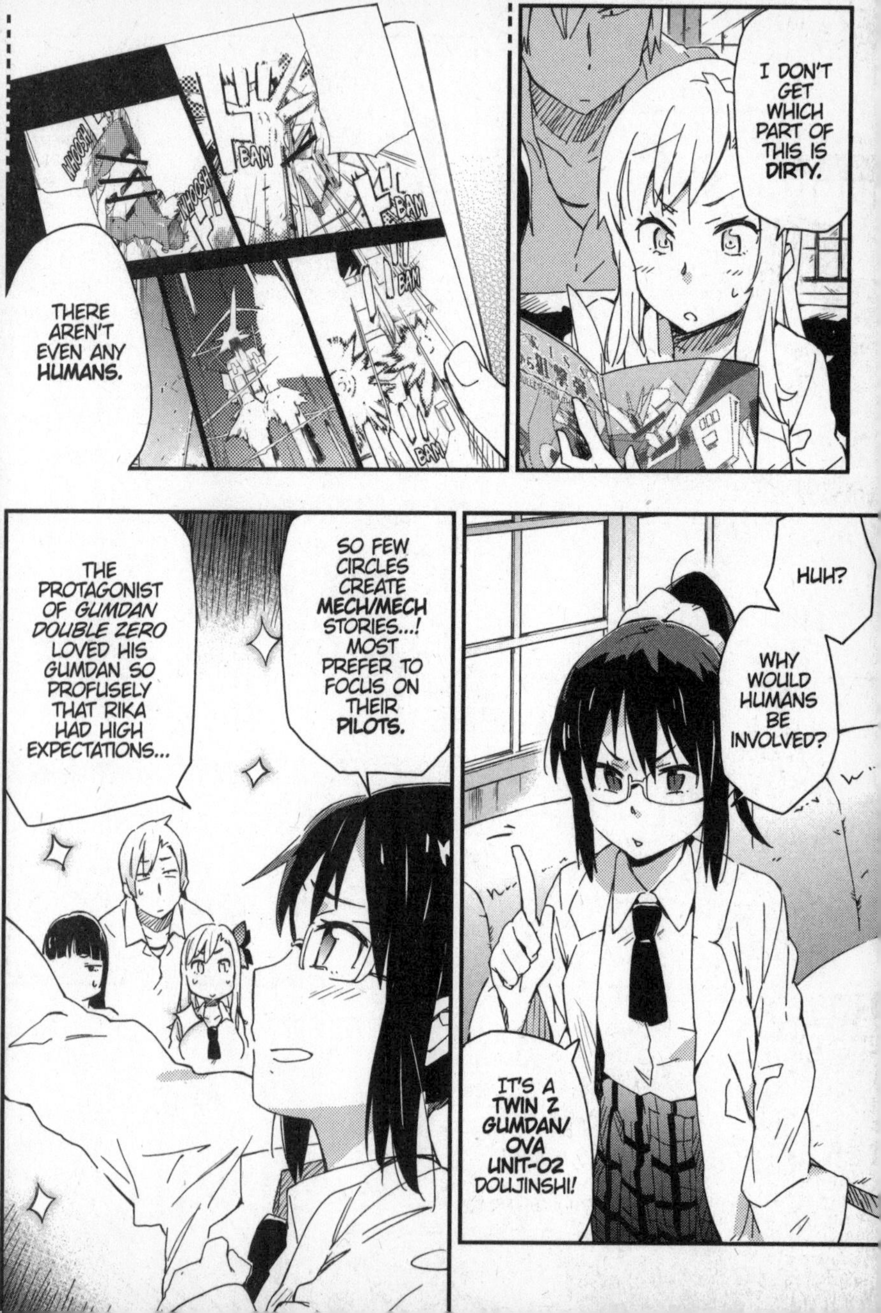
I DON'T GET WHICH PART OF THIS IS DIRTY.
BAM
BAM
WHOOSH
WHOOSH
BAM
BAM
THERE AREN'T EVEN ANY HUMANS.
HUH?
WHY WOULD HUMANS BE INVOLVED?
IT'S A TWIN Z GUMDAN/ OVA UNIT-02 DOUJINSHI!
SO FEW CIRCLES CREATE MECH/MECH STORIES...! MOST PREFER TO FOCUS ON THEIR PILOTS.
THE PROTAGONIST OF GUMDAN DOUBLE ZERO LOVED HIS GUMDAN SO PROFUSELY THAT RIKA HAD HIGH EXPECTATIONS...

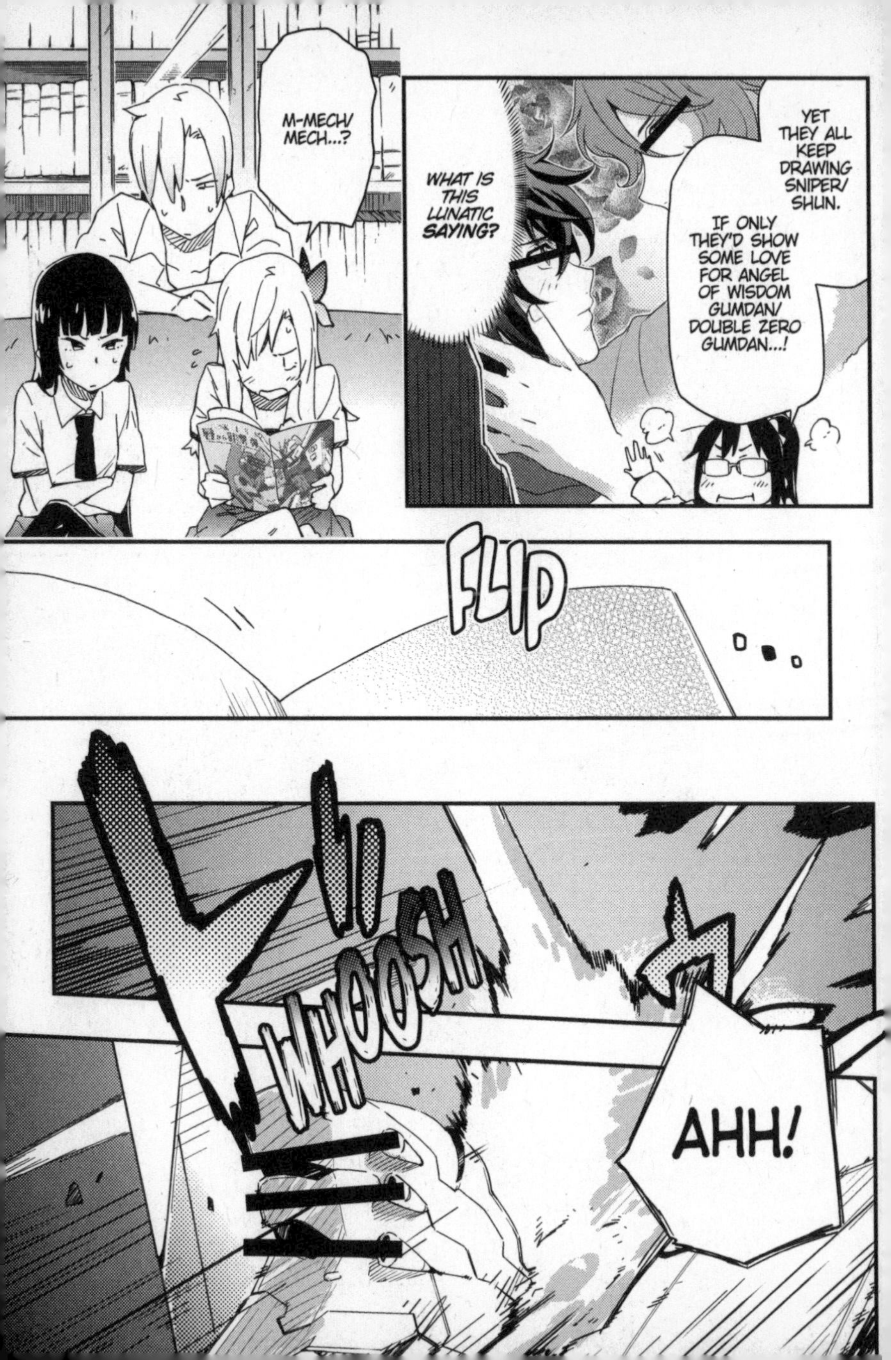
YET THEY ALL KEEP DRAWING SNIPER/SHUN.
IF ONLY THEY'D SHOW SOME LOVE FOR ANGEL OF WISDOM GUMDAN/DOUBLE ZERO GUMDAN...!
WHAT IS THIS LUNATIC SAYING?
M-MECH/MECH...?
FLIP
...
WHOOSH
AHH!

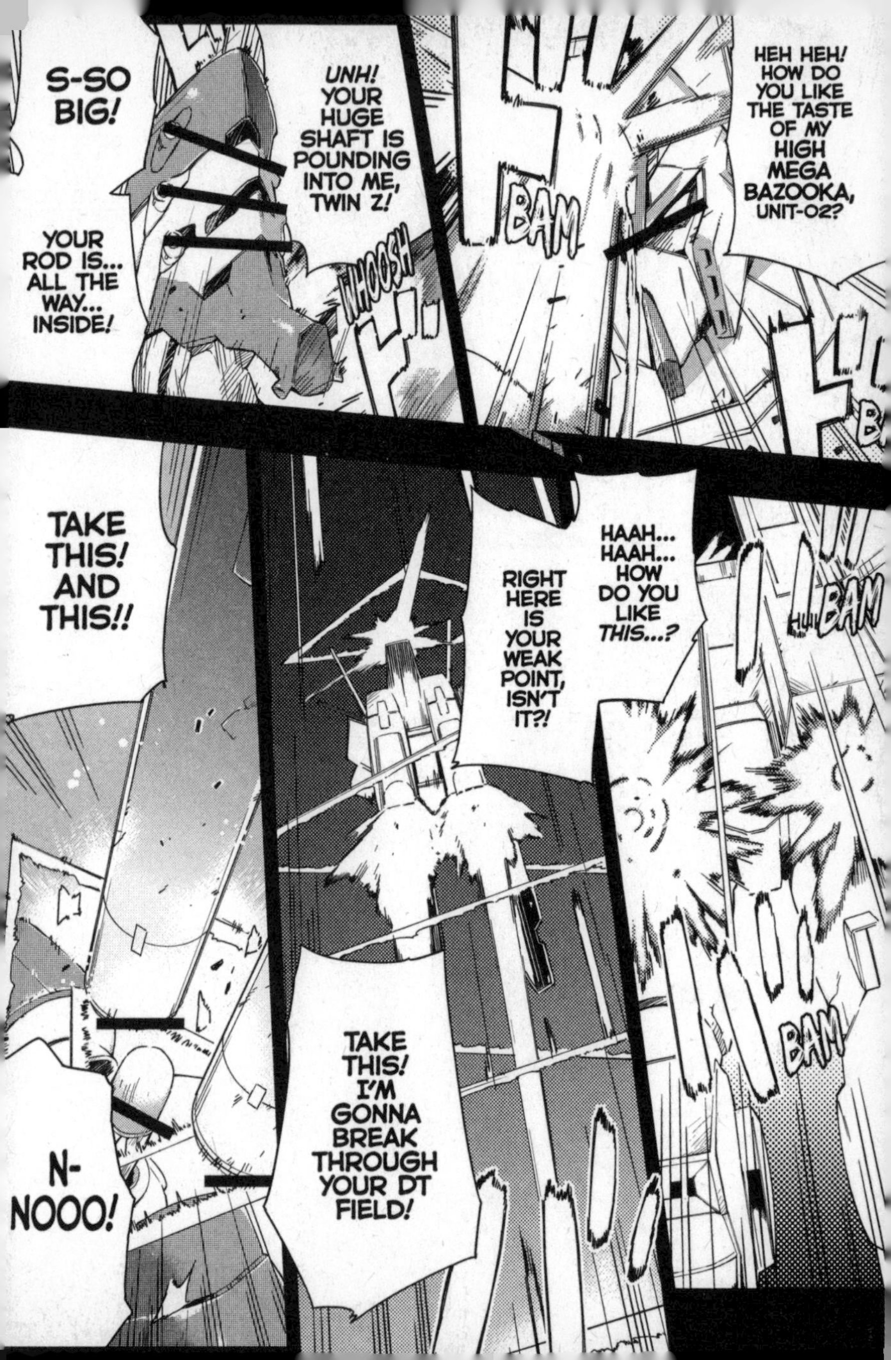
HEH HEH! HOW DO YOU LIKE THE TASTE OF MY HIGH MEGA BAZOOKA, UNIT-02?
BAM
UNH! YOUR HUGE SHAFT IS POUNDING INTO ME, TWIN Z!
WHOOSH
S-SO BIG!
YOUR ROD IS... ALL THE WAY... INSIDE!
HAAH... HAAH... HOW DO YOU LIKE THIS...?
BAM
BAM
RIGHT HERE IS YOUR WEAK POINT, ISN'T IT?!
TAKE THIS! I'M GONNA BREAK THROUGH YOUR DT FIELD!
TAKE THIS! AND THIS!!
N-NOOO!

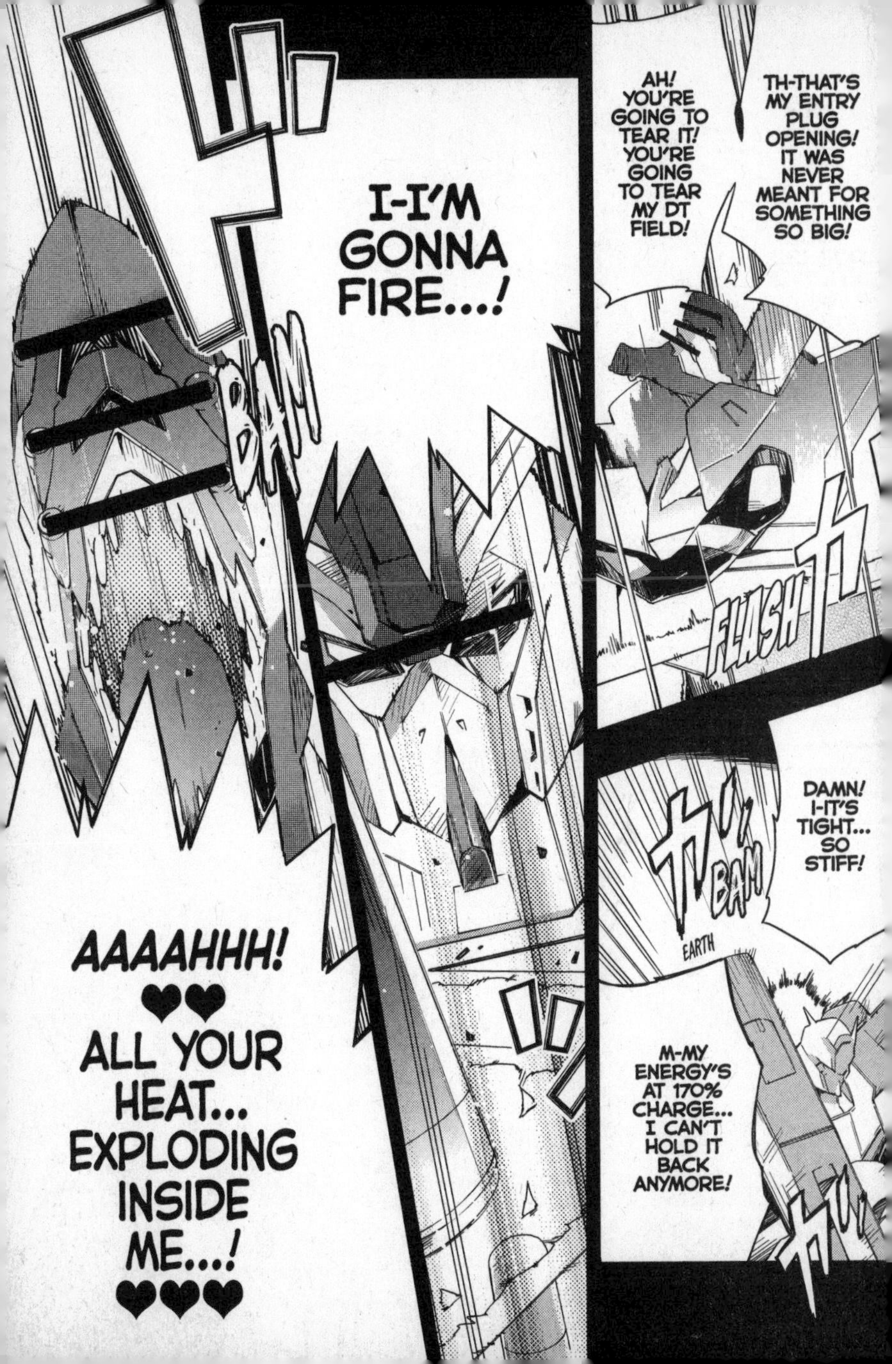

TH-THAT'S MY ENTRY PLUG OPENING! IT WAS NEVER MEANT FOR SOMETHING SO BIG!
AH! YOU'RE GOING TO TEAR IT! YOU'RE GOING TO TEAR MY DT FIELD!
FLASH
DAMN! I-IT'S TIGHT... SO STIFF!
BAM
EARTH
M-MY ENERGY'S AT 170% CHARGE... I CAN'T HOLD IT BACK ANYMORE!
I-I'M GONNA FIRE...!
BAM
AAAAHHH! ♥♥ ALL YOUR HEAT... EXPLODING INSIDE ME...! ♥♥♥

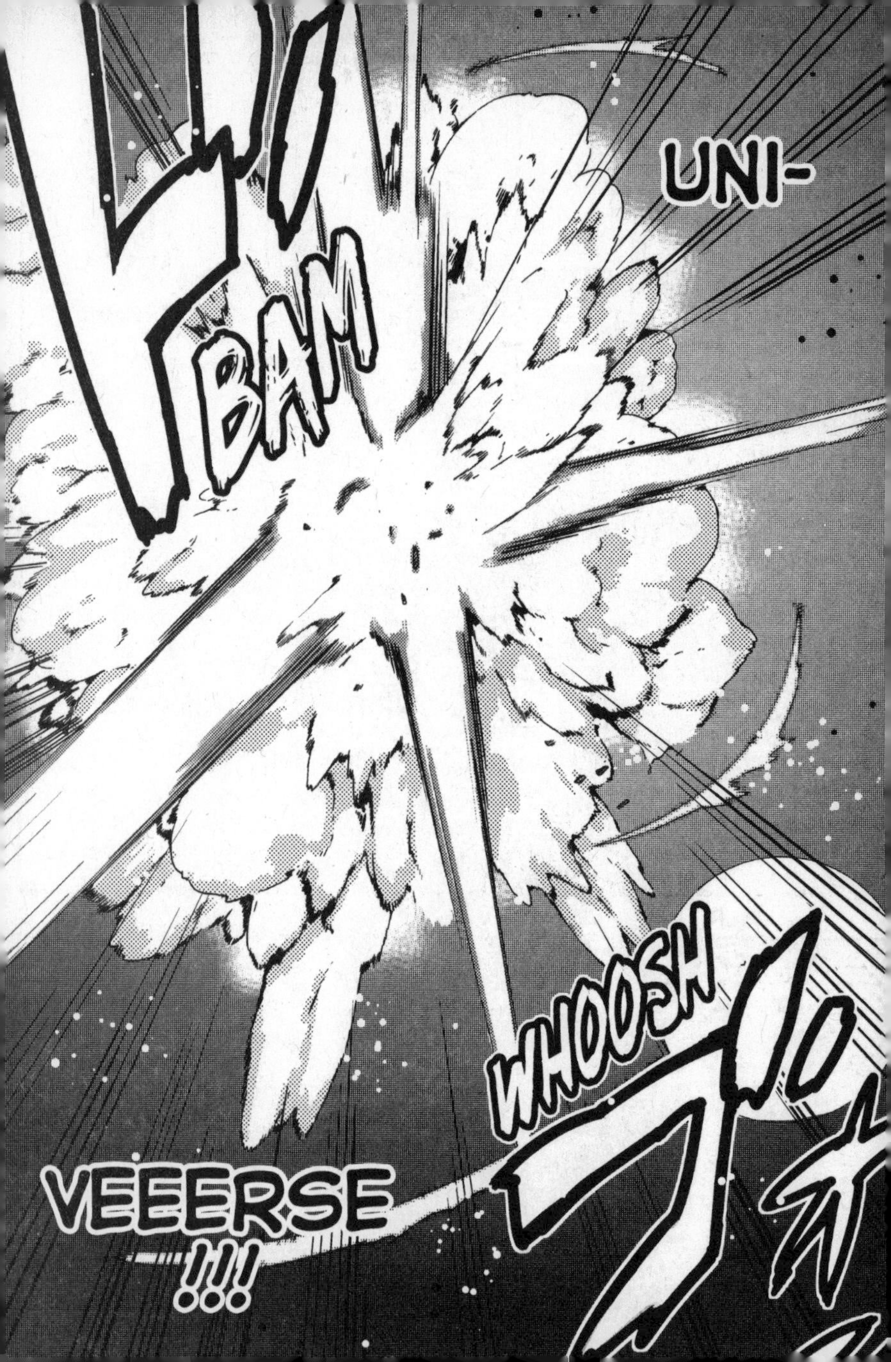
UNI-
BAM
WHOOSH
VEEERSE
—!!!

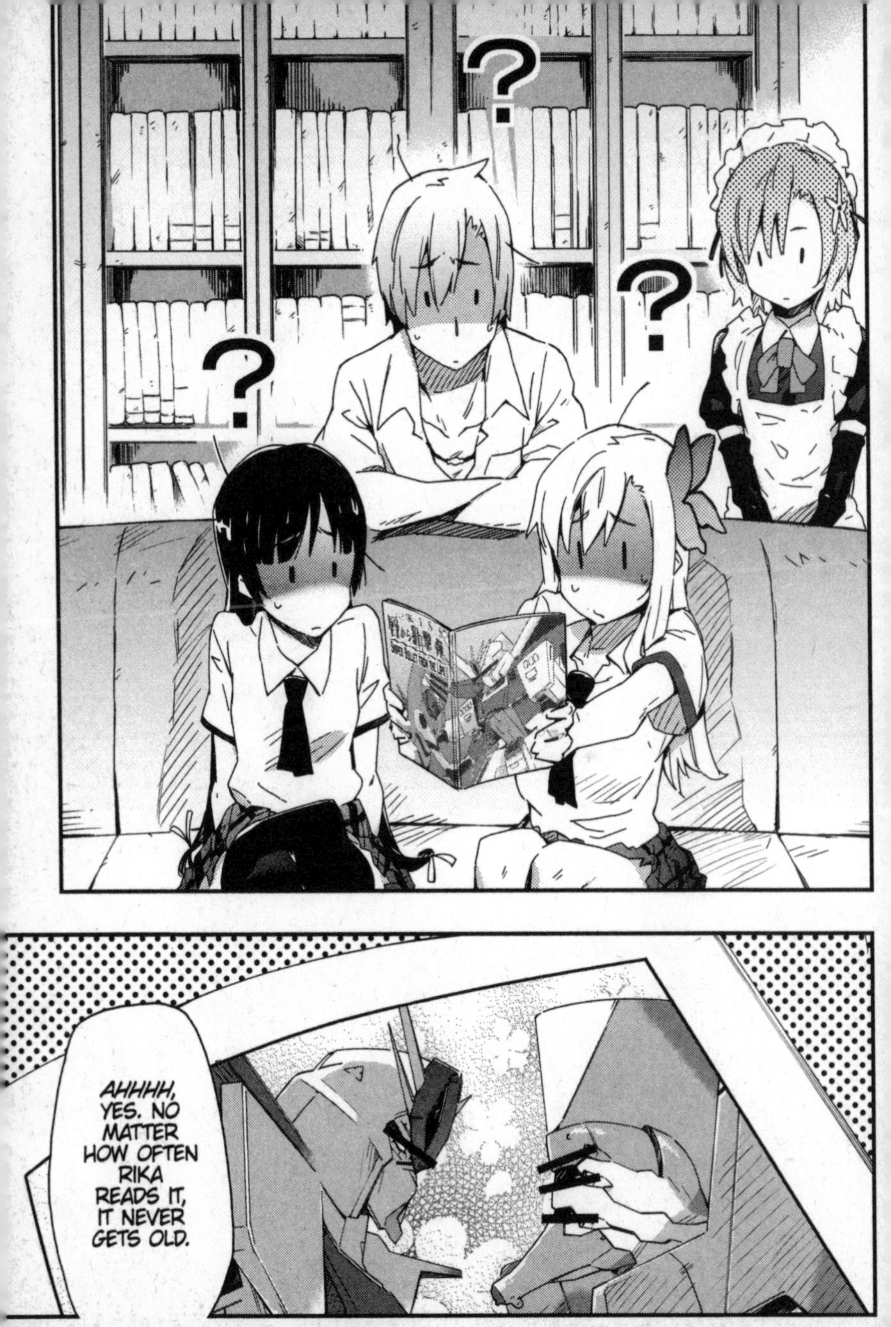
?
?
?
AHHHH, YES. NO MATTER HOW OFTEN RIKA READS IT, IT NEVER GETS OLD.

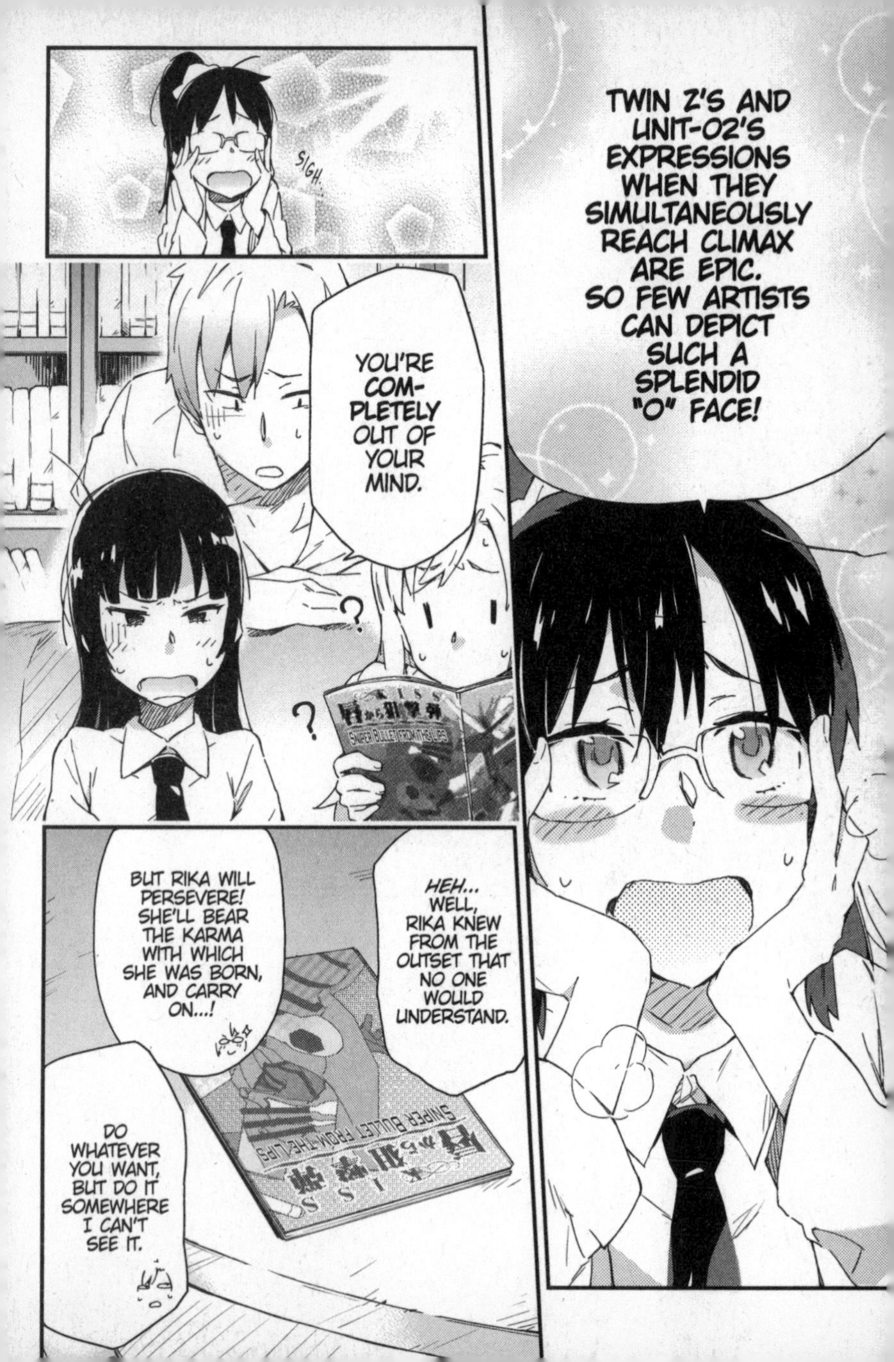
TWIN Z'S AND UNIT-02'S EXPRESSIONS WHEN THEY SIMULTANEOUSLY REACH CLIMAX ARE EPIC. SO FEW ARTISTS CAN DEPICT SUCH A SPLENDID "O" FACE!
SIGH.
YOU'RE COM-PLETELY OUT OF YOUR MIND.
KISS
SNIPER BULLET FROM THE LIPS
HEH... WELL, RIKA KNEW FROM THE OUTSET THAT NO ONE WOULD UNDERSTAND.
BUT RIKA WILL PERSEVERE! SHE'LL BEAR THE KARMA WITH WHICH SHE WAS BORN, AND CARRY ON...!
SNIPER BULLET FROM THE LIPS
KISS
DO WHATEVER YOU WANT, BUT DO IT SOMEWHERE I CAN'T SEE IT.

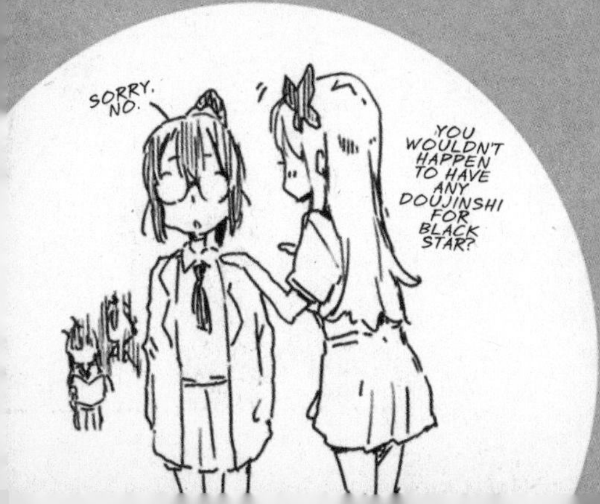
YOU WOULDN'T HAPPEN TO HAVE ANY DOUJINSHI FOR BLACK STAR?
SORRY. NO.

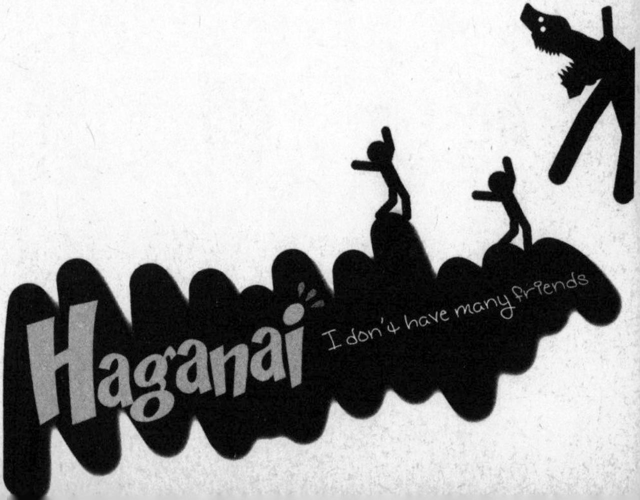
Haganai
I don't have many friends

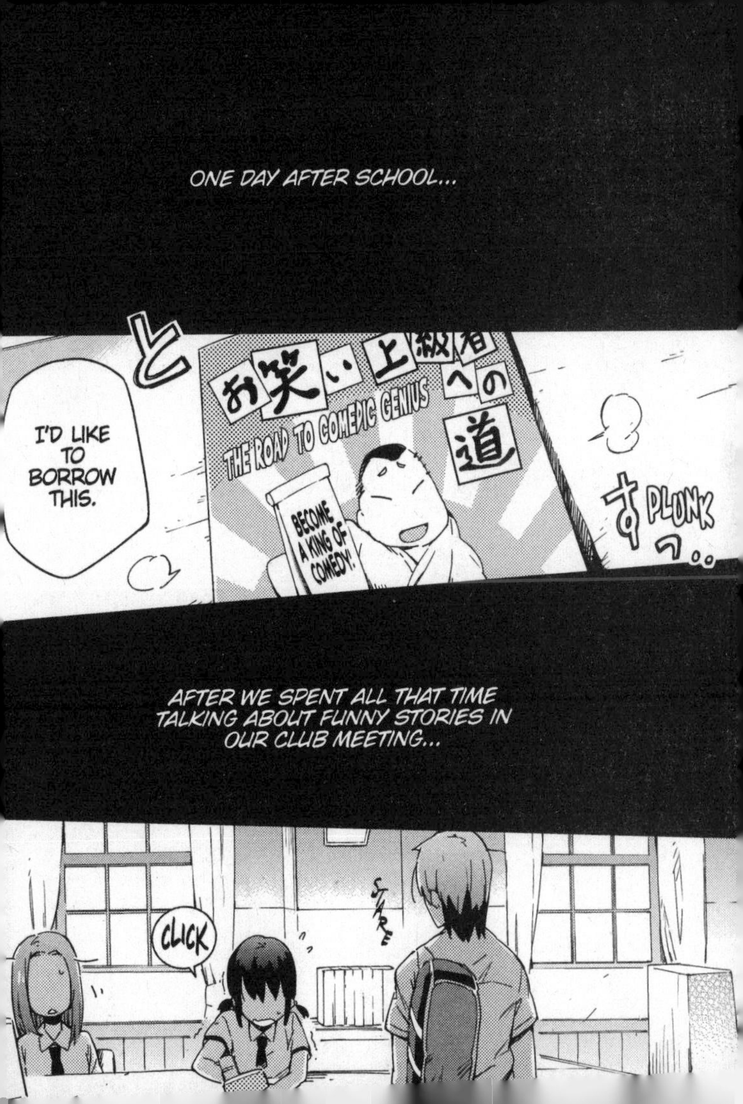
ONE DAY AFTER SCHOOL...
すっ PLUNK
お笑い上級者への道
THE ROAD TO COMEDIC GENIUS
BECOME A KING OF COMEDY!
と
I'D LIKE TO BORROW THIS.
AFTER WE SPENT ALL THAT TIME TALKING ABOUT FUNNY STORIES IN OUR CLUB MEETING...
STARE
CLICK

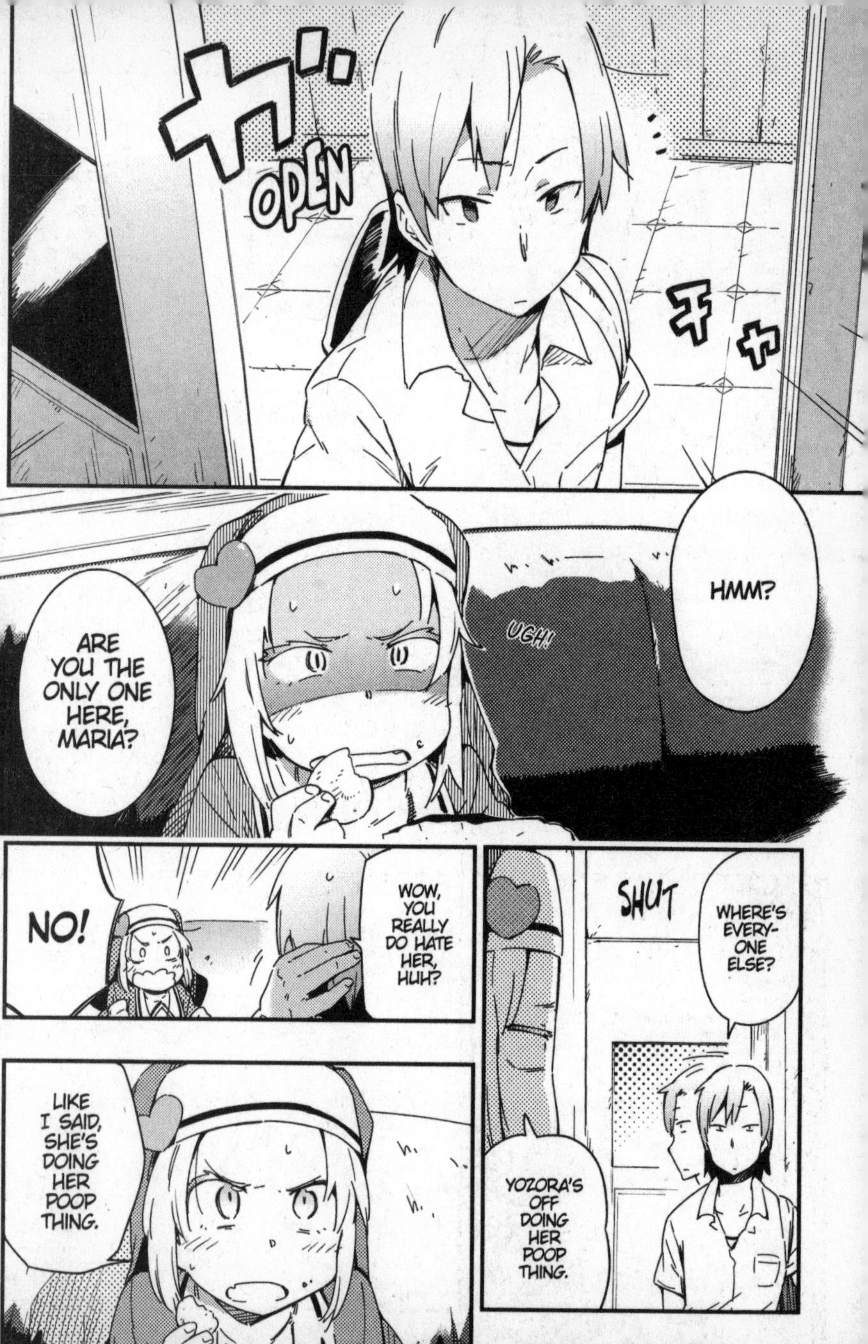

OPEN
HMM?
UGH!
ARE YOU THE ONLY ONE HERE, MARIA?
WHERE'S EVERY-ONE ELSE?
SHUT
YOZORA'S OFF DOING HER POOP THING.
WOW, YOU REALLY DO HATE HER, HUH?
NO!
LIKE I SAID, SHE'S DOING HER POOP THING.

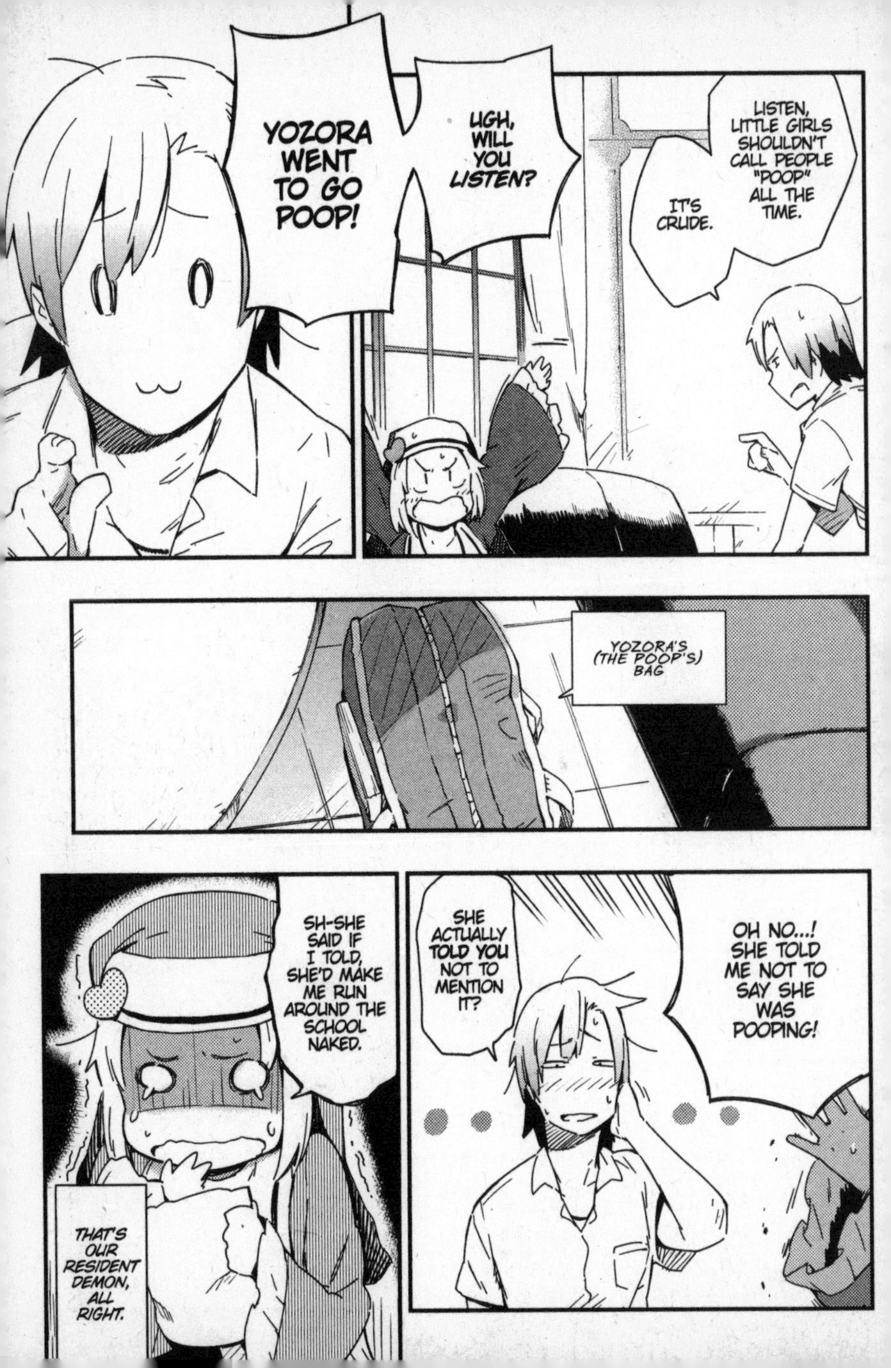
LISTEN, LITTLE GIRLS SHOULDN'T CALL PEOPLE "POOP" ALL THE TIME.
IT'S CRUDE.
UGH, WILL YOU LISTEN?
YOZORA WENT TO GO POOP!
YOZORA'S (THE POOP'S) BAG
OH NO...! SHE TOLD ME NOT TO SAY SHE WAS POOPING!
SHE ACTUALLY TOLD YOU NOT TO MENTION IT?
SH-SHE SAID IF I TOLD, SHE'D MAKE ME RUN AROUND THE SCHOOL NAKED.
THAT'S OUR RESIDENT DEMON, ALL RIGHT.

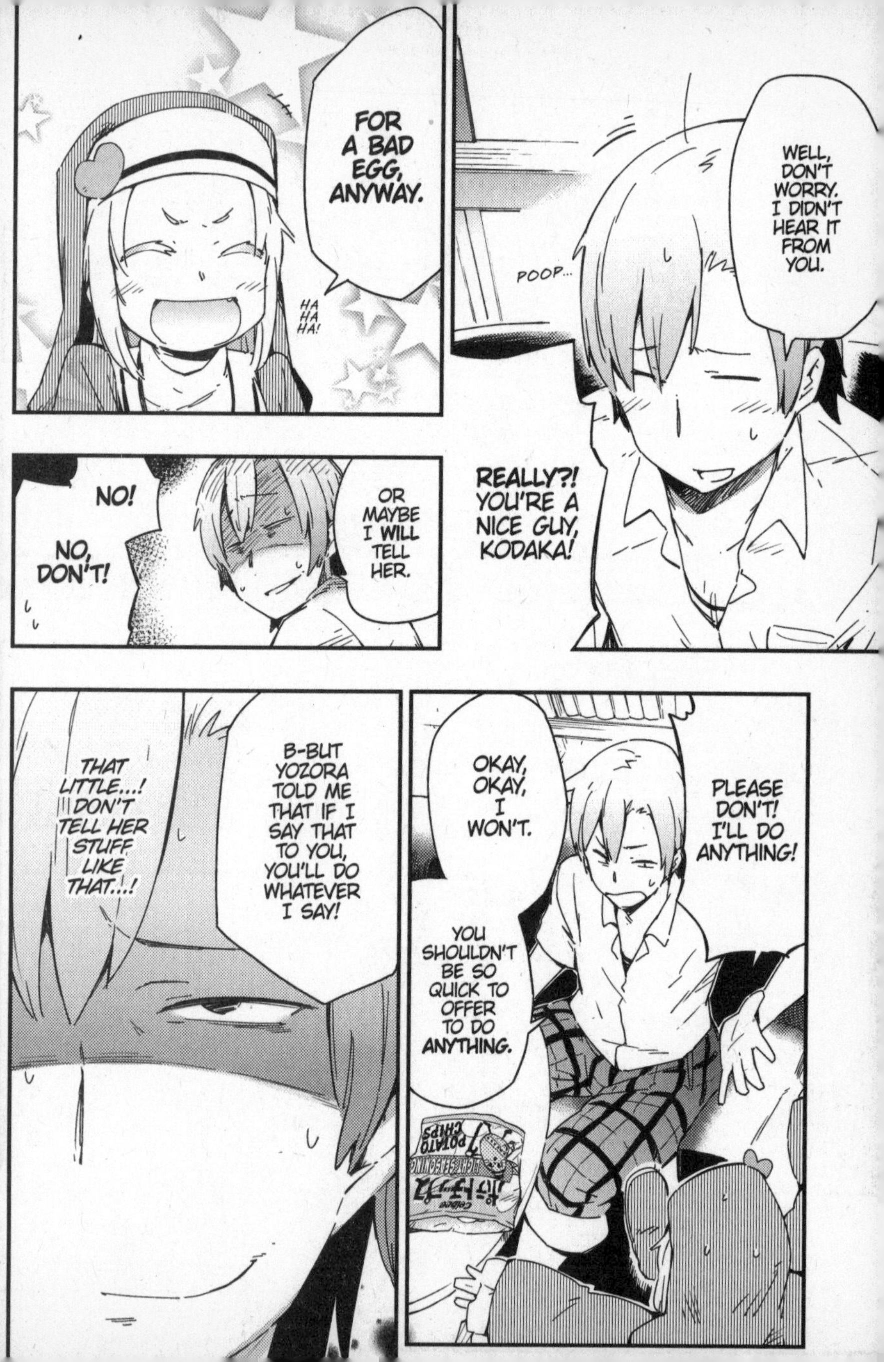
WELL, DON'T WORRY. I DIDN'T HEAR IT FROM YOU.
POOP...
REALLY?! YOU'RE A NICE GUY, KODAKA!
FOR A BAD EGG, ANYWAY.
HA HA HA!
OR MAYBE I WILL TELL HER.
NO!
NO, DON'T!
PLEASE DON'T! I'LL DO ANYTHING!
OKAY, OKAY, I WON'T.
YOU SHOULDN'T BE SO QUICK TO OFFER TO DO ANYTHING.
B-BUT YOZORA TOLD ME THAT IF I SAY THAT TO YOU, YOU'LL DO WHATEVER I SAY!
THAT LITTLE...! DON'T TELL HER STUFF LIKE THAT...!

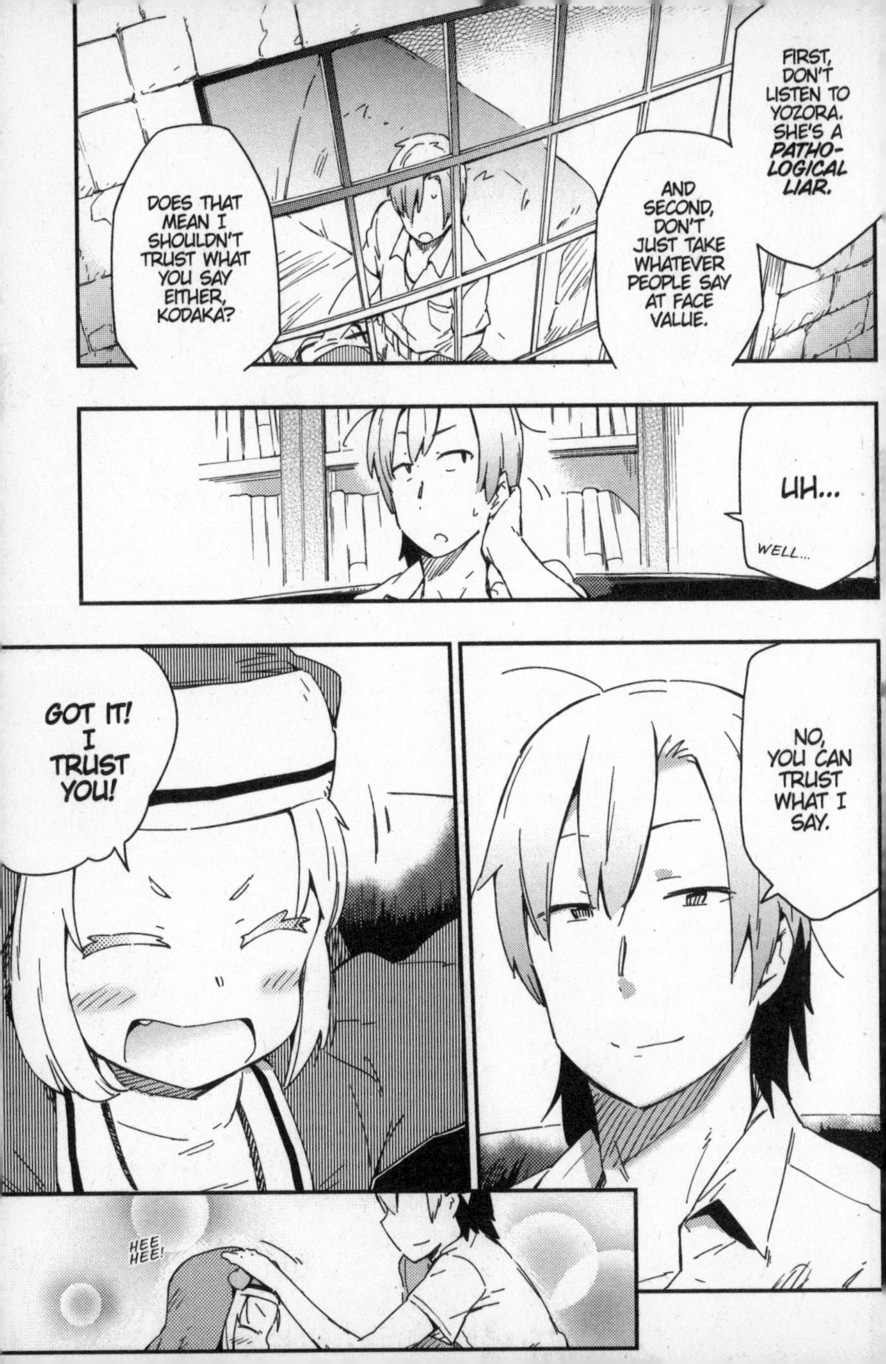
FIRST, DON'T LISTEN TO YOZORA. SHE'S A *PATHOLOGICAL LIAR.*
AND SECOND, DON'T JUST TAKE WHATEVER PEOPLE SAY AT FACE VALUE.
DOES THAT MEAN I SHOULDN'T TRUST WHAT YOU SAY EITHER, KODAKA?
UH...
WELL...
NO, YOU CAN TRUST WHAT I SAY.
GOT IT! I TRUST YOU!
HEE HEE!

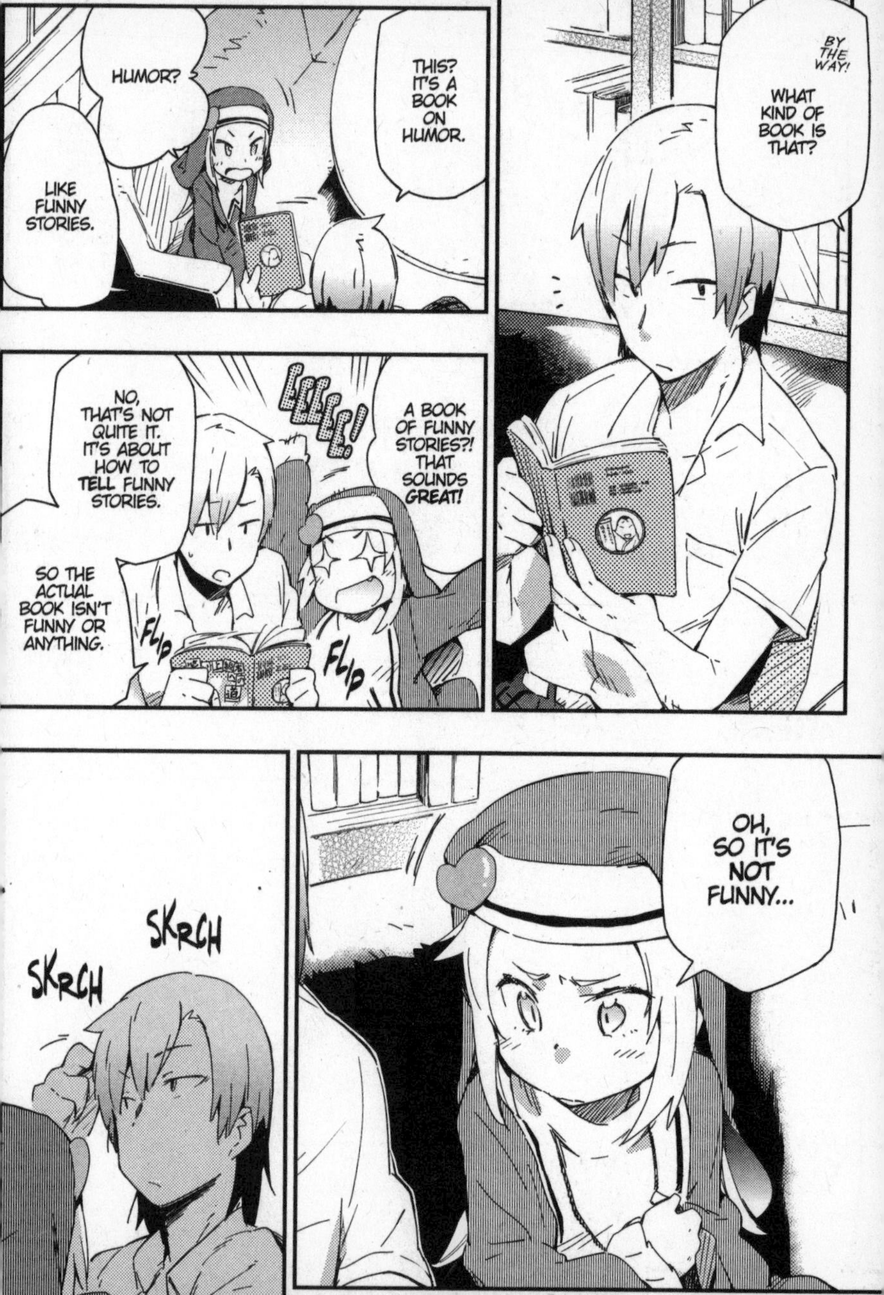
BY THE WAY!
WHAT KIND OF BOOK IS THAT?
THIS? IT'S A BOOK ON HUMOR.
HUMOR?
LIKE FUNNY STORIES.
A BOOK OF FUNNY STORIES?! THAT SOUNDS GREAT!
EEEEE!
NO, THAT'S NOT QUITE IT. IT'S ABOUT HOW TO TELL FUNNY STORIES.
SO THE ACTUAL BOOK ISN'T FUNNY OR ANYTHING.
FLIP
FLIP
OH, SO IT'S NOT FUNNY...
SKRCH
SKRCH

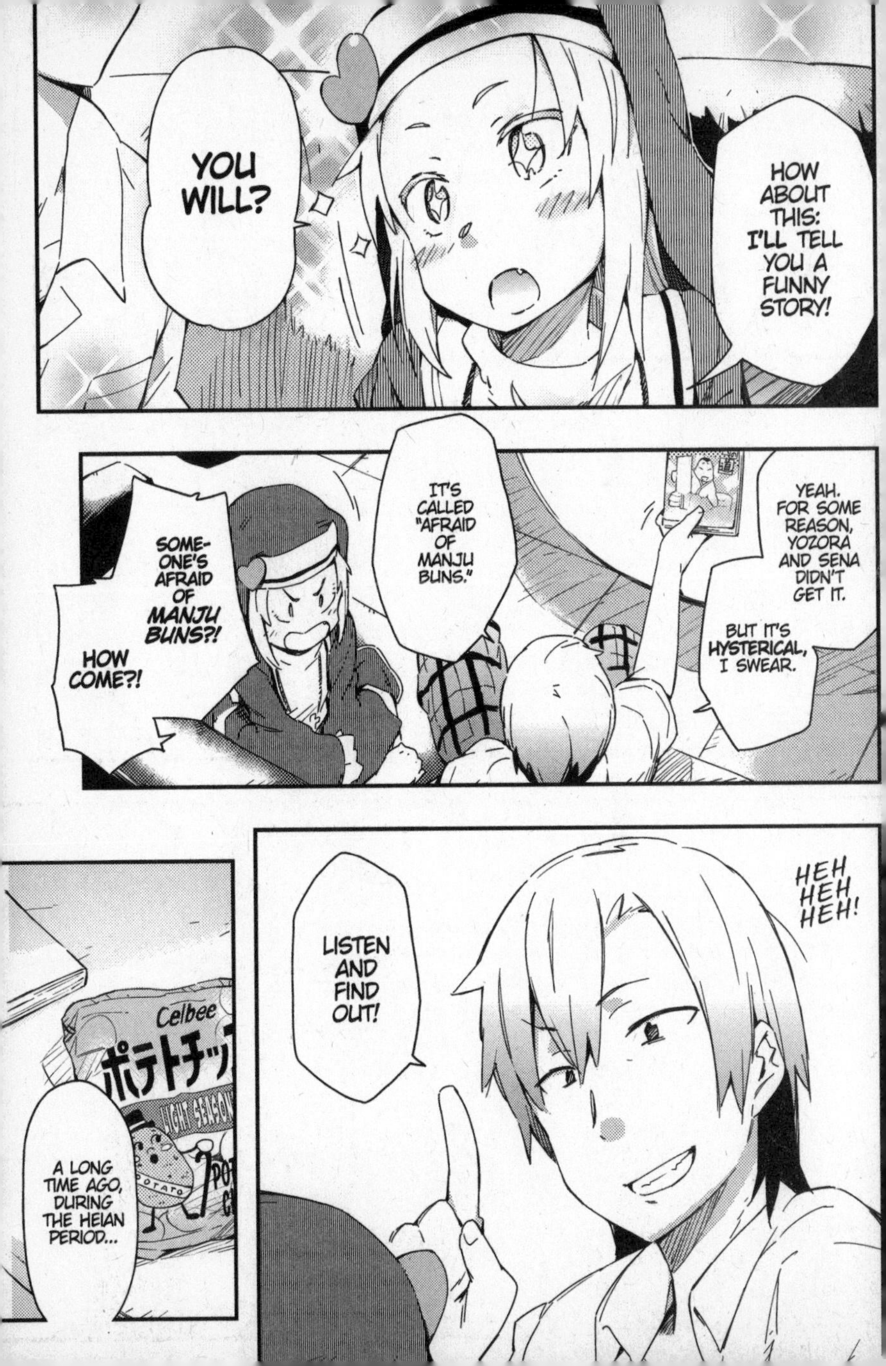
HOW ABOUT THIS: I'LL TELL YOU A FUNNY STORY!
YOU WILL?
YEAH. FOR SOME REASON, YOZORA AND SENA DIDN'T GET IT.
BUT IT'S HYSTERICAL, I SWEAR.
IT'S CALLED "AFRAID OF MANJU BUNS."
SOME-ONE'S AFRAID OF MANJU BUNS?!
HOW COME?!
HEH HEH HEH!
LISTEN AND FIND OUT!
Celbee
A LONG TIME AGO, DURING THE HEIAN PERIOD...

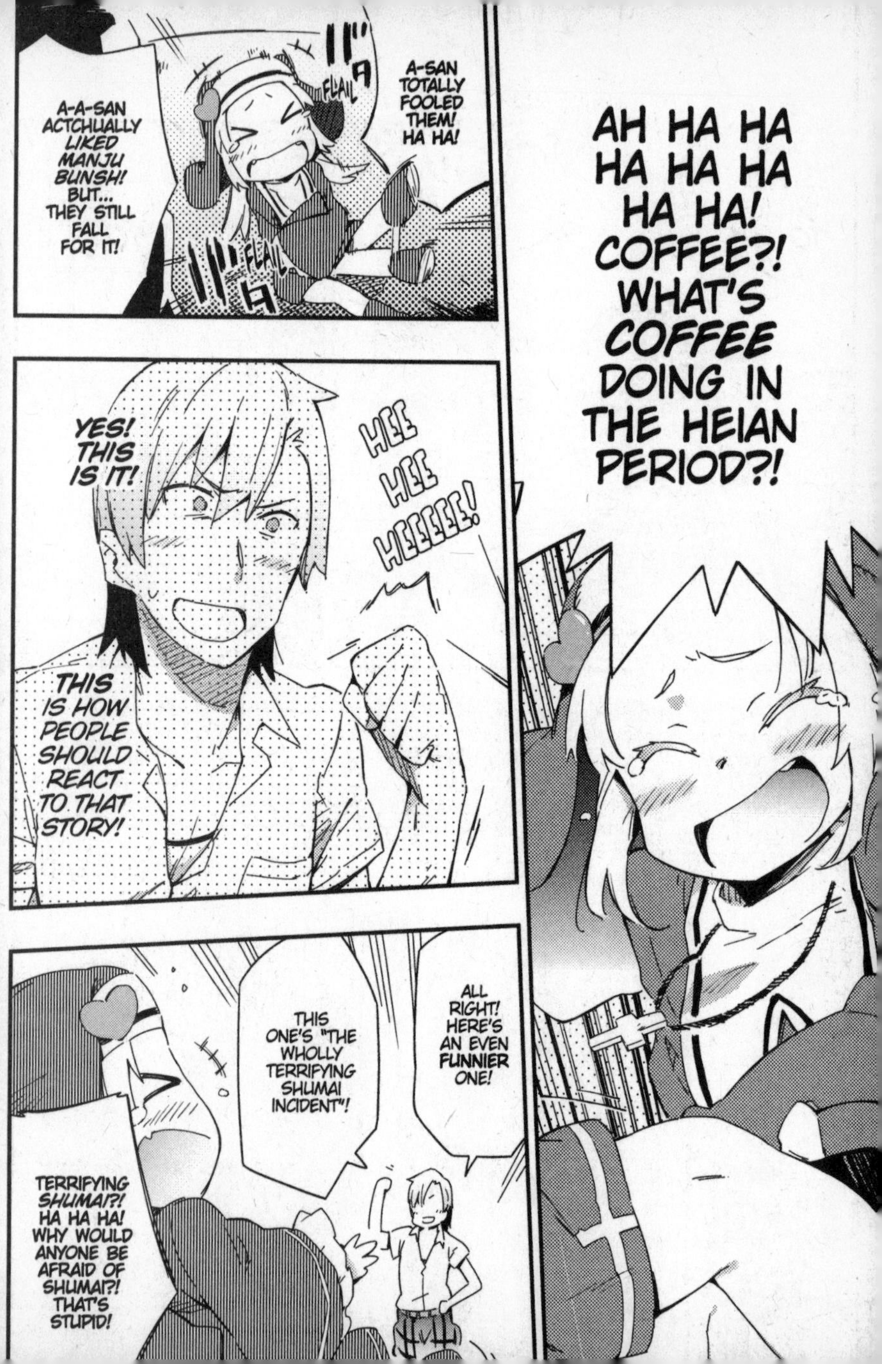
AH HA HA HA HA HA HA HA! COFFEE?! WHAT'S COFFEE DOING IN THE HEIAN PERIOD?!
FLAIL
A-SAN TOTALLY FOOLED THEM! HA HA!
A-A-SAN ACTCHUALLY LIKED MANJU BUNSH! BUT... THEY STILL FALL FOR IT!
FLAIL
HEE HEE HEEEEE!
YES! THIS IS IT!
THIS IS HOW PEOPLE SHOULD REACT TO THAT STORY!
ALL RIGHT! HERE'S AN EVEN FUNNIER ONE!
THIS ONE'S "THE WHOLLY TERRIFYING SHUMAI INCIDENT"!
TERRIFYING SHUMAI?! HA HA HA! WHY WOULD ANYONE BE AFRAID OF SHUMAI?! THAT'S STUPID!

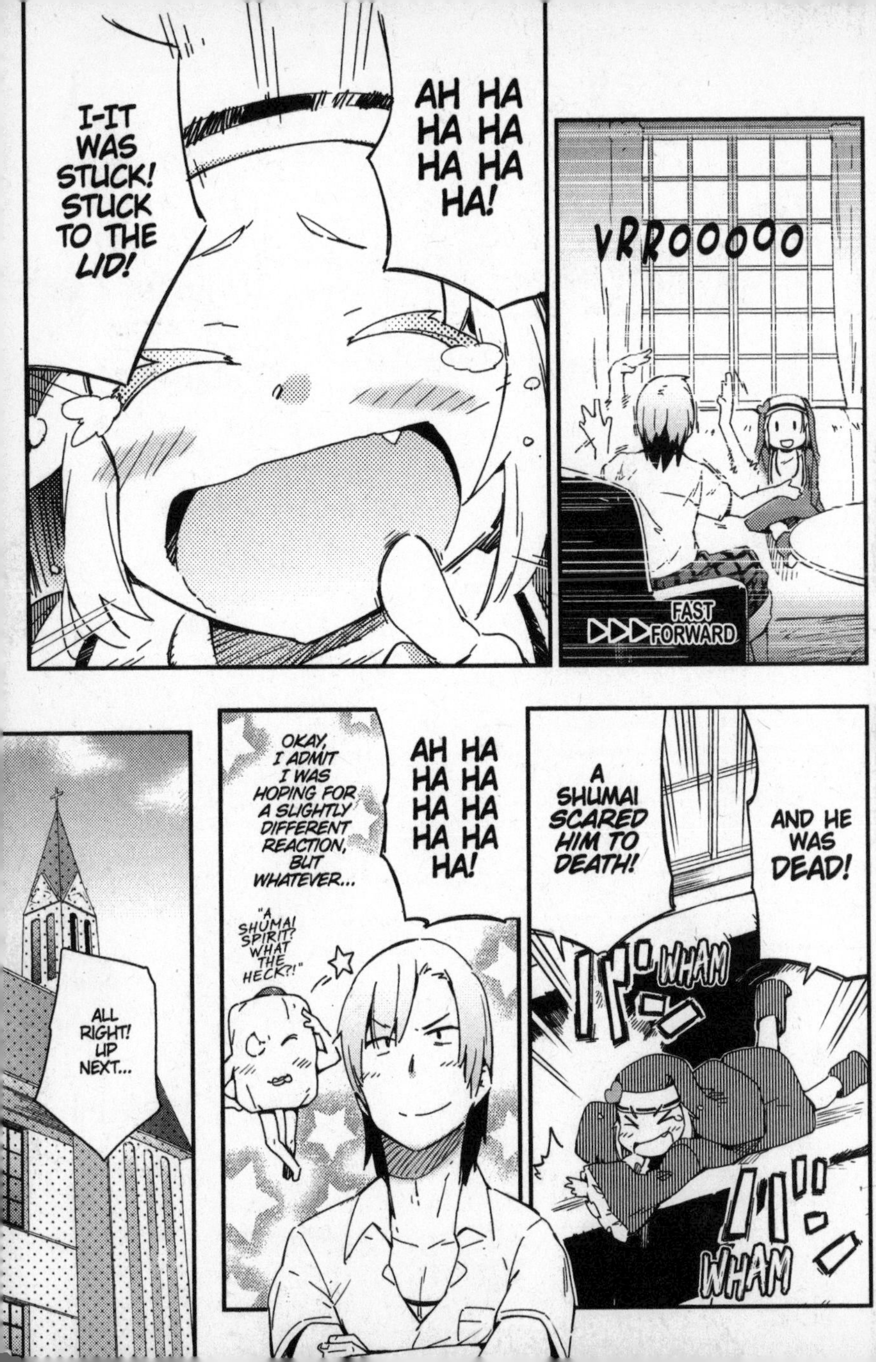
VRROOOOO
FAST FORWARD
AH HA HA HA HA HA HA!
I-IT WAS STUCK! STUCK TO THE LID!
AND HE WAS DEAD!
A SHUMAI SCARED HIM TO DEATH!
WHAM
WHAM
AH HA HA HA HA HA HA HA HA!
OKAY, I ADMIT I WAS HOPING FOR A SLIGHTLY DIFFERENT REACTION, BUT WHATEVER...
"A SHUMAI SPIRIT? WHAT THE HECK?!"
ALL RIGHT! UP NEXT...

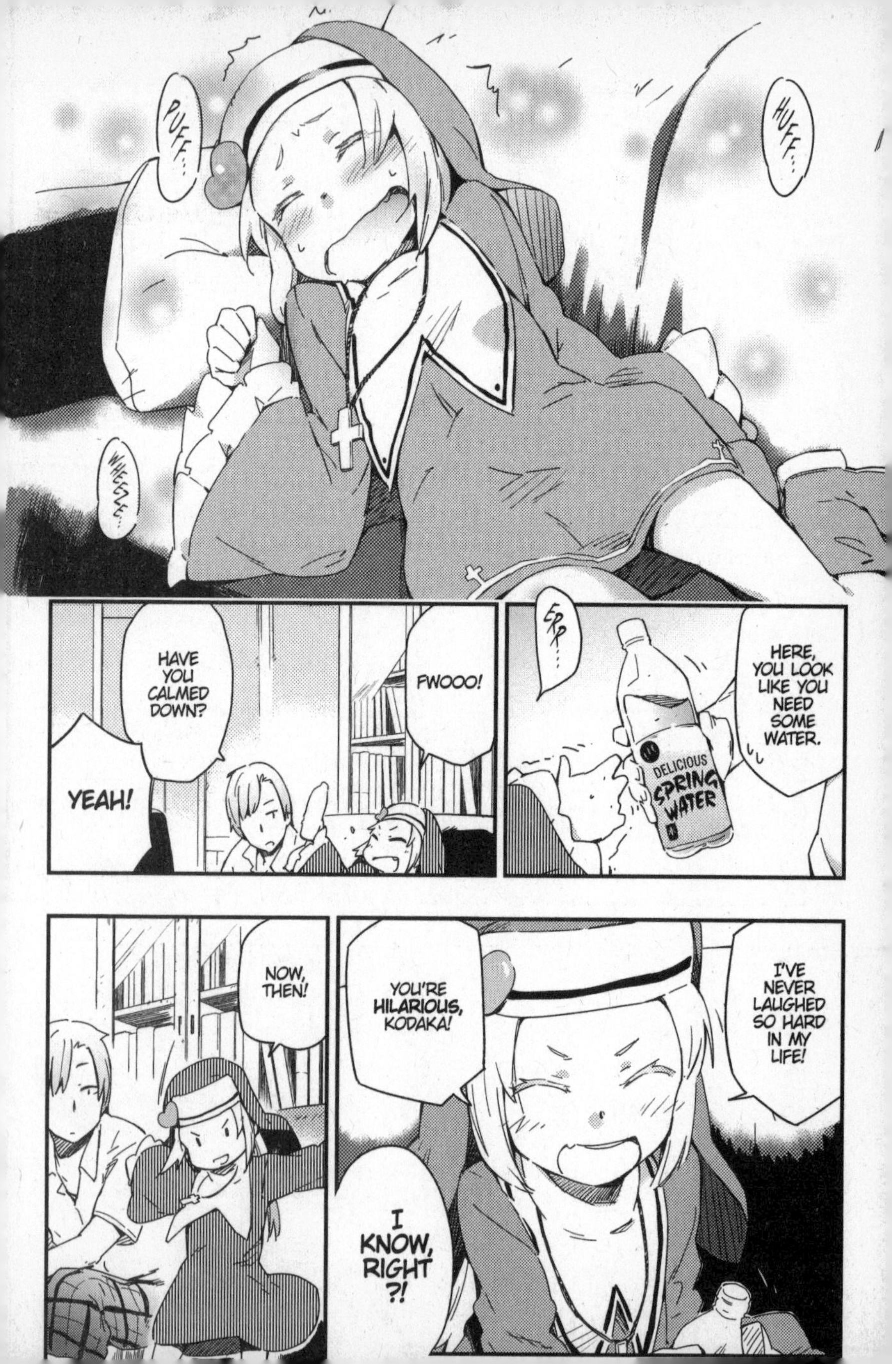
HUFF...
PUFF...
WHEEZE...
HERE, YOU LOOK LIKE YOU NEED SOME WATER.
ERR...
DELICIOUS SPRING WATER
FWOOO!
HAVE YOU CALMED DOWN?
YEAH!
I'VE NEVER LAUGHED SO HARD IN MY LIFE!
YOU'RE HILARIOUS, KODAKA!
I KNOW, RIGHT?!
NOW, THEN!

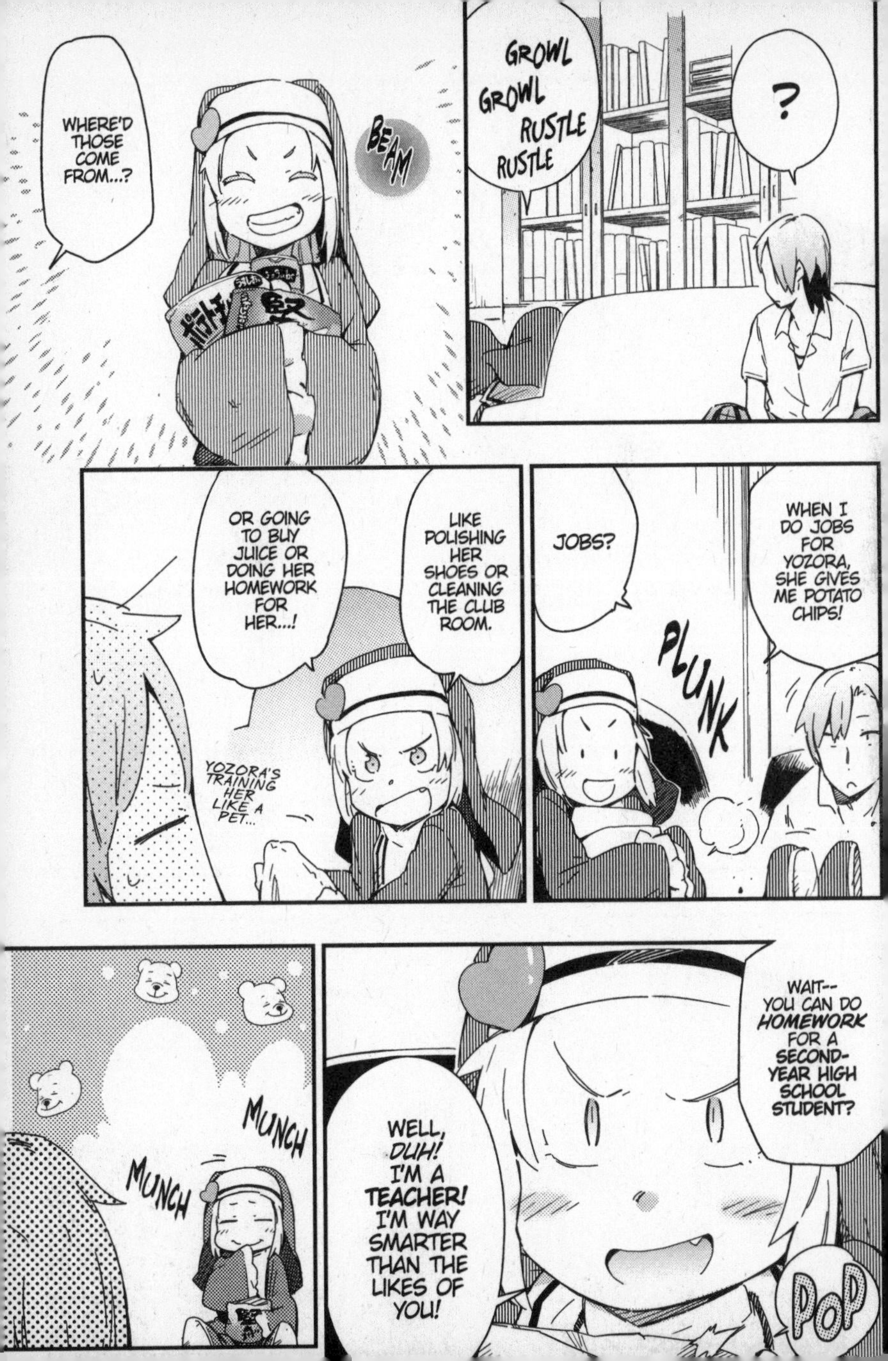
?
GROWL GROWL RUSTLE RUSTLE
WHERE'D THOSE COME FROM...?
BEAM
WHEN I DO JOBS FOR YOZORA, SHE GIVES ME POTATO CHIPS!
JOBS?
PLUNK
LIKE POLISHING HER SHOES OR CLEANING THE CLUB ROOM.
OR GOING TO BUY JUICE OR DOING HER HOMEWORK FOR HER...!
YOZORA'S TRAINING HER LIKE A PET...
WAIT-- YOU CAN DO HOMEWORK FOR A SECOND-YEAR HIGH SCHOOL STUDENT?
WELL, DUH! I'M A TEACHER! I'M WAY SMARTER THAN THE LIKES OF YOU!
POP
MUNCH
MUNCH

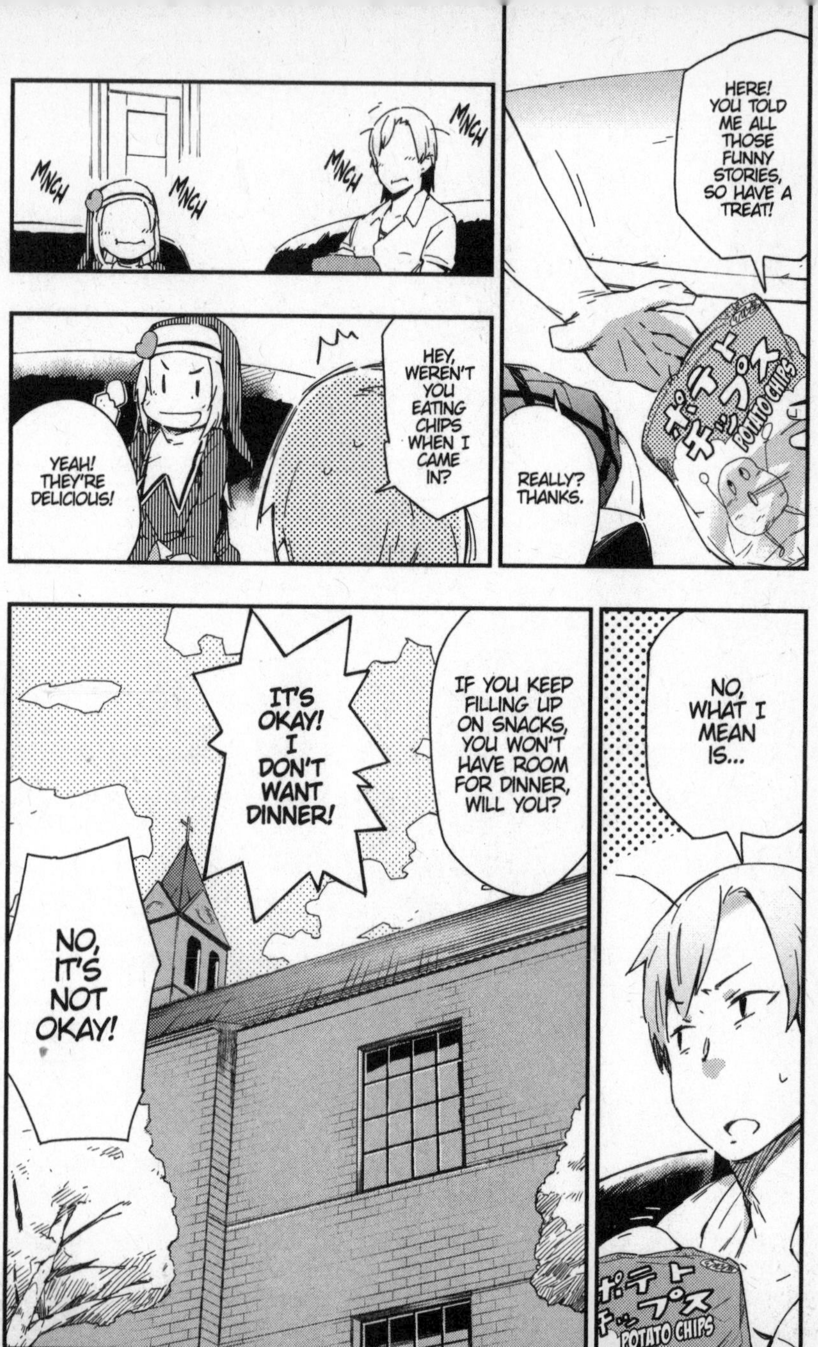
HERE! YOU TOLD ME ALL THOSE FUNNY STORIES, SO HAVE A TREAT!
ポテトチップス POTATO CHIPS
REALLY? THANKS.
MNCH
MNCH
MNCH
MNCH
HEY, WEREN'T YOU EATING CHIPS WHEN I CAME IN?
YEAH! THEY'RE DELICIOUS!
NO, WHAT I MEAN IS...
ポテトチップス POTATO CHIPS
IF YOU KEEP FILLING UP ON SNACKS, YOU WON'T HAVE ROOM FOR DINNER, WILL YOU?
IT'S OKAY! I DON'T WANT DINNER!
NO, IT'S NOT OKAY!

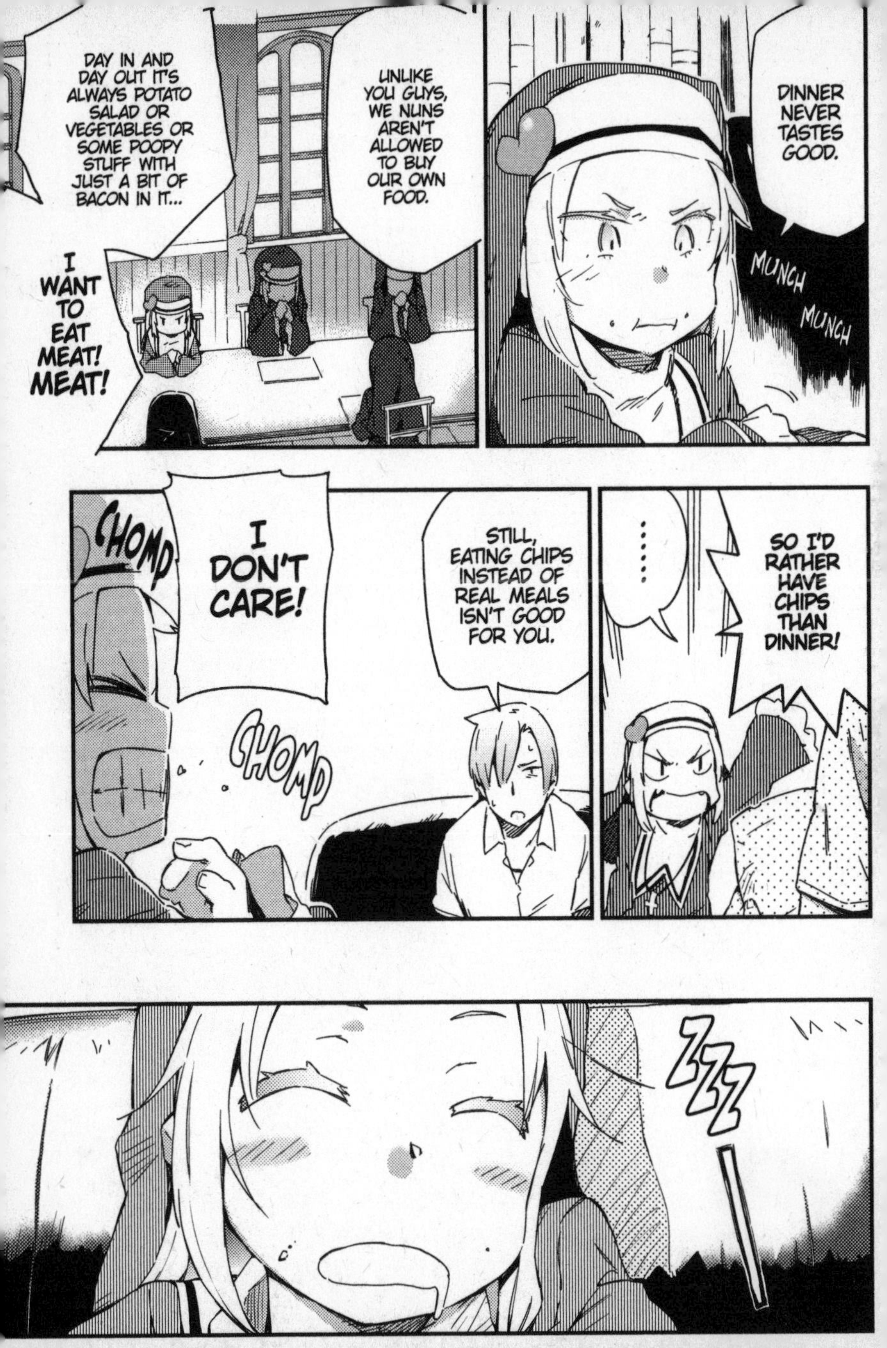
DINNER NEVER TASTES GOOD.
MUNCH
MUNCH
UNLIKE YOU GUYS, WE NUNS AREN'T ALLOWED TO BUY OUR OWN FOOD.
DAY IN AND DAY OUT IT'S ALWAYS POTATO SALAD OR VEGETABLES OR SOME POOPY STUFF WITH JUST A BIT OF BACON IN IT...
I WANT TO EAT MEAT! MEAT!
SO I'D RATHER HAVE CHIPS THAN DINNER!
......
STILL, EATING CHIPS INSTEAD OF REAL MEALS ISN'T GOOD FOR YOU.
I DON'T CARE!
CHOMP
CHOMP
ZZZ

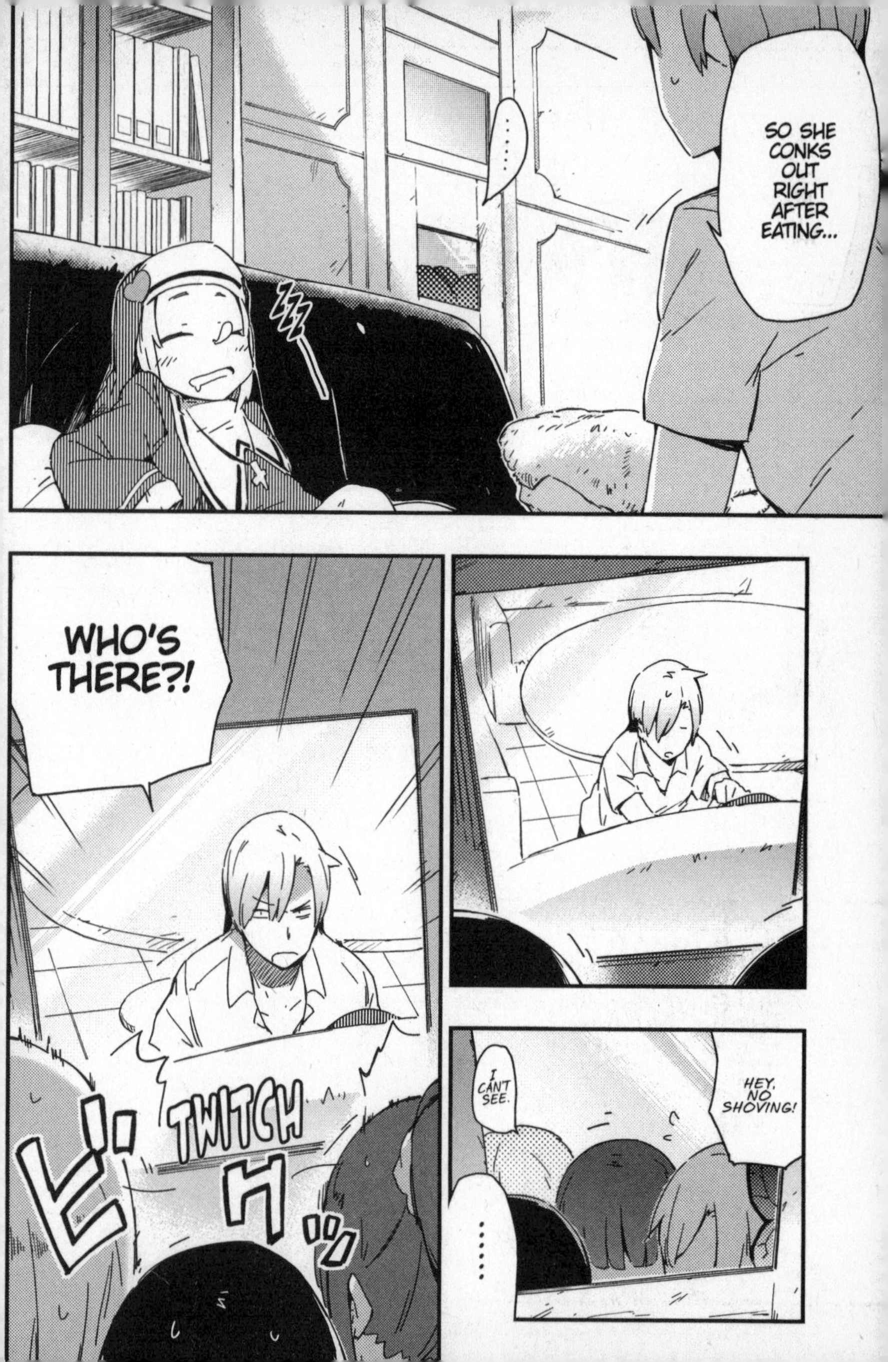
SO SHE CONKS OUT RIGHT AFTER EATING...
...
HEY, NO SHOVING!
I CAN'T SEE.
......
WHO'S THERE?!
ビクッ
TWITCH

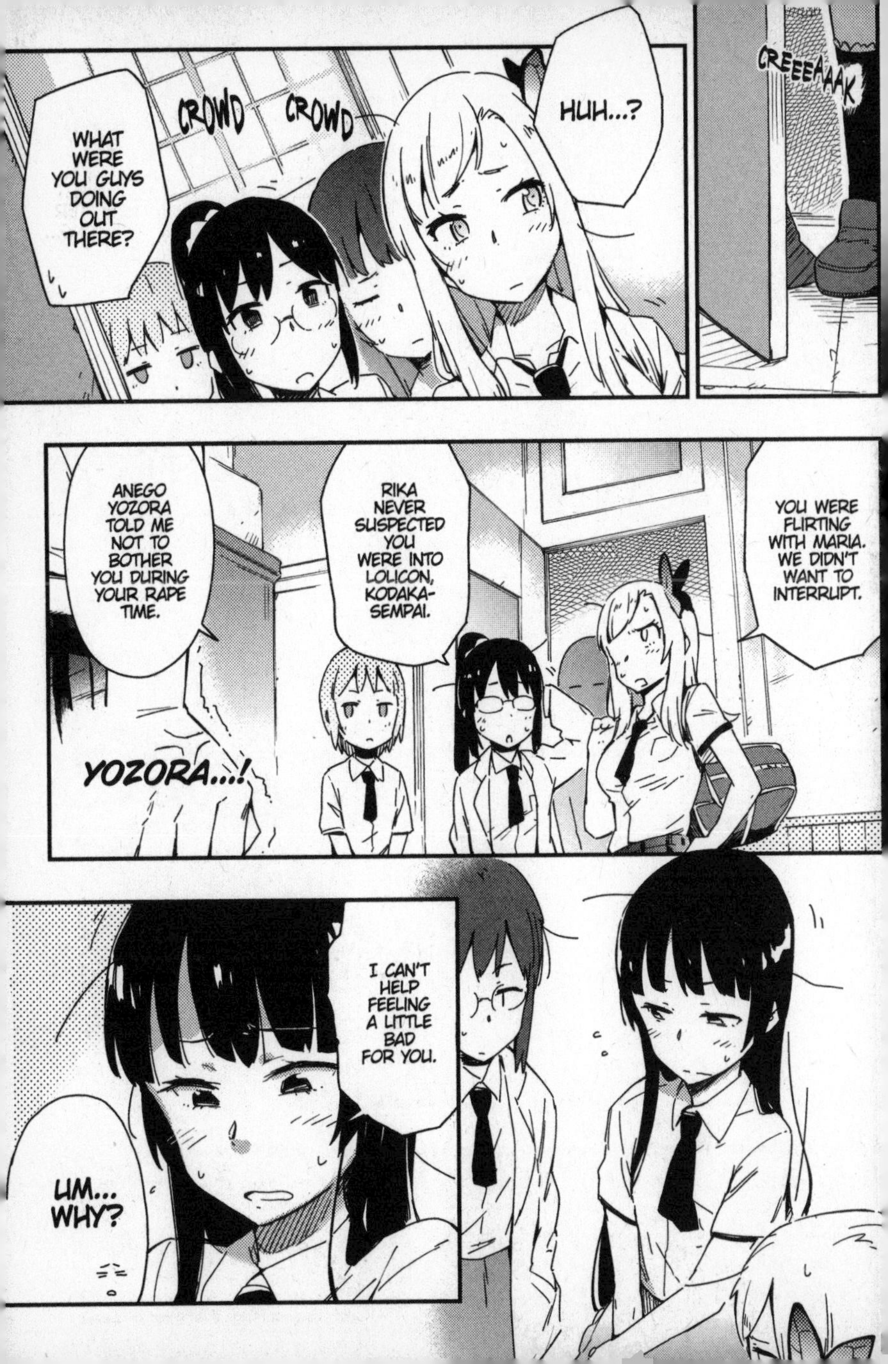
CREEEAAAK
HUH...?
CROWD CROWD
WHAT WERE YOU GUYS DOING OUT THERE?
YOU WERE FLIRTING WITH MARIA. WE DIDN'T WANT TO INTERRUPT.
RIKA NEVER SUSPECTED YOU WERE INTO LOLICON, KODAKA-SEMPAI.
ANEGO YOZORA TOLD ME NOT TO BOTHER YOU DURING YOUR RAPE TIME.
YOZORA...!
I CAN'T HELP FEELING A LITTLE BAD FOR YOU.
UM... WHY?

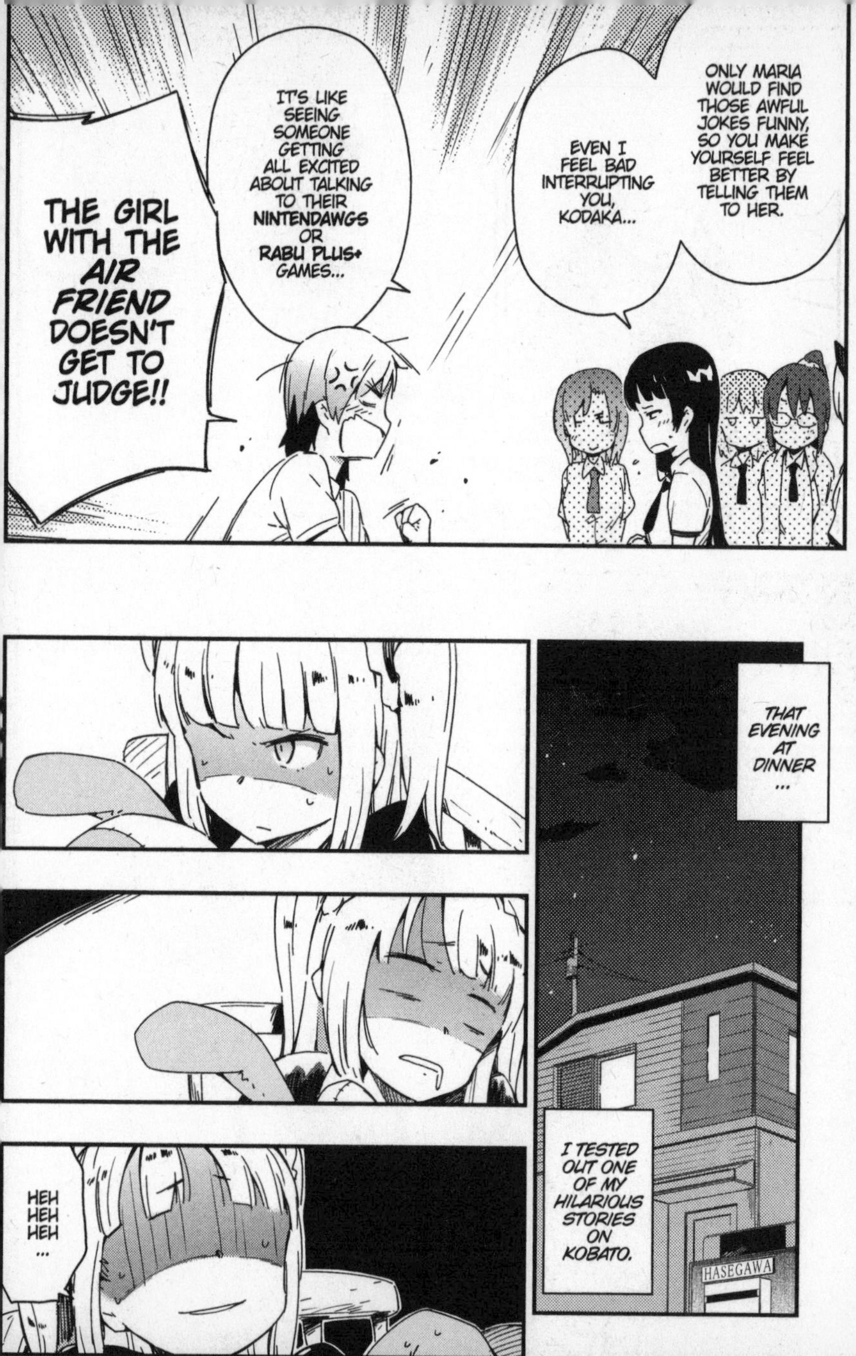
ONLY MARIA WOULD FIND THOSE AWFUL JOKES FUNNY, SO YOU MAKE YOURSELF FEEL BETTER BY TELLING THEM TO HER.
EVEN I FEEL BAD INTERRUPTING YOU, KODAKA...
IT'S LIKE SEEING SOMEONE GETTING ALL EXCITED ABOUT TALKING TO THEIR NINTENDAWGS OR RABU PLUS+ GAMES...
THE GIRL WITH THE *AIR FRIEND* DOESN'T GET TO JUDGE!!
THAT EVENING AT DINNER ...
I TESTED OUT ONE OF MY HILARIOUS STORIES ON KOBATO.
HASEGAWA
HEH HEH HEH ...

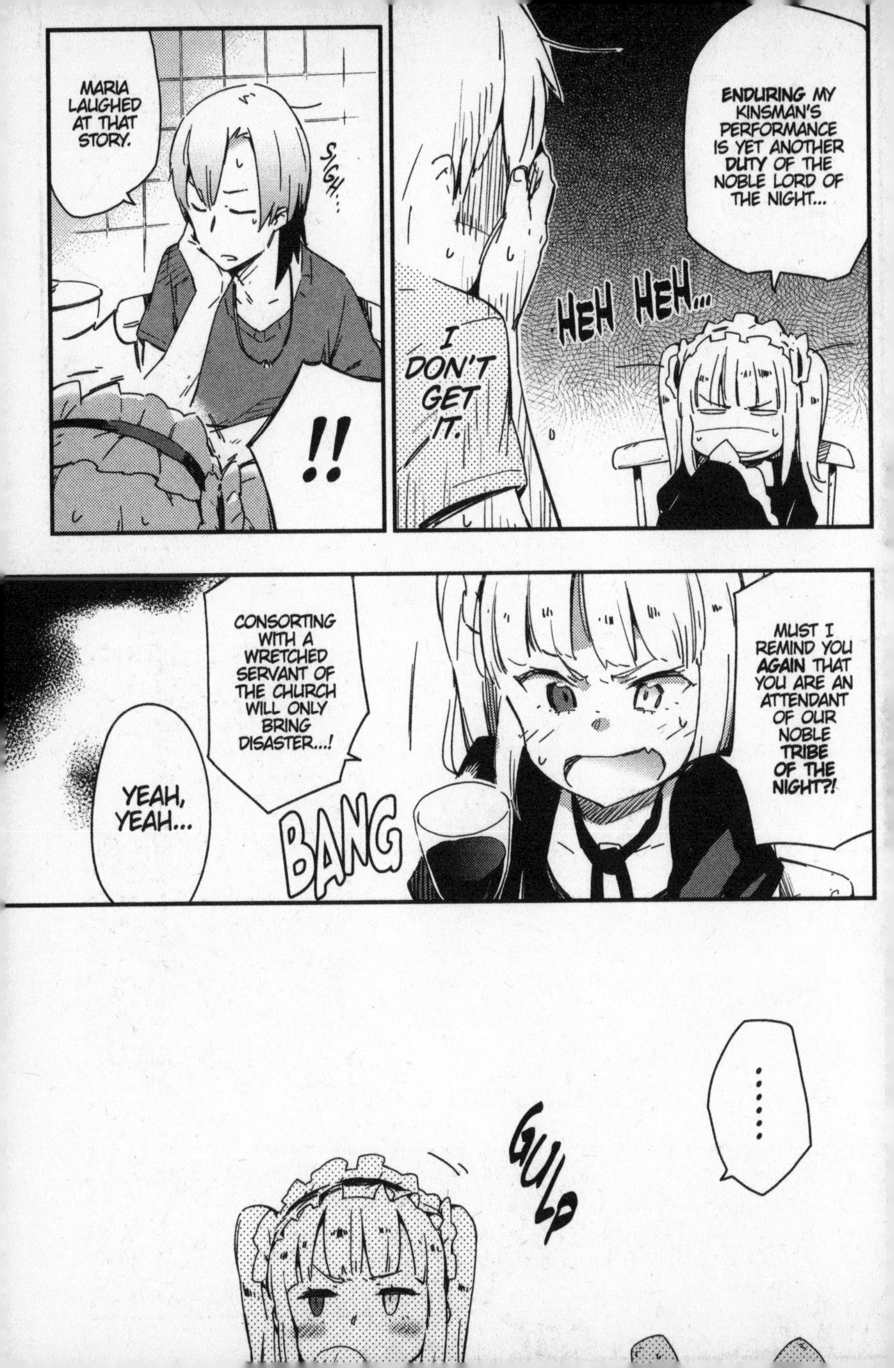
ENDURING MY KINSMAN'S PERFORMANCE IS YET ANOTHER DUTY OF THE NOBLE LORD OF THE NIGHT...
HEH HEH...
I DON'T GET IT.
MARIA LAUGHED AT THAT STORY.
SIGH...
!!
MUST I REMIND YOU AGAIN THAT YOU ARE AN ATTENDANT OF OUR NOBLE TRIBE OF THE NIGHT?!
CONSORTING WITH A WRETCHED SERVANT OF THE CHURCH WILL ONLY BRING DISASTER...!
BANG
YEAH, YEAH...
......
GULP

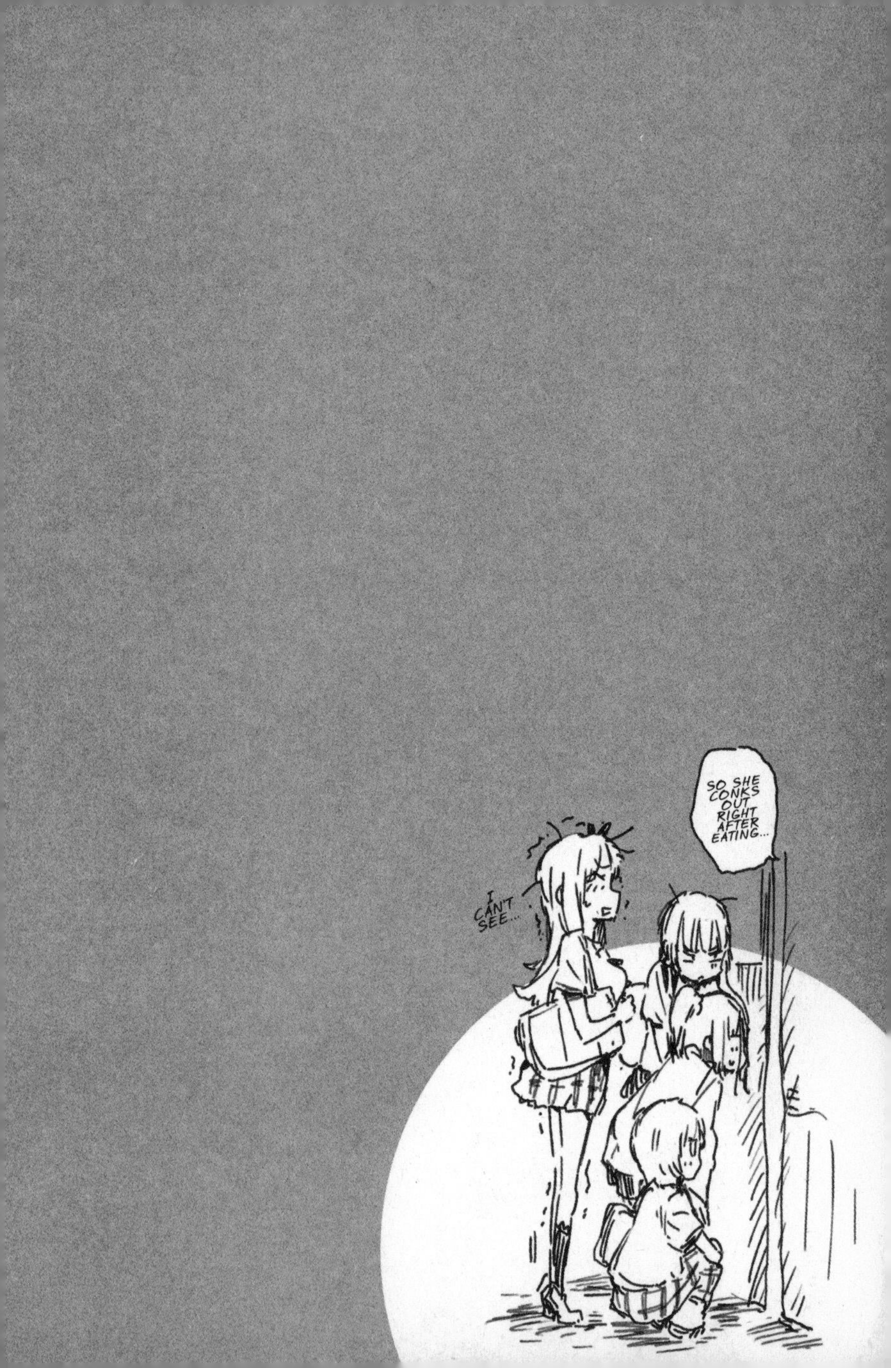
SO SHE CONKS OUT RIGHT AFTER EATING...
I CAN'T SEE...

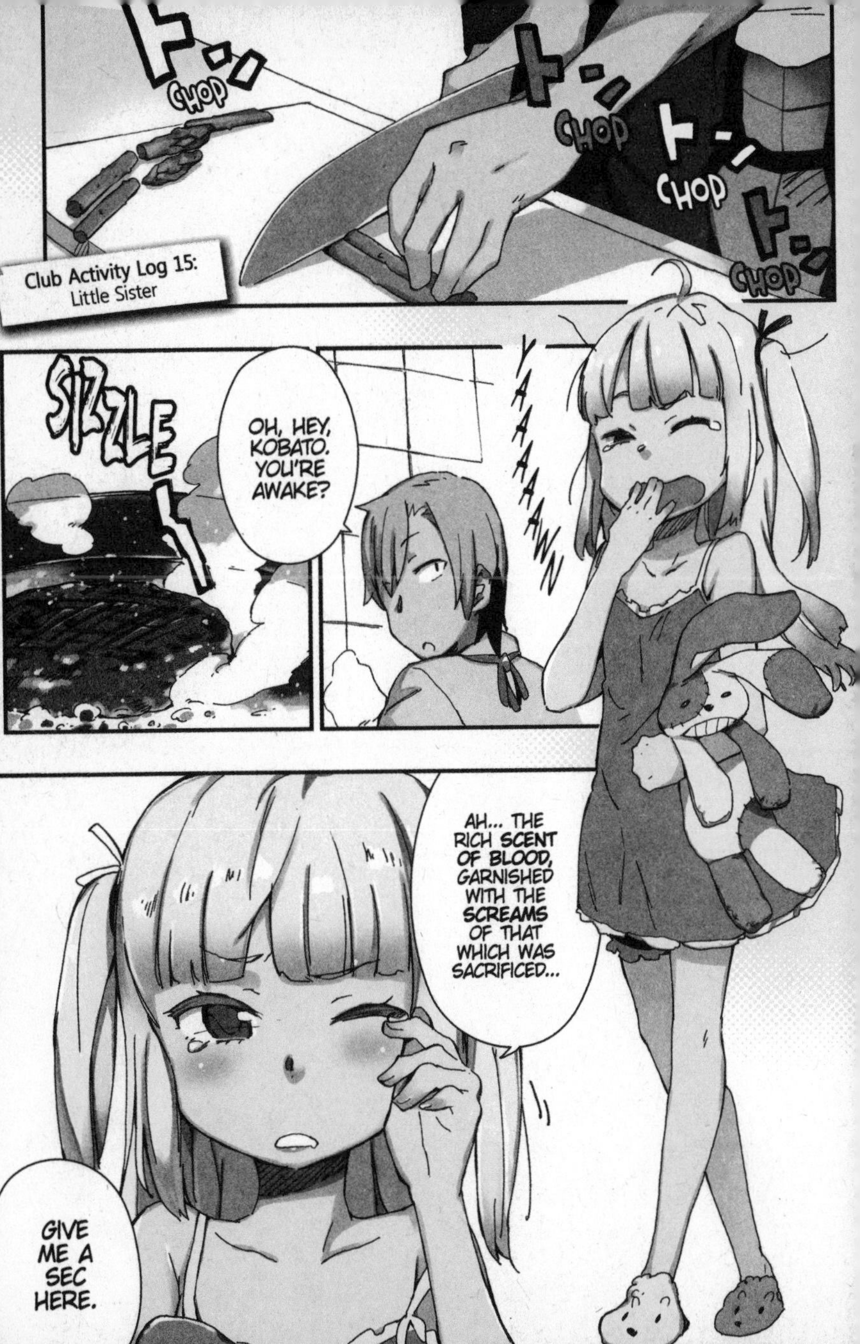
CHOP
CHOP
CHOP
CHOP
Club Activity Log 15:
Little Sister
YAAAAAAAAWN
OH, HEY, KOBATO. YOU'RE AWAKE?
SIZZLE
AH... THE RICH SCENT OF BLOOD, GARNISHED WITH THE SCREAMS OF THAT WHICH WAS SACRIFICED...
GIVE ME A SEC HERE.

Haganai

I don't have many friends

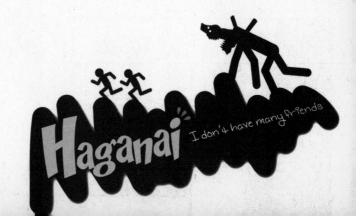

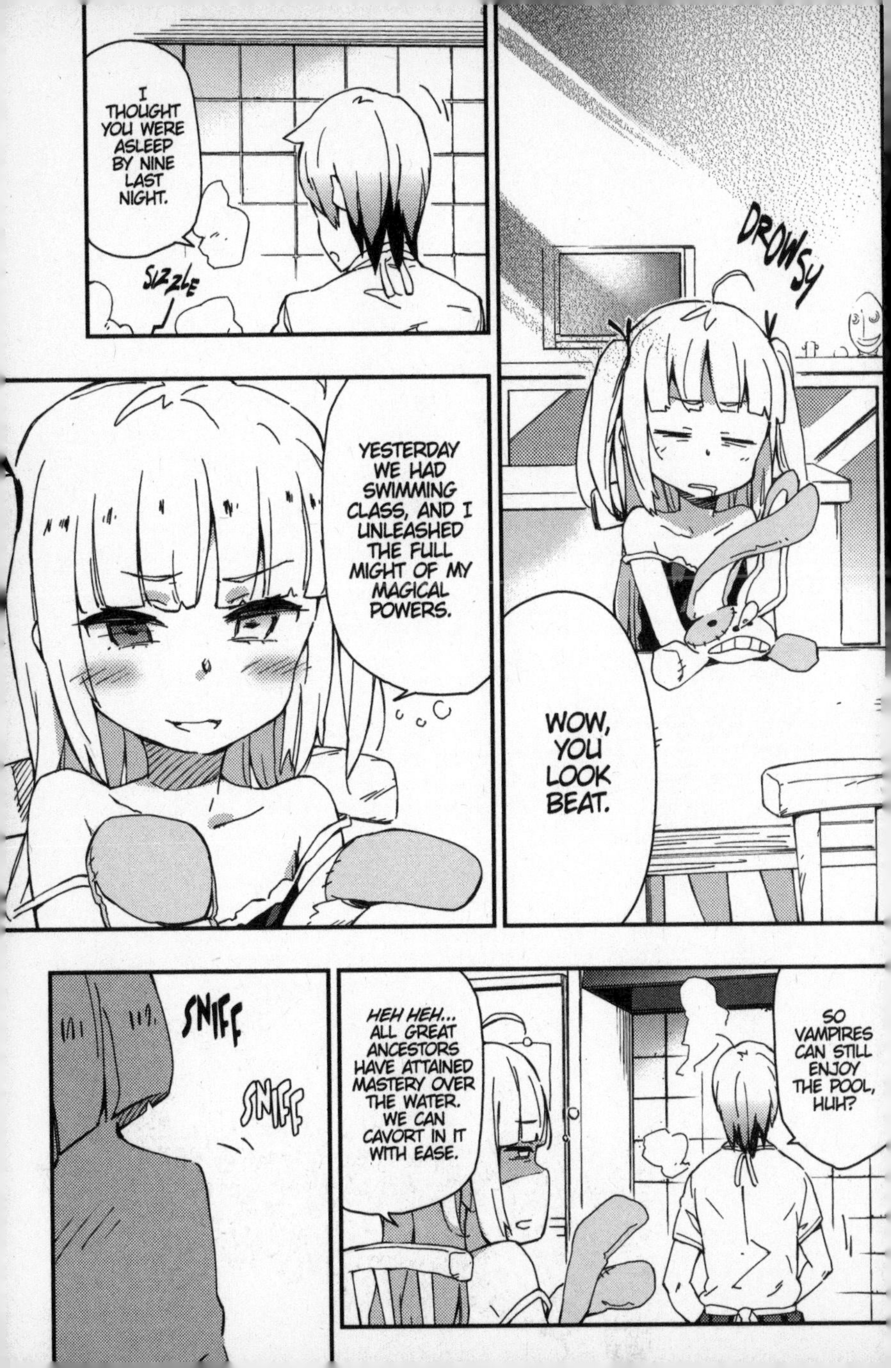
DROWSY
WOW, YOU LOOK BEAT.
I THOUGHT YOU WERE ASLEEP BY NINE LAST NIGHT.
SIZZLE
YESTERDAY WE HAD SWIMMING CLASS, AND I UNLEASHED THE FULL MIGHT OF MY MAGICAL POWERS.
SO VAMPIRES CAN STILL ENJOY THE POOL, HUH?
HEH HEH... ALL GREAT ANCESTORS HAVE ATTAINED MASTERY OVER THE WATER. WE CAN CAVORT IN IT WITH EASE.
SNIFF
SNIFF

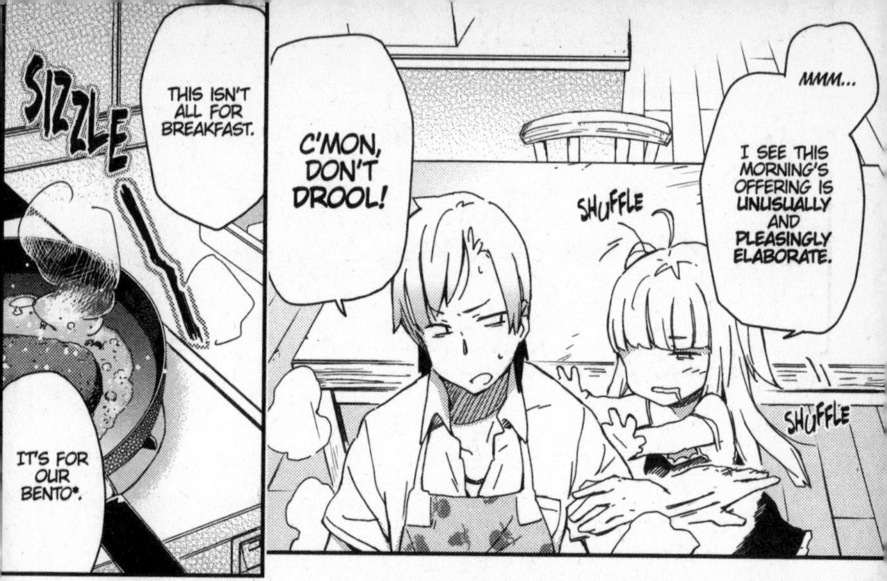
MMM...
I SEE THIS MORNING'S OFFERING IS UNUSUALLY AND PLEASINGLY ELABORATE.
SHUFFLE
SHUFFLE
C'MON, DON'T DROOL!
SIZZLE
THIS ISN'T ALL FOR BREAKFAST.
IT'S FOR OUR BENTO*.

*A packed meal containing a variety of foods. They can be purchased at convenience stores, but homemade bento require a lot of time and effort and are accordingly romanticized.

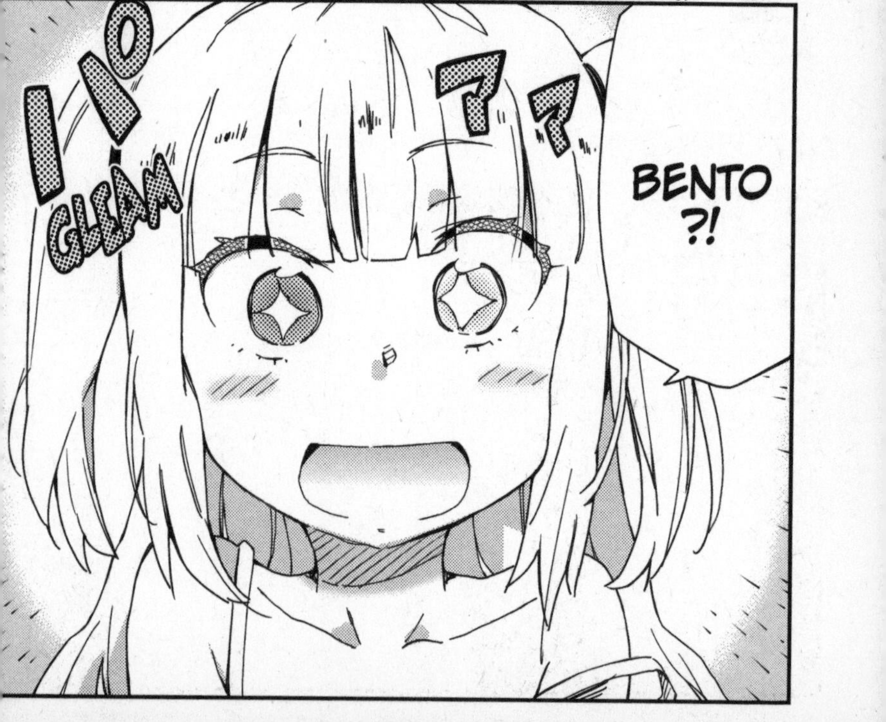
BENTO ?!
パアア
GLEAM

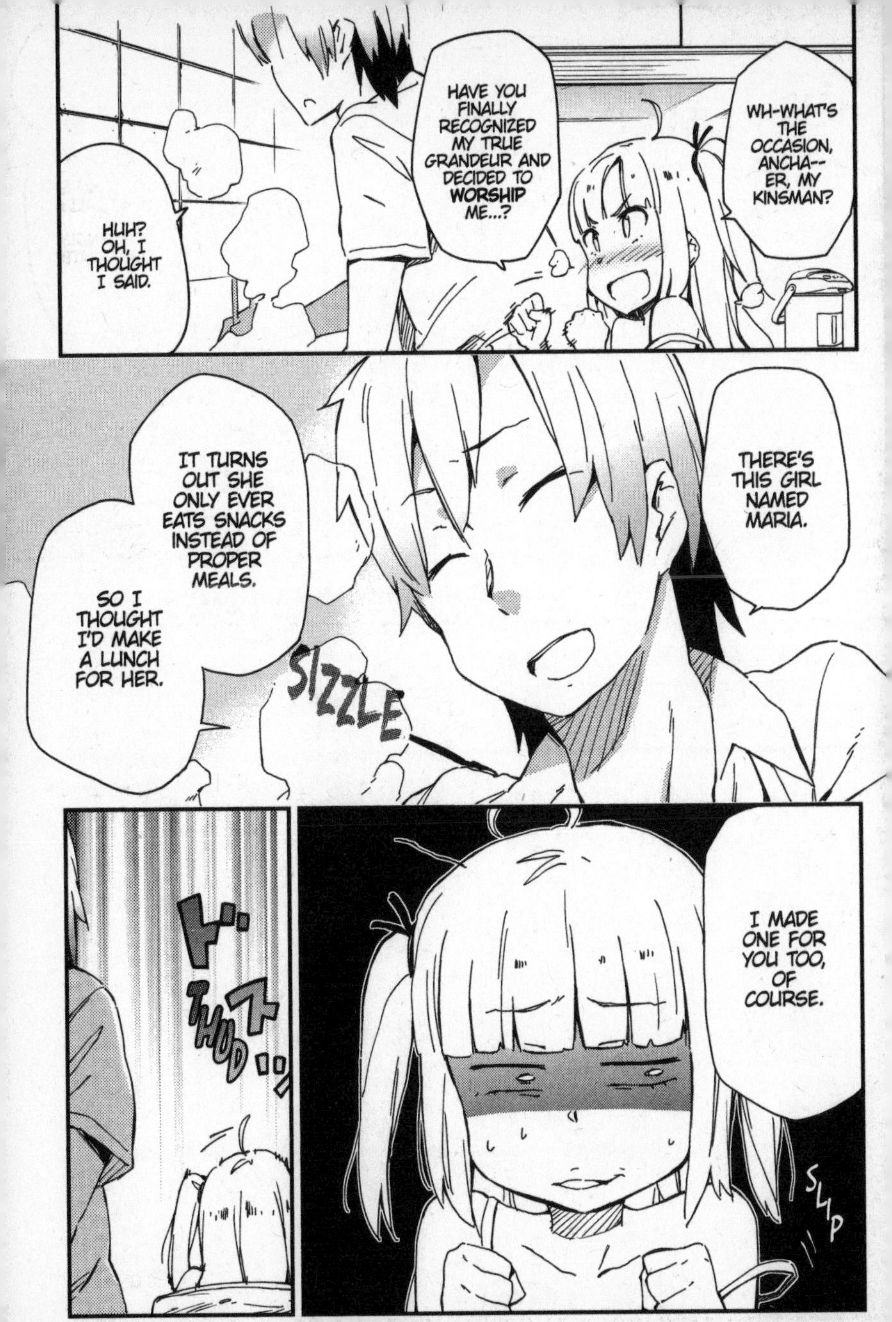
WH-WHAT'S THE OCCASION, ANCHA-- ER, MY KINSMAN?
HAVE YOU FINALLY RECOGNIZED MY TRUE GRANDEUR AND DECIDED TO WORSHIP ME...?
HUH? OH, I THOUGHT I SAID.
THERE'S THIS GIRL NAMED MARIA.
IT TURNS OUT SHE ONLY EVER EATS SNACKS INSTEAD OF PROPER MEALS.
SO I THOUGHT I'D MAKE A LUNCH FOR HER.
SIZZLE
I MADE ONE FOR YOU TOO, OF COURSE.
SLIP
THUD

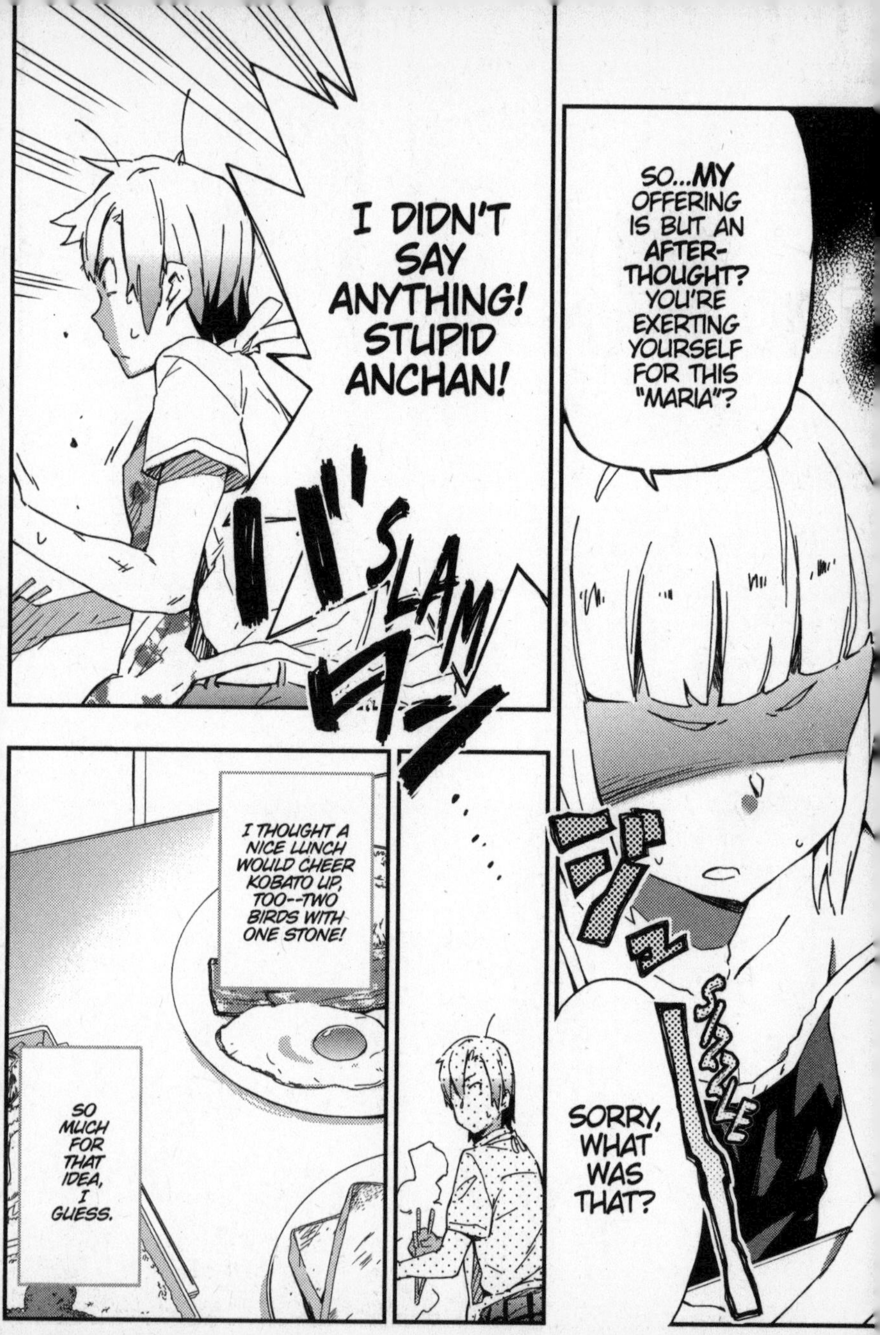
SO...MY OFFERING IS BUT AN AFTER-THOUGHT? YOU'RE EXERTING YOURSELF FOR THIS "MARIA"?
SIZZLE
SORRY, WHAT WAS THAT?
I DIDN'T SAY ANYTHING! STUPID ANCHAN!
SLAM
...
I THOUGHT A NICE LUNCH WOULD CHEER KOBATO UP, TOO--TWO BIRDS WITH ONE STONE!
SO MUCH FOR THAT IDEA, I GUESS.

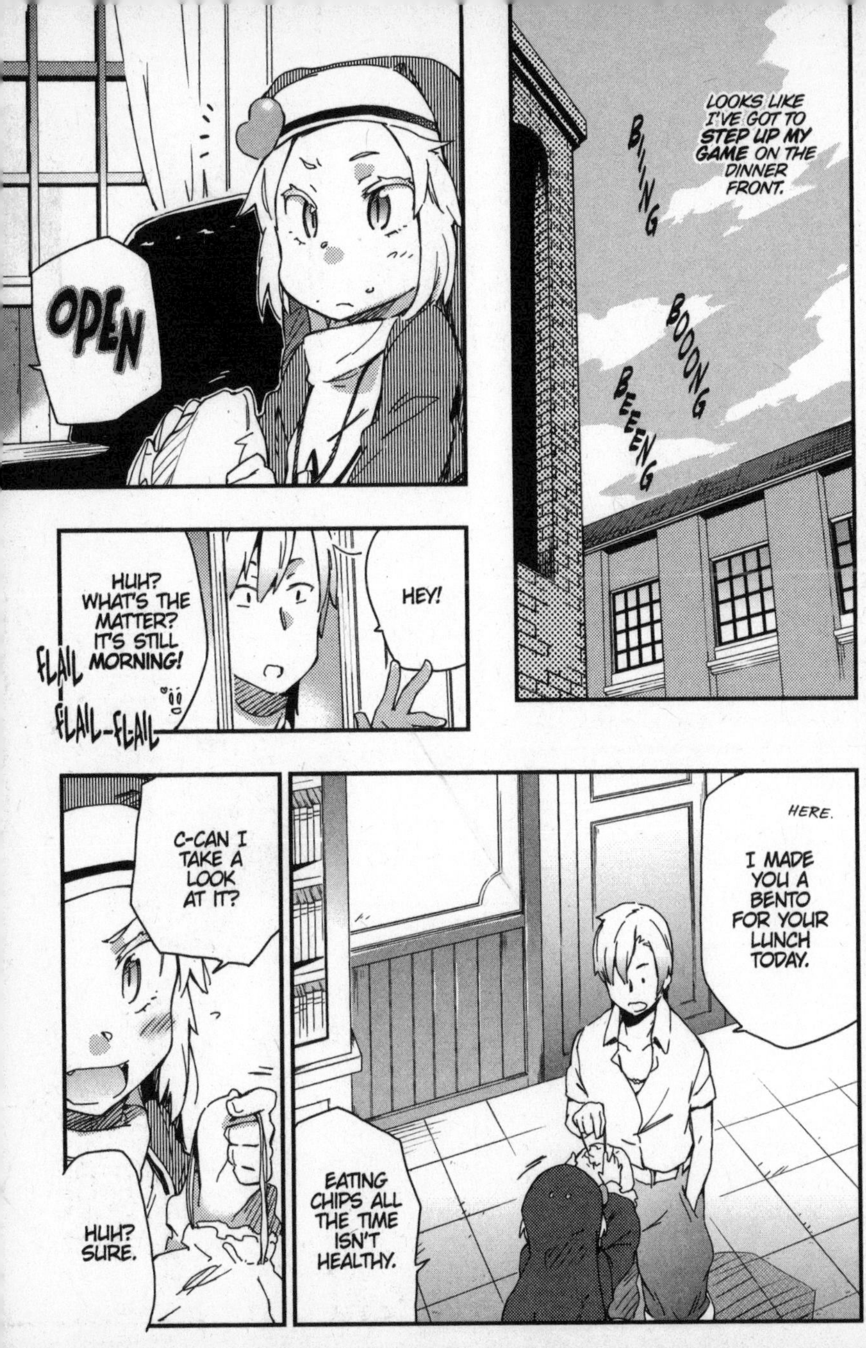
LOOKS LIKE I'VE GOT TO **STEP UP MY GAME** ON THE DINNER FRONT.
BIIING
BOOONG
BEEENG
OPEN
HEY!
HUH? WHAT'S THE MATTER? IT'S STILL MORNING!
FLAIL
FLAIL-FLAIL
HERE.
I MADE YOU A BENTO FOR YOUR LUNCH TODAY.
EATING CHIPS ALL THE TIME ISN'T HEALTHY.
C-CAN I TAKE A LOOK AT IT?
HUH? SURE.

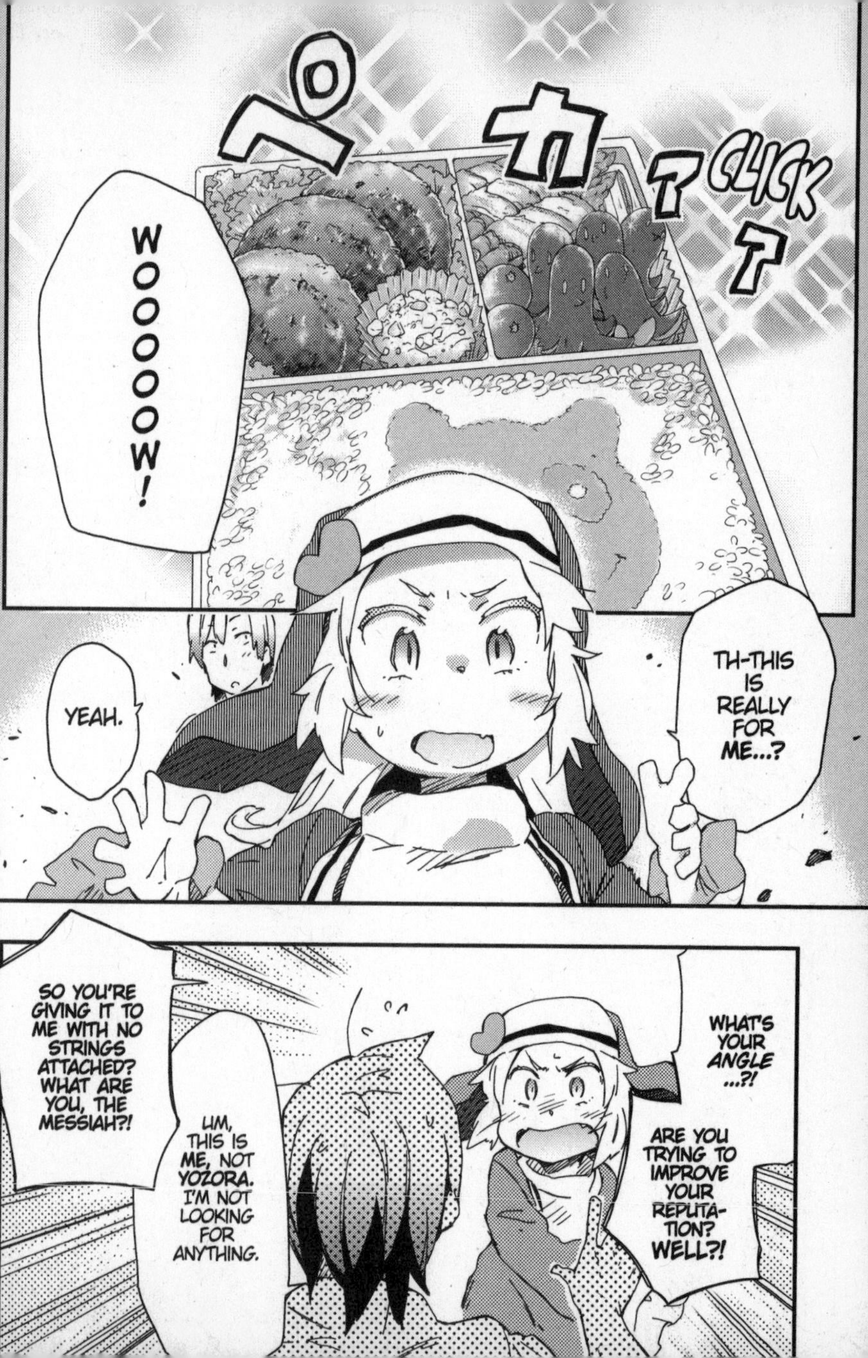
CLICK
パカァァ
WOOOOOOW!
TH-THIS IS REALLY FOR ME...?
YEAH.
WHAT'S YOUR ANGLE ...?!
SO YOU'RE GIVING IT TO ME WITH NO STRINGS ATTACHED? WHAT ARE YOU, THE MESSIAH?!
ARE YOU TRYING TO IMPROVE YOUR REPUTA-TION? WELL?!
UM, THIS IS ME, NOT YOZORA. I'M NOT LOOKING FOR ANYTHING.

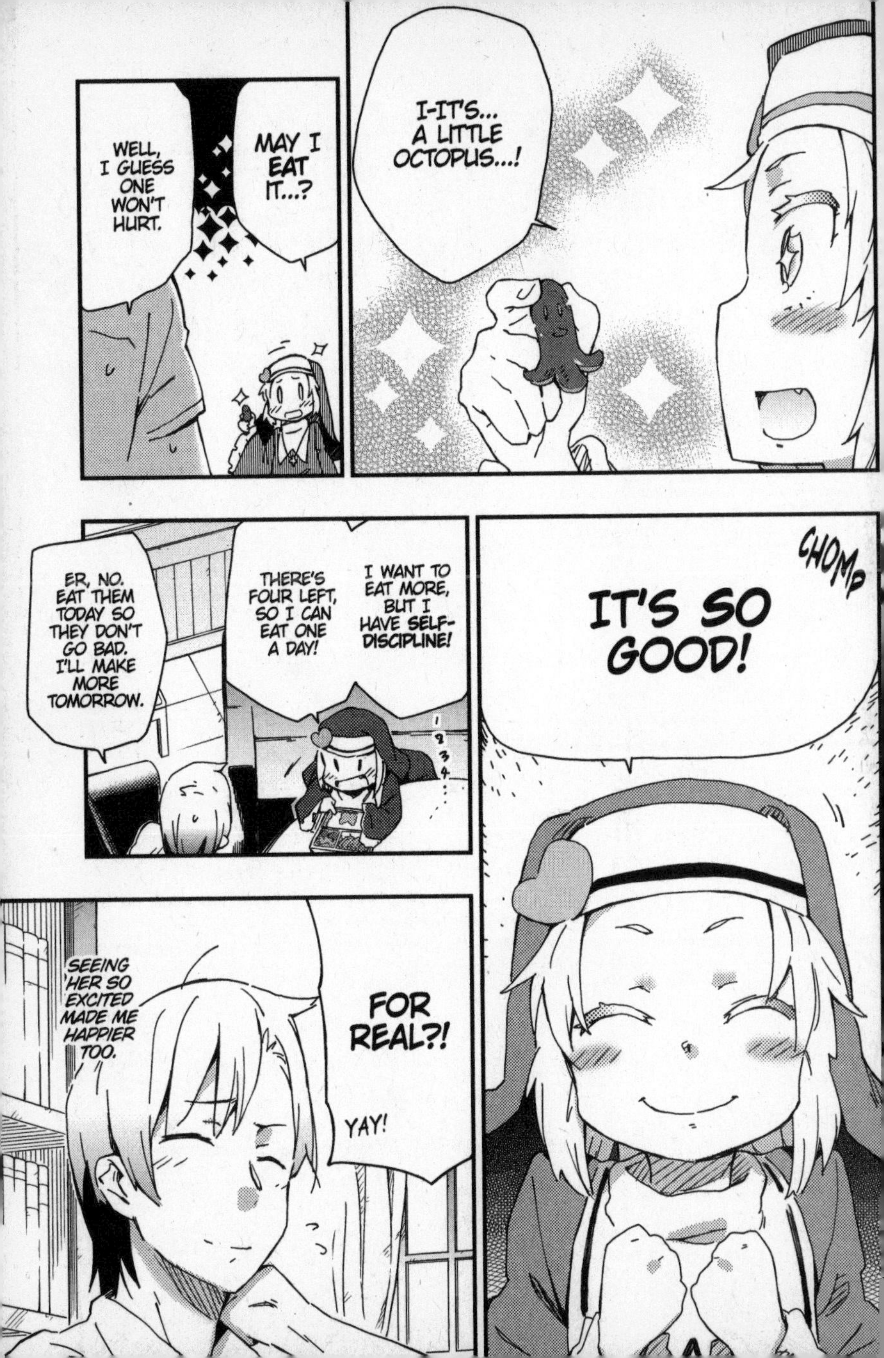

I-IT'S... A LITTLE OCTOPUS...!
MAY I EAT IT...?
WELL, I GUESS ONE WON'T HURT.
CHOMP
IT'S SO GOOD!
I WANT TO EAT MORE, BUT I HAVE SELF-DISCIPLINE!
THERE'S FOUR LEFT, SO I CAN EAT ONE A DAY!
ER, NO. EAT THEM TODAY SO THEY DON'T GO BAD. I'LL MAKE MORE TOMORROW.
FOR REAL?!
YAY!
SEEING HER SO EXCITED MADE ME HAPPIER TOO.

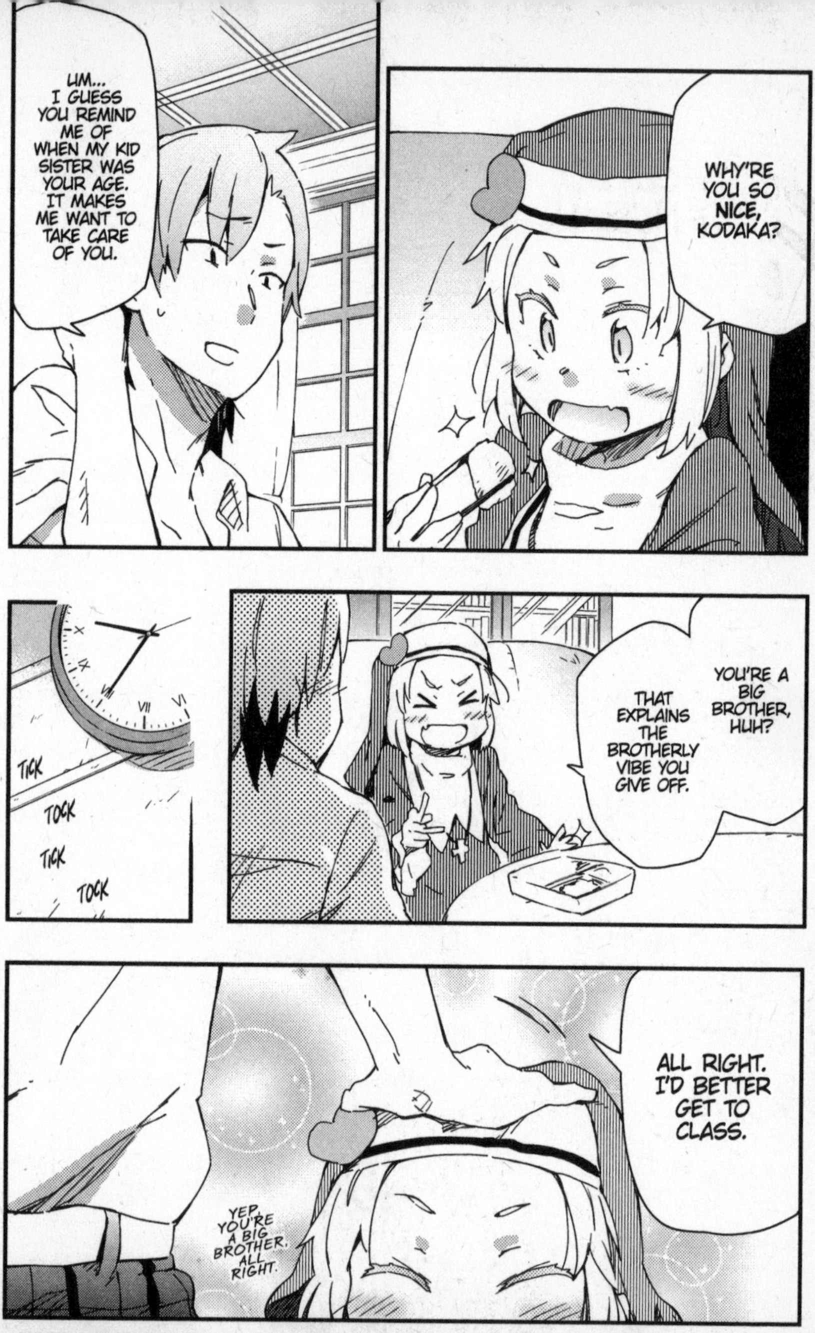
WHY'RE YOU SO NICE, KODAKA?
UM... I GUESS YOU REMIND ME OF WHEN MY KID SISTER WAS YOUR AGE. IT MAKES ME WANT TO TAKE CARE OF YOU.
YOU'RE A BIG BROTHER, HUH?
THAT EXPLAINS THE BROTHERLY VIBE YOU GIVE OFF.
TICK
TOCK
TICK
TOCK
ALL RIGHT. I'D BETTER GET TO CLASS.
YEP, YOU'RE A BIG BROTHER, ALL RIGHT.

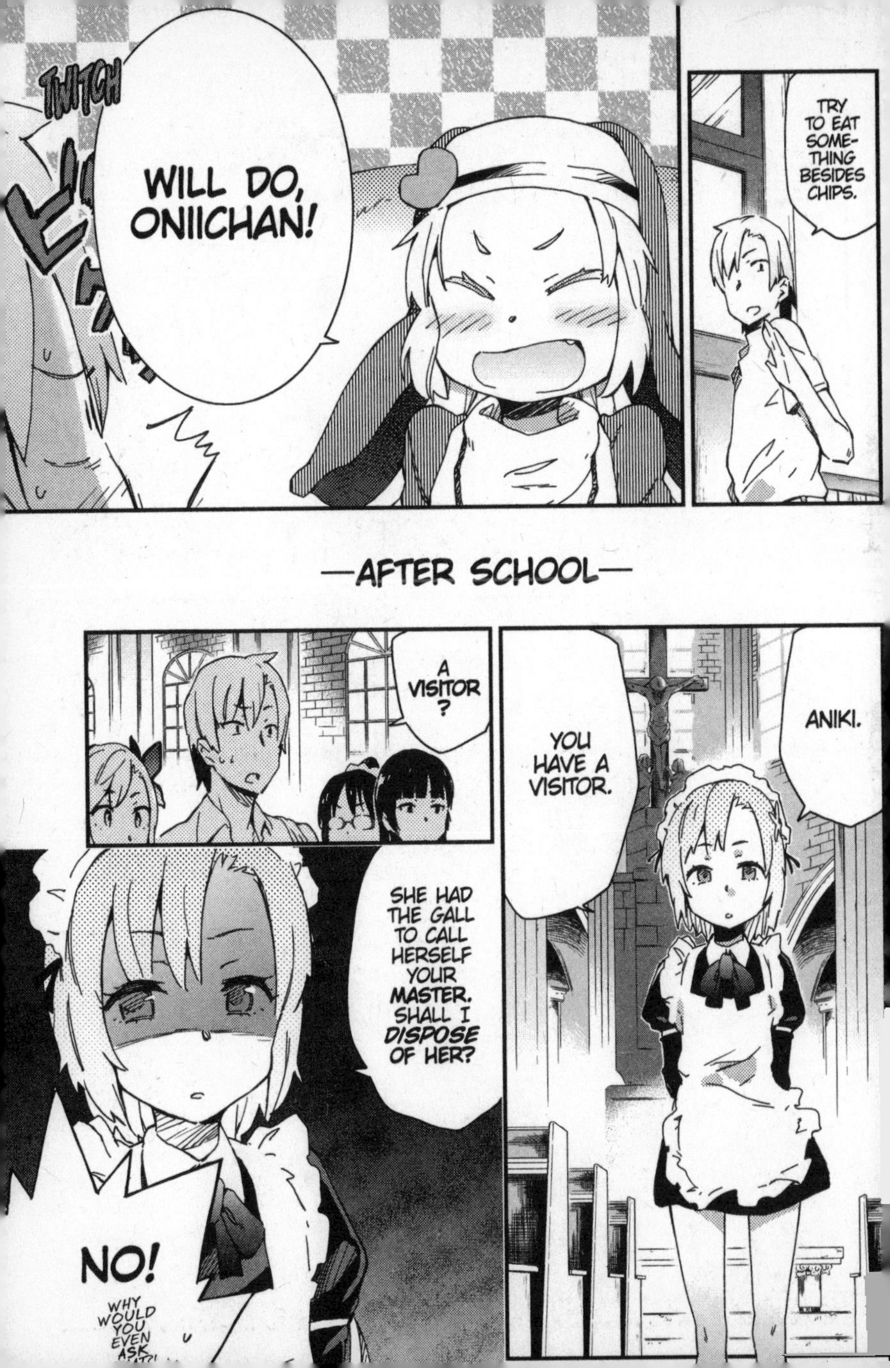

TRY TO EAT SOMETHING BESIDES CHIPS.
TWITCH
WILL DO, ONIICHAN!
—AFTER SCHOOL—
ANIKI.
YOU HAVE A VISITOR.
A VISITOR?
SHE HAD THE GALL TO CALL HERSELF YOUR MASTER. SHALL I DISPOSE OF HER?
NO!
WHY WOULD YOU EVEN ASK

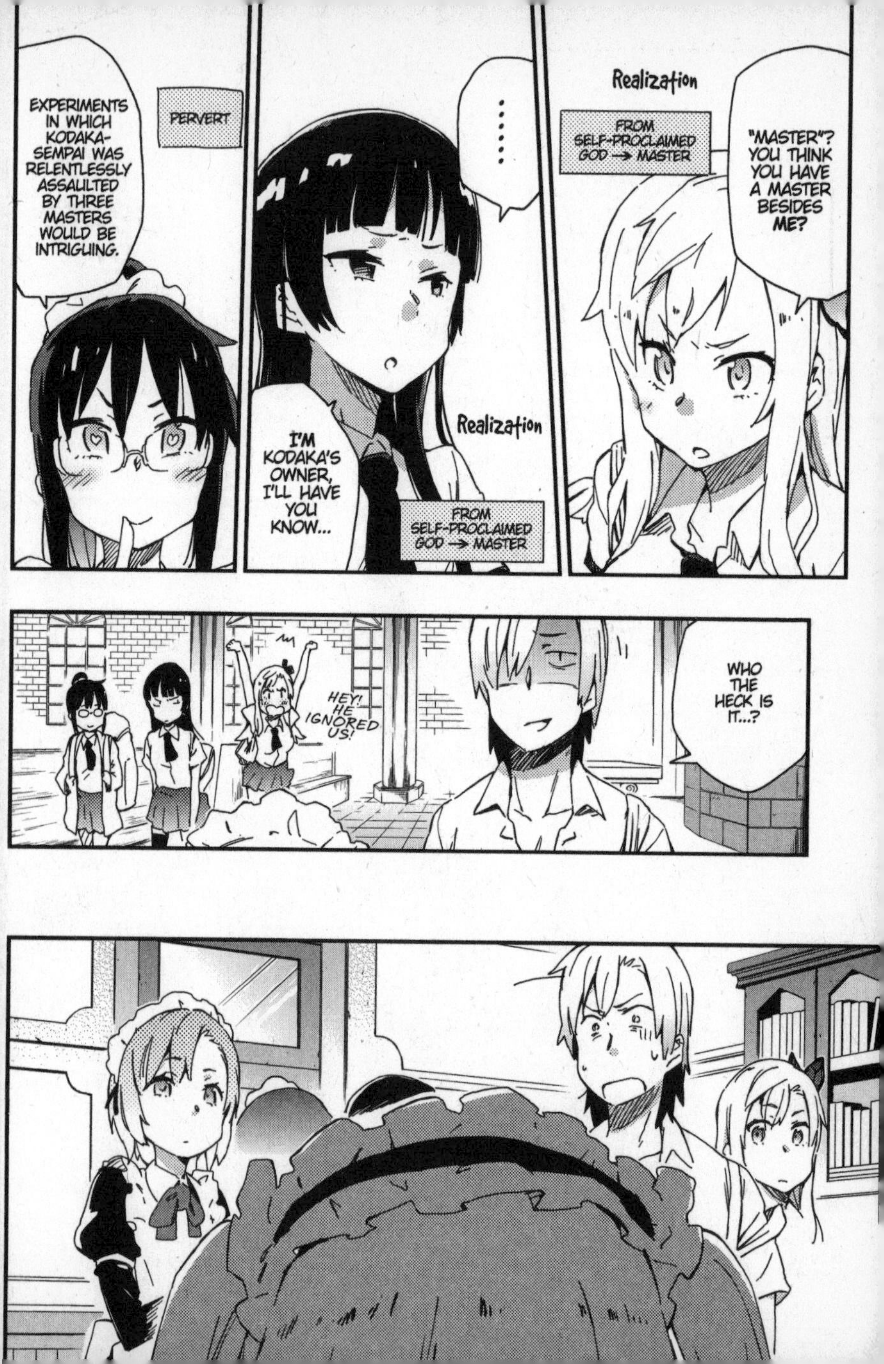
Realization
FROM SELF-PROCLAIMED GOD → MASTER
"MASTER"? YOU THINK YOU HAVE A MASTER BESIDES ME?
......
Realization
I'M KODAKA'S OWNER, I'LL HAVE YOU KNOW...
FROM SELF-PROCLAIMED GOD → MASTER
PERVERT
EXPERIMENTS IN WHICH KODAKA-SEMPAI WAS RELENTLESSLY ASSAULTED BY THREE MASTERS WOULD BE INTRIGUING.
WHO THE HECK IS IT...?
HEY! HE IGNORED US!

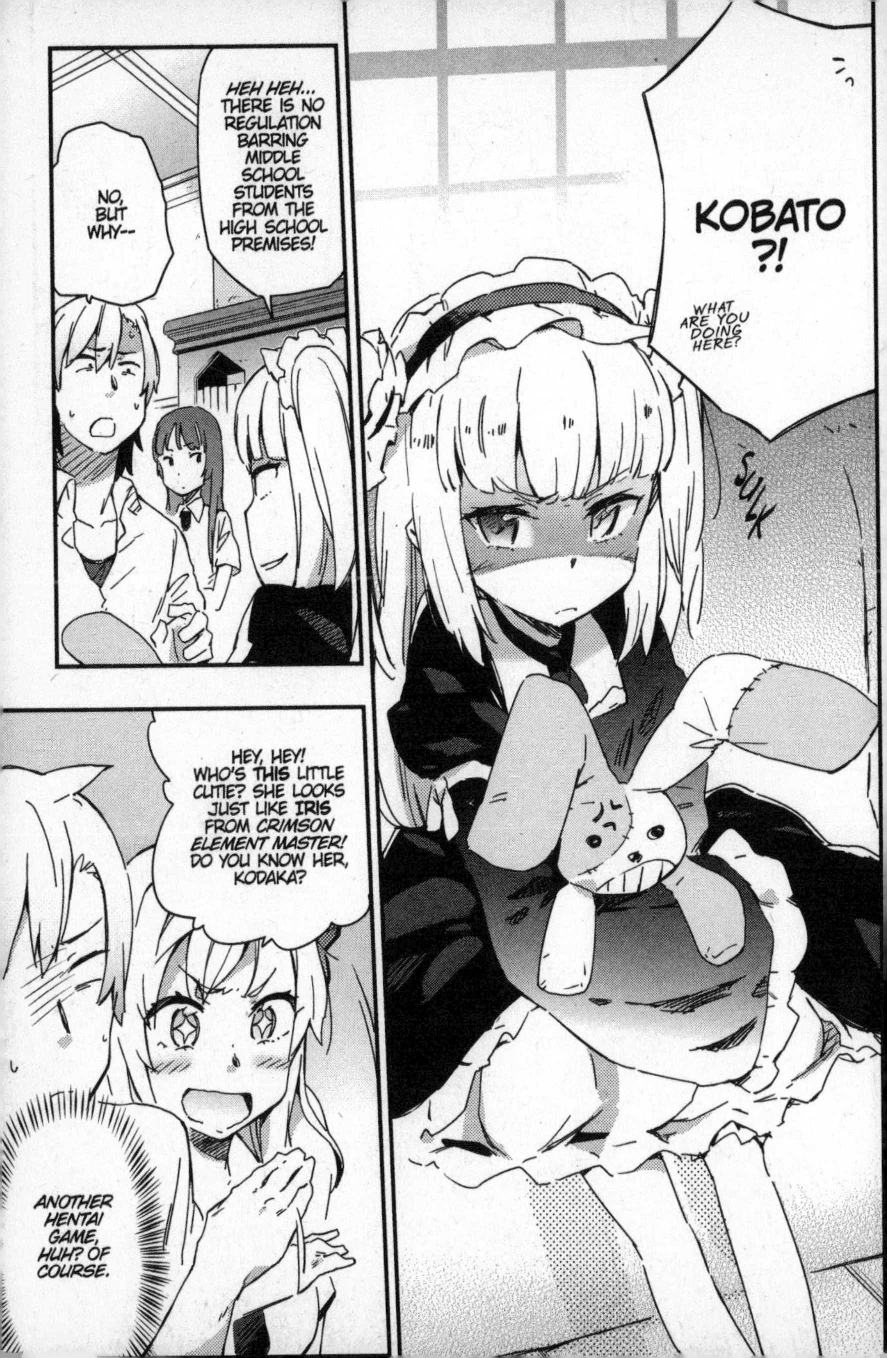
KOBATO ?!
WHAT ARE YOU DOING HERE?
SULK
HEH HEH... THERE IS NO REGULATION BARRING MIDDLE SCHOOL STUDENTS FROM THE HIGH SCHOOL PREMISES!
NO, BUT WHY--
HEY, HEY! WHO'S THIS LITTLE CUTIE? SHE LOOKS JUST LIKE IRIS FROM CRIMSON ELEMENT MASTER! DO YOU KNOW HER, KODAKA?
ANOTHER HENTAI GAME, HUH? OF COURSE.

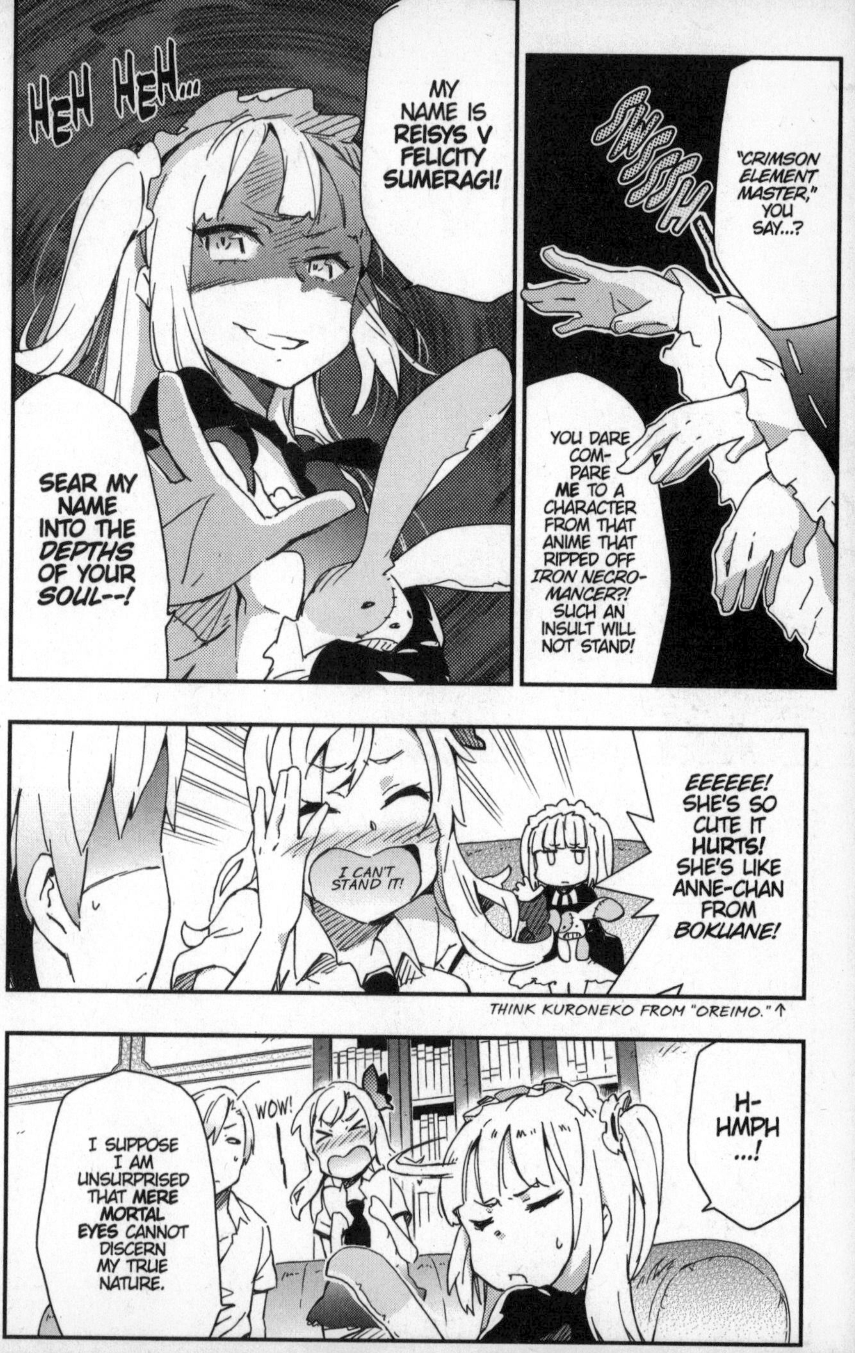
"CRIMSON ELEMENT MASTER," YOU SAY...?
YOU DARE COMPARE ME TO A CHARACTER FROM THAT ANIME THAT RIPPED OFF *IRON NECROMANCER*?! SUCH AN INSULT WILL NOT STAND!
MY NAME IS REISYS V FELICITY SUMERAGI!
HEH HEH...
SEAR MY NAME INTO THE *DEPTHS* OF YOUR SOUL--!
EEEEEE! SHE'S SO CUTE IT HURTS! SHE'S LIKE ANNE-CHAN FROM *BOKUANE!*
I CAN'T STAND IT!
THINK KURONEKO FROM "OREIMO." ↑
H-HMPH ...!
WOW!
I SUPPOSE I AM UNSURPRISED THAT MERE MORTAL EYES CANNOT DISCERN MY TRUE NATURE.

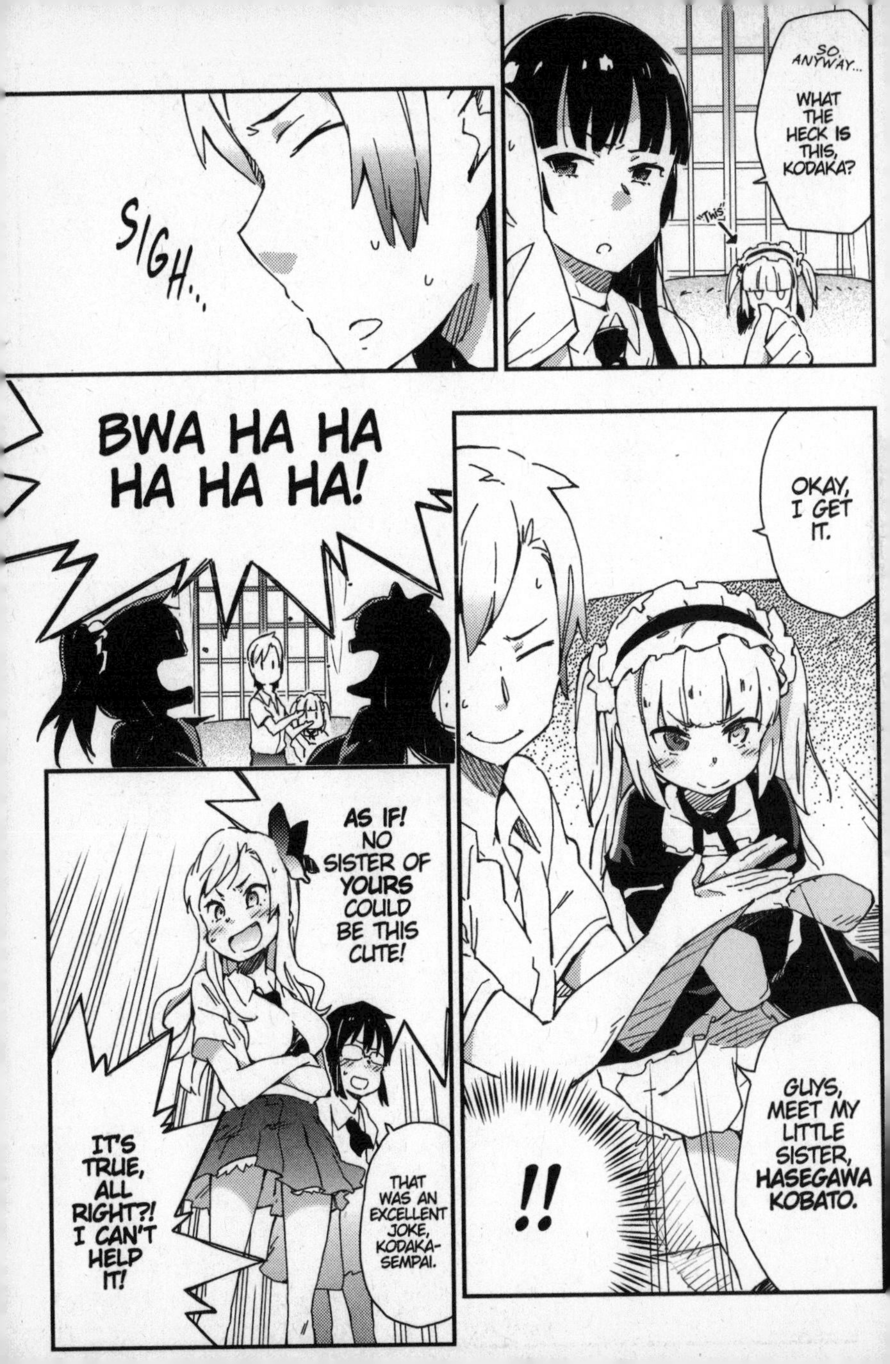
SO, ANYWAY...
WHAT THE HECK IS THIS, KODAKA?
"THIS"
SIGH...
OKAY, I GET IT.
GUYS, MEET MY LITTLE SISTER, HASEGAWA KOBATO.
!!
BWA HA HA HA HA HA!
AS IF! NO SISTER OF YOURS COULD BE THIS CUTE!
THAT WAS AN EXCELLENT JOKE, KODAKA-SEMPAI.
IT'S TRUE, ALL RIGHT?! I CAN'T HELP IT!

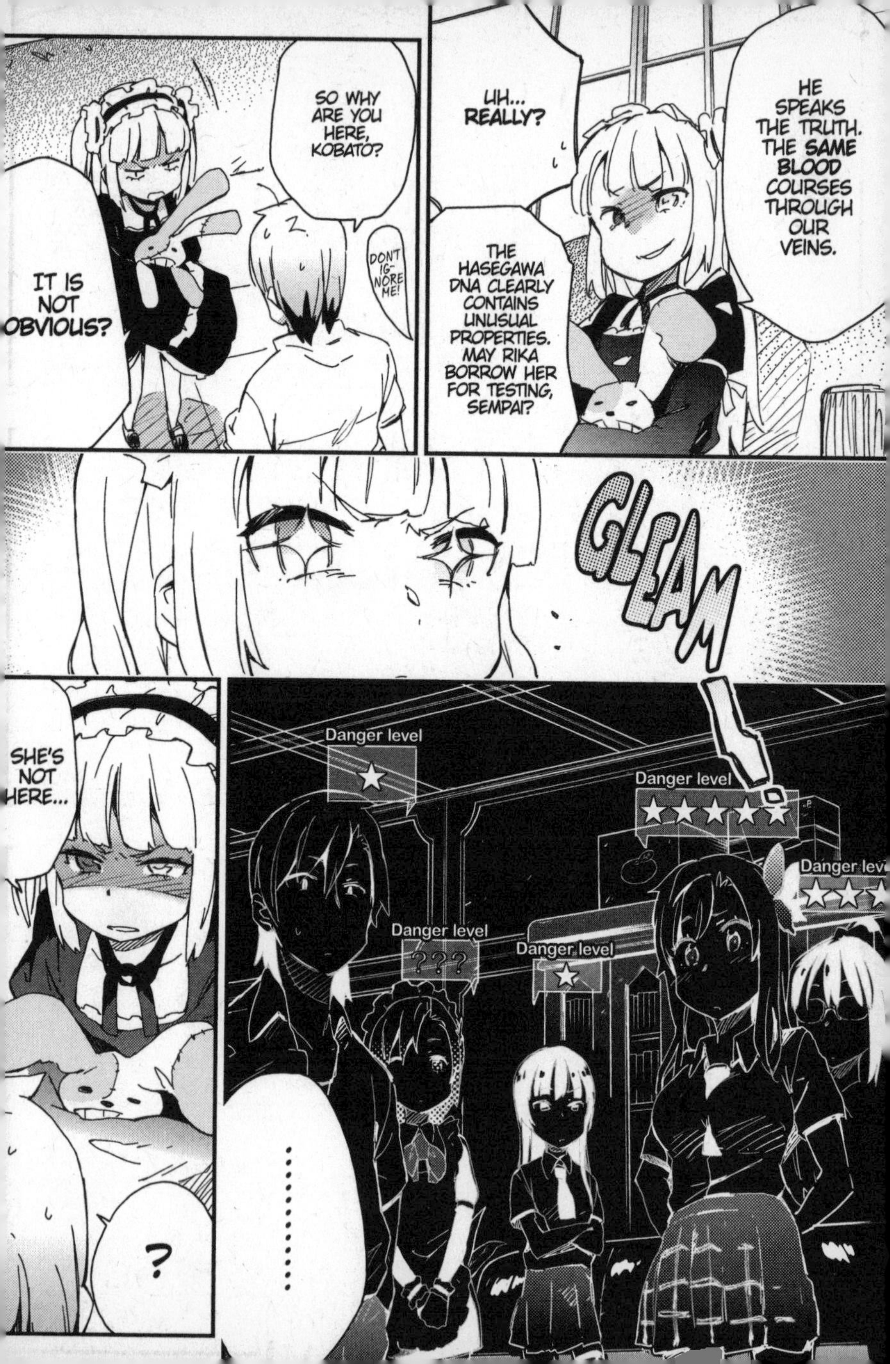
HE SPEAKS THE TRUTH. THE SAME BLOOD COURSES THROUGH OUR VEINS.
UH... REALLY?
THE HASEGAWA DNA CLEARLY CONTAINS UNUSUAL PROPERTIES. MAY RIKA BORROW HER FOR TESTING, SEMPAI?
SO WHY ARE YOU HERE, KOBATO?
DON'T IG-NORE ME!
IT IS NOT OBVIOUS?
GLEAM
!
Danger level ★★★★★
Danger lev ★★★
Danger level ★
Danger level ★
Danger level ???
SHE'S NOT HERE...
......
?

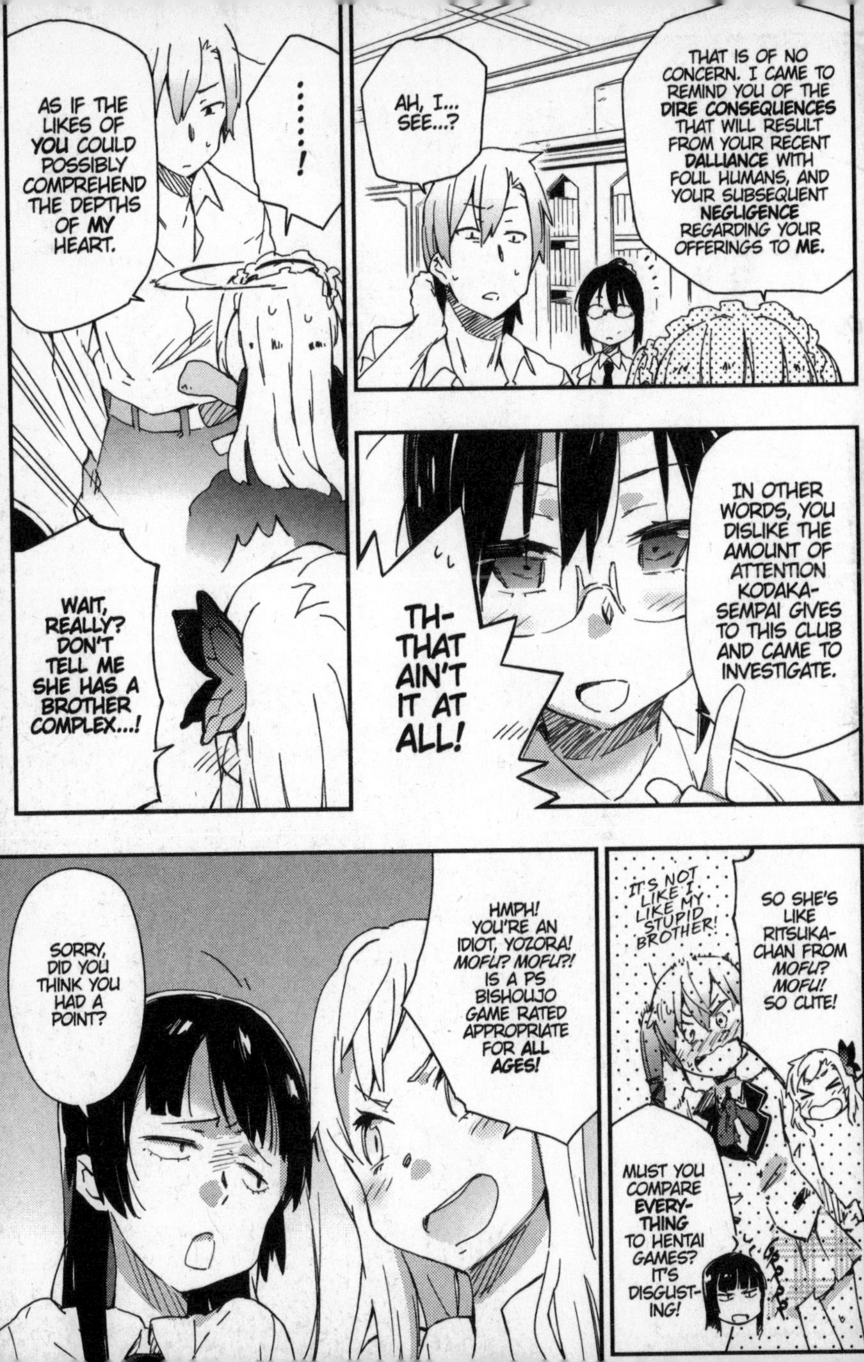
THAT IS OF NO CONCERN. I CAME TO REMIND YOU OF THE DIRE CONSEQUENCES THAT WILL RESULT FROM YOUR RECENT DALLIANCE WITH FOUL HUMANS, AND YOUR SUBSEQUENT NEGLIGENCE REGARDING YOUR OFFERINGS TO ME.
AH, I... SEE...?
IN OTHER WORDS, YOU DISLIKE THE AMOUNT OF ATTENTION KODAKA-SEMPAI GIVES TO THIS CLUB AND CAME TO INVESTIGATE.
TH-THAT AIN'T IT AT ALL!
......!
AS IF THE LIKES OF YOU COULD POSSIBLY COMPREHEND THE DEPTHS OF MY HEART.
WAIT, REALLY? DON'T TELL ME SHE HAS A BROTHER COMPLEX...!
SO SHE'S LIKE RITSUKA-CHAN FROM MOFU? MOFU! SO CUTE!
IT'S NOT LIKE I LIKE MY STUPID BROTHER!
MUST YOU COMPARE EVERY-THING TO HENTAI GAMES? IT'S DISGUST-ING!
HMPH! YOU'RE AN IDIOT, YOZORA! MOFU? MOFU?! IS A PS BISHOUJO GAME RATED APPROPRIATE FOR ALL AGES!
SORRY, DID YOU THINK YOU HAD A POINT?

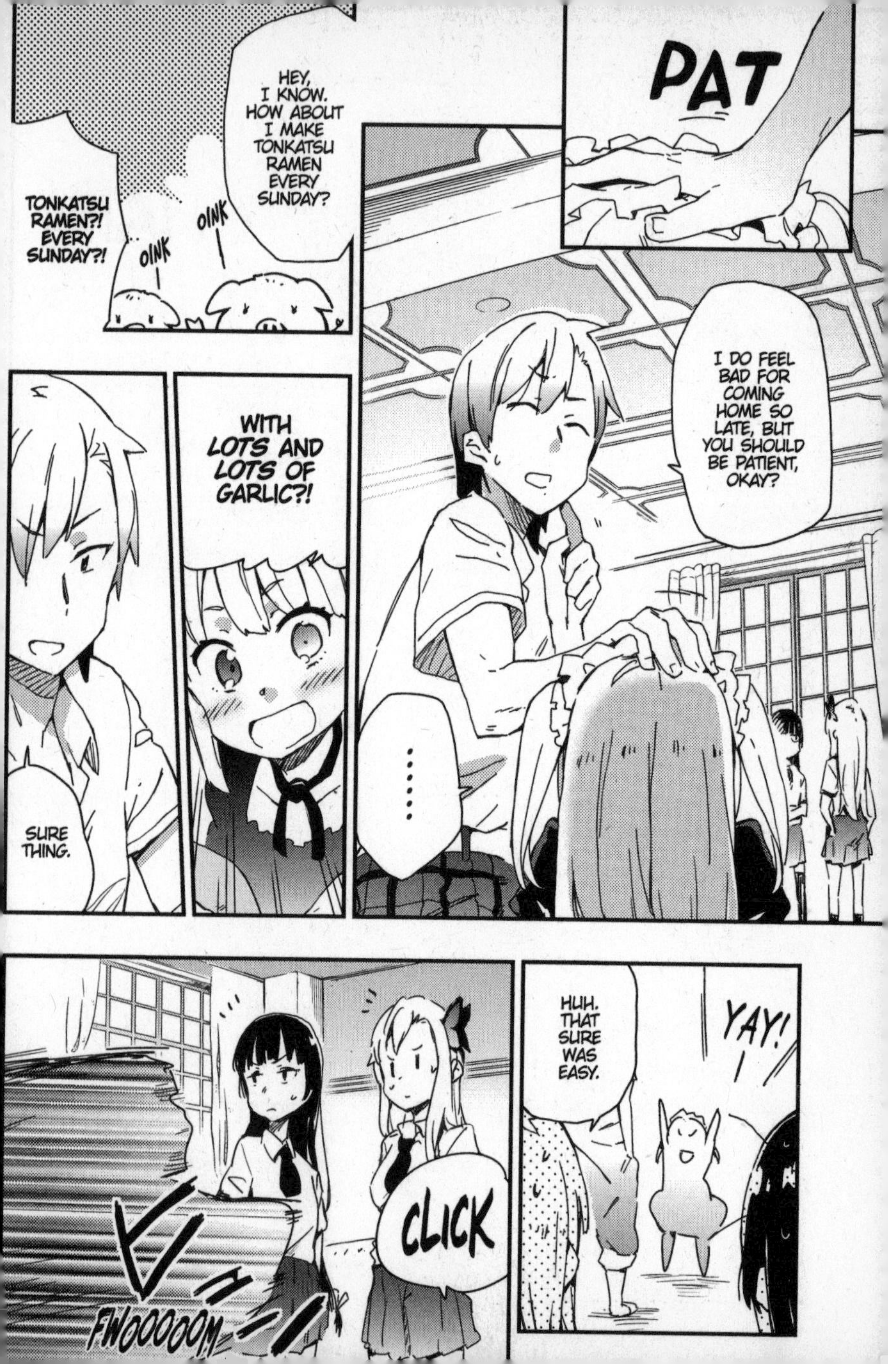
PAT
I DO FEEL BAD FOR COMING HOME SO LATE, BUT YOU SHOULD BE PATIENT, OKAY?
......
HEY, I KNOW. HOW ABOUT I MAKE TONKATSU RAMEN EVERY SUNDAY?
TONKATSU RAMEN?! EVERY SUNDAY?!
OINK
OINK
WITH LOTS AND LOTS OF GARLIC?!
SURE THING.
YAY!
HUH. THAT SURE WAS EASY.
CLICK
FWOOOOOM

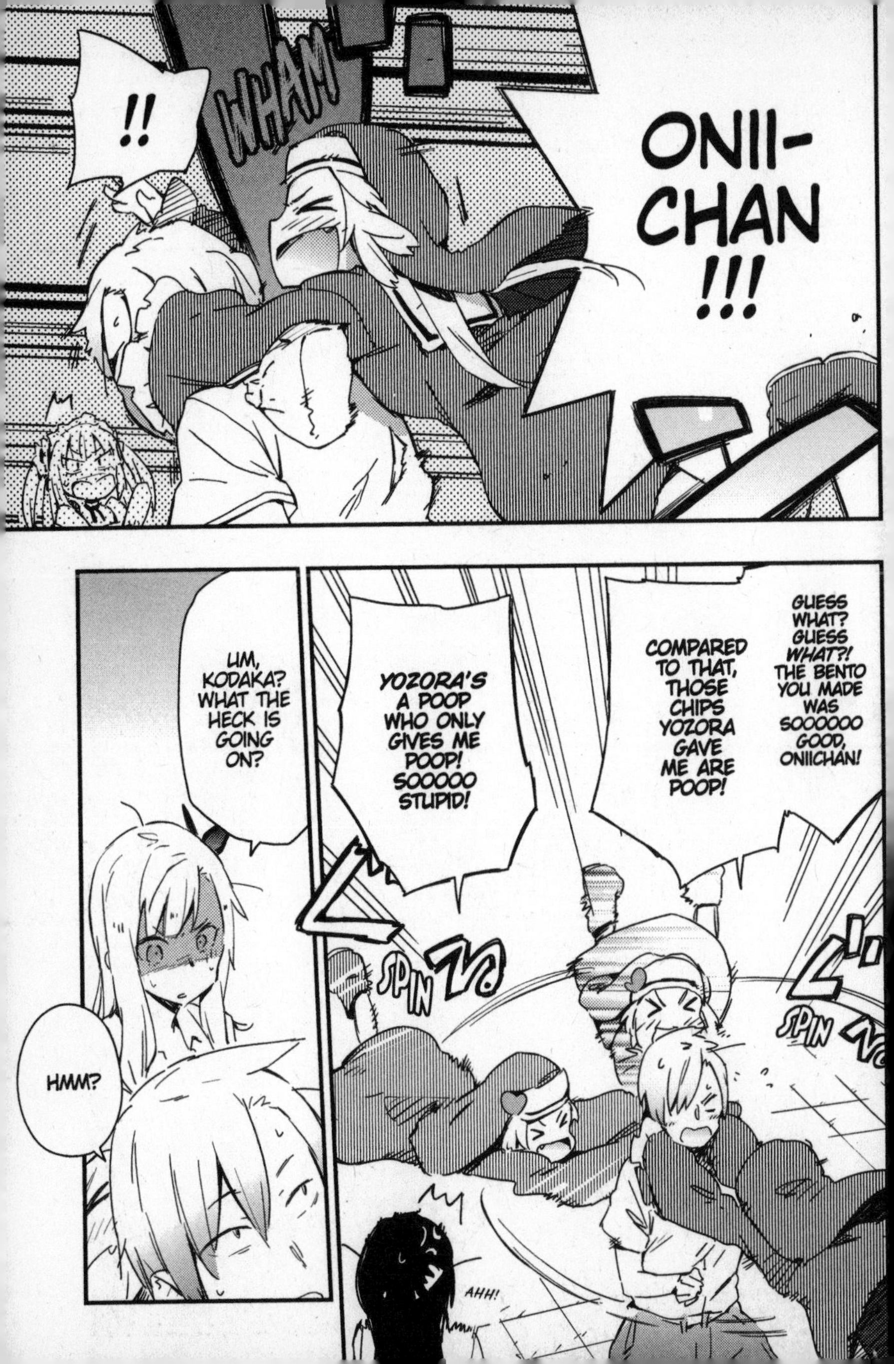
ONII-CHAN!!!
WHAM
!!
GUESS WHAT? GUESS WHAT?! THE BENTO YOU MADE WAS SOOOOOO GOOD, ONIICHAN!
COMPARED TO THAT, THOSE CHIPS YOZORA GAVE ME ARE POOP!
YOZORA'S A POOP WHO ONLY GIVES ME POOP! SOOOOO STUPID!
SPIN
SPIN
AHH!
UM, KODAKA? WHAT THE HECK IS GOING ON?
HMM?

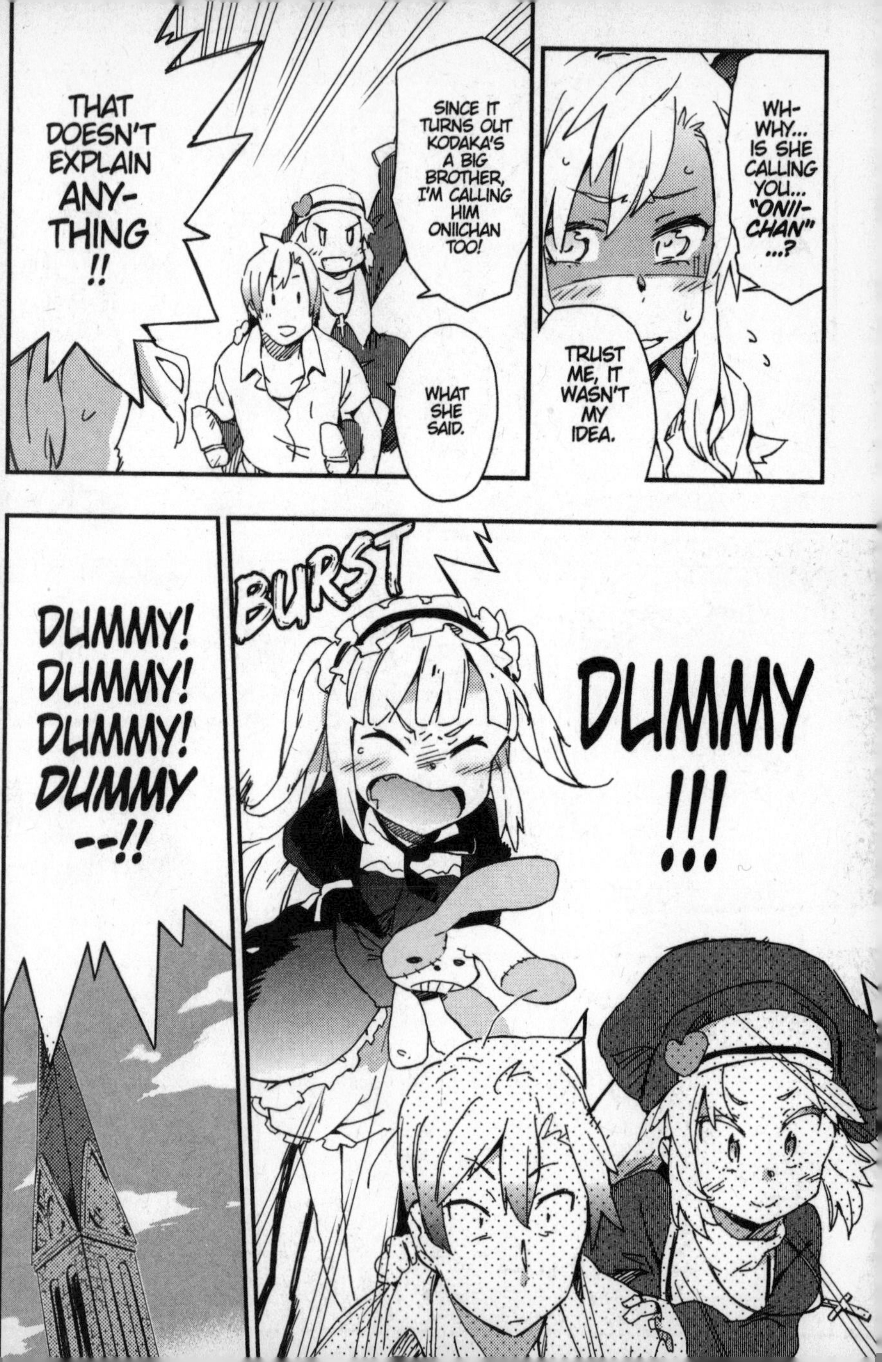
WH-WHY... IS SHE CALLING YOU... "ONII-CHAN" ...?
TRUST ME, IT WASN'T MY IDEA.
SINCE IT TURNS OUT KODAKA'S A BIG BROTHER, I'M CALLING HIM ONIICHAN TOO!
WHAT SHE SAID.
THAT DOESN'T EXPLAIN ANY-THING!!
BURST
DUMMY!!!
DUMMY! DUMMY! DUMMY! DUMMY--!!

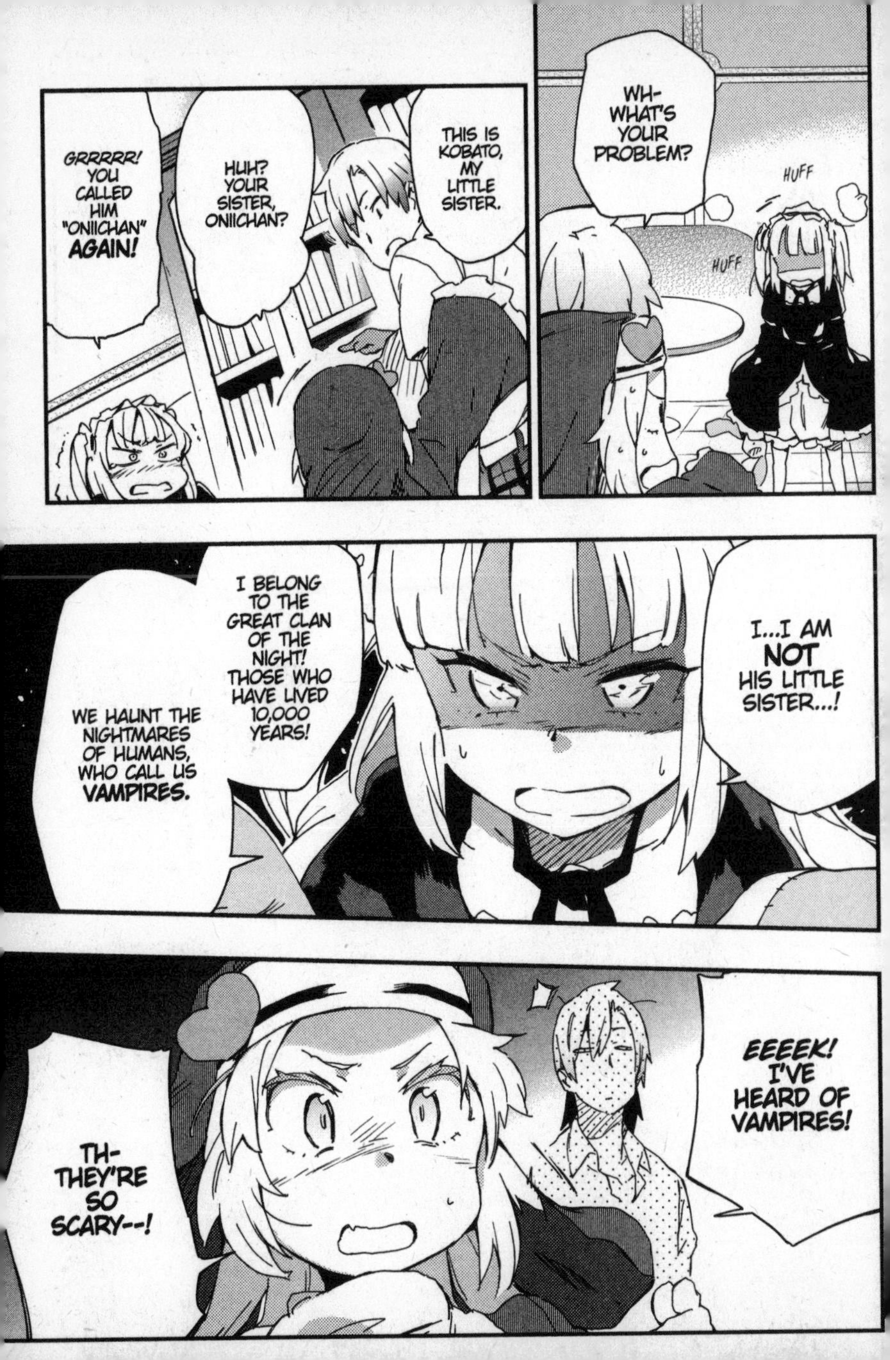
WH-WHAT'S YOUR PROBLEM?
HUFF
HUFF
THIS IS KOBATO, MY LITTLE SISTER.
HUH? YOUR SISTER, ONIICHAN?
GRRRRR! YOU CALLED HIM "ONIICHAN" AGAIN!
I...I AM NOT HIS LITTLE SISTER...!
I BELONG TO THE GREAT CLAN OF THE NIGHT! THOSE WHO HAVE LIVED 10,000 YEARS!
WE HAUNT THE NIGHTMARES OF HUMANS, WHO CALL US VAMPIRES.
EEEEK! I'VE HEARD OF VAMPIRES!
TH-THEY'RE SO SCARY--!

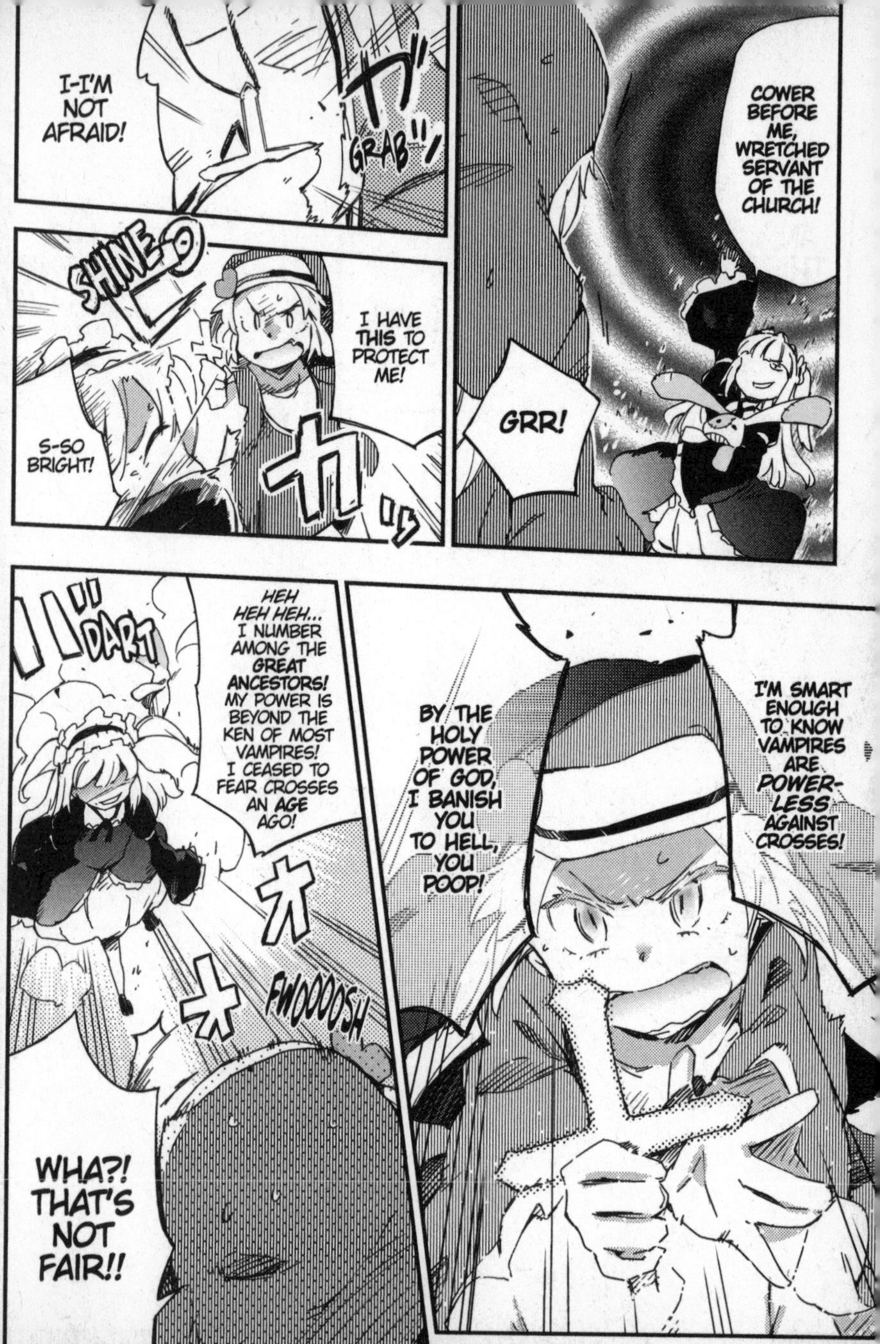
COWER BEFORE ME, WRETCHED SERVANT OF THE CHURCH!
GRR!
I-I'M NOT AFRAID!
GRAB
SHINE
I HAVE THIS TO PROTECT ME!
S-SO BRIGHT!
I'M SMART ENOUGH TO KNOW VAMPIRES ARE *POWERLESS* AGAINST CROSSES!
BY THE HOLY POWER OF GOD, I BANISH YOU TO HELL, YOU POOP!
HEH HEH HEH... I NUMBER AMONG THE **GREAT ANCESTORS!** MY POWER IS BEYOND THE KEN OF MOST VAMPIRES! I CEASED TO FEAR CROSSES AN AGE AGO!
DART
FWOOOOSH
WHA?! THAT'S NOT FAIR!!

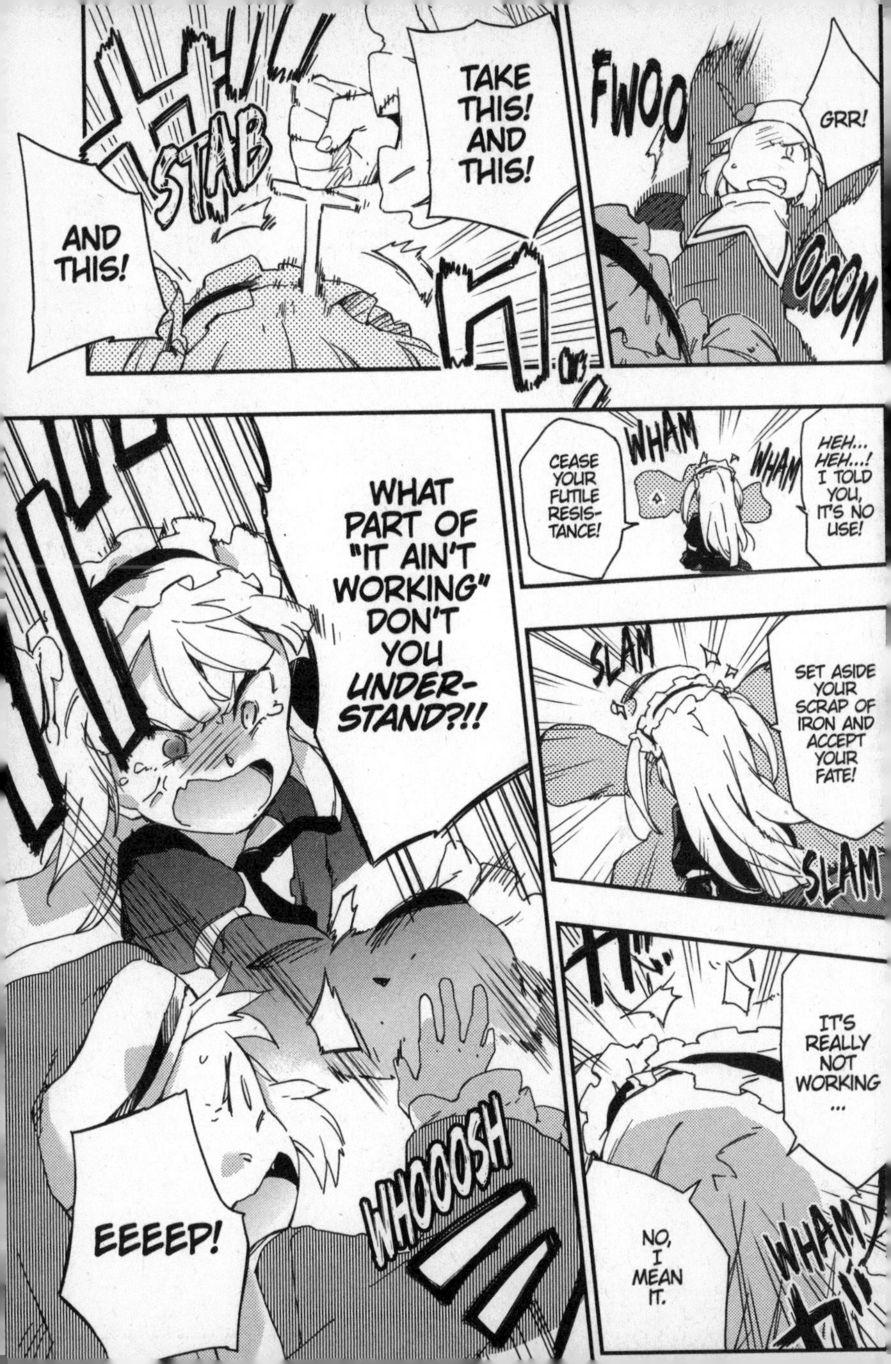
FWOOOOOM
GRR!
TAKE THIS! AND THIS!
STAB
AND THIS!
HEH... HEH...! I TOLD YOU, IT'S NO USE!
WHAM
WHAM
CEASE YOUR FUTILE RESISTANCE!
SET ASIDE YOUR SCRAP OF IRON AND ACCEPT YOUR FATE!
SLAM
SLAM
IT'S REALLY NOT WORKING...
NO, I MEAN IT.
WHAM
WHAT PART OF "IT AIN'T WORKING" DON'T YOU UNDERSTAND?!!
WHOOOSH
EEEEP!

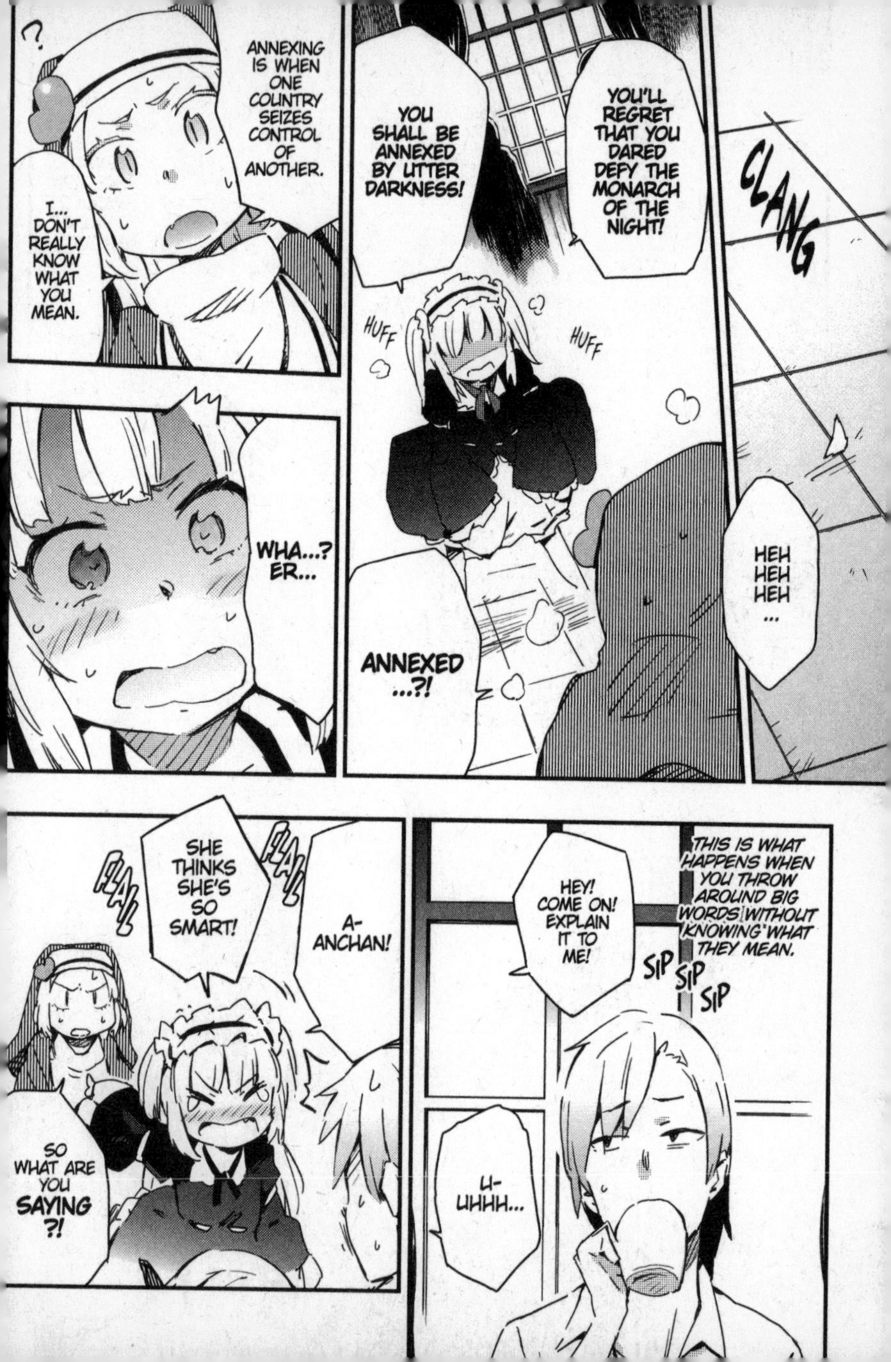
CLANG
HEH HEH HEH...
YOU'LL REGRET THAT YOU DARED DEFY THE MONARCH OF THE NIGHT!
YOU SHALL BE ANNEXED BY UTTER DARKNESS!
HUFF
HUFF
ANNEXED...?!
ANNEXING IS WHEN ONE COUNTRY SEIZES CONTROL OF ANOTHER.
?
I... DON'T REALLY KNOW WHAT YOU MEAN.
WHA...? ER...
THIS IS WHAT HAPPENS WHEN YOU THROW AROUND BIG WORDS WITHOUT KNOWING WHAT THEY MEAN.
HEY! COME ON! EXPLAIN IT TO ME!
SIP SIP SIP
U-UHHH...
A-ANCHAN!
FLAIL
FLAIL
SHE THINKS SHE'S SO SMART!
SO WHAT ARE YOU SAYING?!

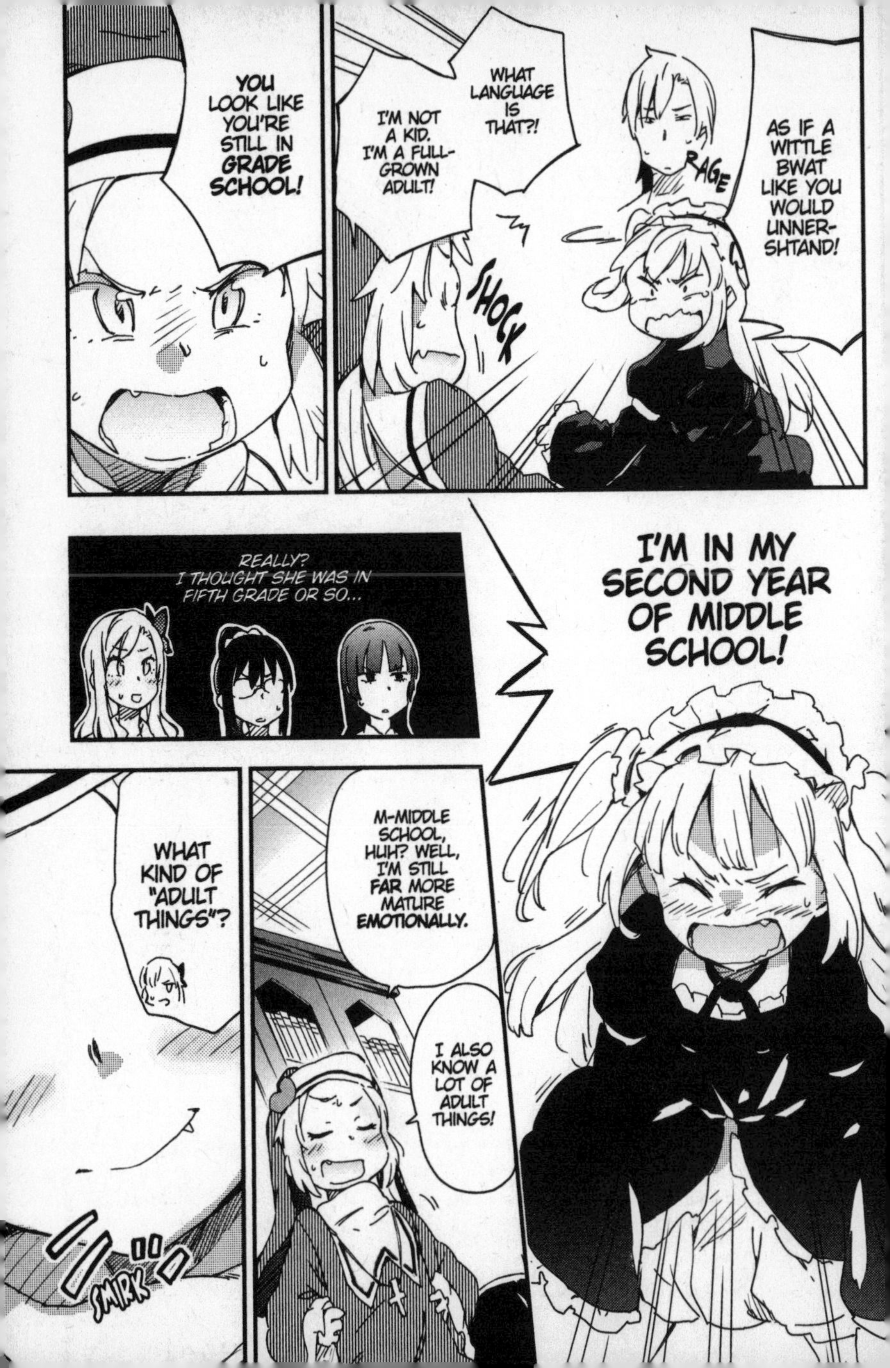
AS IF A WITTLE BWAT LIKE YOU WOULD UNNER-SHTAND!
RAGE
WHAT LANGUAGE IS THAT?!
I'M NOT A KID. I'M A FULL-GROWN ADULT!
SHOCK
YOU LOOK LIKE YOU'RE STILL IN GRADE SCHOOL!
I'M IN MY SECOND YEAR OF MIDDLE SCHOOL!
REALLY? I THOUGHT SHE WAS IN FIFTH GRADE OR SO...
M-MIDDLE SCHOOL, HUH? WELL, I'M STILL FAR MORE MATURE EMOTIONALLY.
I ALSO KNOW A LOT OF ADULT THINGS!
WHAT KIND OF "ADULT THINGS"?
SMIRK

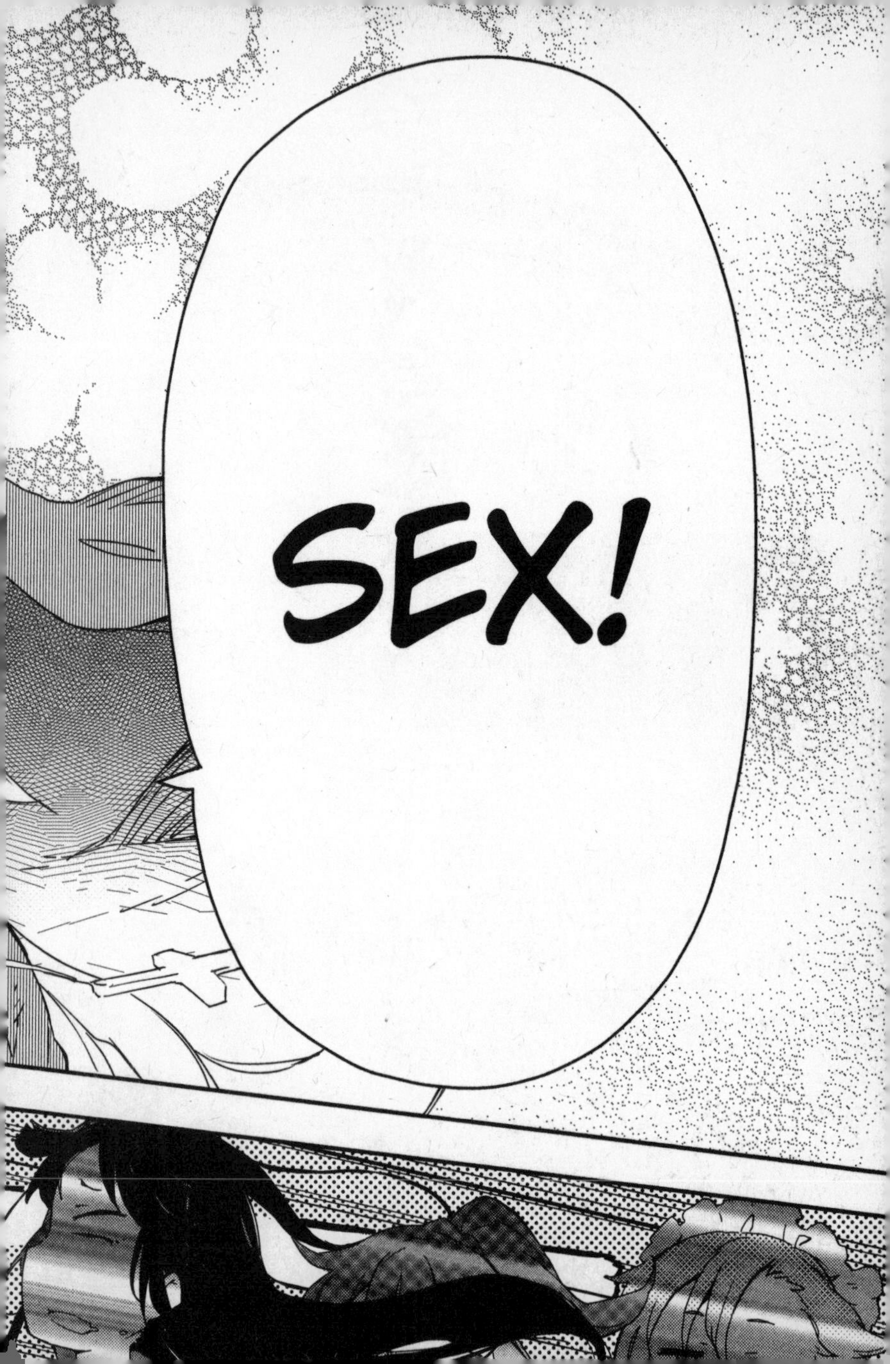
SEX!

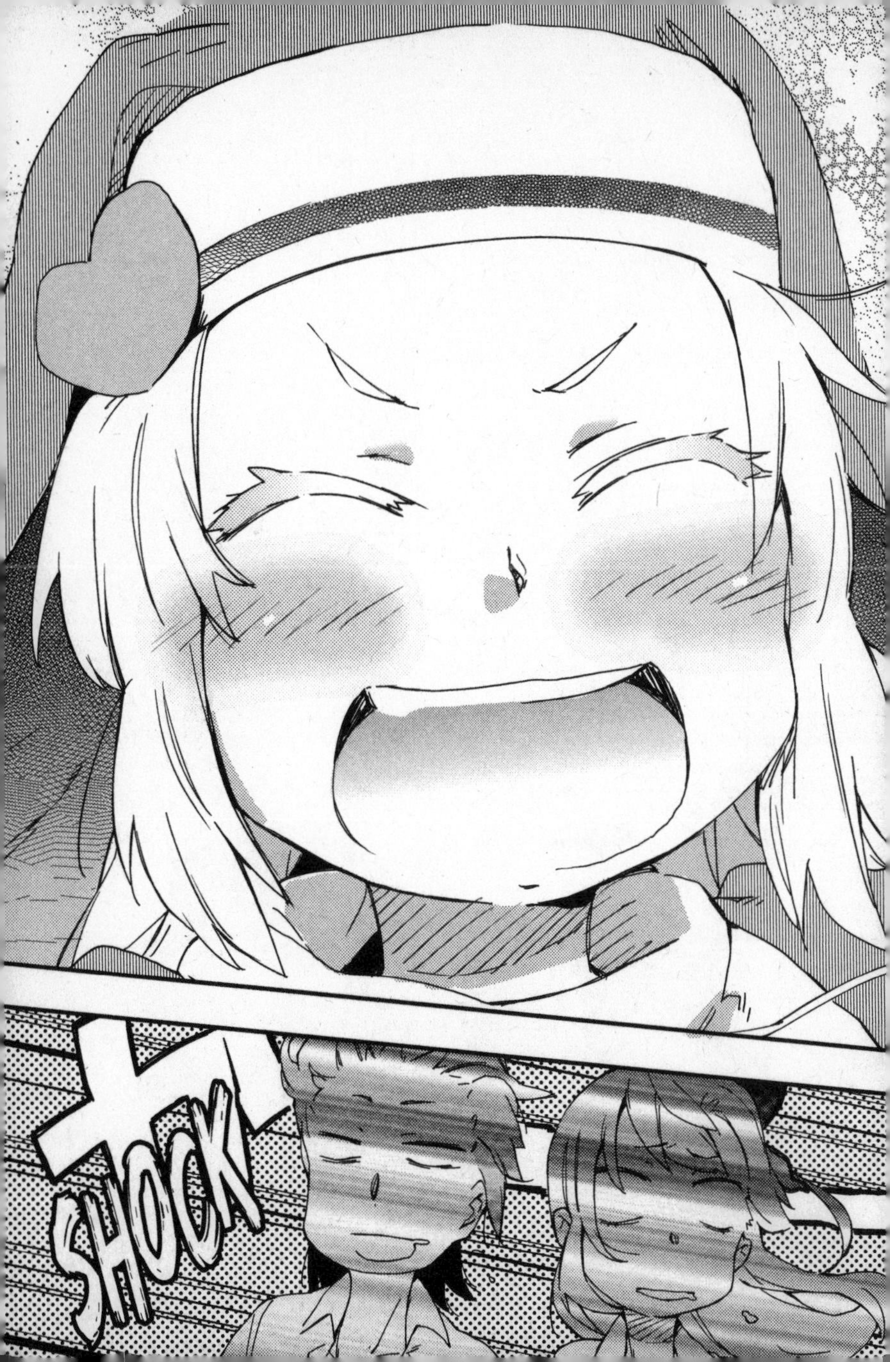
SHOCK

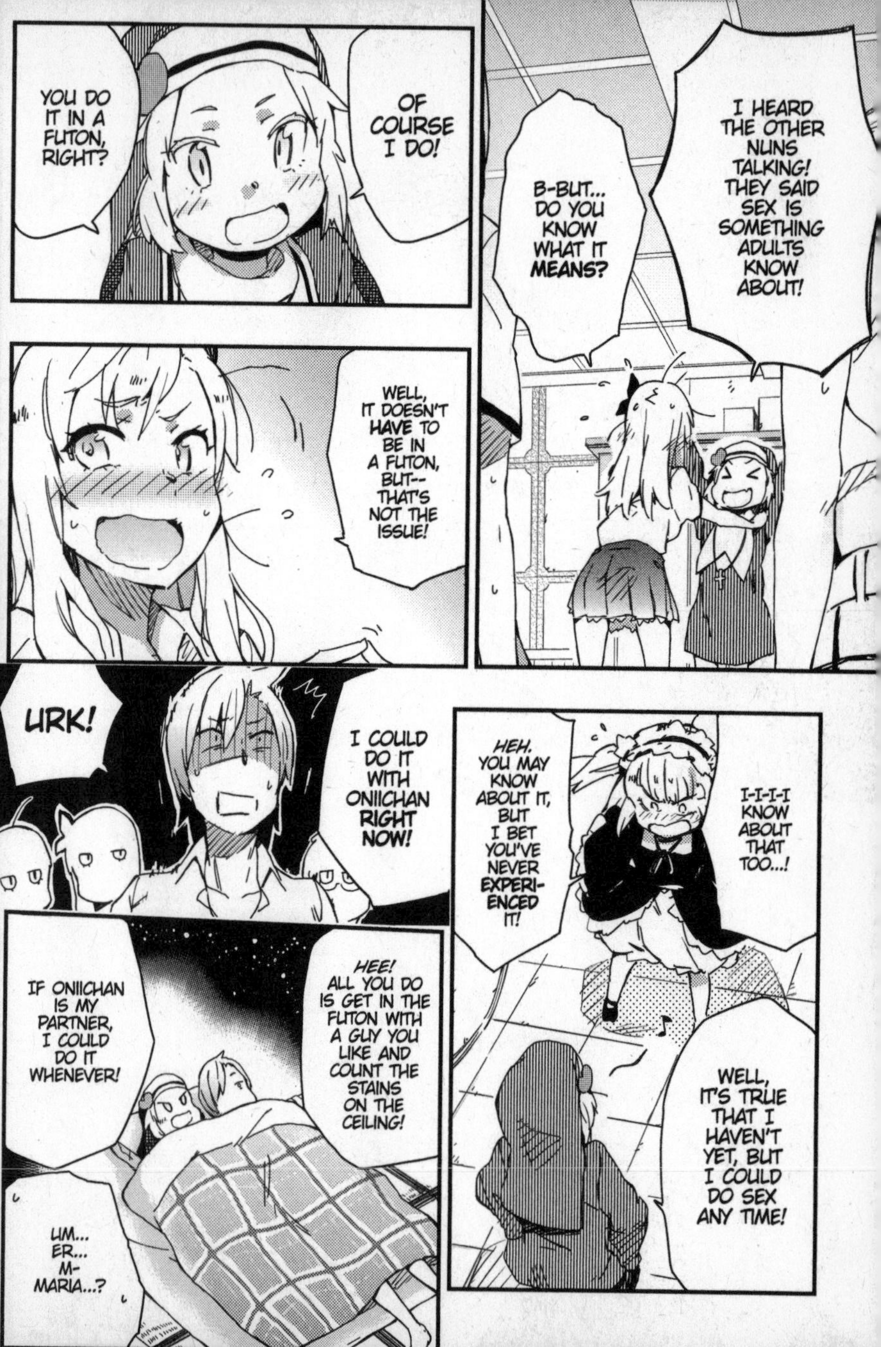

I HEARD THE OTHER NUNS TALKING! THEY SAID SEX IS SOMETHING ADULTS KNOW ABOUT!
B-BUT... DO YOU KNOW WHAT IT MEANS?
OF COURSE I DO!
YOU DO IT IN A FUTON, RIGHT?
WELL, IT DOESN'T HAVE TO BE IN A FUTON, BUT-- THAT'S NOT THE ISSUE!
HEH. YOU MAY KNOW ABOUT IT, BUT I BET YOU'VE NEVER EXPERI-ENCED IT!
I-I-I-I KNOW ABOUT THAT TOO...!
WELL, IT'S TRUE THAT I HAVEN'T YET, BUT I COULD DO SEX ANY TIME!
I COULD DO IT WITH ONIICHAN RIGHT NOW!
URK!
HEE! ALL YOU DO IS GET IN THE FUTON WITH A GUY YOU LIKE AND COUNT THE STAINS ON THE CEILING!
IF ONIICHAN IS MY PARTNER, I COULD DO IT WHENEVER!
UM... ER... M-MARIA...?

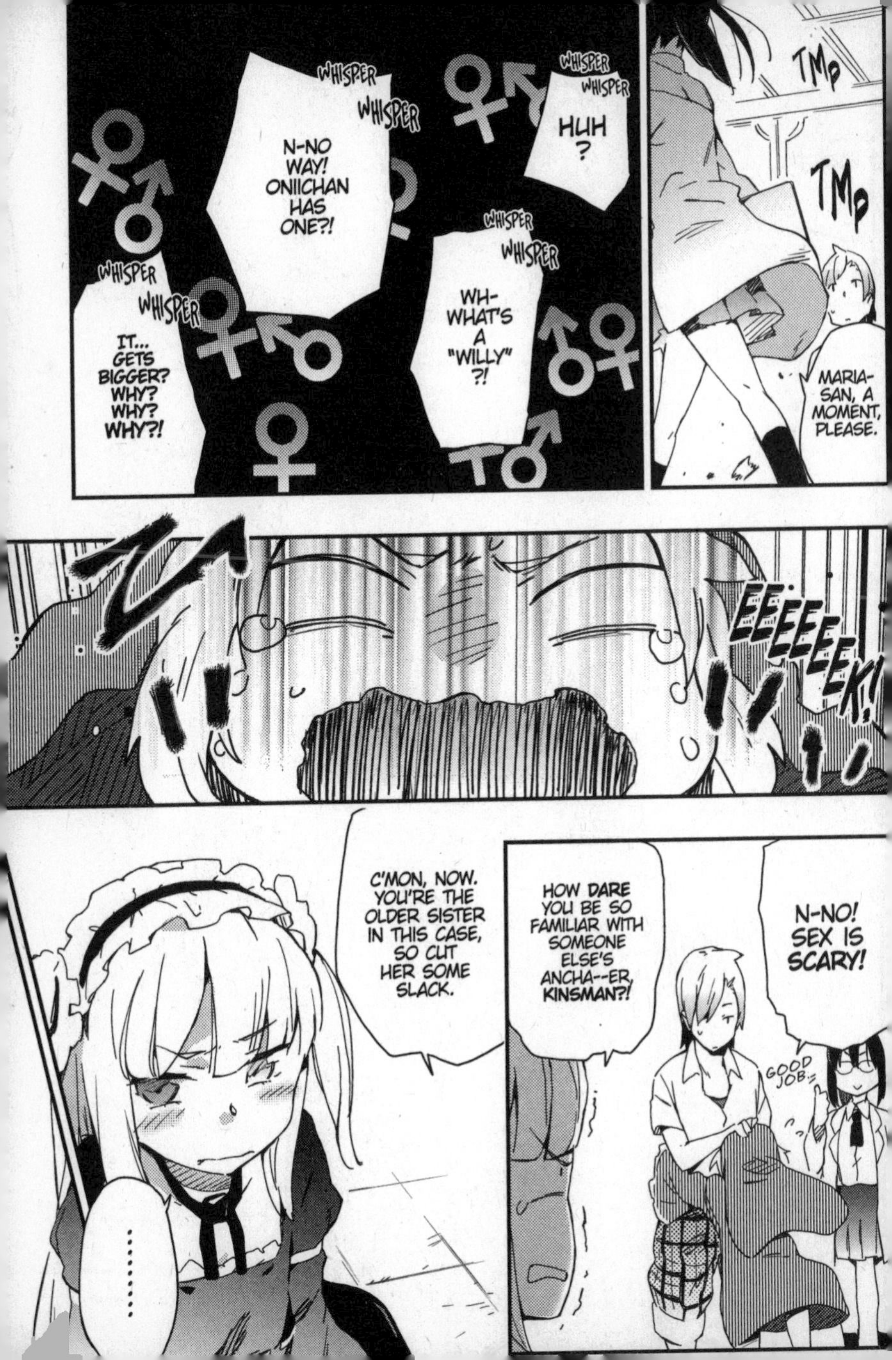
TMP
TMP
MARIA-SAN, A MOMENT, PLEASE.
WHISPER WHISPER
HUH?
WHISPER WHISPER
N-NO WAY! ONIICHAN HAS ONE?!
WHISPER WHISPER
WH-WHAT'S A "WILLY"?!
WHISPER WHISPER
IT... GETS BIGGER? WHY? WHY? WHY?!
EEEEEEK!!
N-NO! SEX IS SCARY!
HOW DARE YOU BE SO FAMILIAR WITH SOMEONE ELSE'S ANCHA--ER, KINSMAN?!
GOOD JOB
C'MON, NOW. YOU'RE THE OLDER SISTER IN THIS CASE, SO CUT HER SOME SLACK.
....

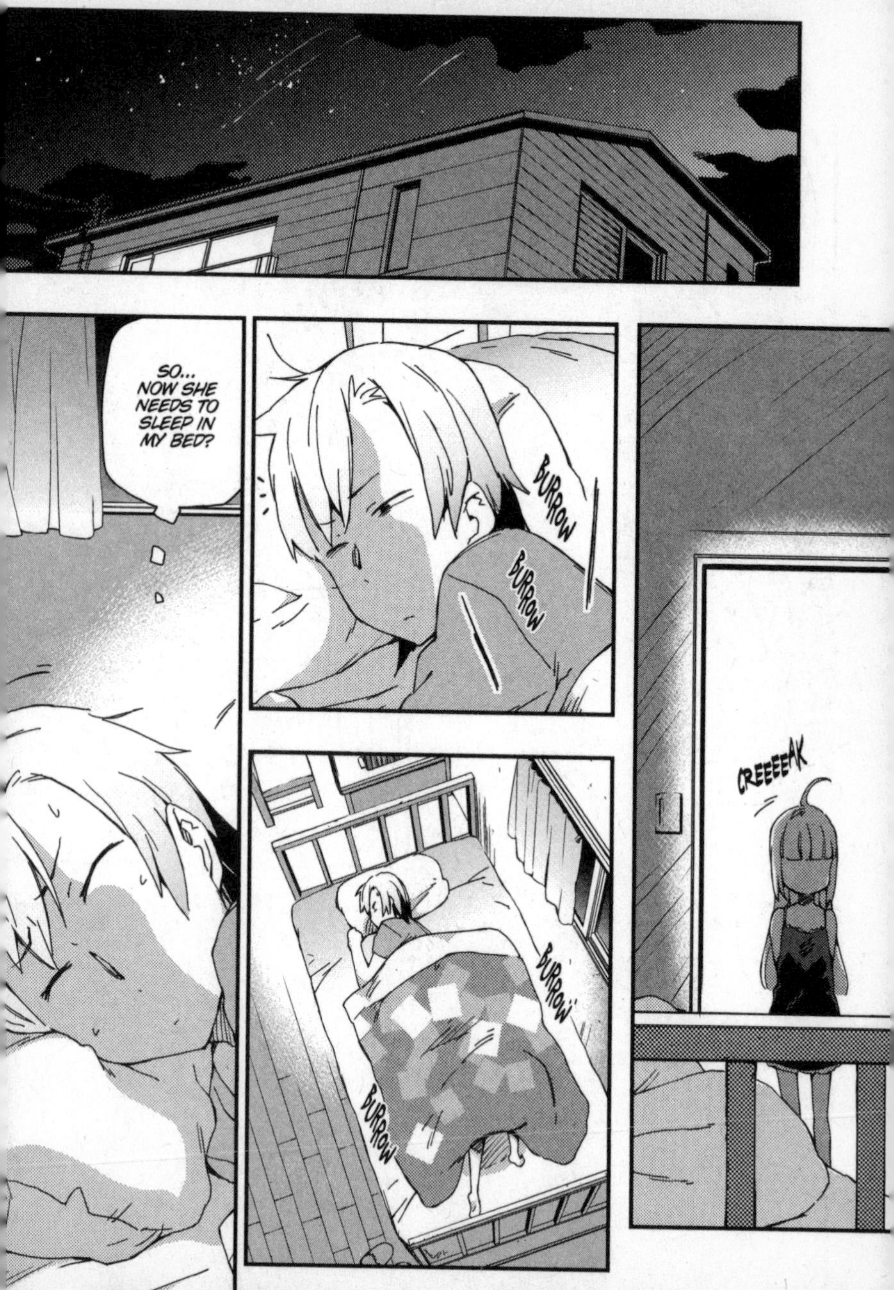
CREEEEAK
BURROW
BURROW
BURROW
BURROW
SO... NOW SHE NEEDS TO SLEEP IN MY BED?

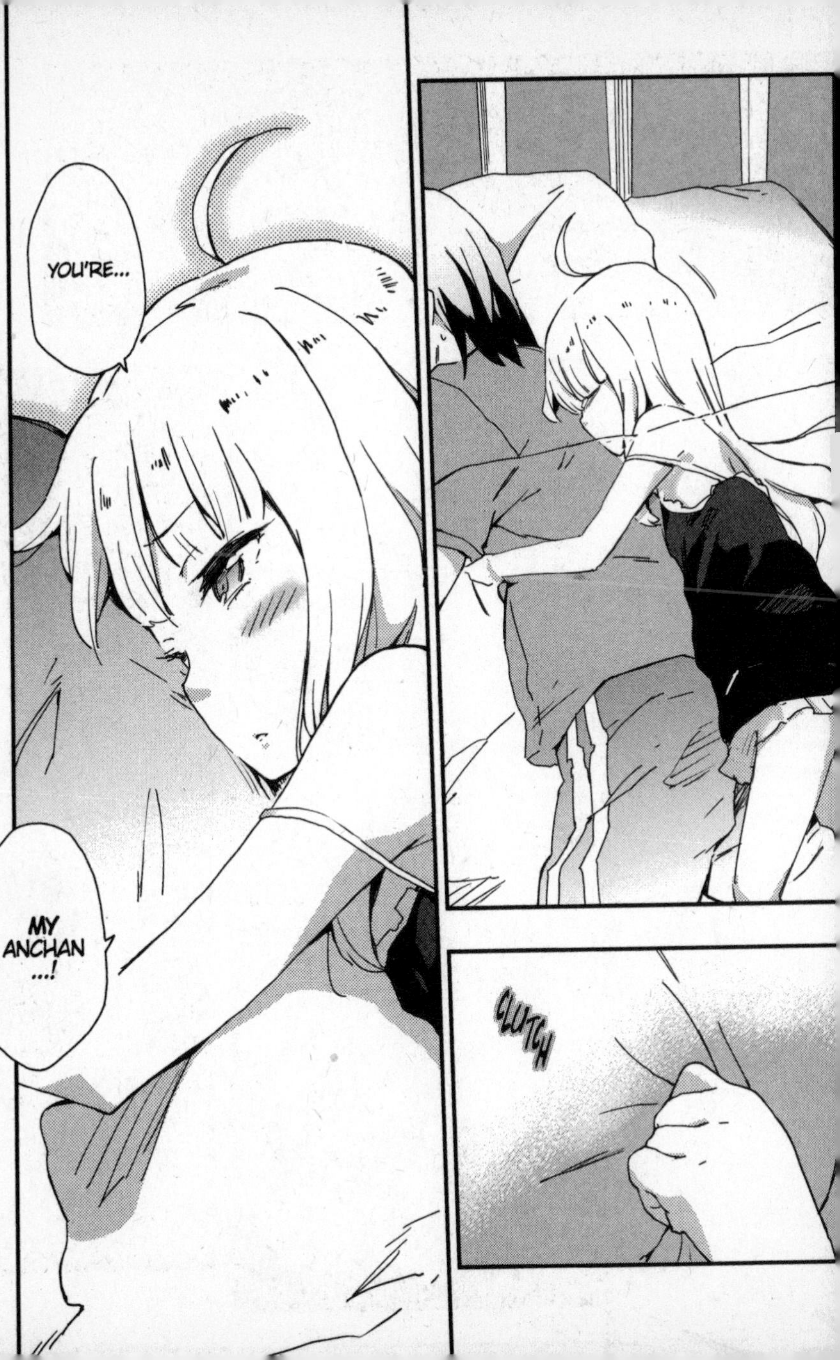
CLUTCH
YOU'RE...
MY ANCHAN ...!

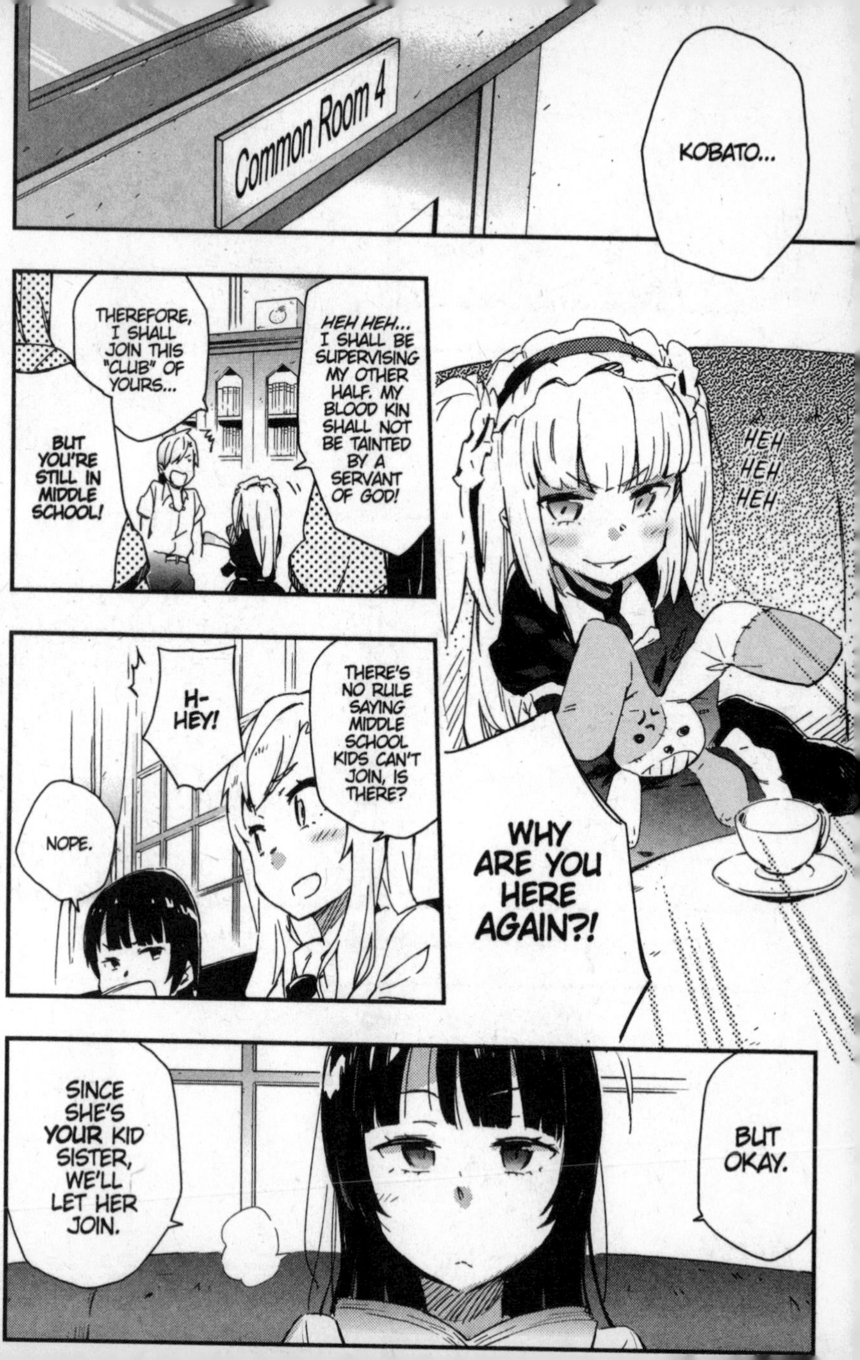
Common Room 4
KOBATO...
WHY ARE YOU HERE AGAIN?!
HEH HEH HEH
HEH HEH... I SHALL BE SUPERVISING MY OTHER HALF. MY BLOOD KIN SHALL NOT BE TAINTED BY A SERVANT OF GOD!
THEREFORE, I SHALL JOIN THIS "CLUB" OF YOURS...
BUT YOU'RE STILL IN MIDDLE SCHOOL!
THERE'S NO RULE SAYING MIDDLE SCHOOL KIDS CAN'T JOIN, IS THERE?
H-HEY!
NOPE.
BUT OKAY.
SINCE SHE'S YOUR KID SISTER, WE'LL LET HER JOIN.

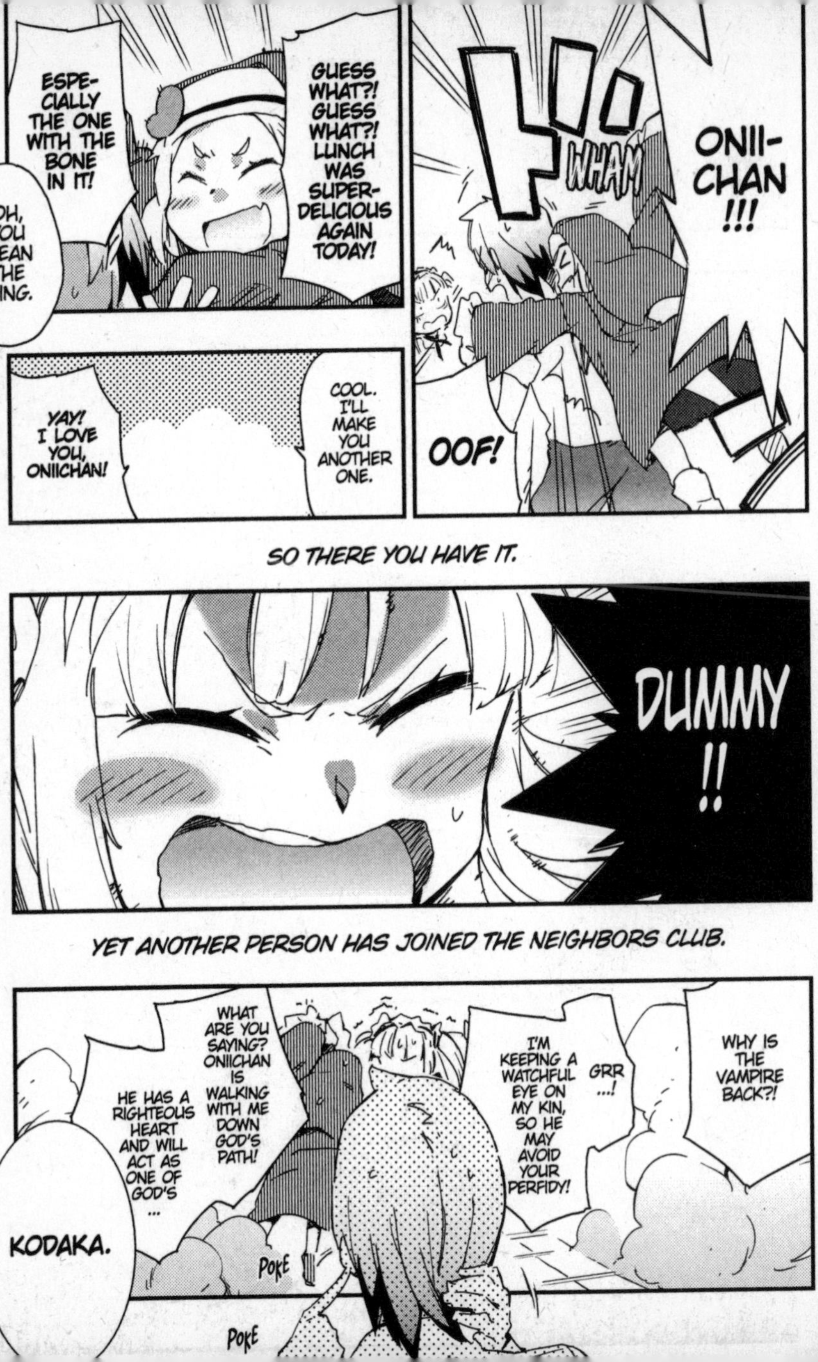
ONII-CHAN!!!
WHAM
OOF!
GUESS WHAT?! GUESS WHAT?! LUNCH WAS SUPER-DELICIOUS AGAIN TODAY!
ESPE-CIALLY THE ONE WITH THE BONE IN IT!
OH, YOU MEAN THE WING.
COOL. I'LL MAKE YOU ANOTHER ONE.
YAY! I LOVE YOU, ONIICHAN!
SO THERE YOU HAVE IT.
DUMMY!!
YET ANOTHER PERSON HAS JOINED THE NEIGHBORS CLUB.
WHY IS THE VAMPIRE BACK?!
I'M KEEPING A WATCHFUL EYE ON MY KIN, SO HE MAY AVOID YOUR PERFIDY!
GRR...!
WHAT ARE YOU SAYING? ONIICHAN IS WALKING WITH ME DOWN GOD'S PATH!
HE HAS A RIGHTEOUS HEART AND WILL ACT AS ONE OF GOD'S ...
KODAKA.
POKE
POKE

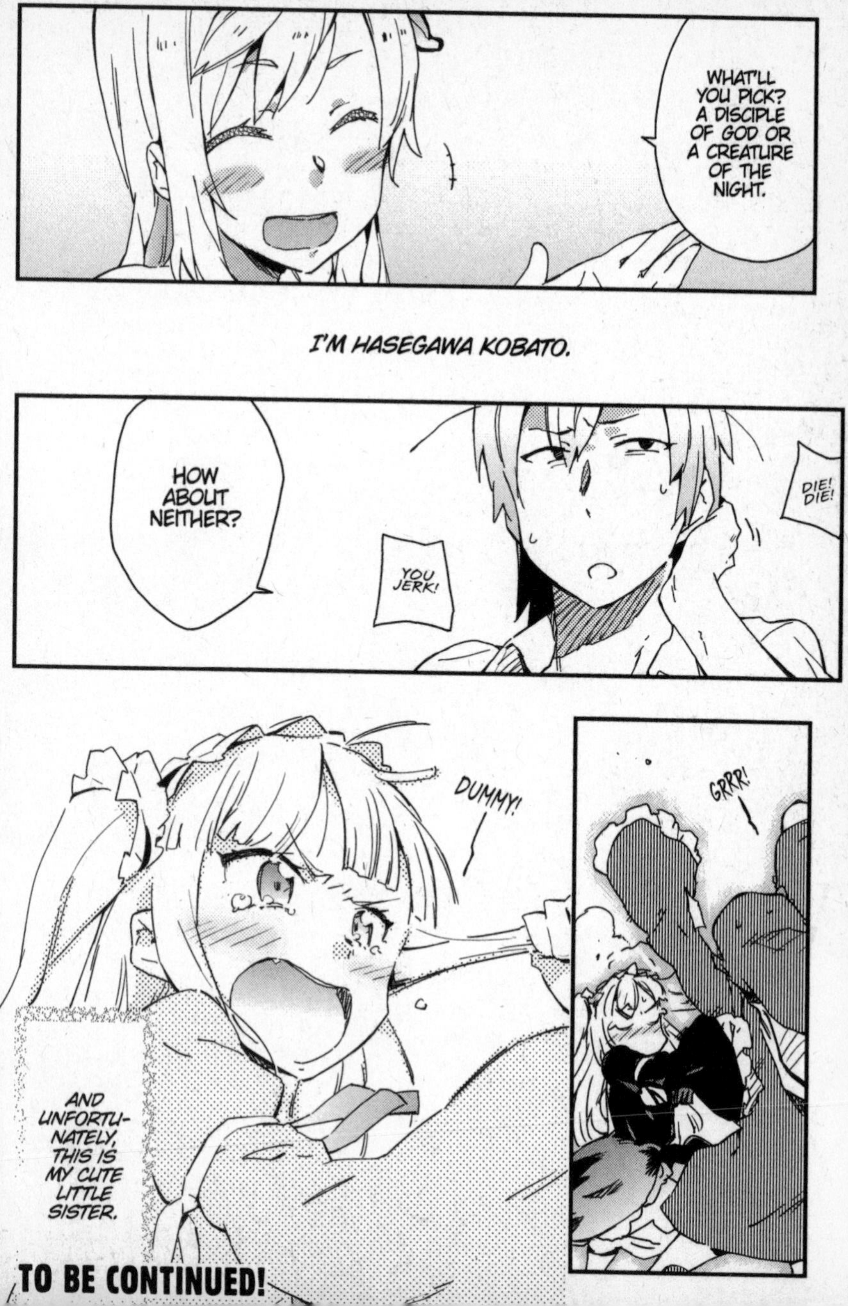
WHAT'LL YOU PICK? A DISCIPLE OF GOD OR A CREATURE OF THE NIGHT.
I'M HASEGAWA KOBATO.
DIE! DIE!
YOU JERK!
HOW ABOUT NEITHER?
GRRR!
DUMMY!
AND UNFORTUNATELY, THIS IS MY CUTE LITTLE SISTER.
TO BE CONTINUED!

LATER...
HASE-GAWA COOTIE TOUCH!
TRAUMA RESURFACING!
WHA--?
HA! IT'S USELESS! IT WON'T WORK ON MY HYPER BARRIER!
TOUCH-BACK!
CROSS BARRIER!
WHAT?! THAT'S NOT FAIR!
IS TOO!!

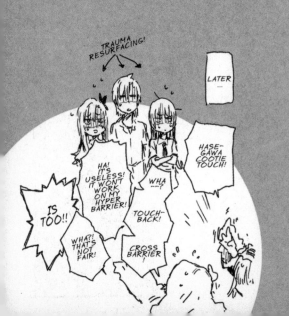

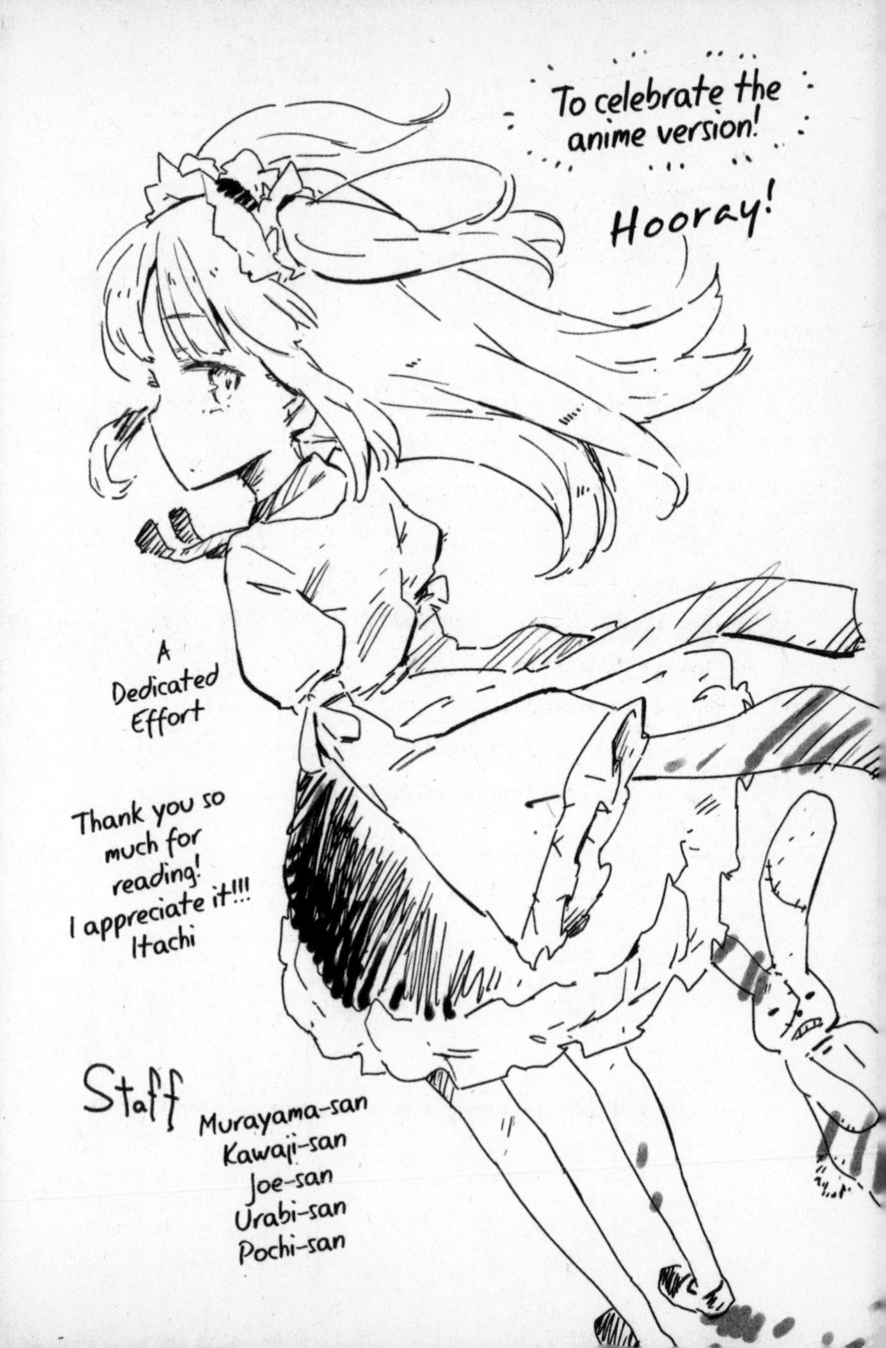
To celebrate the anime version!
Hooray!
A Dedicated Effort
Thank you so much for reading! I appreciate it!!! Itachi
Staff
Murayama-san
Kawaji-san
Joe-san
Urabi-san
Pochi-san

Hello! This is Hirasaka, the original series creator. Thank you very much for purchasing the third volume of *Haganai: I Don't Have Many Friends*. Now that the little sister, the even littler nun, and the perverted scientist have joined the fray, all of the members of the Neighbors Club are finally here! Please enjoy their daily misadventures as they descend into further chaos. I was personally moved by how adorable and vividly violent Rika and Maria are in the manga version compared to the original light novels. I can't wait to see future chapters!

Yomi Hirasaka

A Guest Comment from Haganai+ serialized in Shueisha's Jump SQ.19

It's a pleasure to meet you. I'm Misaki Harukawa, and I'm in charge of the script for *Haganai+*. Every month, I look forward to seeing the very unfortunate appearances of the Neighbors Club members as drawn by Itachi-sensei--especially Yozora! I just love the lively look on her face as she torments Sena...

I continue to look forward to Itachi-sensei's ever-expanding *Haganai* world. I'll have to work hard to avoid being left behind! Please check out *Haganai+!* And congratulations on making it to volume 3, Itachi-sensei!

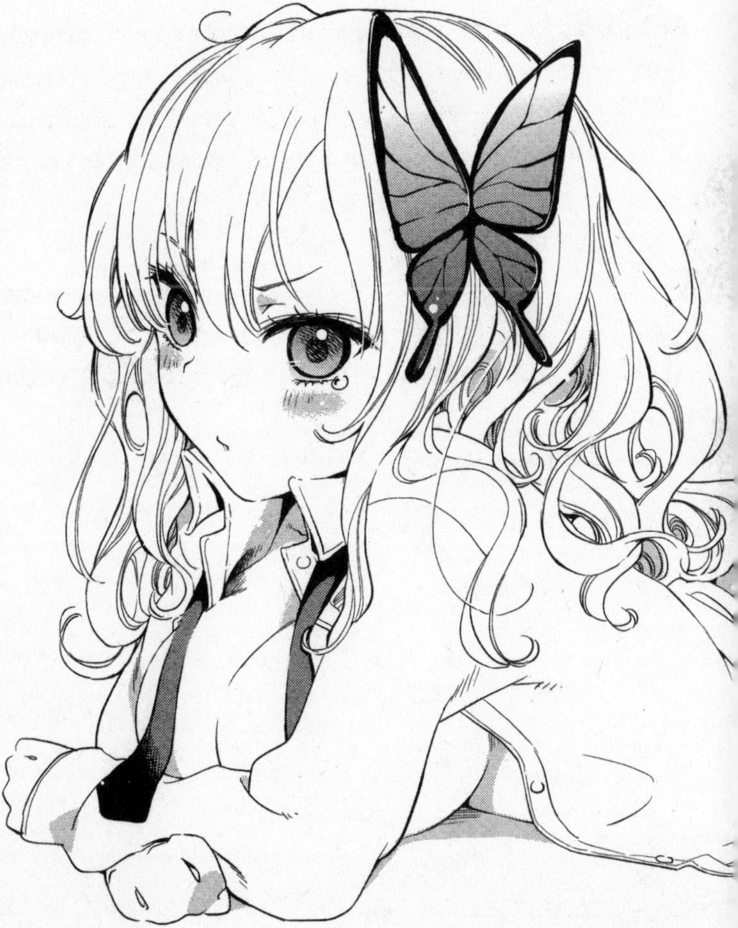

Art: Shouichi Taguchi

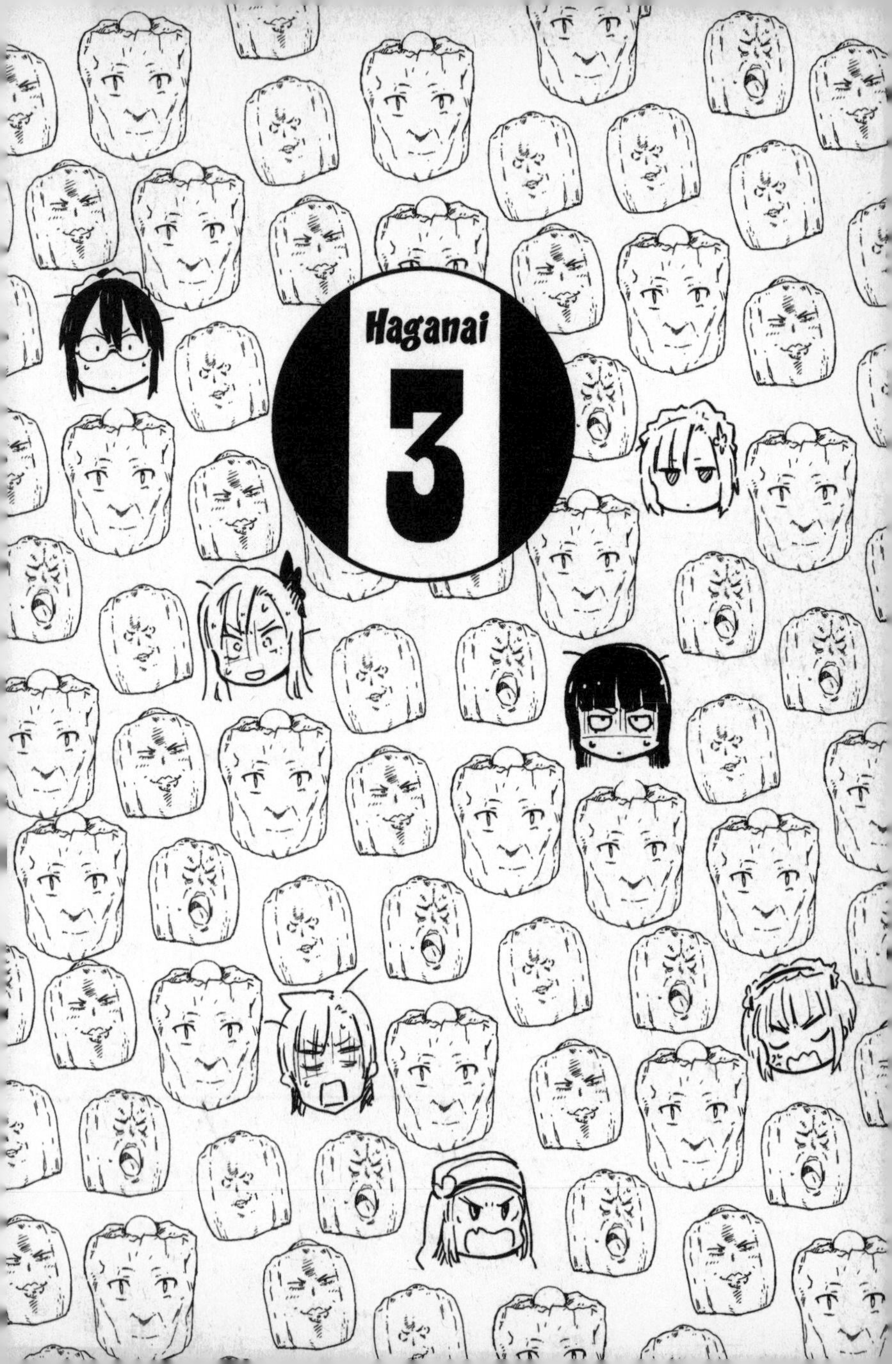
Haganai
3

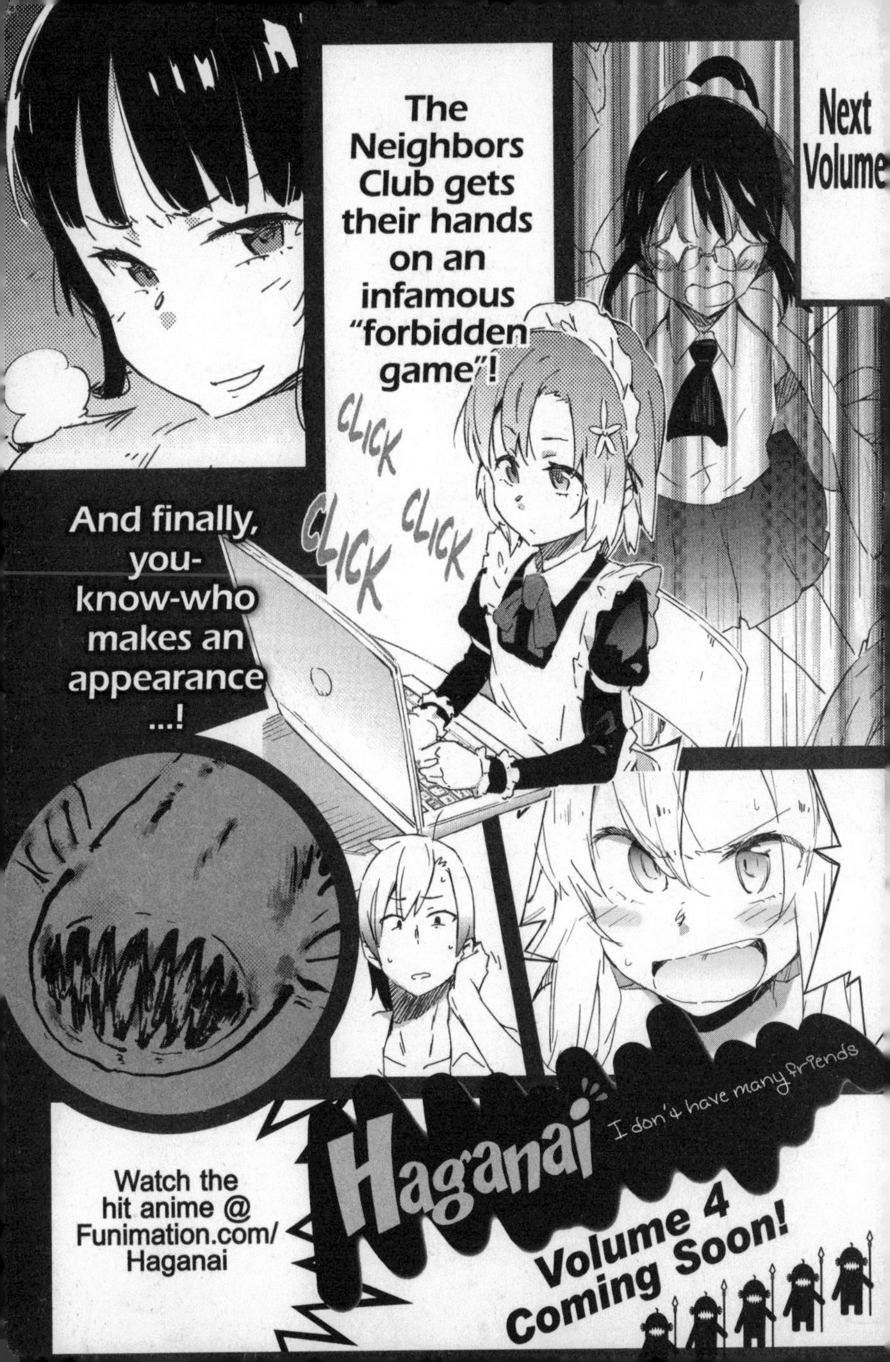

Next Volume
The Neighbors Club gets their hands on an infamous "forbidden game"!
CLICK
CLICK
CLICK
And finally, you-know-who makes an appearance ...!
Haganai
I don't have many friends
Volume 4 Coming Soon!
Watch the hit anime @ Funimation.com/ Haganai

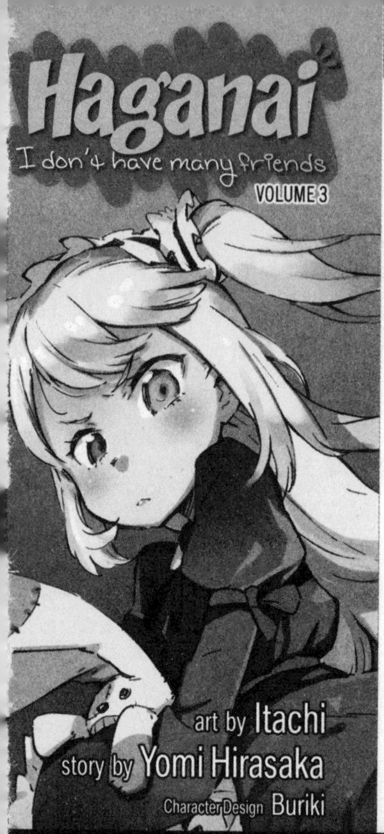
Haganai
I don't have many friends
VOLUME 3
art by Itachi
story by Yomi Hirasaka
Character Design Buriki

STAFF CREDITS

translation	Ryan Peterson
adaptation	Ysabet Reinhardt MacFarlane
lettering	Roland Amago
layout	Bambi Eloriaga-Amago
cover design	Nicky Lim
copy editor	Shanti Whitesides
editor	Adam Arnold
publisher	Jason DeAngelis Seven Seas Entertainment

This is a work of fiction. Names, characters, places, and incidents are the products of the author's imagination or are used fictitiously. Any resemblance to actual events, locales, or persons, living or dead, is entirely coincidental.

ISBN: 978-1-937867-30-0

Printed in Canada

First Printing: June 2013

10 9 8 7 6 5 4 3 2 1

Seven Seas

FOLLOW US ONLINE: ***www.gomanga.com***

READING DIRECTIONS

This book reads from *right to left*, Japanese style. If this is your first time reading manga, you start reading from the top right panel on each page and take it from there. If you get lost, just follow the numbered diagram here. It may seem backwards at first, but you'll get the hang of it! Have fun!!

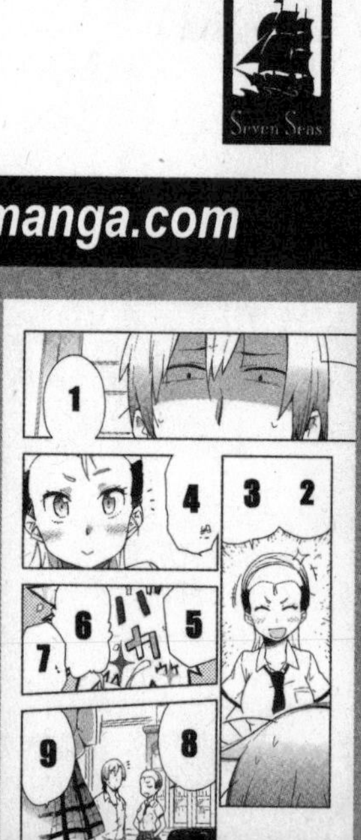
1
2
3
4
5
6
7
8
9